The United Nations and the Independence of Eritrea

The United Nations
Blue Books Series, Volume XII

The United Nations and the
Independence of Eritrea

With an introduction by
Boutros Boutros-Ghali,
Secretary-General of the United Nations

Department of Public Information
United Nations, New York

Published by the United Nations
Department of Public Information
New York, NY 10017

Editor's note:
Each of the United Nations documents and other materials reproduced in this book ("Texts of documents", pages 51-263) has been assigned a number (e.g. Document 1, Document 2, etc.). This number is used throughout the Introduction and other parts of this book to guide readers to the document texts. For other documents mentioned in the book but not reproduced, the United Nations document symbol (e.g., S/1994/933) is provided. With this symbol, such documents can be consulted at the Dag Hammarskjöld Library at United Nations Headquarters in New York, at other libraries in the United Nations system or at libraries around the world which have been designated as depository libraries for United Nations documents. The information contained in this volume is correct as at August 1996.

Copyright © 1996 United Nations

The United Nations and the Independence of Eritrea
The United Nations Blue Books Series
Volume XII
ISBN 92-1-100605-8
United Nations Publication
Sales No. E. 96.I.10

Printed by the United Nations Reproduction Section
New York, NY

Contents

Section One:
Introduction by Boutros Boutros-Ghali, Secretary-General of the United Nations

I	Overview	3
II	Background	6
III	The struggle for independence	14
IV	The referendum	19
V	Reconstruction and long-term development	32
VI	Conclusion	36

Section Two:
Chronology and Documents

I	Chronology of events	41
II	List of reproduced documents	45
III	Other documents	49
IV	Texts of documents	51
V	Subject index to documents	265
VI	Index	271

Maps

Eritrea	17
Voting outside Eritrea	28

Section One
Introduction

I Overview

1   When Eritreans went to the polls in April 1993, their resounding vote in favour of becoming a sovereign State brought a formal end to one of Africa's longest wars, which killed tens of thousands of combatants and civilians and created several hundred thousand refugees. It severely damaged the economy and contributed significantly to regional instability. It was exacerbated at times by a devastating cycle of drought and famine. But the war finally came to an end, with Eritreans exercising their right to self-determination in a free and fair referendum on the issue for which they had long campaigned and fought: independence. In so doing, the Eritrean people advanced the cause of democracy, and contributed greatly to the post-conflict consolidation of peace in the Horn of Africa during a volatile period in the region's history. The successful referendum in Eritrea offered yet another illustration of the links between democratization, development and peace.

2   The United Nations played a crucial role in this transition. Its involvement reflected both the international dimension of the situation — the threat to the peace and security of several Member States — and the increasing demands for the Organization's participation in electoral assistance and democratization. Accordingly, the United Nations Observer Mission to Verify the Referendum in Eritrea (UNOVER) carried out a programme that can be thought of as "referendum-plus", undertaking not only the technical task of assessing the conduct of the electoral process but also promoting the right to popular participation in government and development and coordinating large-scale post-conflict peace-building. Eritrean independence involved the redrawing of colonial borders, until then considered inviolable. Given fears expressed in Africa and elsewhere that Eritrea's secession from Ethiopia would encourage other separatist movements, the United Nations presence also proved effective in bringing legitimacy and orderliness to the transition process. The Organization of African Unity (OAU), for its part, participated in the early diplomacy over the holding of a referendum and, later, as an observer of the actual voting.

3   The referendum results revealed overwhelming backing for independence. The seemingly smooth process, however, masked the diverse obstacles faced by UNOVER in fulfilling its responsibilities. Logistically, the mission was deployed in a country where war had destroyed critical communications and other infrastructure and where most prospective voters were illiterate and unfamiliar with basic voting practices. Organizationally, UNOVER had to ensure that eligible voters among the 750,000 Eritrean refugees — out of a total population of approximately 3.5 million people — spread over more than 40 countries, the majority of them in the Sudan, were given an opportunity to participate. And politically, UNOVER had to make polling arrangements for Eritreans in Saudi Arabia, a nation without regular voting experience, as well as in Ethiopia, where, despite the coming to power of a new Government that officially supported Eritrean independence, the issue remained controversial.

4   Underlying these various considerations was the legacy of the United Nations General Assembly's decision, taken in 1950, that Eritrea, a former Italian colony, should be federated with Ethiopia under the Ethiopian Crown following Italy's defeat in the Second World War. Although the Assembly decided that Italy's other colonies, Libya and Italian Somaliland, were to become sovereign States, a majority of Member States favoured a federal solution for Eritrea on the grounds that it provided the only solution for fostering stability in the region by meeting the legitimate interests of Ethiopia while assuring for the people of Eritrea the power to manage their own local affairs and safeguard their institutions and culture. Still, there was support from many Member States for Eritrean independence, either immediately or following a trusteeship arrangement. Anything less, these States said, would be a denial of Eritreans' right to self-determination. In Eritrea itself, there was a range of views concerning federation with Ethiopia. However, when Ethiopia abrogated the federal agreement and annexed Eritrea in 1962, a movement of resistance to Ethiopian rule was ignited.

5   Because many Eritreans felt the United Nations had failed to adequately support their right to self-determination, UNOVER observers were received at first politely, but not enthusiastically, upon their arrival in Eritrea in early 1993. Following the collapse of the Ethiopian Government in May 1991, the Provisional Government of Eritrea had scheduled a referendum on self-determination for 1993 and requested United Nations involvement in the referendum process. The new Government of Ethiopia, whose leaders had fought alongside the Eritreans, had formally recognized the right of the Eritrean people to determine their political future by an internationally supervised referendum. But these facts alone were not enough to overcome Eritrean concerns about the Organization's intentions. UNOVER's most formidable challenge, then, was to earn the public trust by establishing a credible, impartial and transparent presence.

6   Towards this end, UNOVER took an activist approach to its mandate, reaching out to all regions and individuals and meeting not just with government officials but with village elders, religious leaders, teachers and women's groups. The core element of this effort was a multimedia informational and educational campaign aimed at explaining the

practice of voting as well as its place in a democratic society. By the time the days of voting arrived in April 1993, Eritreans turned out in great numbers to effect a peaceful end to a long and ruinous conflict. By this time as well, positive attitudes towards the United Nations had taken root throughout the country, ushering in a new era in relations between Eritrea and the United Nations. In a symbolic display of this new state of affairs, on the opening day of the polls, the Secretary-General of the Provisional Government of Eritrea — who had been the leader of the main movement of resistance to Ethiopian rule — cast his vote accompanied by my Special Representative.

7   This volume chronicles the entire referendum process of 1991-1993. Following this Overview, Part II of the Introduction discusses the debate over the status of Eritrea following the Second World War, and the General Assembly's decision to federate Eritrea with Ethiopia. Part III briefly recounts the Eritrean struggle for independence and the decision to hold an internationally supervised referendum. Part IV tells the full story of UNOVER, culminating in the voting in April 1993 and Eritrea's accession to United Nations membership one month later. Part V describes how United Nations humanitarian and development agencies, including the Bretton Woods institutions, have worked closely with the new Government and with each other to make an investment in peace — to help Eritrea move from a state of national emergency into an era of reconstruction and recovery, and to create conditions in which a return to war would be unthinkable. Finally, in Part VI, I offer some thoughts on the significance of the United Nations involvement in Eritrea's transition to independence.

8   The documents in Section Two, which make up the bulk of this volume, comprise essential United Nations materials relating to the Organization's involvement in Eritrea, primarily the General Assembly's consideration of the territory's future from 1948 to 1951, the referendum process of 1991-1993 and subsequent programmes for reconstruction and recovery. Included are resolutions of the General Assembly and Security Council, reports and letters of the Secretary-General, reports of the United Nations Commissioner in Eritrea and communications from United Nations Member States. The "Other documents of interest" listing on page 49 guides readers to additional United Nations documents of value.

II Background

9   The question of Eritrea first came before the United Nations in 1948, as part of diplomatic efforts to determine the future status of the former Italian colonies, which had been detached from Italy as a result of its defeat in the Second World War. Deliberations on Eritrea revealed considerable differences among the Organization's Member States, and among Eritreans themselves. In 1950, the General Assembly decided that Eritrea should become an autonomous unit federated with Ethiopia under the Ethiopian Crown. When Ethiopia abrogated the federal agreement in 1962 and made Eritrea an Ethiopian province, an Eritrean independence movement began a political and military campaign of resistance to Ethiopian rule. This war was to last nearly 30 years.

Eritrea under Italian rule

10   For the better part of the first millennium A.D., the territory of present-day Eritrea was part of the Axumite kingdom, a mercantile State with an important seaport near modern Massawa. Control of the area or parts of the area in subsequent centuries fell to a number of kingdoms and powers, among them Ethiopia, Egypt and the Ottoman Empire. In the latter half of the nineteenth century, the territory gradually came under Italian rule as part of the latter's growing colonial presence in Africa. Italian power in Eritrea was formalized on 2 May 1889 with the signing of the Treaty of Wich'alē (Uccialli) by Italy and the Emperor of Ethiopia. On 1 January 1890, Italy proclaimed Eritrea to be an Italian colony. When Italy subsequently attempted to colonize Ethiopia, war broke out. After Ethiopian forces defeated Italy in 1896, Italy recognized Ethiopia's independence but retained control over Eritrea.

11   The roots of modern Eritrean nationalism date to this period. During the years of colonial rule, Italian farmers and settlers established industries, plantations and networks for transportation and communications. Eritreans, while subjected to the foreign exploitation of their land, labour and resources, also formed trade unions, social movements, civic organizations and other institutions which helped foster a sense of common experience and struggle among the country's nine major ethnic and linguistic groups. The number of adherents of the two main religions in Eritrea — Christianity and Islam — was roughly equal at this time, and remains so today.

12 In 1935-1936, again using Eritrea as a base, Italy invaded Ethiopia for a second time. Ethiopia had beseeched the League of Nations for help against Italian aggression, but the League's response — the application of financial and economic sanctions — came only after Italy had occupied the country, and failed to have any tangible effect. On 1 June 1936, Italy united Ethiopia with Eritrea and Italian Somaliland to constitute Italian East Africa.

13 With Italy's defeat in the Second World War, Ethiopia regained its independence. Pursuant to a decision by France, the United Kingdom of Great Britain and Northern Ireland, the United States of America and the Union of Soviet Socialist Republics, Italy's colonies of Eritrea, Italian Somaliland and most of Libya were placed under temporary British administration. Under the terms of the Treaty of Peace with Italy, signed in Paris on 10 February 1947, Italy renounced all claims to the three Territories. The Treaty further stated that the final disposition of the Territories was to be determined by France, the United Kingdom, the United States and the Soviet Union within one year of the Treaty's entry into force — that is, by 15 September 1948. If no agreement was reached by that time, the Treaty provided for the question to be taken up by the United Nations. A four-Power Commission of Investigation visited Eritrea and held numerous consultations on the question, but by the end of the stipulated one-year period no agreement had been reached. Accordingly, on 15 September 1948, the question was referred to the United Nations.[1]

1/Document 1
See page 51

Initial consideration by the General Assembly

14 During discussions in the General Assembly's First Committee in April-May 1949, a wide variety of proposals was presented for each of the three Territories, reflecting significant differences of opinion. Some delegations proposed the granting of immediate independence for certain of the former colonies, whereas others suggested placing the Territories under the International Trusteeship System but could not agree on the modalities of establishing the trusteeship. The Secretary-General at the time, Trygve Lie, reported in June 1949 that each of the three forms of administration provided for in the Charter of the United Nations — administration by the United Nations itself, by a group of States or by one country alone — had its advocates and its opponents (A/930).

15 With respect to Eritrea, opinions among Member States were predominantly in favour of incorporating part of Eritrea into Ethiopia, but there was wide disagreement as to the exact regions involved. Eritrea's chances of becoming an independent State were thought to be much more remote than those of Libya and Italian Somaliland. Ethiopia favoured the speedy transfer of all of Eritrea to Ethiopia, citing claims to the Territory based on geographical, historical, ethnic and economic grounds, including, in particular, its need for adequate access to the sea. The United Kingdom, the administering Power, and the United States, which supported the Ethiopian Government, proposed that the eastern part of Eritrea be incorporated into Ethiopia and that a separate solution be found for the western part. The Soviet Union favoured a United Nations trusteeship, with territorial concessions to Ethiopia to provide access to the Red Sea through the port of Assab. Eighteen Latin American States favoured independence after an interim period of advice and assistance under the International Trusteeship System. Italy was opposed to the annexation of Eritrea by Ethiopia, and asked that Italy be allowed to take over the administration of the Territory.

16   The First Committee also heard from representatives of Eritrean political parties and organizations. The Muslim League of Eritrea, the New Eritrea Pro-Italia Party and the Italo-Eritrean Association all favoured independence, either immediately or following a period of trusteeship under United Nations or Italian administration. The Unionist Party asked that Eritrea be united with Ethiopia.

17   During discussions of the General Assembly in full plenary session, various proposals concerning all three Territories — Eritrea, Italian Somaliland and Libya — were presented. On 18 May 1949, the Assembly decided to postpone further consideration of the question until its next (fourth) regular session.[2] The Assembly also adopted a resolution asking the Economic and Social Council, in its plans and activities regarding developing regions, to take into consideration the economic and social advancement of the former Italian colonies [A/RES/266 (III)].

2/Document 2
See page 51

United Nations Commission for Eritrea

18   Differences of opinion on the question of Eritrea continued when the First Committee took up the issue in September-October 1949 during the fourth session of the General Assembly. Proposals again varied from independence to union with Ethiopia, but the consensus among Member States was that Ethiopia's rights and claims should be respected. Eritrean political parties and organizations representing the full spectrum of local opinion, from immediate independence to union with Ethiopia, again addressed the Committee.

19   On 21 November 1949, the General Assembly, by a vote of 48 in favour, 1 against (Ethiopia) and 9 abstentions, adopted resolution 289 (IV), which addressed the status of all three former Italian colonies.[3] Libya and Italian Somaliland were to become independent and sovereign

3/Document 3
See page 52

States, the former not later than 1 January 1952 and the latter 10 years from the date of the approval by the Assembly of a trusteeship agreement for the Territory with Italy as the Administering Authority. With regard to Eritrea, the Assembly recommended that a Commission, consisting of the representatives of Burma, Guatemala, Norway, Pakistan and the Union of South Africa, should be dispatched to the Territory to examine the question and prepare a report.

20   The Commission's terms of reference called on it to take into account the wishes and welfare of the inhabitants of Eritrea, including the views of the various racial, religious and political groups; the capacity of the people for self-government; the interests of peace and security in East Africa; and the rights and claims of Ethiopia. After visiting Eritrea and Ethiopia, consulting with the Governments having special interests in the question (Egypt, Ethiopia, France, Italy and the United Kingdom) and hearing the views of the representatives of the principal political parties in Eritrea, the Commission submitted its report to the Secretary-General and the General Assembly in June 1950.[4]

4/Document 4
See page 53

21   Differences of opinion among the members of the Commission prevented it from reaching a unanimous conclusion. Instead, it forwarded two memoranda in its report. One, submitted by Burma, Norway and the Union of South Africa, concluded that the poverty of the country and its dependence "in most vital respects on Ethiopia's rich farming resources and transit trade" precluded its complete independence, and that therefore the best solution would have to be based on Eritrea's close political association with Ethiopia. Towards this end, Burma and the Union of South Africa recommended that Eritrea be constituted a self-governing unit of a federation with Ethiopia, under the sovereignty of the Ethiopian Crown. A separate proposal by Norway recommended the reintegration of Eritrea into Ethiopia. The second memorandum, submitted by Guatemala and Pakistan, recommended that Eritrea be placed under the International Trusteeship System, with the United Nations itself as the Administering Authority, for a maximum period of 10 years, at the end of which Eritrea would become completely independent.

General Assembly decides on federation with Ethiopia

22   During the fifth session of the General Assembly, the Ad Hoc Political Committee considered the report of the Commission for Eritrea as well as a number of draft resolutions submitted by Member States. A majority of the Committee supported a 14-Power draft resolution containing a detailed plan, based on the proposal submitted by Burma

and the Union of South Africa, for Eritrean federation with Ethiopia. The 14 sponsors of the resolution were Bolivia, Brazil, Burma, Canada, Denmark, Ecuador, Greece, Liberia, Mexico, Panama, Paraguay, Peru, Turkey and the United States.

23   Under the plan, Eritrea would constitute an autonomous unit federated with Ethiopia under the sovereignty of the Ethiopian Crown. During a transition period ending not later than 15 September 1952, an Eritrean Representative Assembly would be chosen by the people and an Eritrean Constitution prepared and put into effect. A United Nations Commissioner in Eritrea would be appointed whose principal task would be to prepare the draft Constitution in consultation with the administering Power, the Government of Ethiopia and the inhabitants of Eritrea. The Constitution would then be submitted to the Representative Assembly.

24   The solution of federation, said some of the plan's sponsors, would go a long way towards meeting the fundamental desires of that part of the Eritrean population which desired independence while at the same time preserving the unity of Eritrea and ensuring Ethiopia's access to the sea. The plan, these States said, included provisions to safeguard Eritreans against an abuse of power by the Ethiopian Government and guaranteed equality between the two members of the federation.

25   The plan was criticized by a number of Member States — Cuba, the Dominican Republic, El Salvador, Guatemala, Italy, Pakistan, Saudi Arabia, the Soviet Union and Uruguay, among others — primarily on the grounds that it imposed severe restrictions on the right of the Eritreans to self-determination. The representative of Pakistan urged the adoption of the draft resolution presented by his delegation, which recommended that Eritrea be constituted as an independent and sovereign State not later than 1 January 1953. The representative of the Soviet Union stated that the plan amounted to "a marriage against the will of one of the parties". The representative of Italy stated that he considered it a moral duty to support the independence of Eritrea, particularly as the United Nations had granted independence to Libya and Italian Somaliland.

26   The representative of the Muslim League of Eritrea also addressed the Committee, stating that the Eritrean people wanted immediate independence and were opposed to any plan for the partition or annexation of Eritrea and to any plan of union or federation with Ethiopia. The Unionist Party of Eritrea and the Independent Muslim League of Eritrea subsequently sent a telegram to the Committee protesting the granting of a hearing to the representative of the Muslim League of Eritrea, contending that his statements did not "convey the wishes of Eritreans".

27   On 24 November 1950, the Ad Hoc Political Committee

adopted the 14-Power draft resolution containing the federation plan by a vote of 38 to 14, with 8 abstentions. The General Assembly adopted the plan on 2 December in its resolution 390 (V) by a vote of 46 to 10, with 4 abstentions.[5] Twelve days later, the Assembly elected a Commissioner in Eritrea. As the Commissioner later observed, resolution 390 (V) was a new type of decision for the United Nations: "For the first time, the Assembly appointed a Commissioner who was responsible for ensuring that the resolution was carried out without the assistance of a council composed of Member States. For the first time, too, the Assembly drew up the statute for a federation and laid down the principles on which the Constitution of one of the members of that federation should rest".

5/Document 6
See page 94

Adoption of an Eritrean Constitution

28   The United Nations Commissioner in Eritrea arrived in Asmara on 9 February 1951 and visited Addis Ababa on 18 February. Thereafter, he travelled to other regions and provinces of Eritrea, explaining the purposes of the General Assembly resolution and ascertaining the views of the population. In a progress report dated 16 November 1951, he stated that all political groups and all sections of the population with which he had come into contact had voiced their approval and acceptance of the plan to federate Eritrea with Ethiopia while instituting local autonomy. He stated further that they were prepared to cooperate with the Commissioner and with the British Administration in implementing the Assembly's resolution.[6] He noted, however, that a number of people did not fully believe in the federal solution or in the possibility of it being carried through.

6/Document 7
See page 96

29   After these initial consultations, the Commissioner focused on the drafting of a Constitution. He held numerous meetings with representatives of Eritrean political parties and economic, cultural and social organizations in the capital and throughout the country. Discussions covered such questions as the number of assemblies, the designation and powers of the head of the executive branch, the representation of the Emperor of Ethiopia, the official language or languages and the choice of a flag. In these discussions, religious leaders called for constitutional safeguards regarding religious freedom, and the foreign communities urged safeguards for the rights of minorities. The Commissioner also held consultations with representatives of Ethiopia, the United Kingdom and other interested Governments, and with various legal consultants.

30   Meanwhile, the Administering Authority, in consultation with the Commissioner, made arrangements for the formation of the Eritrean Representative Assembly, as called for in paragraph 11 of resolution 390 (V).[7] In order to provide for an Assembly that would not

7/Document 6
See page 94

be unwieldy in size but would still be large enough to represent the many different communities in Eritrea, the United Kingdom decided to divide Eritrea into 68 constituencies, meaning that there was to be roughly one representative for every 15,000 people. The United Kingdom also established rules governing the eligibility of Eritreans for participation in the voting and for election to the Assembly. To be able to vote a person had, among other things, to be a male inhabitant of Eritrea at least 21 years of age, and be of Eritrean descent and not possess foreign nationality. Candidates for the Assembly had to be at least 30 years of age and to fulfil certain additional requirements.

31   The elections, the first ever held in Eritrea, took place on 25 and 26 March 1952; a second round was held on 12 May to break a tie in two constituencies. Three political parties divided 66 of the 68 seats: the Union and Liberal Unionist parties (32), the Democratic and Independent Front (Muslim League and other parties of the Front) (19) and the Muslim League of the Western Province (15). No single party obtained a clear majority, and the seats were shared equally by Christian and Muslim representatives.

32   The Eritrean Representative Assembly was opened officially on 28 April 1952. On 3 May, the United Nations Commissioner presented to the Assembly the draft Eritrean Constitution (in Arabic, English and Tigrinya) and outlined its contents.[8] On 14 May, the Assembly unanimously adopted article 1, which consisted of paragraphs 1 to 7 of General Assembly resolution 390 (V), relating to the adoption and ratification of the act of federation with Ethiopia. During the next two months, the Representative Assembly considered each article of the draft Constitution, and on 10 July unanimously adopted the Constitution as amended during the deliberations.

33   On 11 August 1952, the Emperor of Ethiopia ratified the Constitution during a formal ceremony in Addis Ababa attended by the United Nations Commissioner. On 28 August, the Chief Executive of the Government of Eritrea and the President of the Eritrean Representative Assembly were elected. With the Emperor's ratification of the Federal Act on 11 September 1952, the Federation of Eritrea with Ethiopia was formally established. On 15 September, the Administering Authority (the United Kingdom) formally handed over the administration of Eritrea to the Federal and Eritrean Governments.

34   With these steps, General Assembly resolution 390 (V) of 2 December 1950 was put into effect. The United Nations Commissioner later reported his view that the Constitution "gives Eritrea a fair and promising start in its existence as an autonomous unit within the Federation . . . The Federation and Eritrea will have to learn to live side by side, each respecting the proper sphere of activity and jurisdiction of the other".[9] The General Assembly welcomed the establishment of the

Eritrean Representative Assembly on 17 December 1952, congratulating the "people and governmental authorities of the Federation for their effective and loyal fulfilment" of resolution 390 (V).[10]

10/Document 11
See page 152

Ethiopia abrogates Federal Act

35   Within a few years, the federal arrangement between Ethiopia and Eritrea began to experience problems that cast doubt on its sustainability. In 1956, Ethiopia established Amharic as the official language of Eritrea, replacing Arabic and Tigrinya, which had been stipulated as official languages under the Eritrean Constitution. Ethiopia next forbade the use of the Eritrean flag, began referring to the Eritrean Government as the Eritrean "Administration" and, in 1959, imposed Ethiopian law on Eritrea. Finally, in November 1962, Emperor Haile Selassie of Ethiopia dissolved the Eritrean Representative Assembly and declared Eritrea's federal status void.

36   The gradual erosion of Eritrea's federal status in the late 1950s had led independence-minded Eritreans to launch a campaign of resistance to Ethiopian rule. With the abrogation of the Federal Act in 1962 and the incorporation of Eritrea into Ethiopia as one of that country's provinces, the movement for secession and self-determination was taken up in earnest.

III The struggle for independence

37   The military conflict between Ethiopia and Eritrea was one of Africa's longest struggles for independence and one of the world's most protracted campaigns for self-determination since the founding of the United Nations. A critical factor in helping the Eritrean resistance achieve its goal was a parallel campaign, beginning in the mid-1970s, waged against the Ethiopian Government by a coalition of non-Eritrean groups. Indeed, when that coalition came to power in Ethiopia in May 1991, it supported Eritrean independence. The Eritreans, for their part, although by then in control of Asmara and the rest of Eritrea, stopped short of declaring full sovereignty and instead agreed to the holding, within two years, of an internationally supervised referendum on the question of independence. The United Nations, which was by then playing an increasingly active role in worldwide democratization and electoral assistance, was asked to observe and verify the entire process.

Eritrea and Ethiopia at war

38   Eritrean opposition to Ethiopian rule was led in its early years by the Eritrean Liberation Front (ELF), which drew its support primarily from Muslim inhabitants of the Eritrean lowlands in the west and which launched an armed struggle in 1961. Dissension within the ELF in the early to mid-1970s led to the emergence of the Eritrean People's Liberation Front (EPLF), a coalition of resistance groups. The two groups fought a civil war in the early 1970s, following which the EPLF became the main resistance movement.

39   On 12 September 1974, the Emperor of Ethiopia was overthrown in a military *coup d'état* following several years of social unrest, increasing public pressure to institute land and other democratic reforms, and a famine that had claimed at least 250,000 lives. There were also reports, at the time of the coup, of tensions within the Ethiopian military over the conduct of the Eritrean war. One year later, the country's new military rulers abolished the monarchy and proclaimed Ethiopia to be a socialist State. On 3 February 1977, Mengistu Haile Mariam assumed the presidency of the Provisional Military Administrative Council (PMAC), also known as the Dergue, the body which exercised executive power in Ethiopia. The Mengistu regime established close ties with the Soviet Union, which replaced the United States as Ethiopia's main ally.

40   The early years of the new Ethiopian regime saw an escalation of the war between Eritrea and the Ethiopian Government. The fortunes of the two sides fluctuated greatly during this period. By 1978, the Government controlled much of Eritrea. But in 1982, a major Government offensive, mounted with support from external Powers, including the Soviet Union, failed to achieve its goal of definitively reclaiming Eritrea. The EPLF seized significant amounts of Government weaponry and, throughout the mid-1980s, carried out a series of effective counter-attacks.

41   By this time, the Eritreans were one of several groups engaging in armed opposition against the Government of Ethiopia. Among them was the Tigre People's Liberation Front (TPLF), which was formed in the late 1970s and was seeking autonomy for the Tigre region. The TPLF received military training and equipment from the EPLF, and supported Eritrea's right to secede from Ethiopia. Other anti-Government groups included the Ethiopian People's Democratic Movement (EPDM), a coalition of non-Eritrean and non-Tigrean Ethiopian dissident groups, and the Omoro Liberation Front, seeking independence in the south for the predominantly Muslim Omoros, Ethiopia's largest ethnic group.

International response to famine

42   As these conflicts continued during the 1980s, Ethiopia suffered from a devastating famine on two separate occasions. The first emergency occurred in 1984, following several consecutive years of severe drought and crop failures. More than 8 million people throughout the country, including Eritreans, were affected, with 1 million facing the prospect of death from starvation and hundreds of thousands forced to flee their homes in search of food. United Nations agencies had been sounding the alarm for many months about conditions in the Horn of Africa and elsewhere on the continent, but the crisis only registered globally in late 1984, following media coverage of Ethiopia's plight. The result was the largest mobilization and delivery of resources to a population in peril since the Second World War. Although 250,000 Ethiopians, including Eritreans, perished, the emergency humanitarian assistance operation carried out by United Nations agencies and other organizations is credited with saving millions of lives. When famine and war-induced starvation struck for a second time in the late 1980s, the United Nations again led the international response. During this second Ethiopian emergency, half the population in need of aid was located in areas totally or partially controlled by anti-Government movements.

Efforts to negotiate a peace get under way

43   In the late 1980s, the EPLF gained control of increasing amounts of Eritrean territory. At the same time, the Ethiopian Army, despite its superiority in troops and armaments, was losing ground to the non-Eritrean opposition groups, most notably the TPLF, which formed an alliance with the EPDM to form the Ethiopian People's Revolutionary Democratic Front (EPRDF). After putting down an attempted coup by military officers in May 1989, the Government agreed in June to hold negotiations with the various opposition factions in an effort to find a peaceful solution to the conflict. The Government invited the United Nations to attend as an observer.

44   The first round of talks between representatives of the Ethiopian Government and the EPLF took place in September 1989 at the Carter Center in Atlanta, Georgia, under the sponsorship of former United States President Jimmy Carter. A second round was held two months later in Nairobi. However, little progress was achieved. In early 1990, the EPRDF intensified its struggle against an increasingly besieged Ethiopian Army. And in February of that year, the EPLF increased its hold on Eritrean territory by capturing Massawa, a major Eritrean port, leaving Asmara, Assab and Keren as the only areas of Eritrea not under the Front's control. A subsequent accord between the World Food Programme (WFP) and the EPLF enabled the port of Massawa to be used for deliveries of emergency food aid, both within Ethiopia and across the border to the Sudan. The agreement was notable for having been reached between the United Nations and an anti-Government movement.

45   Following further heavy fighting, the Government of Ethiopia and the EPLF held new rounds of negotiations in the United States in October 1990 and February 1991. Again, however, no agreement was reached. The United States subsequently announced that peace talks would be held in London at the end of May. By this time, in addition to its heavy losses in Eritrea, the Ethiopian Army had suffered major defeats at the hands of EPRDF forces, which were poised for a final advance on Addis Ababa.

46   On 21 May 1991, the leader of the Ethiopian Government, Mengistu Haile Mariam, fled the country. On 24 May, following the departure of Ethiopian troops from Asmara, the EPLF took control of Eritrea's main city. On 27 May, the Provisional Government of Eritrea was formed, with Mr. Issaias Afwerki, the leader of the EPLF, as Secretary-General. One day later, the EPRDF took control of Addis Ababa and established an interim Government.

47   The peace talks in London were held as scheduled on 27 and 28 May 1991. Representatives of the EPLF, meeting under the auspices

Eritrea

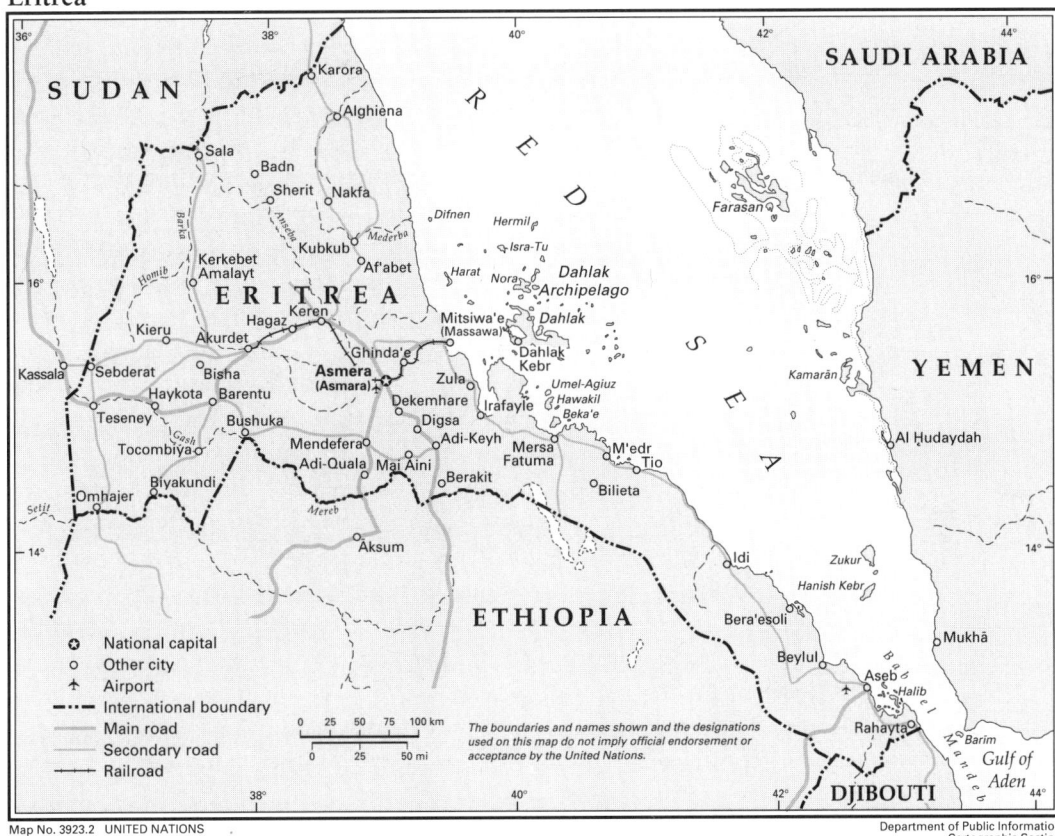

of the United States with representatives of the interim Government of Ethiopia, reaffirmed the intent of the EPLF to hold, within two years, a referendum on the question of independence from Ethiopia. The EPLF had first proposed such a vote in 1980. The interim Government coalition, of which the largest faction was the TPLF, agreed that Eritrea had the right to determine its future, including independence.

48   In adhering to its commitment to hold an internationally supervised referendum, the EPLF decided against an outright declaration of independence, a course which had been favoured by some Eritreans. Instead, the EPLF leadership decided to seek a legal, democratic conclusion to the conflict so as to promote stability and gain the full support of the international community. At the end of the London talks, it was announced that a peace conference had been scheduled for July at which, among other things, a broad-based Ethiopian transitional Government would be formed and the question of Eritrea's future status would be discussed further.

Conference on Peace and Democracy

49 The Conference on Peace and Democracy took place in Addis Ababa from 1 to 5 July 1991 and was attended by almost all the political parties, movements and social organizations in Ethiopia as well as a number of intergovernmental organizations, including the United Nations as an observer. The Conference adopted a Charter affirming that freedom, equal rights and self-determination of all peoples were the cardinal principles governing State affairs in the new Ethiopia. The Charter also set out rules for a transition period, which was to last two years and culminate in multi-party elections, and during which the highest organ of State was to be the Council of Representatives, acting as the transitional Parliament. Mr. Meles Zenawi, the leader of the EPRDF, was named President of this Transitional Government.

50 The EPLF attended the Conference but did not become part of the Transitional Government. With regard to Eritrea, the Conference formally recognized the right of the Eritrean people to determine their political future by an internationally supervised referendum. The Conference also reached agreement on modalities for relations between the Transitional Government of Ethiopia and the Provisional Government of Eritrea for the interim period. In this connection, the two sides discussed Ethiopian access to the ports of Assab and Massawa, decided to form committees on security, immigration and economic matters to advance their mutual interests and committed themselves to respecting the results of a free and fair referendum.

IV   The referendum

51   Owing to the momentous nature of the step being contemplated by Eritrea — the creation of a new African State — extensive consultations were necessary in order to establish the modalities for the referendum and to determine the nature of United Nations involvement in it. Ultimately, the General Assembly decided to create the United Nations Observer Mission to Verify the Referendum in Eritrea (UNOVER), which was deployed to Eritrea in January 1993. The referendum process itself consisted of three stages: the registration of voters, the campaign and the holding of the poll. In fulfilment of its mandate, UNOVER deployed a core team of 21 observers in all districts of Eritrea. They were joined for the voting in April 1993 by an additional 86 observers, while separate arrangements were made to observe the polling in Ethiopia, the Sudan and dozens of other countries where polling-stations were set up for Eritreans living outside the country. Each step of the referendum process was carried out freely and fairly. One month later, a sovereign and independent Eritrea was admitted to the United Nations as the Organization's 182nd Member State.

Invitation to the United Nations

52   Shortly after the July 1991 Conference on Peace and Democracy in Addis Ababa, the Secretary-General of the Provisional Government of Eritrea, Issaias Afwerki, in a letter to my predecessor dated 25 July, invited the United Nations to become involved in the referendum process. My predecessor responded in a letter dated 18 September 1991, stressing that the requirements for the Organization's participation included the agreement of Ethiopia and a clear mandate from the competent organ of the United Nations.

53   Ethiopia's consent was forthcoming in a letter dated 13 December 1991 from the President of the Transitional Government, stating that the United Nations "should play an active role in verifying that the referendum" was free and fair.[11] The Organization, he continued, should "initiate appropriate measures to enable the United Nations to play this role and make the necessary arrangements with the Provisional Government of Eritrea to facilitate the ways and means for United Nations supervision of the referendum".

54   Following receipt of the letter, contacts were undertaken with the Transitional Government of Ethiopia and the Provisional Government

11/Document 13
See page 154

of Eritrea to clarify the role to be played by the Organization. On 21 December 1991, in my capacity as Secretary-General-Designate of the United Nations, I met in Cairo with the Secretary-General of the Provisional Government of Eritrea to discuss the situation in the Horn of Africa and Eritrea in particular. I expressed the willingness of the United Nations to assist the Eritrean people in all fields and requested the Provisional Government to present its requests in this regard officially to the Organization.

55   In his letter of invitation dated 25 July 1991, the Secretary-General of the Provisional Government of Eritrea had also appealed to the world community for assistance in the rehabilitation and reconstruction of the country. In the immediate postwar period, approximately 8 million people in Ethiopia and Eritrea continued to rely on food aid. There was also the challenge of handling the movement and reintegration of ex-soldiers and their families, estimated to number some 400,000, as well as the return of an estimated 500,000 refugees from the Sudan, to which they had fled as a result of the war and famine.

56   The United Nations had maintained a strong humanitarian presence in Ethiopia and Eritrea since 1984-1985, and was well placed to respond. The United Nations Children's Fund (UNICEF), for example, had already established an office in Asmara and planned to embark on a programme of child immunization. The World Food Programme continued to provide essential equipment to the ports of Massawa and Assab to facilitate the delivery of food aid. In September 1991, the United Nations issued an appeal for $400 million in food and other emergency aid to meet humanitarian needs in the Horn of Africa until the end of the year. The Organization also established a Special Emergency Programme for the Horn of Africa (SEPHA) to facilitate the coordination of United Nations relief and short-term rehabilitation efforts in the region.

Working out the modalities

57   In January and February 1992, the first two months of my tenure as Secretary-General, I wrote twice to the President of the Transitional Government of Ethiopia regarding the role the United Nations might play in the referendum process.[12] I presented a number of options, ranging from, at a minimum, the provision of technical assistance without assessment of the referendum process to the organization and conduct of the entire referendum, including the drafting of laws and regulations. Intermediate options included passive observation, which would not involve investigation of complaints or public pronouncements; active observation, which implied interaction with the electoral

12/Document 14
See page 155;
Document 15
See page 155

authorities and the public; observation with independent verification of the results; and organization of the electoral process in cooperation with the appropriate authorities.

58   In subsequent weeks, my representatives carried out consultations and detailed technical discussions on possible arrangements with representatives of both the Transitional Government of Ethiopia and the Provisional Government of Eritrea. One question that arose during this period related to the General Assembly's consideration of the request for United Nations involvement. The Organization of African Unity (OAU) and the African Group at the United Nations took the position that the United Nations could act only upon an invitation from the Government of Ethiopia. These Member States were concerned about the implications the referendum process would have for other potential secessionist movements in Africa, and thus wanted to reaffirm the rights of Member States to guide the involvement of the United Nations in such cases. The Provisional Government of Eritrea, meanwhile, stated on several occasions that the self-determination of the Eritrean people was the sole prerogative of the Eritrean people and did not fall within the jurisdiction or authority of any other party. My approach, in contacts that my representatives and I had with the relevant parties, sought to balance these positions and win the widest possible consensus around a viable plan for United Nations involvement.

59   Separately, the Provisional Government of Eritrea took two important steps. First, on 6 April 1992, it issued a Nationality Proclamation, establishing the criteria for determining Eritrean nationality by birth, naturalization, adoption and marriage.[13] Second, on 7 April, the Provisional Government issued a proclamation announcing that a referendum would be held on or before 3 April 1993 on a question to read as follows: "Do you approve Eritrea to become an independent sovereign State?" The proclamation also established an independent Referendum Commission, headed by a Referendum Commissioner, to organize and conduct the referendum, and set out the rules and regulations governing the identification of voters and other aspects of the process.[14]

60   On 19 May 1992, the Referendum Commissioner, by a letter addressed to me, invited the United Nations to send a delegation "to observe, and to verify the freeness, fairness and impartiality of the entire referendum process from its beginning in July 1992 to its completion in April 1993".[15] Taking into account this invitation, as well as the earlier endorsement of a United Nations role by the Transitional Government of Ethiopia and the historical involvement of the General Assembly with the political evolution of Eritrea, it was my view at this point that the Assembly might wish to authorize the involvement of the United Nations in the referendum.

61   As recently as December 1991, the General Assembly had

13/Document 16
See page 156

14/Document 17
See page 158

15/Document 19
See page 170

affirmed "the value of the electoral assistance that the United Nations [had] provided at the request of some Member States, in the context of full respect for their sovereignty" [A/RES/46/137]. With the end of the cold war and the transition to democracy occurring in many countries, the provision of electoral assistance had become an important new field of endeavour for the Organization. The United Nations had monitored elections in Namibia (as part of the United Nations Transition Assistance Group, or UNTAG), Nicaragua and Haiti, and had provided many other countries with technical assistance in all aspects of voting, drafting constitutions and related matters. An operation in Eritrea, I felt, would be fully in keeping with the mandate of the Organization to support not only democratization but also self-determination, decolonization and post-conflict peace-building. It would also serve as a stabilizing influence at a time of growing turmoil in neighbouring States.

62   Accordingly, on 11 June 1992 I brought the matter to the attention of the General Assembly, and informed it that I had decided to dispatch a technical team to Eritrea in order to gather more information for the Assembly's consideration of the question.[16] The team visited Eritrea from 30 July to 8 August and held in-depth discussions with the Referendum Commission, members of the Provisional Government and representatives of a wide spectrum of political, social and religious organizations. On the basis of United Nations experience in other elections and referenda and of comments received from the United Nations Centre for Human Rights, the team made a number of technical suggestions aimed at improving some operational aspects of the referendum or clarifying articles of the Referendum Proclamation that might be susceptible to misinterpretation. The response of the Referendum Commission to these suggestions was positive in all cases. Later in August, pending the decision of the General Assembly to formally authorize the Organization's involvement, I assigned two officers to Asmara as an "advance team" to assist in the initial preparations for the referendum and to provide such support to the Referendum Commission as might be required.[17]

16/Document 20
See page 171

17/Document 21
See page 172

Report to the General Assembly

63   In October 1992, I submitted a report to the General Assembly in which I strongly recommended that the Assembly give its approval for the establishment of a United Nations observer mission.[18] I proposed the following terms of reference for such a mission:

18/Document 24
See page 173

(a) To verify the impartiality of the referendum authorities and organs, including the Referendum Commission, in all aspects and stages of the referendum process;

(b) To verify that there exists complete freedom of organization, movement, assembly and expression without hindrance or intimidation;

(c) To verify that there is equal access to media facilities and that there is fairness in the allocation of both the timing and length of broadcasts;

(d) To verify that the referendum rolls are properly drawn up and that qualified voters are not denied identification and registration cards or the right to vote;

(e) To report to the referendum authorities on complaints, irregularities and instances of interference reported or observed and, if necessary, to request the referendum authorities to take action to resolve and rectify such complaints, irregularities or interference;

(f) To observe all activities related to the registration of voters, the organization of the poll, the referendum campaign, the poll itself and the counting, computation and announcement of the results.

64   A mission of modest size seemed appropriate given the peaceful situation in Eritrea, the work already carried out by the Referendum Commission and the general lack of political tensions or conflicting positions in relation to the referendum. Therefore, I proposed that a total of 21 international staff, headed by a Special Representative and supported by local personnel, be deployed. These core personnel would be joined during the polling by additional observers from the United Nations Development Programme (UNDP), personnel from other United Nations agencies in Eritrea and neighbouring countries, volunteers from among the international personnel of non-governmental organizations (NGOs) in Eritrea and additional observers from abroad contributed by the United Nations Secretariat and Member States. The total cost of the mission was estimated at just under $3 million.

65   On 16 December 1992, the General Assembly authorized the establishment of the mission, to be known as the United Nations Observer Mission to Verify the Referendum in Eritrea (UNOVER). The Assembly requested that I arrange for the mission's deployment as soon as possible and called upon "the authorities directly concerned to extend their fullest cooperation".[19]

19/Document 25
See page 179

Initial preparations

66   I visited Eritrea in early January 1993 to appraise the situation at first hand and to signal the commitment of the United Nations to the process of democratization in Eritrea. UNOVER was inaugurated during my visit, with headquarters and a regional office in Asmara and regional offices at Keren and Mendefera. (An additional regional centre was

established in March at Adi Qaih.) Later in January, I appointed Mr. Samir Sanbar as my Special Representative and Chief of UNOVER. Also in January, the mission's core team of 21 observers, representing 16 nationalities, received intensive in-depth training before being deployed to their respective regions.

67   UNOVER's guidelines were set out in my report to the General Assembly of 19 October 1992.[20] During all three phases of the referendum process — the registration of voters, the campaign and the polling — the mission's observers were to gather factual information about the conduct of the referendum and evaluate the impartiality of the referendum authorities at all levels. UNOVER staff were instructed to abide by the principle that the ultimate judgement about the referendum process would be made by the voters themselves, to respect the independent character of Eritrea's Referendum Commission and to establish a relationship with the Commission on that basis.

68   The Referendum Commission had ultimate authority for organizing and conducting the referendum in all its aspects, and had begun work immediately upon its establishment in April 1992. It faced two major tasks: to inform each and every citizen about the substantive issues surrounding the referendum question, and to make certain that each voter was familiar with voting techniques and other practical aspects of conducting an election.

69   UNOVER and the Referendum Commission faced similar challenges in carrying out their respective mandates. Foremost among them were the low literacy levels prevailing in Eritrea and the relative lack of voting experience and training in electoral practices. In addition, some Eritreans were reportedly questioning the usefulness or the purpose of a referendum in a country which was seen as having already won its freedom. Finally, there was only a brief period in which to complete technical preparations for the referendum, including arrangements for voting by Eritrean refugees, expatriates and exiles in Ethiopia, Saudi Arabia, the Sudan and elsewhere.

Voter registration

70   The identification and registration of voters began in mid-October 1992. This process was complicated by the lack of a census and the absence of a civil register, a situation which was itself the product of large-scale migrations of people during the colonial and federation periods and during the war.

71   UNOVER's positive interventions smoothed the registration process on a number of occasions. Following reports that some women were being forbidden by their husbands to register, UNOVER personnel

20/Document 24
See page 173

discussed the issue with village elders. In some of these cases, the men's opposition was attributed to cultural sensitivities over women being photographed; after consultations with UNOVER, the elders allowed an exception as they felt it would be for a good cause.

72   UNOVER also raised with the Referendum Commission the question of whether prisoners awaiting trial for their alleged collaboration with the Ethiopian authorities during the war would be permitted to participate in the referendum. The Commission in turn raised the issue with Eritrea's Department of Internal Affairs. UNOVER was subsequently informed that all such prisoners who had not been tried and convicted of crimes would be provided with registration cards and allowed to vote. Mission personnel were also invited to visit the prisons in order to interview prisoners in this category and ensure that they had been registered to vote. This constituted an important and successful assertion by UNOVER of a fundamental electoral principle.

73   By the end of the registration period on 1 March 1993, more than 1.1 million Eritreans had registered: 861,074 persons in Eritrea, 154,136 in the Sudan, 66,022 in Ethiopia, 43,765 in Saudi Arabia and 76,000 in all other countries combined, which included Australia, Belgium, Canada, Côte d'Ivoire, Denmark, Djibouti, Egypt, Finland, France, Germany, Greece, Iceland, India, Iraq, Italy, Kenya, Kuwait, the Netherlands, New Zealand, Nigeria, Norway, Qatar, the Russian Federation, Sweden, Switzerland, Syria, Uganda, the United Arab Emirates, the United Kingdom, the United Republic of Tanzania, the United States, Yemen, Zambia and Zimbabwe.

The campaign period

74   During the campaign, which lasted from 17 February 1993 until 21 April 1993, both UNOVER and the Referendum Commission mounted a massive civic education programme to explain the concept, principles and purposes underlying a referendum and to instruct prospective voters in the actual voting procedures and techniques. The Commission prepared 800,000 posters (in four major languages), voting manuals and curriculum materials for social science classes. Theatrical troupes staged plays containing voting and democracy-related themes. Videos for television (in nine languages) and radio programmes were also produced. The Commission later concluded that, of all the media employed for voter education, radio was the most effective. The Commission also conducted practice sessions in which voters went through simulated polling exercises, and trained 45 teachers in various electoral procedures. These teachers, in turn, instructed 5,000 young

people, who were then deployed as registrars at polling-stations throughout Eritrea.

75   UNOVER teams visited municipalities, villages, mosques and churches in all parts of Eritrea during the campaign, maintaining regular contact with community and religious leaders and social organizations and observing rallies and other referendum-related activities. The most common encounters were with elders, who usually came forward as the village representatives to speak with the observers. UNOVER personnel also monitored the mechanisms through which broadcasting time was allocated as well as the content of the information broadcast.

76   UNOVER's information campaign included radio programmes, posters and other materials stressing the right to vote, the principle of one vote per person and the secrecy of the vote. My Special Representative, for his part, worked closely with Eritrean radio and television, using every available opportunity to speak about the purpose of a free and fair referendum. He also travelled to all of UNOVER's regional offices as well as other areas. In these public visits he was welcomed with great enthusiasm. At Keren, he was received by more than 100,000 people from the town and surrounding villages — indicating the growing excitement with which Eritreans had accepted not just the idea of the referendum but the role of the United Nations in it. Such popular manifestations were notable given the fact that, prior to UNOVER's presence, some Eritreans had continued to harbour negative attitudes towards the United Nations for what they regarded as the Organization's inadequate support for Eritrean self-determination, both in the 1950s and during the long war with Ethiopia.

77   The campaign period presented UNOVER with a number of political obstacles that had to be surmounted. In Ethiopia, UNOVER's contacts with the Government and the preparations for the referendum itself, including a training seminar in Addis Ababa, were carried out in a low-profile manner so as not to provoke those segments of the Ethiopian population which, though a minority, continued to oppose Eritrean independence. In the Sudan, UNOVER maintained contacts with the Government and with the international diplomatic community in Khartoum for the purpose of gaining assistance in making voting arrangements for the large number of Eritrean refugees in that country. The Sudanese mission in Asmara also helped in this effort.

78   Another delicate political situation arose in connection with the presence in Saudi Arabia of more than 40,000 eligible Eritrean voters. Political differences between some Saudi Arabian and Eritrean authorities led to consultations between the Government of Saudi Arabia and my Special Representative within the framework of my good offices. One week before the referendum, the Saudi Government responded

positively to my efforts, enabling voting to take place and creating improved relations between Saudi Arabia and Eritrea.

79   By the beginning of April, the construction of more than 1,000 polling-stations in Eritrea — mat huts called "agnets", made from local materials — had been completed. UNOVER personnel had visited these sites and prepared detailed travel itineraries for those who would actually observe the vote. Areas with hazards such as bad roads or land-mines were identified and reported. Additional polling-stations were established in Ethiopia (202), the Sudan (335) and the other countries where voting was to take place, including Australia, Djibouti, Germany, India, Kuwait, New Zealand, the Nordic countries, Qatar, Saudi Arabia, the United Arab Emirates, the United States and Yemen.

80   Between 12 and 18 April, 86 observers arrived in Eritrea to join UNOVER, among them personnel provided by Member States, specialized agencies of the United Nations system, the Economic Commission for Africa (ECA) and international NGOs. At peak strength, UNOVER fielded personnel from 35 countries. The mission held training seminars to brief the new observers on its *modus operandi* and on the electoral code of conduct issued by the Referendum Commission, and then deployed teams consisting of two observers, a driver and an interpreter.

81   At the invitation of the Referendum Commission, other international observers came to Eritrea for the voting. Operating independently of UNOVER, these included delegations from the OAU, the Movement of Non-Aligned Countries, the European Community, the League of Arab States, Canada (Canadian NGO Observation Delegation), Denmark, Egypt, Ethiopia, the United Kingdom (Catholic Fund for Overseas Development), the United States (African-American Institute) and Yemen. They were deployed following two days of orientation by the Referendum Commission on Eritrean society and history, the liberation struggle and the conditions under which the referendum would be taking place. Among the local groups observing the vote was the Eritrean Citizens' Referendum Monitoring Group.

82   By 20 April, all polling-stations had received the necessary ballot-boxes, ballot papers, voter registers, stamps, indelible ink and other supplies. On 22 April, with all such preparations in order and with all observers in place both in Eritrea and abroad, my Special Representative and the Referendum Commissioner of Eritrea announced the beginning of the referendum.

The polling

83   For three days, from 23 to 25 April, Eritreans went to the polls in an atmosphere approximating that of a national celebration. By the

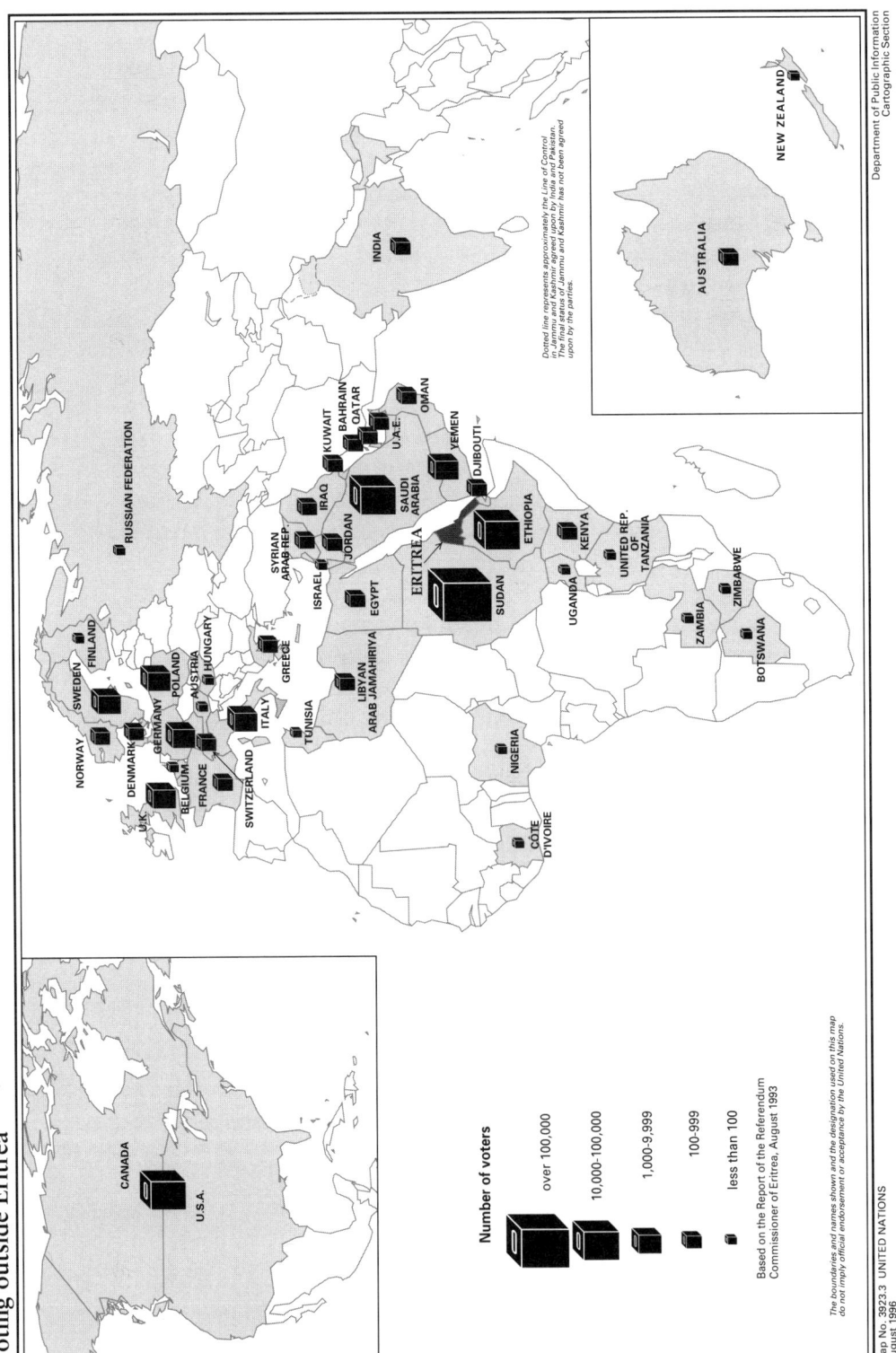

end of the first day, more than 85 per cent of the eligible participants had voted, and the final tally showed a voter turnout of 98.24 per cent. The majority of the polling-stations stayed open from 7 a.m. until 7 p.m. UNOVER observers covered 84 per cent of the 1,044 polling stations in Eritrea, and 90 per cent of the 335 stations in the Sudan were covered.

84   Polling in other countries where the referendum took place was carried out on different dates. Eritreans in Yemen, for example, voted from 16 to 18 April. In the Nordic countries, voting was held on 17 and 18 April, while in New Zealand voting took place on 24 and 25 April. Members of the Eritrean People's Liberation Army (EPLA), the military wing of the EPLF, voted in mid-April in their barracks. This arrangement had been arrived at by the Referendum Commission and UNOVER to permit soldiers to be deployed for duty during the regular polling days and also to avoid the presence of armed, uniformed men in voting booths, which might have been misconstrued by some voters as intimidation.

85   Immediately after the closure of polling-stations at the end of the third day of voting, electoral officials began counting the votes in the presence of observers, elders and representatives of the media. UNOVER conducted a "quick count" and within a few hours was able to provide preliminary — and, as it turned out, highly accurate — results to the Referendum Commission and the Provisional Government.

The results

86   On 27 April 1993, the Referendum Commission announced the official provisional results. Of those who had cast their votes, 1,098,015 had voted "yes" and 1,825 had voted "no"; 323 votes were invalid and 53,838 were tendered ballots, cast at a polling-station at which the voter was not registered. This meant that 99.805 per cent of those participating in the referendum had voted for independence, and only 0.17 per cent had voted against. Eritreans voting in Ethiopia, the Sudan and other countries, as well as members of the EPLA, had voted "yes", again with nearly total unanimity.

87   As I later informed the General Assembly, reports of UNOVER observers from all parts of Eritrea indicated that the referendum had been well organized and conducted in a smooth and orderly manner.[21] No essential electoral materials were missing from the polling-stations, no cases of intimidation were reported or observed and the secrecy of the vote was generally respected, although the lack of an established electoral practice created some minor procedural difficulties. Based on this evaluation, my Special Representative officially announced

21/Document 39
See page 242

on 27 April that "the referendum process in Eritrea can be considered to have been free and fair at every stage, and . . . it has been conducted to my satisfaction".[22] In its subsequent report, the Referendum Commission stressed the good working relationship between it and UNOVER which could be taken "as a model for such future endeavours elsewhere".

22/Document 28
See page 213

88   The observer mission sent by the OAU concurred in this assessment, declaring that the manner in which polling had been conducted in Eritrea was "free, fair and devoid of significant irregularities . . . The referendum marked a happy occasion for the people of Eritrea in particular and for Africa in general considering how the Eritrean people had exercised their freedom of choice through the ballot-box in a peaceful manner without any fear of intimidation and harassment".[23]

23/Document 27
See page 212

89   In a statement on 27 April 1993, the Secretary-General of the Provisional Government of Eritrea congratulated the Eritrean people for what he described as their "historic achievement". He also said that although formal independence would not be declared until 24 May 1993 — the second anniversary of the EPLF's entry into Asmara following the collapse of the former Ethiopian Government — Eritrea was a sovereign country as of 27 April.[24]

24/Document 29
See page 213

90   Separately, in a letter to me dated 29 April, the Secretary-General of the Provisional Government praised the United Nations for the role it had played in the smooth conduct and outcome of the referendum. At the same time, he appealed for substantial assistance from the international community to build peace and heal the wounds and devastation wrought by a long war that had now come to an end through appropriate legal and democratic instruments. I, in turn, congratulated the people of Eritrea on the result of the referendum in a letter dated 13 May 1993 to the Secretary-General of the Provisional Government. I concluded, "The cause of Eritrean independence has been given a resounding endorsement. The foundations have been laid for your country's passage to full nationhood and membership in the international community of nations".

91   A further consolidation of peace and stability in the region came on 29 April 1993, when Ethiopia's Council of Representatives recognized Eritrea's sovereignty and independence. In a statement, Ethiopia's Ministry of Foreign Affairs declared, "It is the conviction of the Transitional Government of Ethiopia that the independence of Eritrea represents a new landmark in relations between the two peoples, ushering in a period of far more enhanced cooperation and the further strengthening of the bonds of brotherhood between them".[25]

25/Document 30
See page 214

Eritrean independence and admission to United Nations

92   A number of significant events occurred during the interim period between the referendum and the ceremonies marking Eritrean independence. The Governments of Djibouti, Egypt, Italy, Saudi Arabia, the Sudan, the United Kingdom, the United States, Yemen and others extended diplomatic recognition to Eritrea. On 12 May 1991, the Provisional Government of Eritrea submitted a formal application for membership in the United Nations,[26] and also applied for membership in the OAU. The Provisional Government proclaimed a transition period of four years' duration, during which a Constitution would be drafted and ratified; laws on political parties and the press would be prepared; and multi-party elections at all levels of government — village, local and provincial — would be held. The EPLF turned itself into a political party known as the People's Front for Democracy and Justice.

93   In a message to the Eritrean people on 24 May 1993, the day independence was celebrated officially, I stated, "Today marks the turning-point in the history of Eritrea and indeed the Horn of Africa region as a whole. The spirit of independence was kept alive by Eritreans for nearly two decades, often under very difficult circumstances. Eritreans have made great sacrifices in order to determine the future of their country as free people. That objective has now been achieved . . . ."[27]

94   Two days later, the Security Council, in its resolution 828 (1993), unanimously recommended to the General Assembly that Eritrea be admitted to membership in the United Nations.[28] In an accompanying statement by its President, the Council noted "with great satisfaction Eritrea's solemn commitment to uphold the purposes and principles of the Charter of the United Nations and to fulfil all the obligations contained therein".[29]

95   On 28 May, pursuant to the recommendation of the Security Council, the General Assembly voted to admit Eritrea as the Organization's 182nd Member State.[30] In a statement to the Assembly following the vote, the Chairman of the delegation of Eritrea to the United Nations said, "Membership in the United Nations is of special significance for Eritrea, because of the United Nations role in deciding Eritrea's future in the 1950s, and because of the Organization's special responsibility . . . We wish to express our commitment to fulfilling our obligations as a State Member of the world community".[31] Immediately after the adjournment of the meeting of the Assembly, the Eritrean flag was raised in a ceremony at United Nations Headquarters in New York.

26/Document 31
See page 215

27/Document 32
See page 216

28/Document 33
See page 217

29/Document 34
See page 217

30/Document 35
See page 217

31/Document 36
See page 218

V Reconstruction and long-term development

96   Independence confronted Eritrea with daunting challenges as well as great opportunities. The country's main priorities were to revitalize the economy, repatriate several hundred thousand refugees, demobilize and reintegrate 70,000 soldiers and provide for the needs of some 2 million people — roughly two thirds of the country's population — who were destitute and dependent on outside relief for their daily survival. It was my view that Eritreans should not be asked to face these challenges alone. I thus appealed to the international community to provide generous and timely assistance. I also gave my commitment to the Eritrean people that the United Nations system would do its part in sustaining the positive momentum generated by Eritrea's successful referendum and accession to United Nations membership.

Resettlement of refugees

97   Between the end of the war in May 1991 and the referendum in April 1993, approximately 70,000 Eritreans returned spontaneously to Eritrea, most of them from the Sudan. At independence, many more were poised for return, including some 430,000 still in the Sudan. The task facing Eritrea was not just to repatriate and reintegrate these individuals, but to rehabilitate the areas to which they were expected to return — primarily the western lowland provinces, which had been the scene of some of the most intense fighting during the war. These areas, where towns and villages had been destroyed and where crops and animal herds had been decimated, were also suffering severe soil erosion, deforestation and other forms of environmental degradation, posing a further obstacle to the resumption of normal life.

98   In June 1993, the Government of Eritrea and the United Nations Department of Humanitarian Affairs issued an appeal to the international community for the resources required to fund a joint Programme for Refugee Reintegration and Rehabilitation of Resettlement Areas in Eritrea (PROFERI).[32] A $262-million, three-and-a-half-year undertaking, PROFERI aimed at providing food aid; initial relief packages for returnees; seeds, tools, livestock and other basic inputs for farmers and herders; and help in building or rehabilitating basic services

32/Document 37
See page 222

such as housing, hospitals, clinics, schools, roads, rails, ports, wells and sanitation systems.

99 On 6 July 1993, a pledging conference was held in Geneva to raise $111 million for the 19 months of the programme's first phase. Both the President of Eritrea and the United Nations Under-Secretary-General for Humanitarian Affairs addressed the gathering.[33] The former stressed that the repatriation of refugees should be "firmly rooted in, and be linked with, programmes of rehabilitation and recovery of the society as a whole", and added that mobilization of the necessary funds would "not only help the Eritrean people stand on their own two feet, but extricate the international community from the vicious circle of emergency assistance". The Under-Secretary-General likewise underlined the importance of the relief-to-development continuum, whereby humanitarian aid agencies, following emergency and short-term rehabilitation activities, would hand over responsibility to development organizations.

33/Document 38
See page 238

100 The initial response by the donor community to the PROFERI appeal — pledges of some $32 million, and actual disbursements of significantly less — was disappointing. The Eritrean Government considered this level of funding insufficient to embark on a large-scale repatriation operation.[34] Instead, the Government and the Department of Humanitarian Affairs agreed to start with a pilot project for the return and integration of some 4,500 families (15,000-20,000 persons) from the Sudan. By July 1995, the pilot programme had assisted in the repatriation of approximately 24,200 Eritrean refugees, while 130,000 to 140,000 Eritreans are estimated to have returned spontaneously. However, the several hundred thousand Eritrean refugees still in the Sudan constitute one of the world's largest refugee populations. In the Horn of Africa, the Office of the United Nations High Commissioner for Refugees (UNHCR) was providing assistance to some 1.6 million refugees and internally displaced persons.

34/Document 43
See page 258

Other programmes of assistance and development

101 To improve operational coordination among United Nations programmes and funds working in support of post-conflict peace-building in Eritrea, the Government and the United Nations signed an agreement in September 1993 to establish a United Nations Integrated Office in Asmara, headed by a United Nations Representative serving as Resident Coordinator. The opening of such an office was not just an administrative exercise but a conceptual step reflecting my continuing efforts to promote a unified United Nations presence and voice at the

country level and to implement a common United Nations system strategy in response to the special and urgent requirements of newly independent countries and States in transition. The Integrated Office in Asmara was the system's ninth, and the first to be established outside the former Soviet Union.

102 In its contacts with the United Nations and other providers of outside assistance, the Government of Eritrea has placed great importance on self-sufficiency. Given that a high percentage of Eritreans are farmers and herders, and that in recent decades the region had experienced regular food shortages and famines, the goal of agricultural self-sufficiency has been pursued with particular intensity and creativity. Thousands of former EPLF soldiers have been deployed to the countryside to assist with small-village infrastructure projects such as microdams and land terracing, while other Eritreans have participated in voluntary food-for-work programmes designed to guard against chronic dependence on emergency relief from abroad, as has occurred in other countries.

103 None the less, outside assistance from the United Nations and others remains a significant element in the Government of Eritrea's overall recovery and rehabilitation programme. The Government estimated the costs involved at $1 billion. PROFERI was just one component of the international community's involvement. Other United Nations assistance was provided under the aegis of the Special Emergency Programme for the Horn of Africa (SEPHA), which in January 1993 issued an appeal for funding totalling $80.5 million for activities to be carried out that year by the Department of Humanitarian Affairs, the Food and Agriculture Organization of the United Nations (FAO), the United Nations Children's Fund (UNICEF), the World Food Programme (WFP), the World Health Organization (WHO) and United Nations Volunteers (UNV). Of this total, the largest amount was for emergency food needs; according to SEPHA, even with good rains Eritrea was expected to need at least several years to attain self- sufficiency in basic foodstuffs.

104 Also in early 1993, a consortium of donors led by the World Bank that included the United Nations Development Programme (UNDP), the European Economic Community, Italy, Germany, the Netherlands and Sweden endorsed a $155-million Recovery and Rehabilitation Programme for Eritrea (RRPE) . The programme was designed to stimulate the economy and gave priority to agriculture, industry, energy, roads, ports and government institutions. At a World Bank Consultative Group meeting in December 1994, Eritrea received further pledges of $250 million for 1995 from donors, who praised the Government for promulgating an investment code, improving access to basic social services and adopting a development strategy promoting private enterprise and a market-based economy.

105 Other United Nations programmes have focused on clean water and sanitation services (UNICEF), fisheries and small-scale irrigation (FAO) and literacy and the reactivation of primary education (United Nations Educational, Scientific and Cultural Organization (UNESCO) and UNICEF). Assistance from WHO has targeted rehabilitation of hospitals and health centres; provision of essential medical/surgical supplies, laboratory equipment and essential drugs; provision of insecticides and spraying equipment for a malaria-control programme; and training for Eritrean health professionals in the control of high-priority communicable diseases, such as malaria, tuberculosis, AIDS and meningitis.

106 In early 1994, FAO and WFP reported that there had been yet another crop failure in Eritrea, that food production had fallen sharply and that there was a shortage of pasture for livestock. With Ethiopia facing a similar predicament, some 17 million people in the Horn of Africa were considered to be at risk of starvation, sparking fears of a repeat of earlier humanitarian tragedies. This time, however, the use of an early-warning system put in place with the help of United Nations agencies led to a swift and generous donor response and an equally rapid and efficient distribution of aid. Helped as well by good rains, the region overcame the threat of a major catastrophe.

VI Conclusion

107   The resolution of one of Africa's longest wars through a free and fair referendum was an important United Nations success, and the United Nations Observer Mission to Verify the Referendum in Eritrea (UNOVER) had an impact far beyond its immediate mandate and jurisdiction.

108   For the war-ravaged people of Eritrea, the experience of the referendum enabled them to become true participants and partners in the decision-making process on a vital issue affecting the viability and well-being of their country. This achievement was particularly welcome given the country's multilingual, multicultural and multi-religious character. UNOVER also helped turn public perception of the United Nations in Eritrea in a positive direction, a factor that bodes well for the Organization's ongoing humanitarian and development activities in the country and the region.

109   For the strife-torn Horn of Africa, the peaceful transition in Eritrea offered a much-needed example of stability and harmony during a time of conflict in the Sudan, anarchic conditions in Somalia and a tension-filled period in Ethiopia. Eritrea established cooperative relations with its former foe, thereby contributing to the consolidation of peace in Ethiopia as well. Moreover, the way in which Eritrean independence was achieved — with the involvement of the United Nations, the Organization of African Unity and the new Government of Ethiopia — eased the concerns expressed in Africa and elsewhere over the revision of the continent's colonial boundaries.

110   UNOVER demonstrated once again the value of United Nations electoral and other technical assistance for countries formerly at war. As an early exercise in post-conflict peace-building, the mission helped Eritrea move towards long-term stability, economic growth, democratization, social justice and the rule of law. Its integrated and focused work validated the evolving international consensus that democracy, development and peace are complementary and mutually reinforcing aspects of the same overall endeavour. Without peace, Eritrea would not have been able to embark on the path of democratization and development. Without a democratic referendum, the Eritrean people would not have had a central voice in that process, as was their right. And without development, the gains Eritreans have made will remain fragile.

111   Eritrea opens a new chapter in its history with a reservoir of goodwill and support from the international community. It possesses maritime and mineral resources with considerable export potential. Its climate and historical attractions are well suited to tourism. Its location makes it a natural regional hub for transport and trade. Many Eritrean expatriates have returned, bringing with them much-needed expertise.

112 Following its acceptance into membership in the United Nations, Eritrea became a member of the International Labour Organization (ILO), UNESCO, WHO and other organizations of the United Nations system. It also joined regional organizations such as the Organization of African Unity (OAU) and the Intergovernmental Authority on Drought and Development (IGADD) — renamed the Intergovernmental Authority on Development (IGAD) in 1996 — whose other members are Djibouti, Ethiopia, Kenya, Somalia, the Sudan and Uganda. International non-governmental organizations opened offices in Asmara. Bilateral relations with Ethiopia were strengthened through agreements addressing trade and transit issues. And with its transition from de facto to legally recognized independence, Eritrea has gained formal access to direct international lending by the World Bank and other intergovernmental institutions, as only States are eligible for such assistance.

113 The international community has provided essential political and material backing for Eritrea's emergence from war and for UNOVER's role in facilitating that transition, and can be proud of the results. It should sustain this effort with similar commitment as Eritrean nation-building enters a new and decisive phase.

BOUTROS BOUTROS-GHALI

Section Two
Chronology and Documents

I Chronology of events

2 May 1889
Italy and the Emperor of Ethiopia sign the Treaty of Wich'alē (Uccialli), giving Italy sovereignty over part of Eritrea.

1 January 1890
Italy proclaims Eritrea a colony.

1896
Ethiopian forces defeat Italy in Ethiopia. Italy retains control over Eritrea.

1935-1936
Italy invades and conquers Ethiopia, and subsequently unites Ethiopia with Eritrea and Italian Somaliland to form Italian East Africa.

1941
After Allied forces defeat Italy in Ethiopia during the Second World War, Eritrea, Italian Somaliland and most of Libya are placed under British administration.

10 February 1947
France, the Union of Soviet Socialist Republics, the United Kingdom and the United States sign the Treaty of Peace with Italy, under which Italy renounces all right and title to its former colonies — Eritrea, Libya and Italian Somaliland. France, the USSR, the United Kingdom and the United States agree to determine the final disposition of the three Territories within one year of the entry into force of the Treaty.

15 September 1947
The Treaty of Peace with Italy enters into force.

15 September 1948
Upon the expiry of the one-year period set in the Treaty of Peace with Italy, France, the USSR, the United Kingdom and the United States request that the question of the disposition of the former Italian colonies be placed on the agenda of the United Nations General Assembly. The Assembly adds the item to its agenda on **24 September**.
See Document 1, page 51

18 May 1949
During its third regular session, the General Assembly decides to postpone further consideration of the question of the disposition of the former Italian colonies until its fourth regular session.
See Document 2, page 51

21 November 1949
The General Assembly recommends the establishment of a United Nations Commission for Eritrea "to ascertain more fully the wishes and the best means of promoting the welfare of the inhabitants of Eritrea, to examine the question of the disposal of Eritrea and to prepare a report for the General Assembly, together with such proposal or proposals as it may deem appropriate for the solution of the problem of Eritrea".
See Document 3, page 52

14 February 1950
The United Nations Commission for Eritrea holds its first meeting in Asmara.

8 June 1950
The United Nations Commission for Eritrea submits its report.
See Document 4, page 53

2 December 1950
Following lengthy deliberations, the General Assembly adopts resolution 390 A (V), recommending that Eritrea "shall constitute an autonomous unit federated with Ethiopia under the sovereignty of the Ethiopian Crown" not later than 15 September 1952.
See Document 6, page 94

16 November 1951
The United Nations Commissioner in Eritrea, appointed pursuant to General Assembly resolution 390 A (V), reports to the General Assembly on his consultations with the Administering Authority (United Kingdom), the Government of Ethiopia and the inhabitants of Eritrea in connection with drafting an Eritrean Constitution in preparation for Eritrea's federation with Ethiopia.
See Document 7, page 96

29 January 1952
The General Assembly adopts economic and financial provisions relating to Eritrea that are to form part of the arrangements for the final disposition of the Territory.
See Document 8, page 109

25-26 March 1952
Elections for an Eritrean Representative Assembly are held. The Assembly convenes on **28 April 1952**.
See Document 10, page 146

3 May 1952
The United Nations Commissioner in Eritrea presents a draft Constitution to the Eritrean Assembly.

10 July 1952
The Eritrean Assembly unanimously adopts the Constitution as amended during its deliberations.

11 August 1952
The Emperor of Ethiopia ratifies the Constitution.

11 September 1952
With ratification of the Federal Act by the Emperor of Ethiopia, the Eritrean Constitution enters into force and the Federation of Eritrea with Ethiopia is formally established.

15/16 September 1952
The United Kingdom formally hands over the administration of Eritrea to the Federal and Eritrean governments.

17 October 1952
The United Nations Commissioner in Eritrea submits his final report.
See Document 9, page 113

27 October 1952
The United Kingdom reports to the General Assembly on the administration of Eritrea for the period from December 1950 to September 1952.
See Document 10, page 146

17 December 1952
The General Assembly welcomes the establishment of the Federation of Eritrea with Ethiopia under the sovereignty of the Ethiopian Crown.
See Document 11, page 152

14 November 1962
Ethiopia declares the Eritrean Constitution void, ends the federal status of Eritrea, dissolves the Eritrean parliament, and incorporates Eritrea into Ethiopia as a province. Following these events, an Eritrean resistance movement begins a campaign of armed struggle against Ethiopian rule.

12 September 1974
The Ethiopian armed forces depose Emperor Haile Selassie of Ethiopia.

3 February 1977
Mengistu Haile Mariam assumes the presidency of the Provisional Military Administrative Council (PMAC), also known as the Dergue, which exercises executive power in Ethiopia.

1978-1989
Ethiopian armed forces and the Eritrean People's Liberation Front (EPLF) wage an ongoing military conflict. By the latter part of this period, Ethiopian forces have withdrawn from several major cities and towns, and the EPLF controls most of Eritrea except for Asmara and Massawa, a major port on the Red Sea. Non-Eritrean opposition groups also make significant gains against the Ethiopian Army.

September-November 1989
In an attempt to find a negotiated solution to the conflict, former United States President Jimmy Carter sponsors two rounds of talks, first in Atlanta and later in Nairobi, between representatives of the Government of Ethiopia and the EPLF; a United Nations delegation attends the talks as an observer.

February 1990
The EPLF captures Massawa.

October 1990–February 1991
As fighting continues, the Government of Ethiopia and the EPLF hold talks in the United States.

21 May 1991
Mengistu Haile Mariam flees Ethiopia.

24 May 1991
The EPLF takes over control of Asmara.

28 May 1991
The Ethiopian People's Revolutionary Democratic Front (EPRDF) captures Addis Ababa and establishes an interim Government. At peace talks held in London under the auspices of the United States, representatives of the EPLF meet with a delegation from Ethiopia and commit to holding a referendum on the future of Eritrea within two years.

29 May 1991
The EPLF establishes a Provisional Government of Eritrea.

1-5 July 1991
The Conference on Peace and Democracy, held in Addis Ababa and attended by almost all the political parties, movements and social organizations in Ethiopia, establishes a Transitional Government in Ethiopia and formally recognizes the right of the Eritrean people to determine its political future by an internationally supervised referendum.

25 July 1991
The Secretary-General of the Provisional Government of Eritrea, in a letter to the Secretary-General of the United Nations, invites the United Nations to become involved in the Eritrean referendum process.

September 1991
The United Nations issues an appeal for $400 million in food and other emergency aid to meet humanitarian needs in the Horn of Africa until the end of the year, and establishes a Special Emergency Programme for the Horn of Africa (SEPHA) to strengthen humanitarian assistance efforts for people threatened by famine and disease.

13 December 1991
The President of the Transitional Government of Ethiopia, in a letter to the Secretary-General of the United Nations, requests that the United Nations play an active role in verifying a free and fair referendum.
See Document 13, page 154

21 December 1991
Boutros Boutros-Ghali, in his capacity as Secretary-General-Designate of the United Nations, meets in Cairo with the Secretary-General of the Provisional Government of Eritrea to discuss the situation in the Horn of Africa.

6 April 1992
The Provisional Government of Eritrea issues a nationality proclamation, defining the general conditions for qualifying as an Eritrean citizen.
See Document 16, page 156

7 April 1992
The Provisional Government of Eritrea issues a referendum proclamation, setting out rules and regulations to govern the referendum process and establishing a Referendum Commission and Referendum Court.
See Document 17, page 158

19 May 1992
The Referendum Commissioner of Eritrea, in a letter to the Secretary-General of the United Nations, invites the United Nations to observe and verify the freeness, fairness and impartiality of the entire referendum process from its beginning in July 1992 to its completion in April 1993.
See Document 19, page 170

11 June 1992
The Secretary-General of the United Nations informs the President of the General Assembly that he plans to dispatch a technical team to Eritrea to gather information for the preparation of a report on the details of potential involvement by the United Nations in the referendum process.
See Document 20, page 171

30 July–8 August 1992
A United Nations technical team visits Eritrea and holds discussions with the Referendum Commission, members of the Provisional Government of Eritrea and representatives of a wide spectrum of political, social and religious organizations.
See Document 24, page 173

Mid-October 1992
Voter registration begins.

19 October 1992
The Secretary-General, in a report to the General Assembly, recommends the establishment of a United Nations Observer Mission to Verify the Referendum in Eritrea (UNOVER).
See Document 24, page 173

November 1992
The Provisional Government of Eritrea announces that the referendum will be held in April 1993.

16 December 1992
The General Assembly authorizes the Secretary-General to establish UNOVER.
See Document 25, page 179

January 1993
As part of the Special Emergency Programme for the Horn of Africa, the United Nations issues a consolidated inter-agency appeal for $80.5 million in funding for relief and short-term rehabilitation activities in Eritrea — including $51.4 million for emergency food needs for some 1.5 million war- and drought-affected Eritreans, of whom 200,000 are internally displaced persons.
See Document 26, page 180

6 January 1993
The Secretary-General visits Eritrea to appraise the referendum process.

7 January 1993
UNOVER, consisting of 21 international staff members supported by local personnel, is inaugurated.

25 January 1993
The Secretary-General appoints Mr. Samir Sanbar as his Special Representative and Chief of UNOVER.

17 February 1993
The referendum campaign begins.

1 March 1993
Voter registration is completed.

12-18 April 1993
Eighty-six international observers join the 21 core members of UNOVER for the last phase of the referendum process.

21 April 1993
The referendum campaign ends.

23-25 April 1993
The referendum is held, with a voter turnout of more than 98 per cent. Polling takes place in Eritrea, Ethiopia, the Sudan and over 40 other countries, in some cases on different dates.

27 April 1993
The Eritrean Referendum Commission announces the official provisional results, indicating that 99.805 per cent of those who participated voted for independence. The Special Representative of the Secretary-General announces: "On the whole, the referendum process in Eritrea can be considered to have been free and fair at every stage, and that it has been conducted to my satisfaction."
See Document 28, page 213; and Document 39, page 242

29 April 1993
Ethiopia recognizes Eritrea's sovereignty and independence.

12 May 1993
Eritrea formally applies for membership in the United Nations.
See Document 31, page 215

24 May 1993
On the second anniversary of the EPLF's entry into Asmara, Eritrea formally declares itself to be an independent, sovereign State and declares a four-year transition period.
See Document 32, page 216

26 May 1993
The Security Council recommends to the General Assembly that Eritrea be admitted to membership in the United Nations.
See Document 33, page 217; and Document 34, page 217

28 May 1993
The General Assembly decides to admit Eritrea to membership in the United Nations.
See Document 35, page 217; and Document 36, page 218

June 1993
The Government of Eritrea and the United Nations launch a joint appeal for $262 million in funding required to implement the Programme for Refugee Reintegration and Rehabilitation of Resettlement Areas in Eritrea (PROFERI), which seeks to repatriate up to 500,000 Eritrean refugees from the Sudan over a three-and-a-half-year period and to rehabilitate their resettlement areas.
See Document 37, page 222

June 1993
Eritrea is admitted to the Organization of African Unity (OAU).

6 July 1993
A pledging conference for PROFERI is held in Geneva.
See Document 38, page 238

11 August 1993
The Secretary-General reports to the General Assembly on UNOVER.
See Document 39, page 242

29 September 1993
Eritrea and the United Nations sign an agreement to establish the United Nations Integrated Office in Eritrea to facilitate inter-agency coordination in support of Eritrea's post-conflict nation-building efforts.

30 September 1993
The President of Eritrea addresses the forty-eighth session of the General Assembly.
See Document 40, page 251

February 1994
The EPLF decides to transform itself into a political party called the People's Front for Democracy and Justice.

II List of reproduced documents

The documents reproduced on pages 51-263 include resolutions of the General Assembly and of the Security Council, reports and letters of the Secretary-General, reports of the United Nations Commissioner in Eritrea, communications from United Nations Member States and other materials.

1948

Document 1
Letter dated 15 September 1948 from France, the Union of Soviet Socialist Republics, the United Kingdom of Great Britain and Northern Ireland and the United States of America requesting that the question of the disposal of the former Italian colonies be added to the agenda of the General Assembly.
A/645, 16 September 1948
See page 51

1949

Document 2
General Assembly resolution concerning the question of the disposal of the former Italian colonies.
A/RES/287 (III), 18 May 1949
See page 51

Document 3
General Assembly resolution concerning the question of the disposal of the former Italian colonies.
A/RES/289 (IV), 21 November 1949
See page 52

1950

Document 4
Report of the United Nations Commission for Eritrea (excerpt).
A/1285, 8 June 1950
See page 53

Document 5
Report of the Interim Committee of the General Assembly: Consideration of the Report of the United Nations Commission for Eritrea.
A/1388, 1950
See page 93

Document 6
General Assembly resolution concerning the report of the United Nations Commission for Eritrea and the report of the Interim Committee of the General Assembly.
A/RES/390 (V), 2 December 1950
See page 94

1951

Document 7
Progress report of the United Nations Commissioner in Eritrea during the year 1951 (excerpt).
A/1959, 16 November 1951
See page 96

1952

Document 8
General Assembly resolution on economic and financial provisions relating to Eritrea.
A/RES/530 (VI), 29 January 1952
See page 109

Document 9
Final report of the United Nations Commissioner in Eritrea (excerpt).
A/2188, 17 October 1952
See page 113

Document 10
Report of the Government of the United Kingdom concerning the administration of Eritrea for the period from December 1950 to September 1952 (excerpt).
A/2233, 27 October 1952
See page 146

Document 11
General Assembly resolution concerning the report of the United Nations Commissioner in Eritrea.
A/RES/617 (VII), 17 December 1952
See page 152

1990

Document 12
Urgent appeal to the forty-sixth session of the Commission on Human Rights submitted by several non-governmental organizations.
E/CN.4/1990/NGO/75, 7 March 1990
See page 153

1991

Document 13
Letter dated 13 December 1991 from the President of the Transitional Government of Ethiopia to the Secretary-General of the United Nations concerning the results of the Conference on Peace and Democracy held in Ethiopia in July 1991.
A/C.3/47/5, Annex II, 29 October 1992
See page 154

1992

Document 14
Letter dated 15 January 1992 from the Secretary-General of the United Nations to the President of the Transitional Government of Ethiopia concerning United Nations involvement in the referendum process in Eritrea.
Not issued as a United Nations document.
See page 155

Document 15
Letter dated 19 February 1992 from the Secretary-General of the United Nations to the President of the Transitional Government of Ethiopia concerning United Nations involvement in the referendum process in Eritrea.
Not issued as a United Nations document.
See page 155

Document 16
Eritrean Nationality Proclamation, issued on 6 April 1992 in Asmara.
Not issued as a United Nations document.
See page 156

Document 17
Eritrean Referendum Proclamation, issued on 7 April 1992 in Asmara.
Not issued as a United Nations document.
See page 158

Document 18
Letter dated 9 April 1992 from Denmark, Finland, Iceland, Norway and Sweden to the Secretary-General of the United Nations concerning the dispatch of a technical survey mission to Eritrea and Ethiopia.
Not issued as a United Nations document.
See page 169

Document 19
Letter dated 19 May 1992 from the Commissioner of the Referendum Commission of Eritrea to the Secretary-General of the United Nations inviting the United Nations to observe and verify the referendum process.
A/C.3/47/5, Annex III, 29 October 1992
See page 170

Document 20
Letter dated 11 June 1992 from the Secretary-General of the United Nations to the President of the General Assembly concerning developments pertaining to the political status of Eritrea.
A/C.3/47/5, Annex I, 29 October 1992
See page 171

Document 21
Letter dated 18 June 1992 from the Secretary-General of the United Nations to the Secretary-General of the Provisional Government of Eritrea concerning United Nations involvement in the referendum process.
Not issued as a United Nations document.
See page 172

Document 22
Letter dated 24 August 1992 from the Secretary-General of the United Nations to the President of the Transitional Government of Ethiopia concerning United Nations involvement in the referendum process in Eritrea.
Not issued as a United Nations document.
See page 172

Document 23
Letter dated 24 August 1992 from the Secretary-General of the United Nations to the Secretary-General of the Provisional Government of Eritrea concerning United Nations involvement in the referendum process.
Not issued as a United Nations document.
See page 173

Document 24
Report of the Secretary-General on the request to the United Nations to observe the referendum process.
A/47/544, 19 October 1992
See page 173

Document 25
General Assembly resolution authorizing the Secretary-General to establish the United Nations Observer Mission to Verify the Referendum in Eritrea (UNOVER).
A/RES/47/114, 16 December 1992
See page 179

1993

Document 26
United Nations 1993 Consolidated Inter-agency appeal: Eritrea. Special Emergency Programme for the Horn of Africa (SEPHA).
January 1993
See page 180

Document 27
Statement of 26 April 1993 by the Organization of African Unity Observer Mission to the Eritrean Referendum.
Not issued as a United Nations document.
See page 212

Document 28
Announcement of 27 April 1993 by the Special Representative of the Secretary-General on the referendum.
Not issued as a United Nations document.
See page 213

Document 29
Statement of 27 April 1993 by the Secretary-General of the Provisional Government of Eritrea on the referendum.
Not issued as a United Nations document.
See page 213

Document 30
Statement of 4 May 1993 by the Ministry of Foreign Affairs of the Transitional Government of Ethiopia on the recognition by Ethiopia of the sovereignty and independence of Eritrea.
Not issued as a United Nations document.
See page 214

Document 31
Letter dated 12 May 1993 from the Secretary-General of the Provisional Government of Eritrea to the Secretary-General of the United Nations submitting Eritrea's application for membership in the United Nations.
A/47/948-S/25793, 18 May 1993
See page 215

Document 32
Message of 24 May 1993 by the Secretary-General of the United Nations on the occasion of the independence celebrations in Eritrea.
Not issued as a United Nations document.
See page 216

Document 33
Security Council resolution recommending to the General Assembly that Eritrea be admitted to membership in the United Nations.
S/RES/828 (1993), 26 May 1993
See page 217

Document 34
Statement by the President of the Security Council concerning the Council's recommendation to the General Assembly that Eritrea be admitted to membership in the United Nations.
S/25847, 26 May 1993
See page 217

Document 35
General Assembly resolution admitting Eritrea to membership in the United Nations.
A/RES/47/230, 28 May 1993
See page 217

Document 36
Provisional verbatim record of the 104th meeting of the 47th session of the General Assembly, at which Eritrea was admitted to membership in the United Nations.
A/47/PV.104, 28 May 1993
See page 218

Document 37
Joint Government of Eritrea and United Nations Appeal for Eritrea: Programme for Refugee Reintegration and Rehabilitation of Resettlement Areas in Eritrea (PROFERI).
June 1993 (Volume I: Main Appeal Document)
See page 222

Document 38
Statements made by the President of Eritrea and by the United Nations Under-Secretary-General for Humanitarian Affairs at the Pledging Conference for the Programme for Refugee Reintegration and Rehabilitation of Resettlement Areas in Eritrea (PROFERI), held in Geneva on 6 July 1993.
10 August 1993
See page 238

Document 39
Report of the Secretary-General on UNOVER.
A/48/283, 11 August 1993
See page 242

Document 40
Statement dated 30 September 1993 by the President of Eritrea at the 48th Session of the United Nations General Assembly.
Not issued as a United Nations document.
See page 251

Document 41
Executive Summary of a report by the United Nations Economic Commission for Africa, the United Nations Development Programme and the Department of Humanitarian Affairs on formulating the master plan for rehabilitation, reconstruction and development of Eritrea.
October 1993
See page 254

Document 42
Letter from Chargé d'affaires a.i. of the Permanent Mission of Eritrea to the United Nations addressed to the Secretary-General of the United Nations concerning UNOVER.
A/48/643, 24 November 1993
See page 256

1994

Document 43
Activities of the United Nations High Commissioner for Refugees financed by voluntary funds: Report on Eritrea for 1993-1994 and proposed programmes and budget for 1995.
A/AC.96/825/Part I/8, 23 August 1994
See page 258

1995

Document 44
Activities of the United Nations High Commissioner for Refugees financed by voluntary funds: Report on Eritrea for 1994-1995 and proposed programmes and budget for 1996.
A/AC.96/846/Part I/7, 24 July 1995
See page 260

The following is a breakdown, by category, of the documents reproduced in this volume.

Resolutions of the General Assembly
Documents 2, 3, 6, 8, 11, 25, 35

Resolution of the Security Council
Document 33

Statement by the President of the Security Council
Document 34

Reports of the Secretary-General
Documents 24, 39

Correspondence of the Secretary-General
Documents 14, 15, 20, 21, 22, 23

Statements by the Secretary-General
Document 32

Reports of the United Nations Commissioner in Eritrea
Documents 7, 9

Communications and statements by Member States
Documents 1, 10, 13, 16, 17, 18, 19, 29, 30, 31, 40, 42

Other
Documents 4, 5, 12, 26, 27, 28, 36, 37, 38, 41, 43, 44

III Other documents of interest

Readers seeking additional information about the involvement of the United Nations in Eritrea might wish to consult the following documents, which are available in the Dag Hammarskjöld Library at United Nations Headquarters in New York, at other libraries in the United Nations system or at libraries around the world which have been designated as depository libraries for United Nations documents.

1948-1953

Annual reports of the Secretary-General

A/930, covering the period from 1 July 1948 to 30 June 1949

A/1287, covering the period from 1 July 1949 to 30 June 1950

A/1844, covering the period from 1 July 1950 to 30 June 1951

A/2141, covering the period from 1 July 1951 to 30 June 1952

A/2404, covering the period from 1 July 1952 to 30 June 1953

Reports of the First Committee of the General Assembly on the question of the disposal of the former Italian colonies

A/873, 14 May 1949 (contains draft resolution rejected by the General Assembly)

A/1089, 15 November 1949

Communications from Ethiopia

Telegram dated 14 May 1949 from the Emperor of Ethiopia to the Secretary-General.
A/882, 16 May 1949

Letter dated 9 August 1950 from the Chairman of the Ethiopian delegation to the United Nations to the Secretary-General.
A/1389, 23 September 1950

Telegram dated 19 September 1950 from the Emperor of Ethiopia to the Secretary-General.
A/1374, 20 September 1950

1993-1996

Resolutions of the General Assembly

Assistance to refugees, returnees and displaced persons in Africa.
A/RES/48/118, 20 December 1993
A/RES/49/174, 23 December 1994
A/RES/50/149, 21 December 1995

Reports of the Secretary-General

Assistance to refugees, returnees and displaced persons in Africa.
A/48/444, 15 October 1993
A/49/578, 26 October 1994
A/50/413, 7 September 1995

Enhancing the effectiveness of the principle of periodic and genuine elections.
A/48/590, 18 November 1993

Support by the United Nations system for the efforts of Governments to promote and consolidate new or restored democracies.
A/50/332, 7 August 1995

IV Texts of documents

The texts of the 44 documents listed on the preceding pages are reproduced below. The appearance of ellipses (. . .) in the text indicates that portions of the document have been omitted. A subject index to the documents begins on page 265.

Document 1

Letter dated 15 September 1948 from France, the Union of Soviet Socialist Republics, the United Kingdom of Great Britain and Northern Ireland and the United States of America requesting that the question of the disposal of the former Italian colonies be added to the agenda of the General Assembly

A/645, 16 September 1948

Note from the Secretary-General

The Secretary-General has the honour to communicate to Members of the General Assembly the following communication received by him from the Governments of the United States of America, France, the United Kingdom and the Union of Soviet Socialist Republics:

Paris, 15 September 1948

On the instructions of the Governments of the United States of America, France, the United Kingdom of Great Britain and Northern Ireland and of the Union of Soviet Socialist Republics we have the honour to inform you that in application of Article 23 and Paragraph 3 of Annex XI of the Treaty of Peace with Italy, the question of the disposal of the former Italian colonies is referred to the General Assembly in order that, in conformity with its Rules of Procedure, the General Assembly may examine this question during the Session which is to open on 21 September.

For the Government of the United States of America
(*Signed*) L.W. DOUGLAS

For the Government of France
(*Signed*) SCHUMAN

For the Government of the United Kingdom of Great Britain and Northern Ireland
(*Signed*) Hector MCNEIL

For the Government of the Union of Soviet Socialist Republics
(*Signed*) A. VYSHINSKY

Document 2

General Assembly resolution concerning the question of the disposal of the former Italian colonies

A/RES/287 (III), 18 May 1949

The General Assembly

Decides to postpone further consideration of the item "Question of the disposal of the former Italian colonies" until the fourth regular session of the General Assembly. 1/

1/ See also resolution 266 (III), page 6.

Document 3

General Assembly resolution concerning the question of the disposal of the former Italian colonies

A/RES/289 (IV), 21 November 1949

The General Assembly,

In accordance with Annex XI, paragraph 3, of the Treaty of Peace with Italy, 1947, whereby the Powers concerned have agreed to accept the recommendation of the General Assembly on the disposal of the former Italian colonies and to take appropriate measures for giving effect to it,

Having taken note of the report 1/ of the Four Power Commission of Investigation, having heard spokesmen of organizations representing substantial sections of opinion in the territories concerned, and having taken into consideration the wishes and welfare of the inhabitants of the territories, the interests of peace and security, the views of the interested Governments and the relevant provisions of the Charter,

...

C. *With respect to Eritrea, recommends:*

1. That a Commission consisting of representatives of not more than five Member States, as follows, Burma, Guatemala, Norway, Pakistan and the Union of South Africa, shall be established to ascertain more fully the wishes and the best means of promoting the welfare of the inhabitants of Eritrea, to examine the question of the disposal of Eritrea and to prepare a report for the General Assembly, together with such proposal or proposals as it may deem appropriate for the solution of the problem of Eritrea;

2. That in carrying out its responsibilities the Commission shall ascertain all the relevant facts, including written or oral information from the present administering Power, from representatives of the population of the territory, including minorities, from Governments and from such organizations and individuals as it may deem necessary. In particular, the Commission shall take into account:

(a) The wishes and welfare of the inhabitants of Eritrea, including the views of the various racial, religious and political groups of the provinces of the territory and the capacity of the people for self-government;

(b) The interests of peace and security in East Africa;

(c) The rights and claims of Ethiopia based on geographical, historical, ethnic or economic reasons, including in particular Ethiopia's legitimate need for adequate access to the sea;

3. That in considering its proposals the Commission shall take into account the various suggestions for the disposal of Eritrea submitted during the fourth regular session of the General Assembly;

4. That the Commission shall assemble at the Headquarters of the United Nations as soon as possible. It shall travel to Eritrea and may visit such other places as in its judgment may be necessary in carrying out its responsibilities. The Commission shall adopt its own rules of procedure. Its report and proposal or proposals shall be communicated to the Secretary-General not later than 15 June 1950 for distribution to Member States so as to enable final consideration during the fifth regular session of the General Assembly. The Interim Committee of the General Assembly shall consider the report and proposal or proposals of the Commission and report, with conclusions, to the fifth regular session of the General Assembly;

D. *With respect to the above provisions:*

1. *Invites* the Secretary-General to request the necessary facilities from the competent authorities of each of the States in whose territory it may be necessary for the Commission for Eritrea to meet or travel;

2. *Authorizes* the Secretary-General, in accordance with established practices,

(a) To arrange for the payment of an appropriate remuneration to the United Nations Commissioner in Libya;

(b) To reimburse the travelling and subsistence expenses of the members of the Council for Libya, of one representative from each Government represented on the Advisory Council for Somaliland, and of one representative and one alternate from each Government represented on the Commission for Eritrea;

(c) To assign to the United Nations Commissioner in Libya, to the Advisory Council for Somaliland, and to the United Nations Commission for Eritrea such staff and to provide such facilities as the Secretary-General may consider necessary to carry out the terms of the present resolution.

...

1/ See *Four Power Commission of Investigation for the former Italian Colonies*, volumes I-III.

Document 4

Report of the United Nations Commission for Eritrea (excerpt)

A/1285, 8 June 1950

Letter of transmittal

Geneva, 8 June 1950

Sir,

The United Nations Commission for Eritrea has the honour to communicate to you herewith its report in accordance with section C, paragraph 4, of resolution 289 A (IV), which provides that the report of the Commission shall be communicated to the Secretary-General not later than 15 June 1950 for distribution to Member States.

We have the honour to be, Sir, Your obedient Servants,

(*Signed*) Aung KHINE (*Burma*)

Carlos GARCÍA BAUER (*Guatemala*)

Erling QVALE (*Norway*)

Mian ZIAUD-DIN (*Pakistan*)

F. H. THERON (*Union of South Africa*)

Petrus J. SCHMIDT (*Principal Secretary*)

Mr. Trygve Lie
Secretary-General
United Nations
Lake Success
New York, USA

Chapter I
Historical background, establishment and organization of the United Nations Commission for Eritrea

Section I. Historical Introduction

(a) Submission of the question of Eritrea to the United Nations

1. Article 10 of the Conditions of Armistice signed by Italy on 3 September 1943 provided that the Commander-in-Chief of the Allied Forces "will establish Allied military government over such parts of Italian territory as he may deem necessary in the military interests of the Allied nations". The administration of Eritrea which had been occupied in 1941 by the Allied armed forces was undertaken by the British Authorities, first through the Occupied Enemy Territories' Administration and later through the Foreign Office Administration of African Territories.

2. Under the terms of the agreement establishing the Council of Foreign Ministers adopted at the Berlin Conference of 17 July-24 August 1945, it was agreed at the Moscow Conference of 16-27 December 1945 that the terms of the Treaty of Peace with Italy would be drafted by the Foreign Ministers of the United Kingdom, the United States of America, the Soviet Union and France.

3. At a meeting in Paris, the Council of Foreign Ministers adopted, on 3 July 1946, a draft article on the former Italian colonies and a draft joint declaration by the Four Powers, which, in conformity with decisions taken at the Paris Conference of 29 July-15 October 1946, became respectively article 23 and annex XI of the Treaty of Peace with Italy.

"*Article 23*

"1. Italy renounces all right and title to the Italian territorial possessions in Africa, i.e., Libya, Eritrea and Italian Somaliland.

"2. Pending their final disposal, the said possessions shall continue under their present administration.

"3. The final disposal of these possessions shall be determined jointly by the Governments of the Soviet Union, of the United Kingdom, of the United States of America, and of France within one year from the coming into force of the present Treaty, in the manner laid down in the joint declaration of 10 February 1947, issued by the said Governments, which is reproduced in annex XI.

"*Annex XI*

"1. The Governments of the Union of Soviet Socialist Republics, of the United Kingdom of Great Britain and Northern Ireland, of the United States of America, and of France agree that they will, within one year from the coming into force of the Treaty of Peace with Italy bearing the date of 10 February 1947, jointly determine the final disposal of Italy's territorial possessions in Africa, to which, in accordance with article 23 of the Treaty, Italy renounces all right and title.

"2. The final disposal of the territories concerned and the appropriate adjustment of their boundaries shall be made by the Four Powers in the light of the wishes and welfare of the inhabitants and the interests of peace and security, taking into consideration the views of other interested Governments.

"3. If with respect to any of these territories the Four Powers are unable to agree upon their disposal within one year from the coming into force of the Treaty of Peace with Italy, the matter shall be referred to the General Assembly of the United Nations for a recommendation, and the Four Powers agree to accept the recommendation and to take appropriate measures for giving effect to it.

"4. The Deputies of the Foreign Ministers shall continue the consideration of the question of the disposal of the former Italian colonies with a view to submitting to the Council of Foreign Ministers their recommendations on this matter. They shall also send out commissions of investigation to any of the former Italian colonies in order to supply the Deputies with the necessary data on this question and to ascertain the views of the local population".

4. The period of one year, referred to in paragraph 3 of the above joint declaration, began to run from 15 September 1947, in accordance with article 90 of the Treaty of Peace.

5. On 3 October 1947, the Deputies of the Foreign Ministers took up the question of the disposal of the former colonies in accordance with paragraph 4 of annex XI of the Treaty of Peace. It was decided that an investigation on the spot by representatives of the Four Powers would be carried out in the three former Italian colonies. The Four-Power Commission of Investigation for the former Italian colonies stayed in Eritrea from 12 November 1947 to 3 January 1948 and its report is dated 31 August 1948. It was also agreed to recognize as "interested Governments", for the purposes of paragraph 2 of annex XI of the Treaty of Peace, the Governments of the other Allied and Associated Powers having signed the Treaty of Peace with Italy, including both India and Pakistan, and also the Governments of Italy and Egypt. It was further decided that interested Governments should submit their views to the Deputies to be studied between the time the Commission left and the receipt of its report. Nineteen Governments were thus invited in the capacity of "interested Governments".

6. In the report of the Deputies of the four Foreign Ministers to the Council dated 1 September 1948, 1/ and in accordance with the views held by the four Governments at that time, which have been modified since, France proposed that "with the exception of the territories situated between the Gulf of Zula and French Somaliland, Eritrea should be placed under the trusteeship of Italy" and that "the territories situated between the Gulf of Zula and French Somaliland should be assigned to Ethiopia in full sovereignty". The Soviet Union recommended placing the former Italian colony of Eritrea "under the trusteeship of Italy for a definite acceptable term". The United Kingdom proposed that "Ethiopia should be appointed to be Administering Authority in Eritrea for a period of ten years"—after which "the General Assembly of the United Nations would decide whether, and if so under what conditions, Ethiopian administration should continue indefinitely". There should be set up an advisory council with the right to suspend any legislation on certain reserved subjects introduced by the Ethiopian Administration and a special Eritrean commission of the United Nations to which the advisory council and the Ethiopian Administration would report from time to time; this commission would be quite distinct either from the Trusteeship Council or the Trusteeship Committee of the General Assembly. The United States of America proposed that "the southern section of Eritrea (including the Danakil coast, and the districts of Akkele Guzai and Serae...)" be ceded to Ethiopia, and that the Foreign Ministers recommend to the General Assembly of the United Nations that the question of the disposition of "the remainder of Eritrea, that is, the northern and predominantly Moslem portion including Asmara and Massawa, be postponed for one year".

7. While the Soviet Union recommended that, in the case of all three former Italian colonies, the "frontiers which existed on 1 January 1934, fixed in accordance with treaties and agreements in force at that time concluded between the interested Governments concerned" should be maintained, the United Kingdom, the United States of America and France recommended that "the frontier between the territories assigned to Ethiopia and French Somaliland should follow the course of the Wadi Weima".

8. Upon the expiry of the period set in annex XI of the Treaty of Peace with Italy, the Council of Foreign Ministers had not reached any agreement.

(b) The question of Eritrea at the third and fourth regular sessions of the General Assembly of the United Nations

9. On 15 September 1948, the Governments of France, the United Kingdom, the United States of Amer-

---

1/ Document C.F.M./D/L/48/IC/202 of the Council of Foreign Ministers (Deputies).

ica and the Union of Soviet Socialist Republics addressed the following communication to the Secretary-General of the United Nations: 2/

"Paris, 15 September 1948

"On the instructions of the Governments of the United States of America, France, the United Kingdom of Great Britain and Northern Ireland and of the Union of Soviet Socialist Republics we have the honour to inform you that in application of article 23 and paragraph 3 of annex XI of the Treaty of Peace with Italy, the question of the disposal of the former Italian colonies is referred to the General Assembly in order that, in conformity with its rules of procedure, the General Assembly may examine this question during the session which is to open on 21 September".

10. The question of the disposal of the former Italian colonies was considered at the second part of the third regular session by the First Committee which, on 13 May 1949, by 34 votes to 16, with 7 abstentions, 3/ decided to recommend the adoption by the General Assembly of a resolution providing *inter alia* that Eritrea, except for the Western Province, be incorporated into Ethiopia. 4/ However, the General Assembly, by 37 votes to 14, with 7 abstentions, rejected the draft resolution 5/ and decided to postpone further consideration of the question of the disposal of the former Italian colonies until its fourth regular session. 6/

11. At the fourth regular session, the First Committee appointed Sub-Committee 17 for the purpose of studying all drafts and suggestions and to propose a draft resolution or draft resolutions to settle the question of the former Italian colonies. 7/ Due to the fact that the available information on Eritrea was considered insufficient by several delegations, Sub-Committee 17 recommended the establishment of a United Nations Commision for Eritrea. 8/ On the report of this Sub-Committee, the First Committee recommended the adoption by the General Assembly of three resolutions, of which resolution A, section C, approved by the First Committee by 47 votes to 5, with 6 abstentions, 9/ provided for the establishment of this Commission. Resolution A as a whole which dealt with all three former Italian colonies was adopted by 49 votes to 1, with 8 abstentions. 10/

12. Section C of this resolution, concerning Eritrea, was adopted by the General Assembly on 21 November 1949 by 47 votes to 5, with 6 abstentions, 11/ and resolution A as a whole was adopted by 48 votes to 1, with 9 abstentions. 12/ This resolution was given the number 289 A (IV).

(c) Terms of Reference of the United Nations Commission for Eritrea

13. Section C of resolution 289(IV) reads as follows:

"With respect to Eritrea, [the General Assembly] *recommends*:

"1. That a Commission consisting of representatives of not more than five Member States, as follows: Burma, Guatemala, Norway, Pakistan and the Union of South Africa, shall be established to ascertain more fully the wishes and the best means of promoting the welfare of the inhabitants of Eritrea, to examine the question of the disposal of Eritrea and to prepare a report for the General Assembly, together with such proposal or proposals as it may deem appropriate for the solution of the problem of Eritrea;

"2. That in carrying out its responsibilities the Commission shall ascertain all the relevant facts, including written or oral information from the present administering Power, from representatives of the population of the territory, including minorities, from Governments and from such organizations and individuals as it may deem necessary. In particular, the Commission shall take into account:

(a) The wishes and welfare of the inhabitants of Eritrea, including the views of the various racial,

---

2/ A/645 (*Official Records of the third session of the General Assembly*, Part I, Plenary Meetings, Annexes to the summary records of meetings, pages 149-150).
3/ *Official Records of the third session of the General Assembly, Part II*, First Committee, summary records of meetings, page 394.
4/ Concerning the votes on the various paragraphs, paragraph 3 dealing with Eritrea was voted upon in two parts. The part referring to the disposal of Eritrea except for the Western Province was adopted by roll-call, by 36 votes to 6, with 15 abstentions. The part of paragraph 3 dealing with the disposal of the Western Province was rejected by roll-call, by 19 votes to 16, with 21 abstentions (*Official Records of the third session of the General Assembly, Part II*, First Committee, summary records of meetings, pages 393-394).
5/ Paragraph 3 dealing with Eritrea had been adopted by 37 votes to 11, with 10 abstentions (*Official Records of the third session of the General Assembly, Part II*, Plenary Meetings, summary records of meetings, pages 593-596).
6/ *Official Records of the third session of the General Assembly Part II*, Plenary Meetings, summary records of meetings, page 608.
7/ A/C.1/498 (*Official Records of the fourth session of the General Assembly*, First Committee, annexes to the summary records of meetings, page 24).
8/ A/C.1/522 (*Official Records of the fourth session of the General Assembly*, First Committee, Annexes to the summary records of meetings, page 25).
9/ A/1089 (*Official Records of the fourth session of the General Assembly*, Plenary Meetings, Annexes to the summary records of meetings, page 58).
10/ *Ibid.*
11/ *Official Records of the fourth session of the General Assembly*, Plenary Meetings, summary records of meetings, page 302.
12/ *Ibid.*

religious and political groups of the provinces of the territory and the capacity of the people for self-government;

(b) The interests of peace and security in East Africa;

(c) The rights and claims of Ethiopia based on geographical, historical, ethnic or economic reasons, including in particular Ethiopia's legitimate need for adequate access to the sea;

"3. That in considering its proposals the Commission shall take into account the various suggestions for the disposal of Eritrea submitted during the fourth regular session of the General Assembly;

"4. That the Commission shall assemble at the Headquarters of the United Nations as soon as possible. It shall travel to Eritrea and may visit such other places as in its judgment may be necessary in carrying out its responsibilities. The Commission shall adopt its own rules of procedure. Its report and proposal or proposals shall be communicated to the Secretary-General not later than 15 June 1950 for distribution to Member States so as to enable final consideration during the fifth regular session of the General Assembly. The Interim Committee of the General Assembly shall consider the report and proposal or proposals of the Commission and report, with conclusions, to the fifth regular session of the General Assembly".

Paragraph 1 of section D reads as follows:

"D. *With respect to the above provisions* [the General Assembly]:

"1. *Invites* the Secretary-General to request the necessary facilities from the competent authorities of each of the States in whose territory it may be necessary for the Commission for Eritrea to meet or travel".

Section II. Organization of the Commission

(a) Composition of the Commission and Secretariat 13/

14. In accordance with resolution 289 (IV), the Commission consisted of representatives of Burma, Guatemala, Norway, Pakistan and the Union of South Africa. The following representatives and alternates were appointed to constitute the Commission in representation of their respective countries: Mr. Justice Aung Khine and U Maung Maung Soe (Burma), Mr. Carlos García Bauer and Mr. Jose Luis Mendoza (Guatemala), Mr. Justice Erling Qvale and Mr. Ivar Lunde (Norway), Mr. Mian Ziaud-Din and Mr. Mir Mohamed Shaikh (Pakistan), Major-General F. H. Theron and Mr. F. J. van Biljon (Union of South Africa). Their credentials were found to be in due form.

15. The Secretariat of the Commission, totalling twenty persons, was headed by Mr. Petrus J. Schmidt as Principal Secretary, together with a Deputy Principal Secretary, Mr. David Blickenstaff, and two Assistant Secretaries.

(b) Rules of procedure

16. At the third meeting, held on 7 February 1950, the Commission adopted 14/ its rules of procedure. 15/

(c) Election of officers

17. All the representatives on the Commission were not present at the first meeting held at Lake Success on 10 January 1950, and as the Commission had not yet considered its rules of procedure, it was decided to elect a temporary Chairman. Mr. Justice Aung Khine (Burma) was unanimously elected temporary Chairman. 16/

18. At its third meeting, held on 7 February 1950, the Commission elected Mr. Justice Erling Qvale (Norway) Chairman, and Mr. Mian Ziaud-Din (Pakistan) Rapporteur.

19. At the 36th meeting, held on 31 March 1950, the Commission decided unanimously to amend its rules of procedure to provide that the office of Chairman would be assumed in future by representatives in rotation in the English alphabetical order of the names of the members for a period of seven days at a time. 17/ Accordingly, the Chairmanship of the Commission was assumed by representatives as follows:

31 March-6 April: Mr. Aung Khine (Burma);

7 April-13 April: Mr. Carlos García Bauer (Guatemala);

14 April-20 April: Mr. Erling Qvale (Norway);

21 April-27 April: Mr. Mian Ziaud-Din (Pakistan);

28 April-4 May: Major-General F. H. Theron (Union of South Africa);

5 May-11 May: Mr. Aung Khine (Burma);

12 May-18 May: Mr. Carlos García Bauer 18/ (Guatemala);

13/ Complete lists of delegations and Secretariat staff are given in annexes 1, 2 and 3 of this report.
14/ A/AC.34/SR.3, paragraph 38.
15/ A/AC.34/R.4.
16/ A/AC.34/SR.1, paragraph 14.
17/ A/AC.34/SR.36, paragraph 2, and A/AC.34/R.153.
18/ Due to the resignation on 16 May 1950 of Mr. García Bauer, he was replaced for the remainder of his term as Chairman by Mr. Qvale who served as Acting Chairman.

19 May-25 May: Mr. Erling Qvale (Norway);

26 May-1 June: Mr. Mian Ziaud-Din (Pakistan);

2 June-8 June: Major-General F. H. Theron (Union of South Africa).

(d) Subsidiary bodies

20. Sub-Commission I, comprising representatives of all five members of the Commission, was established by a resolution adopted at the seventh meeting, held on 18 February 1950, to investigate all the economic aspects of the evidence presented and available to the Commission. 19/

21. Sub-Commission I elected Mr. van Biljon (Union of South Africa) and Mr. Maung Maung Soe (Burma) as Chairman and Rapporteur, respectively. It held twenty-two meetings and submitted its report to the Commission on 8 May 1950. 20/

22. The Commission also set up three working groups at various stages in its work. When it became necessary, the Commission divided itself into two field groups.

Chapter II
Summary of the main activities of the Commission

Section I. Programme of Work

23. The Commission held seventy meetings, of which forty were public meetings and forty-four private in all or in part. 21/ The first and last meetings were held on 10 January 1950 and 8 June 1950 respectively.

24. On 15 February 1950, at 10 a.m., the flag of the United Nations was raised at the gate of the Palace grounds at Asmara by the Principal Secretary. The Chairman of the Commission addressed those attending the ceremony, who included members of the Commission and the Secretariat, officials of the British Administration and local Press representatives.

25. The Commission established a Working Group to prepare a programme of work and visits which was adopted and later adjusted as circumstances required. A complete schedule of the day-to-day meetings, visits and hearings of the Commission, detailing the witnesses heard, is included in annex 17 [not reproduced here].

Section II. Information from and Relations with the Administering Power

26. The Commission addressed to the British Administration-Eritrea four questionnaires or requests for information 22/ on political, economic and ethnographic subjects.

27. Following a communication from the British Administration, 23/ the Commission, at its 12th meeting, held on 24 February 1950, adopted 24/ the following statement: 25/

"The Commission has no intention to disclose at the moment any information received from the British Administration. The papers submitted by the Chief Administrator will be given a restricted circulation and their contents will not be disclosed until the drafting of the report of the Commission, when disclosure might be necessary for that purpose." 26/

The British Administration thereafter addressed a series of replies to the Commission's communications. 27/

28. Further, the Commission communicated with the British Administration on various subjects when clarification or explanations were required in connexion with its work or that of its subsidiary bodies and when it was considered that the Administration could provide information on the matter.

Section III. Information from Representatives of the Population of the Territory, including Minorities

(a) Communiqué to the inhabitants of Eritrea

29. At the fifth meeting, held on 14 February 1950, the Commission approved the following communiqué: 28/

"*Communiqué by the Commission to the inhabitants of Eritrea inviting written statements by individuals or groups*:

"The United Nations Commission for Eritrea extends its greetings to the people of Eritrea.

19/ A/AC.34/R.15.
20/ *Reservation by the delegation of Guatemala*:
"In the meeting held on 29 April 1950, the Guatemalan delegation requested that the part of the rules of procedure relating to the rotation of Chairmanship should be applied in Sub-Commission I. The Chairman, Mr. van Biljon, refused to apply this rule."
21/ *Reservation by the delegation of Guatemala*:
"The Guatemalan delegation places on record that it was always opposed to the practice of holding private meetings without justified reason as it considers this contrary to the tradition of the United Nations."
22/ A/AC.34/R.21, A/AC.34/R.28, A/AC.34/R.58 and A/AC.34/R.84.
23/ A/AC.34/R.27.
24/ A/AC.34/SR.12, paragraph 14.
25/ A/AC.34/R.34.
26/ *Reservation by the delegation of Guatemala*:
"The Guatemalan delegation was opposed to the adoption of this resolution because this secrecy obstructed or made difficult the necessary verifying of information received from an interested source."
27/ A/AC.34/R.47, A/AC.34/R.49, A/AC.34/R.81 and Add.1. A/AC.34/R.68, A/AC.34/R.69, A/AC.34/R.70, A/AC.34/R.101, A/AC.34/R.132, A/AC.34/R.133, A/AC.34/R.129, A/AC.34/R.163, A/AC.34/R.166.

"The Commission has been appointed by the General Assembly of the United Nations with instructions to ascertain the wishes and the best means of promoting the welfare of the inhabitants of Eritrea, and to report to the General Assembly with proposals for the future of Eritrea.

"In carrying out its responsibilities, the Commission will ascertain all the relevant facts and will consult the present Administering Power, other Governments, and representatives of the population, including such minorities, organizations and individuals as it may deem necessary. The Commission will take into account the views of the various racial, religious and political groups of Eritrea.

"The Commission has, therefore, decided to invite any individual or any group of individuals from among the inhabitants of Eritrea who so desire to send, as soon as possible and not later than 28 February 1950, to the Commission at its headquarters in Asmara any written statement relating to the future status of Eritrea.

"Such statements may, if it is desired, give the names of representatives whom the Commission might invite for oral hearings. The Commission may, in the future, issue further invitations with regard to the consultations which it may desire to hold with the inhabitants of Eritrea".

(b) Request that the British Administration issue a proclamation

30. At the 12th and 13th meetings of the Commission, the representatives of a political group requested guarantees that all persons should be allowed to appear freely before the Commission, and an allegation, subsequently denied by the persons concerned, was also made that the leader of the parties of the group had been prevented from appearing by the Administration. The following resolution was adopted by the Commission at its 15th meeting, held on 25 February 1950: 29/

"*The United Nations Commission for Eritrea*

"*Decides*

"That in order to avoid all likelihood of certain allegations as made yesterday before the Commission, the Commission requests the British Administration in Eritrea to issue a proclamation to the population that all persons are free to express to the Commission their views about the future of Eritrea, and that any such expressions will not render them liable to disapprobation of any kind on the part of the Administration, and that they will receive all possible protection".

31. A letter dated 28 February 1950 30/ was addressed by the Administering Authority to the Principal Secretary together with the following draft notice to the public:

"The Chief Administrator wishes to emphasize that all persons resident in Eritrea enjoy the utmost freedom to express to the United Nations Commission their views about the future of Eritrea, and that they will be afforded all possible protection by the Administration in the expression of such views both at the time and subsequently during the continuance of the British Administration. He wishes also to mention that, because of the limited time available to the Commission, and the importance of the work on which they are engaged, all statements made should be relevant to the terms of reference of the Commission and should, furthermore, when dealing with matters of fact only consist of such information as can be substantiated. He regrets to observe that many statements have been made in public to the Commission which are untrue and can be of no value to the Commission in their difficult task".

The Commission, at its 18th meeting, held on 3 March 1950, took note of the British communication. 31/

32. The Administering Authority published the proclamation in the Eritrean Press on 19 March 1950.

(c) Hearings and visits 32/

33. The Commission heard representatives of the various political parties, of commercial and other organizations, of the Coptic Church and Moslem religious personages, at Asmara. It visited the other main centres of Eritrea and toured the countryside, either as a whole or in two field groups, and held sixty-four hearings at thirty-seven centres with the local representatives of the inhabitants. Where possible, the Commission inspected manufacturing and other establishments of interest.

(d) Resolution of thanks to the people of Eritrea

34. The Commission, at its 42nd meeting, held on 6 April 1950, adopted the following resolution: 33/

"*The United Nations Commission for Eritrea*

"*Resolves*

29/ A/AC.34/R.35.
30/ A/AC.34/R.40.
31/ A/AC.34/SR.18, paragraph 1.
32/ See annexes 17 and 18, Map 2 of this report [not reproduced here].
33/ A/AC.34/R.175.

"To thank the people of Eritrea for their hospitality and co-operation with the Commission and for their commendable conduct at the hearings in Asmara as well as in the field, thus contributing largely towards the completion of its task in this country".

Section IV. Consultations with the Governments of Egypt, Ethiopia, France, Italy and the United Kingdom

(a) Invitation to the Governments of Egypt, Ethiopia, France, Italy and the United Kingdom

35. Pursuant to General Assembly resolution 289 A (IV), section C, the Commission decided to invite the Governments of Egypt, Ethiopia, France, Italy and the United Kingdom to express their views concerning the future of Eritrea and to provide such information as they might believe useful to the Commission. Suitable letters were addressed to these Governments on 3 March 1950 in which it was indicated that the Commission would be prepared, provided the respective Governments so desired, to engage in direct consultations with each of them:

(*a*) At Addis Ababa during the first week of April (letter to Ethiopia);

(*b*) At Cairo during the second week of April (letter to Egypt);

(*c*) At Rome during the third week of April (letter to Italy);

(*d*) During the first three weeks of April at a time and place found to be mutually convenient (letters to France and to the United Kingdom).

The programme of work was subsequently modified and the changed dates for the visits were later communicated to the respective Governments.

(b) Consultations with the Government of the United Kingdom

36. The following letter, dated 24 February 1050, 34/ was addressed to the Principal Secretary by the Special Liaison Officer of the British Administration-Eritrea to the Commission:

"I have, as agreed between us, consulted my Government informally as to the manner in which they wish, as an interested Government, to place their views before the Commission and I have been informed that they are quite willing to present them in written form to the Commission here in Asmara, provided that those views are not published so long as the Commission is actually in this territory. They would wish of course to be in a position to answer any questions upon their views and to submit any supplementary oral testimony at a later stage, but to avoid complications it would be preferable if this stage could be delayed until the Commission has written its report, which I understand will take place in Geneva.

"Perhaps you would let me know what the next step should be".

37. The Commission, at its 16th meeting, held on 28 February 1950, adopted the following resolution: 35/

"Considering the letter from the Special Liaison Officer, B.A.E., dated 24 February 1950.

"*The United Nations Commission for Eritrea*

"*Decides* to inform the British Administration that the Commission will gladly accept the views of the United Kingdom Government in written form here in Asmara, and

"*Agrees* not to publish these views so long as the Commission is actually in this territory".

38. The Special Liaison Officer, British Administration-Eritrea, transmitted to the Commission a "Statement of the views of His Majesty's Government regarding the disposal of Eritrea laid before the United Nations Commission for Eritrea at Asmara on 18 March 1950". 36/

39. Further, the Commission, during its 50th meeting, held on 28 April in Geneva, heard the representative of the United Kingdom Government, Mr. Frank E. Stafford, Special Liaison Officer. 37/

(c) Consultations with the Government of Ethiopia

40. The Commission, at its 24 meeting, held on 13 March 1950, adopted the following resolution: 38/

"*The United Nations Commission for Eritrea*

"*Decides*

"To visit such other towns and places in Ethiopia besides Addis Ababa as can be conveniently arranged in consultation with the Ethiopian Government".

41. The Commission further discussed the matter of its consultations with the Government of, and its visit to, Ethiopia at its 29th, 30th, 31st, 34th, 36th, 37th and 42nd meetings and it adopted various resolutions. 39/ In this connexion, a number of communications 40/ were received from the Government of Ethiopia, and the Commission at its

---

34/ A/AC.34/R.32.
35/ A/AC.34/R.43.
36/ A/AC.34/R.89 (annex 4 of this report [not reproduced here]).
37/ A/AC.34/SR.50, Part I (see annex 5 of this report [not reproduced here]).
38/ **A/AC.34/R.73.**
39/ A/AC.34/R.119, A/AC.34/R.122, A/AC.34/SR.36.
40/ A/AC.34/R.98, A/AC.34/R.99, A/AC.34/R.118, A/AC.34/R.128, A/AC.34/R.156, A/AC.34/R.158.

31st meeting, held on 25 March 1950, heard Mr. Deressa, the Ethiopian Minister of Commerce and Industry.

42. In conformity with its revised programme of work, 41/ the Commission was in Ethiopia, on the invitation of that Government, between 9 and 12 April, when it visited Gondar, educational, medical and other establishments in and around Addis Ababa and the Ethiopian Air Force training school at Bishoftu. 42/

43. At the 43rd meeting of the Commission, held on 10 April, 43/ Mr. Aklilou Abte Wold, the Minister for Foreign Affairs, made a statement giving the views of the Ethiopian Government. 44/ Consultations with the Government of Ethiopia continued during the 44th meeting, held on 11 April, 43/ and a letter dated 28 April 1950, transmitting "Supplementary remarks and observations" was addressed to the Commission by the Ethiopian Minister of Foreign Affairs. 45/

(d) Consultations with the Government of Egypt

44. The Commission visited Egypt between 12 and 17 April 1950. At its 46th meeting, held on 15 April, it heard Mohamed Salah El-Din Bey, the Minister for Foreign Affairs, who made a statement giving the views of the Government of Egypt. 46/

(e) Consultations with the Government of Italy

45. The Commission visited Italy between 17 and 20 April. A letter dated 17 April from Count Sforza, the Minister for Foreign Affairs, giving the views of the Italian Government, was addressed to the Chairman of the Commission. 47/

(f) Consultations with the Government of France

46. On 20 April 1950, in Rome, a letter was received by the Chairman of the Commission from the French Ambassador to the Italian Government, transmitting a communication from Mr. Robert Schuman, the French Minister for Foreign Affairs and giving the views of the French Government. 48/

Section V. Drafting of the Report

47. The general debate on the question of the disposal of Eritrea took place at Geneva during the 51st, 52nd, 58th, 59th, 63rd and 64th meetings held between 3 and 17 May 1950.

48. After the draft of chapters I and II of the report 49/ had been considered in the first reading, the Commission discussed the procedure to be followed with regard to subsequent chapters of the report and adopted, at its 65th meeting, held on 19 May 1950, the following resolution: 50/

"*The United Nations Commission for Eritrea*

"*Decides*

"That its report to the General Assembly will contain chapters I and II of the draft report as they will be approved in the second reading, to which will be attached any memoranda submitted individually or jointly by the various delegations, setting forth their views regarding the relevant facts and the solutions which they consider appropriate for the disposal of Eritrea, and a volume of annexes, containing the documents which the Commission may decide to include;

"That delegations are requested that their memoranda should not exceed twenty-five double-space typed pages per delegation;

"That these memoranda will be conveyed to the Rapporteur as early as possible and not later than 2 June 1950 and will be distributed by the Secretariat to the members of the Commission as soon as they are received;

"That after the receipt of the memoranda by the Rapporteur, a meeting of the Commission will be convened for the purpose of including these memoranda in the report and of approving the ultimate paragraphs of the report and its subsequent presentation".

49. Draft chapters I and II as approved during the first reading 51/ were considered in the second reading at the 66th meeting of the Commission, held on 20 May 1950. The memoranda submitted by the various delegations on 2 June 1950, in accordance with the above resolution, were subsequently included in the report and not discussed by the Commission.

50. The final draft report, drawn up in accordance with the above resolution, was submitted to the Commission during its 67th meeting held on 6 June 1950, and was approved by the Commission during its 69th meeting, held on 8 June 1950.

40/ A/AC.34/R.98, A/AC.34/R.99, A/AC.34/R.118, A/AC.34/R.128, A/AC.34/R.156, A/AC.34/R.158.
41/ A/AC.34/R.157.
42/ A/AC.34/R.169.
43/ See annex 7 of this report.
44/ A/AC.34/SR.43, appendix A (annex 6 of this report [not reproduced here]).
45/ A/AC.34/R.187 (annex 8 of this report [not reproduced here]).
46/ A/AC.34/SR.46, Part I (see annexes 9 and 10 of this report [not reproduced here]).
47/ A/AC.34/SR.47, appendix A (annex 11 of this report [not reproduced here]).
48/ A/AC.34/R.182 (annex 12 of this report [not reproduced here]).
49/ A/AC.34/R.183/Rev.1, A/AC.34/R.186, A/AC.34/R.192, A/AC.34/R.195.
50/ A/AC.34/R.197.
51/ A/AC.34/R.196 and Add.1.

51. The Commission desires to express to the British Administration-Eritrea, and to the Governments of Egypt, Ethiopia and Italy its appreciation for the courtesies and facilities which were extended to it during the course of its work.

52. The Commission also expresses it appreciation of the work of the Secretariat and the service which it rendered in the arduous task of the Commission. 52/

MEMORANDUM SUBMITTED BY THE DELEGATIONS OF BURMA, NORWAY AND THE UNION OF SOUTH AFRICA

Part I: Factual Review of the Problem of Eritrea

I. *Introductory statement*

53. In terms of resolution 289 A (IV) of the General Assembly, the Commission's report has to be in the hands of the Secretary-General not later than 15 June 1950. By 19 May 1950, the Commission had, however, only concluded the first reading of the two opening chapters of the report. The drafting of the substantive chapters of the report had not even been commenced; indeed, their draft outline had not by then been examined by the Commission in order to give a guide to the Rapporteur.

54. The Commission had concluded its general debate on the problem of Eritrea, but this discussion had shown that, as between some delegations, there were marked differences in regard to essential factual matters, and no way of bridging them had been revealed. An objective approach to the facts of the case, leading to a measure of agreement on them, is clearly a prerequisite to the formulation of the best solution for Eritrea. But in the circumstances mentioned, an agreed factual report by the Commission was precluded.

55. In addition, only three more weeks were available to the Commission and it was obvious that a far longer time would be needed for the Commission to prepare a comprehensive report, with the lengthy discussion, roll-call votes and numerous reservations which would certainly have been entailed.

56. The delegations of Burma, Norway and the Union of South Africa accordingly felt themselves compelled to support a resolution by the Commission on 19 May 1950, that chapters I and II, together with joint or separate memoranda on their views by the various delegations and a selected appendix of documents, be submitted as the Commission's report.

57. The delegations of Burma, Norway and the Union of South Africa herewith submit a memorandum consisting of two parts. Part I outlines the facts surrounding the problem of Eritrea. Part II contains the proposals by the three delegations for a solution of the problem.

II. *Eritrea, its people and economy*

A. Geography and population

Size and location

58. Eritrea is about 50,000 square miles in size. It adjoins Ethiopia along a broad front on the south, largely following the upper reaches of the Gash and Setit rivers. It stretches northwards triangularly, along the bulging Sudan border on the west and from the south of Port Sudan for 200 miles along the Red Sea to the Gulf of Zula. Below Zula, Eritrea has a long, narrow appendage, a strip of Dankalia desert, stretching a further 250 miles south along the Red Sea as far as French Somaliland, but only some 40 miles inland along an imaginary line parallel to the coast and forming Eritrea's western border with Ethiopia.

Topography and density of population

59. The Ethiopian uplands abut into Eritrea on its south, to form the central Eritrean plateau, often fragmented by sheer mountains and with an altitude ranging from 6,000 to 8,000 feet. These highlands comprise the administrative Divisions of Serae and Akkele Guzai in the south and the Division of Hamasien, with the capital, Asmara, towards the north. Though only 24 per cent of the area of Eritrea, these three Divisions have 56 per cent of the population.

60. The central highlands fall off steeply to the east where Massawa and the surrounding area, together with the Zula peninsula and Dankalia, form the Red Sea administrative Division, a dry, torrid and scantily populated region. It represents 22 per cent of the total area but has only 11 per cent of the population of Eritrea.

61. North of Asmara, around Keren, the altitude falls to 4,000 feet and the mountains become very broken. In the far north they become hilly in their descent to the Tokar region of the Sudan; to the east they slope steeply to the Red Sea plain but to the west more gradually to the Sudan plains. This whole area forms the Western Province Administrative Division, comprising 54 per cent of the area of Eritrea and a third of its people. The eastern Red Sea plain of this Division, like the northern hill country and the north-western steppe region, is dry and hot; only the Keren mountain area and the hilly and wooden region between the Setit river bordering Ethiopia and the Gash river have a better climate.

The diversity of the Eritrean people

62. The indigenous Eritreans are estimated at one million and, according to available statistics, have trebled

---

52/ *Reservation by the delegation of Guatemala*: "The delegation of Guatemala while recognizing the worthy and valuable contribution of a certain part of the staff of the Secretariat regrets that it is not able to accept a declaration of such general character."

in the last fifty years. The two principal language groups are in origin Semitic and their Tigrinya and Tigré languages, like Amharic which is spoken in Central Ethiopia and is the official language of the Ethiopian Empire, spring from a common root, Geez, the ancient language of Ethiopia which has survived only in Coptic liturgy. Tigrinya uses Geez characters; Tigré can be written both in Geez and Arabic script. The Tigrinya and Tigré languages are based on a common origin and structure rather than on recognizable similarity, and as now spoken they are mutually unintelligible. The Tigrinya-speaking people are mostly Copts and the Tigré-speaking groups mostly Moslem. In the west and east of Eritrea are representatives of the race habitually using languages of the Hamitic type, principally the Beni-Amer tribes, some of whom still use Beja, the tribes of the Danakil who speak a language of their own, and possibly the tribes on the eastern edge of the central plateau speaking a language called Saho; most of these tribes are Moslem. Arabic has been adopted as a second language by sections of the western tribes to whom Arab culture has spread, and it is almost the lingua franca of the Mohammedan quarter in the Eritrean towns. Neither the Hamitic nor Semitic linguistic groups are racially pure, they have absorbed so much alien blood from each other and from negroid and other groups that the term race is hardly applicable to them. A distinctive racial group is represented by small tribes of negroid or nilotic origin in the south-west of Eritrea.

63. These various population groups have different economic habits, different forms of social organization and largely live in different areas though the boundaries are blurred by seasonal migrations and overlapping of tribal areas. The central Eritrean highlands have a practically solid block of some 470,000 settled cultivators, Coptic in religion and Tigrinya-speaking. They live in villages, nestling against the mountains with a Coptic church prominent on the hill-top. These people are organized in kinship groups of families claiming descent from a common ancestor, but they, in effect, form small territorial units since the hereditary land right is corporate and vested in the kinship group. Elected councils of elders manage the communal affairs and chiefs were unknown until appointed by the Italians. There are close affinities between the highland dwellers and those of the adjoining Tigrai Province of Ethiopia. Their language and religion are the same; inter-marriage is frequent, and so is migratory use of grazing in the Tigrai. The central highlands have only 72,000 rural Moslems; some are settled in small groups throughout the area, but the main concentration is toward the eastern escarpment where the semi-nomadic Saho-speaking tribes live. In winter they move to the Red Sea foothills for grazing where, if possible, some cultivate quick-maturing crops, returning to the plateau in the summer.

64. Adjoining the Saho trioes are the Danakil tribes, pure nomads speaking Danakil, a language distantly related to Saho. Both groups are organized on a kinship basis, with an elective chieftainship for each kinship group. Appointed tribal chiefs were introduced by the Italians. The Saho-speaking tribes never acquired any unity. A common language and religion and a common need for protection have developed a sense of cohesion amongst the Danakil.

65. Western, northern and eastern Eritrea are inhabited by numerous nomadic tribes of greatly varying size and language, yet united to some extent by the common religion of Islam. The Beni-Amer tribes predominate in numbers and mostly speak Tigré, but some speak Beja or are bilingual. With the advent long ago of new tribes in the north-west, a division of society into aristocratic and serf classes occurred, which in part still exists although feudal dues have been abolished by the British Administration. Tribal organization on a territorial basis is precluded by the nomadic nature of the tribes; it, therefore, developed on a kinship basis, with elective councils of elders and elective chiefs. Tribal chieftainship by appointment was introduced by the Italians and still exists.

66. The Keren mountain area, owing to its better rainfall, is largely inhabited by sedentary peasants. There is a block of Tigrinya-speaking Copts south of Keren in the so-called Abyssinian Districts, and a distinctive Belein-speaking tribe lives around Keren. The negroid or nilotic groups of Eritrea are located in the south-west, between the Setit and Gash rivers; they are mainly agriculturalists, speak two languages of their own and are still regarded as an inferior race by their Coptic and Moslem neighbours.

67. The bulk of the population of Eritrea is rural and 847,000 or 78 per cent of the estimated total of 1,067,000 are so classified. Since 1933, considerable urbanization of the indigenous Eritreans has, however, occurred. The main concentrations are in the capital, Asmara, and in the Red Sea port, Massawa, which respectively account for 126,000 and 26,000, or for a total of 152,000 of the estimated urban population of 219,000. The indigenous population of Asmara is predominantly Coptic, that of Massawa and other centres mainly Moslem. Many rural Eritreans have become detribalized and in their new surroundings have acquired a use of Italian.

68. In the light of the foregoing, the population statistics of Eritrea are tabulated below, showing the diversity of the situation in broad outline:

Estimated geographical distribution, religion, language and way of life
of the Eritrean people by administrative divisions

Grouping	Highlands	Red Sea	Western Province	Total
(a) Size and density:				
Percentage of total area	24	22	54	100
Percentage of population:				
Rural	53	8	39	100
Rural + urban	56	11	33	100
(b) Religion of indigenous people:				
Moslem	104,000	105,000	315,000	524,000
Christian	470,000	2,000	34,000	506,000
Pagan	-	-	8,000	8,000
Total	574,000	107,000	357,000	1,038,000
(c) Rural population:				
(i) Way of life:				
Settled agriculturalists	388,000	17,000	80,000	485,000
Nomadic	62,000	47,000	254,000	363,000
Total	450,000	64,000	334,000	848,000
(ii) Language:				
Tigrinya	387,000	-	9,000	396,000
Tigré	-	29,000	243,000	272,000
Saho	63,000	7,000	-	70,000
Belein	-	-	37,000	37,000
Danakil	-	28,000	-	28,000
Other	-	-	45,000	45,000
Total	450,000	64,000	334,000	848,000
(d) Urban population:				
Moslem	31,000	41,000	17,000	89,000
Christian	93,000	2,000	6,000	101,000
Asiatic	5,000	1,000	2,000	8,000
European	19,000	1,500	500	21,000
Total	148,000	45,500	25,500	219,000
TOTAL RURAL AND URBAN POPULATION ((c)(i)+(d))	598,000	109,500	359,500	1,067,000

The administrative and judicial system

69. In view of the form of social organization existent in the village communities and amongst the nomadic kinship groups, their day-to-day affairs are regulated internally through that medium. District and tribal chiefs, appointed and paid by the Administration as in Italian times, are, however, responsible for the relations with the Administration of the groups of villages and nomads under their control. These chiefs act as the general agents of the Administration in their areas and tribes, collect the annual Native tribute, perform certain judicial functions and convey administrative orders to the population. The chiefs act through unpaid subordinate chiefs, village headmen and heads of tribal sections designated by the Administration. It maintains direct contact with the rural communities through senior divisional officers, assisted by divisional officers. The main towns

of Eritrea are generally divided into European and non-European quarters; the affairs of the former are conducted by municipalities under close supervision of the Administration, while the latter are administered through chiefs appointed and paid by the Administration.

70. Apart from the employment of Eritreans in subordinate clerical and other grades, the British Administration has sought to train Eritreans for superior posts, but few have the requisite education. Eighteen Eritrean administrative assistants are being trained to replace British administrative officers and other Eritreans are being recruited. In the police, fifty-five Eritreans hold posts of police inspectors, and in accordance with their capacity some of them have been put in charge of the smaller police stations.

71. In the judicial system, the Eritreans play a growing role. The tribunals which have jurisdiction in all civil cases as between Europeans, and as between Europeans and non-Europeans, have Italian judges appointed by the Administration. The village headmen and heads of tribal sections appointed by the Administration have jurisdiction as judges of the first instance in civil cases between parties of the same religion and community. Sharia courts administer Sharia law in civil cases as between Moslems. The British Administration has, in addition, created Native courts, whose members are Eritreans, with jurisdiction in penal cases against non-Europeans under specific Italian or British laws, and also in civil cases between non-Europeans if customary law is applicable. There are three courts of appeal in the territory, presided over by European judges.

Educational standards of the Eritrean people

72. The educational standard of the Eritrean people is low. According to the Intellectual Association of Eritreans, only one of whose members holds a university degree, some 70 per cent of the people are illiterate. As yet, a little less than 10,000 Eritrean children attend school, which is approximately 6 per cent of the Eritrean population of school age.

Other communities in Eritrea

73. There are small Greek, Arab, Jewish, Indian and Sudanese communities in the Eritrean towns, mainly engaged in trading, though many of the Arabs are labourers. The Italian communities are larger and occupy a special position in that they supply the country with artisans, technicians, professional men and entrepreneurs, in view of the inadequate standards of eduction and training of the Eritreans. Before the preparations for the Italo-Ethiopian war, the number of Italians living in Eritrea, mainly in the towns but sometimes as farm colonists, was limited to about 5,000. Thereafter the number of Italians increased considerably but figures of the Italian civil population are not available. Since the British occupation of Eritrea, the Italian population has progressively declined, from 60,000 in 1941 to 20,000 by March 1950. The Associazione Meticci dell'Eritrea estimates that the territory has 25,000 half-castes (including Eritrean mothers); many of them are associated with the Italians in the economic role they play in Eritrea.

Capacity of the people for self-government

74. Despite its small population, Eritrea is, therefore, a mosaic of religious and linguistic groups, and as will be shown later, acute political differences have now arisen on the basic question of its future. To govern such a country would be no easy task and the fact cannot be escaped that at present the Eritrean people lack the capacity for the self-government of Eritrea entirely on their own. There is no Eritrean intelligentsia to draw on for the purpose; the bulk of the people are illiterate; and only 6 per cent of the children attend school. Moreover, the leaders of the community have no knowledge of the responsibilities of government and possess no administrative or judicial experience other than in the regulation of tribal affairs and the application of customary law.

B. Eritrea's farming resources

Climate, land-use and waterworks

75. The rainfall map published as appendix D of annex 13 [not reproduced here] is based on official Italian and British rainfall records since 1938. It shows that the territory is largely sub-desert, and not a tenth of it receives twenty inches of rain a year, the minimum needed for stable crop production in warm climates.

76. The Red Sea plain receives winter rains, almost nil in Dankalia and only eight inches in the north, so that the whole area is largely desert; in summer the heat is intense. The rest of Eritrea has summer rains, except a small area on the eastern slopes of the highlands, around Ghinda and Fil-Fil, which receives summer and winter rains; with a total of forty inches this small area is a green oasis. On the highlands, the climate is equable and a rainfall of twenty inches fairly assured, but it is torrential and restricted to three to four months; the other months are dry and dusty. Around Keren the rainfall declines to fourteen inches, and to less in the north and south-west, so that most of the extensive western lowlands are too dry for crops; in summer they are hot and malarial. In the south-western corner, between the Setit and Gash rivers, the rainfall averages twenty inches, but it rains in strips and there are wide seasonal fluctuations so that crop production is shifting and precarious; the scarcity of

underground supplies of drinking water, common to the adjoining Sudanese plains, is a further obstacle.

77. The low rainfall permanently limits crop production in Eritrea. It severely hampers afforestation too as seedlings in plantations actually have to be watered in the dry months, otherwise less than 15 per cent survive after three years; in addition, the highland mountains which need re-afforestation most have often been eroded down to the bare rock. On account of the low rainfall, most of Eritrea is fit only for a migratory form of animal husbandry. The pattern of land-use is as follows:

Possibilities of land-use in Eritrea

	Acres	Percentage
Cultivable land	780,000	2.6
Wooded	1,520,000	5.0
Scrub	1,843,000	6.0
Grazing	23,069,000	74.7
Waste land	3,525,000	11.5
Mineral reservations	55,000	0.2
Total	30,792,000	100.0

The low percentage of cultivable land in Eritrea is common to other arid regions of Africa and not to its centre or south. In comparison with other African countries, however, the pressure of population in Eritrea is inordinate; the density of population per square mile of cultivable land is 700 in Eritrea, as against 30 in Ethiopia 53/ where the rainfall is much higher, and 1,420 in Egypt 53/ with its assured water supply and fertile delta.

78. The low rainfall, furthermore, limits the possibilities of irrigation in Eritrea. There is not a single river that runs for more than three months of the year, except the Setit on the frontier which originates in Ethiopia. River irrigation takes the form of flooding. The flood water is diverted to adjacent banked-in fields, either by means of a series of earth banks in the river beds as in the eastern lowlands, where little water now reaches the sea, or by permanent works as at Tessenei on the Gash river; most of its water which has not to be diverted to the Sudan cotton fields by agreement between the Governments is used by the Ali Gidr estate at Tessenei. On the Setit, to the northern bank of which Eritrea has access, little irrigation development has yet occurred and would involve pumping.

79. Extensive waterworks and hydro-electric development in the territory are also precluded by the low and seasonal rainfall. Twenty years ago, 54/ the popular theory was that the many gorges from the highlands to the eastern lowlands should be dammed in order to regulate the flood flow. Today, the Eritrean Chamber of Commerce and the Italo-Eritrean Association assert that the deficient agricultural output and the absence of power supplies could both be solved by series of small dams on the highlands, to catch the run-off by means of canals and to regulate the flow to the eastern lowlands for irrigation purposes, coupled with hydroelectric works along the steep decline. The author of this plan, however, declared that security conditions had prevented him from traversing the territory to test "its real possibilities". It does not in any case seem to bear examination. Regularity of flow is a first principle of hydro-electric generation, whereas the lowland cultivators need the water over a few months; surplus flood water which now disappears in the sandy river-beds, moreover, feeds the water-holes of the nomadic herdsmen lower down. Furthermore, the recordings at the series of catchment dams supplying Asmara show an annual evaporation loss of 50 per cent, with the high altitude of 8,000 feet and warm cloudless days. The optimistic view of the Italo-Eritrean Association 55/ that apart from the projected long-term waterworks, it would be possible to raise Eritrea's cereal yields seven-fold by planting the seed in rows instead of sowing it, has no basis in fact.

80. While the Eritrean highlands have the best rainfall, the region is very broken except around Asmara and in the Serae, where they flatten out. In consequence cultivable soil is extremely scarce. The small fields hug the mountain sides and are very stony so that the steel-pointed wooden plough, drawn by two oxen, and merely scratching the meagre soil, is the only suitable implement in most of the highlands. Rudimentary terracing is practised but proper levelling is rare and the communal system of land tenure does not make for improvement as it provides no individual security of occupation. The highland mountains have themselves long been denuded of trees and soil. In result, this densely populated region, so vital to the agricultural economy of Eritrea, has lost much of its fertility and is rapidly eroding further. The food waters of the Gash river, which originates in the highlands, carry as much as 8 to 10 per cent of soil particles. The soil thus carried away by the seasonal run-off is deposited in the eastern and western lowlands of Eritrea or outside its borders. It is there that irrigation is practised on the rich alluvial soil, to the extent that the supply of flood water permits.

Farming output and productivity

81. It is apparent that Eritrea is an inherently poor agricultural country. It is short of water, and short of cultivable land where there is water. As a result, an

---

53/ H. Shantz, "Agricultural Regions of Africa", *Economic Geography*, March 1943, page 157.
54/ G. Dainelli, "The Italian Colonies", *The Geographical Review*, July 1929.
55/ A/AC.34/SR.26, paragraph 37.

average of only 250 lbs. of cereals and legumes are produced yearly per rural dweller, with an average per capita holding of 1 1/2 cattle and 2 1/2 goats. Compared with Egypt's yield of 2.3 metric tons of cereals and pulses per hectare, or 0.8 to 1 metric ton per hectare in the Middle East, Eritrea's yield is only 0.5. 56/ As 78 per cent of Eritrea's population subsists on farming, the effect of its low productivity on the economy of Eritrea as a whole is obvious, both now and in the future, since no large-scale alternative form of employment exists.

82. In view of shortages and payment difficulties, a determined effort was made by the British Administration, after the occupation in 1941 and the release of manpower, to step up the production of food in Eritrea and reduce the food deficit. By giving priority to cereals over other crops on the concessions and by means of propaganda amongst the Eritreans, the output of cereals and pulses was progressively increased, from the order of 50,000 to 100,000 tons per annum, and the area cultivated from 300,000 to 600,000 acres. Livestock numbers nearly doubled over the same period, and have quadrupled in fifty years with the extended application of animal medicine, though droughts still take their toll. Eritrea, however, still has to import 12,500 tons of cereals yearly, one-eighth of its requirements, and future possibilities of expansion are restricted. Over-stocking is a serious problem in the highlands, and there practically all the available cultivable land is occupied. In the eastern lowlands a modest expansion under flood irrigation is possible and the western lowlands alone still have considerable scope for irrigation development. If and when the 170,000 additional acres capable of being watered in Eritrea have been put under irrigation, the human and animal population would also undoubtedly have grown. The main problem facing Eritrean farming is in fact not an expansion of acreage under irrigation but the rehabilitation of the densely-populated denuded highlands; this represents a task in terracing, levelling, re-afforestation and the inculcation of the first elements of rotation and manuring, which will involve very considerable expenditure, labour and time.

Farming regions

83. The table below compares the farm output, livestock, crop land and forestry resources of Eritrea's natural agricultural regions. Although these regions do not coincide with the administrative divisions, the table is complementary to the divisional analysis of the Eritrean population in paragraph 68.

Estimated size, output and livestock of Eritrea's natural farming regions

	Highlands	Western lowlands	Eastern lowlands	Total
Area in acres	10,680,000	10,880,000	9,232,000	30,792,000
Acreage cultivated	392,000	135,000	33,500	560,500
Percentage	3.7	1.25	0.36	1.82
Acreage still cultivable	48,000	165,000	6,500	219,500
Total percentage cultivable	4.15	2.75	0.43	2.57
Average output of cereals and pulses, 1947-1949 (tons)	71,760	21,900	6,450	100,110
Cattle	740,000	360,000	100,000	1,200,000
Goats and sheep	900,000	800,000	450,000	2,150,000
Camels	30,800	70,000	5,000	105,000
Horses, mules and donkeys	65,000	17,000	1,000	83,000
Tonnage of timber available	3,600,000	4,500,000	900,000	9,000,000

84. There is a natural measure of specialization and hence a degree of inter-dependence between these different farming regions. The western lowlands, for instance, help to meet the total cereal deficit of the other areas. On account of differences in seasons and inadequate grazing on the highlands, the tribes in the south-east move to the Ghinda area of the eastern slopes for grazing and cultivation in the winter and those from

---

56/ Yields derived from data in the report of the United Nations Food and Agriculture Organization Near East Pre-Conference Regional Meeting in Beirut during September 1949. (FAO document C.49/1/6).

Keren to the Sheb area. There also is a regular migration of cattle from the Serae and the western lowlands down to the Setit, and when grazing is bad, beyond the river into Ethiopia. On the other hand, many cattle from the highlands move into the Tigrai, and Ethiopia, moreover, is the main source of supply to meet Eritrea's food deficit in cereals, coffee, etc.

European farming concessions

85. About 78,000 acres of State lands have been issued under concessions, principally to Italian settlers. Farmed along modern lines, they produce most of the fresh milk, vegetables and fruit needed in the towns and limited quantities of sisal, coffee and tobacco. Sisal and bananas are exported, the latter under preferential arrangement to Italy. A number of the farming concessions have lately been practically abandoned on account of insecurity. The experimental nature of these concessions has been most instructive, but since they often are exceptional in being well-watered, they have had little influence on Eritrean dry-land farming. They, however, provide considerable employment to Eritreans. The Ali Gidr estate at Tessenei is, for instance, worked on a share basis and as the operations are not mechanized, employment during planting and harvesting reaches 5,000.

C. Other economic activities in Eritrea

Employment outside farming

86. As against about 850,000 people dependent on farming, the table below shows the relative importance of the other avenues of employment in Eritrea, except commerce and domestic service for which no figures are available:

Principal avenues of employment outside farming

Occupation	Eritreans	Europeans	Total
Manufacturing (1947)	23,900	5,000	28,900
Mining (1947)	3,200	400	3,600
Rail and road transport	900	2,800	3,700
Administration and public utilities	3,500	12,000	15,500

Manufacturing industry

87. Eritrea's manufacturing activities date mainly from 1936. Ancillary to the road construction and building programme launched by Italy, cement, brick and tile factories were established, and many servicing and electrical workshops, food plants, etc., were started to cater for the transport fleet and the enlarged Italian population. Many of the transport and construction works were no longer needed after the liberation of Ethiopia and the British occupation of Eritrea, and today, after the departure of two-thirds of the Italian civilians, rows of derelict buildings mark the scene in the smaller towns en route to Ethiopia and in the partly demolished Italian and Allied military and naval bases.

88. In the few big towns, however, a new phase of industrial expansion set in after 1943. When the wartime shortages threw the territory back on its own supplies, Italian ingenuity and enterprise played an important role in improvising new factories, to make such consumer goods as bottles, glassware, matches, beer, wine, paper and soap. The pre-existing cereal factories, edible oil plants, the tobacco monopoly, and chinaware and furniture factories supply food needs and conventional necessities. In addition, there are various fishmeal, mother-of-pearl and dum-nut button factories and vegetable fibre plants which cater largely for export overseas and two large salt-works which export sizeable quantities to Ethiopia and overseas. Also the beer, wine, glass, chinaware and match factories have come to rely on export, principally to the Sudan and to a lesser extent to Ethiopia, for a half and more of their sales. Some of these different factories are modern, but many are not and most are small. Their principal advantage seems to be the low level of Eritrean wages. Child labour, of both sexes, is extensively employed at still lower wages.

89. Lacking domestic sources of supply, imported petroleum and coal are used on the railways and for the generation of electricity, so that in this respect Eritrea has no advantage. The annual output of electricity is now about 22,500,000 kwh, a tenth of which is generated at hydro-electric works, and in view of the low rainfall and seasonal stream-flow, further development is inevitably restricted. Industrial minerals and agricultural and forestry raw materials in the territory are limited, though the marine resources and animal products still offer scope for further industrial development. The severe obstacles to re-afforestation have previously been noted and today reliance is largely placed on the limited supply of indigenous trees. The match factory, for instance, has to rely on the euphorbia candelabra tree, which is not very suitable for the purpose and takes fifty years to mature so that, at the present rate of match production, the supplies are visibly diminishing. Again, the dum palms, the nuts and leaves of which are used in industry, occur only in narrow fringes along the river banks of the eastern lowlands so that supplies are expensive to collect and limited, while also occupying some of the land still available for irrigation. The Eritrean market is, moreover, small and while the ingenuity of the Italians in using such raw materials as do exist, including substitutes, is remarkable and the low wage level is of advantage, it would be unwarranted to expect further considerable industrial expansion. The statement by the Italo-Eritrean Associa-

tion that, given a decision on the future of Eritrea which would provide the requisite political and financial security now lacking, the industrial employment could be readily stepped up to 100,000 people, has not been supported by any concrete facts.

Mining

90. Organized mineral exploration was undertaken in Eritrea late in the Italian regime by three semi-public concerns. One explored for gold in the western lowlands; another for copper, nickel and iron in the north; and the third drilled for oil on the Dahlak Islands off Massawa. No records of the oil drillings are available, but no discoveries are known, and the records of the two other concerns are not complete. The gold veins found and later worked are not of high value and though sometimes thick, they are vertical and often discontinuous. The northern region of Eritrea is potentially mineralized, but it is dry and difficult of access from the sea. The nickel ore located there is of low quality and the size of the deposits, like those of copper and white asbestos found in association, are not known; traces of manganese, titanium and chromium were also found. Mica, in very broken form, and vermiculite occur elsewhere in small quantities. Small seams of lignite, incapable of commercial exploitation, have been found. The known iron ore deposits total only 17 million tons. Marble and road stone abound. Kaolin and feldspar of good quality exist. The limited area of the torrid Dankalia depression falling within Eritrea, the greater part of it being in Ethiopia, contains sodium and potassium salts in considerable and payable quantities.

91. The limited mineral deposits which have been located and considerations connected with the geological history of the country, of which a certain knowledge was disclosed by the explorations carried out, suggest that Eritrea cannot be considered as a region favoured by mineral wealth. On the other hand, it could not be stated definitely that Eritrea is poor in minerals; her geology is too incompletely known and much further study and capital would be required to complete the task. The Red Sea plain north of Massawa, for instance, has sediments of miocenic age which have not yet been drilled for petroleum. It would, however, clearly be unwarranted and rash to assess Eritrea's economic future on an assumption that oil mineral deposits of real value are going to be discovered.

92. In view of the limited known mineral deposits, and the fact that most is known of the gold occurrences, their extraction is the principal mining activity. Gold production, which commenced mainly after 1937, reached 17,000 ounces by 1940. Dismantling for war purposes, the damage done to five mines since 1948 by terrorists and the closing of a further nine on account of insecurity and for economic reasons have reduced the gold output to as low as 2,800 ounces. Sale is allowed on the free market at a premium as it appears that working costs exceed the official gold price. Kaolin and feldspar are worked only to the extent of local requirements. No other mines exist.

Transport, foreign trade and balance of payments

93. Eritrea has one railroad. It links the port of Massawa with the highland capital Asmara, and as it was not designed to serve Ethiopian trade, it thence links up with Eritrea's own western hinterland. Traffic on the latter section is scarce, averaging 60 tons of goods and 800 passengers per day; the traffic density is somewhat higher, 220 tons of goods and 550 passengers per day, on the shorter section from Asmara to Massawa harbour, which is conveniently situated for traffic to and from the Tigrai and Gondar regions of Ethiopia. Notwithstanding that competing motor transport parallel to the railroad is largely prohibited, the rail traffic barely produces enough revenue to meet current costs, with no provision for depreciation and renewal. The Italian ropeway between Massawa and Asmara is inoperative as there is not enough traffic even for the railway.

94. The Eritrean road system, comprising 485 miles of main roads and 1,400 miles of secondary dirt roads, is an engineering feat. Constructed largely after 1935, the roads not only link the territory internally but also northern Ethiopia with Massawa, the Dessie region with Assab, and Eritrea's west and centre with the Sudan. The road motor fleet conveys some 70,000 tons of goods yearly to and from Ethiopia and probably 50,000 tons internally.

95. The Eritrean Chamber of Commerce has stressed the importance of the transport earnings on the Ethiopian transit trade and of the additional income secured as commission, harbour revenue, freight and insurance. A related source of earnings is the value added to Ethiopian primary products, resorted, cleaned or processed in Eritrea for re-export. The inward and outward transit trade to and from Ethiopia totals about £3,000,000 a year, compared with Eritrea's own import-export trade total of £4,700,000. From this comparison, the vital economic significance to Eritrea of her location, astride the Red Sea trade route and with the potentially rich Ethiopian hinterland behind her, is self-evident. The *entrepôt* earnings from Ethiopian trade, together with dollar remittances to American personnel in Eritrea, have the result that Eritrea's own adverse trade balance of over £1,500,000 is largely wiped out. For the past three years foreign receipts and payments have been in approximate

balance, so that import control has been considerably relaxed.

96. Eritrea's own foreign trade conforms to the pattern of her domestic economy. Her principal exports are hides, skins, salt and other marine products; exports of manufactures are far smaller. On the other hand, due to the low rainfall and scarcity of cultivable soil, cereals and other foodstuffs bulk large in her imports, as do textiles, fuel and tires. As a source of cereals and other foodstuffs, Ethiopia ranks first and enjoys tariff preference. The distribution between countries of the import trade in manufactured goods seems to have been influenced considerably by import control and Britain now is the main supplier. Italy has, however, remained the principal market for Eritrean primary produce.

Taxation and finance

97. The Italian tax system for Eritrea is still in force, with a large variety of direct and indirect taxes. Customs duties (averaging 10 per cent), income tax (levied at progressive rates on incomes over £60 and averaging 10 to 12 per cent), a monopoly tax on tobacco goods of over 100 per cent, and the surcharges on petrol (88 per cent), spirits (89 per cent) and beer (43 per cent) provide three-fourths of the revenue. The annual tax yield of £1,200,000 is only about £1 per head of population. The Eritrean Chamber of Commerce has assessed the incidence of taxation at £46 per head for Europeans and at four shillings per Eritrean.

98. Budgetary expenditure exceeds the revenue of Eritrea, and the accumulated deficit met by the British Treasury over the past nine years is £1,508,200, of which £970,000 were spent on Italian relief repatriation, leaving a net deficit of £538,000. This figure excludes the costs of the British military forces and further understates the true budgetary deficit in that the administration has been conducted on a care-and-maintenance basis only; no provision for renewal of capital has been made and avoidable capital expenditure has been deferred. The charges for posts, telegraphs and veterinary services cover costs, but the medical, railway and port services are rendered at rates which would not nearly cover costs if due provision were made for capital depreciation. Inclusive of certain capital expenditure which could no longer be deferred, the estimate deficit for the current financial year has risen to nearly £450,000.

Is Eritrea economically viable?

99. Eritrea is largely sub-desert and an inherently poor farming country. Her known mineral deposits are negligible. She has practically no local sources of power. In the absence of any rich sources of raw materials, of domestic power or of widespread industrial skill, Eritrea can have no real industrial future. A number of manufacturing industries exist, and some can develop further, but they are small and their principal advantage is the low wage level of the Eritreans, including the extensive child labour force. Eritrea's road links with Ethiopia and her two harbours, however, enable her to profit from the conveyance and handling of a large transit trade with Ethiopia, the resultant earnings contributing greatly to offset her own large adverse trade balance. Eritrea is closely linked with the Ethiopian economy in other respects as well. Ethiopian grazing lands are extensively used; Ethiopia is the most convenient supplier of Eritrea's cereal deficit, and if the population of Eritrea's densely-occupied highlands continues to increase, emigration to the sparsely inhabited Ethiopian uplands will become a necessity. Furthermore, Ethiopia and the Sudan provide the largest export markets for Eritrean manufactures. In view of the paucity of her resources, Eritrea regularly has a budgetary deficit, even without provision being made for capital depreciation. The average tax yield is only £1 per head, the Europeans being estimated to contribute £46 each and Eritreans four shillings. The budget deficit cannot, however, be wiped out simply by inventing new tax formulae, since the Eritrean peasantry, comprising 78 per cent of the population, have a very low per capita output; crop yields in Eritrea are half those in the Middle East. In these circumstances outside financial assistance had to be provided to Eritrea, first by the Italians and then by the British Administration. Further assistance would be needed for the extension of medical services and educational facilities, for the rehabilitation of the denuded highlands which are the mainstay of Eritrean agriculture, and for exploration to discover minerals. The costs of defence are today met by the British Treasury.

100. Eritrea has, therefore, neither the resources nor the revenue to make her economically viable in the foreseeable future. Her economic dependence on Ethiopian economy is very great. And in view of the absence of any technical proficiency on the part of the Eritreans themselves, the continued presence of a sufficient number of foreign technicians, Italian and other, to operate her manufacturing industries and technical services, is vital to the maintenance of the present level of economic activity as well as for any possible increase in industrial development.

III. Political wishes of the people

A. *Recent changes in political groupings in Eritrea*

101. Since the survey made by the Four-Power Commission in Eritrea in 1947, important changes in the attitude of the different political parties have led to a new line-up of the main political organizations of the territory.

These developments have partly altered the situation which existed two years earlier.

102. The main change which has occurred since 1947 is the formation of the Independence Bloc and the subsequent development of new political parties. The Independence Bloc was formed in New York during the 1949 spring session of the General Assembly by a coalition of the Moslem League, the Liberal Progressive Party, the New Eritrea Party (formerly the Pro-Italia Party), the Nationalist Party, the Veterans' Association and the Italo-Eritrean Association. These parties had variously favoured independence, Italian trusteeship or continued British Administration, but now united in a demand for the immediate independence of Eritrea. The Bloc was joined by two new organizations, the Independent Eritrea Party (composed mostly of former Unionists from the Keren District) and the Intellectual Association of Eritreans (composed of a small number of individuals).

103. This concentration of parties and groups around a common programme for independence was soon followed by important secessions from the Bloc and by the establishment of new parties by dissident elements. The groups concerned all stated that they seceded because of their conviction that Italian interests and interferences influence the policy of the Bloc, but in some cases personal division of opinion between different party leaders was also a probable cause. The first change of allegiance occurred with the formation of the Independent Moslem League of Massawa, mainly amongst Moslem residents of the Red Sea, Hamasien and Akkele Guzai Divisions; this group has come out in favour of union with Ethiopia under conditions designed to protect Moslem interests. After the arrival of the Commission in Eritrea, three new parties were organized by groups breaking away from the Independence Bloc. Two of these are the Liberal Unionist Party (composed of former members of the Liberal Progressive Party) and the Independent Eritrea United to Ethiopia Party (composed of former members of the Independent Eritrea Party) who both favour union with Ethiopia, the former under certain conditions. The third is the Moslem League of the Western Province (composed of former members of the Moslem League) which advocates the continuance of the present British Administration in the Western Province for a period of ten years, leaving the rest of the territory to decide its future for itself. The Independence Bloc, favouring an independent Eritrea, therefore now consists of seven political parties, of which the Moslem League is numerically the largest.

104. The Unionist Party has remained the biggest single party in Eritrea and has continued to urge the reunion of the whole of Eritrea with Ethiopia. In this it is supported by three smaller parties. Recently, in the circumstances explained more fully in paragraph 110, the Unionist and allied parties signified that, if the majority of the inhabitants of the Western Province were found to oppose reunion, they would not oppose a separate solution for it, provided that the remainder of Eritrea were then united with Ethiopia.

105. These political shifts are indicative of the state of feeling and uncertainty which has been engendered in Eritrea by the long delay in applying a final political solution. The continued uncertainty also is a root cause of the insecurity and violence which have marked the past months. It must be stressed that while the major political parties are active in propagating their views and enlisting the support of the people, they are not as highly organized as in other countries and have little appreciation of the practical responsibilities of government.

B. Assessment of the political wishes of the parties and people

106. The Commission sought to ascertain the political views and wishes of the population through hearings of representatives of the different political parties and other associations as well as by inquiries in the country. The leaders were called to state their opinions before the Commission in Asmara, and the different parties and associations also submitted written statements to the Commission. Furthermore, during the field hearings in the countryside and other towns, representatives of local branches of the various organizations were questioned by the Commission or its field groups.

107. The questions put to the representatives who met the Commission in Asmara and in the field were designed to establish as much information as possible about the membership and numerical support claimed by the different associations, parties and leaders of the local political groups. The questions were also framed so as to elicit their main political views on the future government of the territory and their wishes with reference to independence, union or association with Ethiopia, trusteeship, continuation of the present Administration, the disposal of the territory as an undivided entity under these different solutions, and partition of Eritrea with the view to according separate treatment to the Western Province. Additional questions ranging over a diverse field were put by the different delegations.

C. Views of the principal political parties and associations

108. The Commission gave hearings in Asmara to the eighteen political and other associations which desired to be heard. The views expressed by the leading parties and allied organizations during these hearings are briefly summarized.

The Unionist Party and allied parties

109. *The Unionist Party* 57/ desired the immediate and unconditional reunion of Eritrea with Ethiopia, basing its claims on the close links of race, geography, history and economy between the two countries. It asserted that this course was favoured by the great majority of the Eritrean population (including 75 per cent of the inhabitants of the Western Province). The Party was against independence without association with Ethiopia, stressing that real independence for a poor country such as Eritrea could not thereby result. It opposed the Independence Bloc on the grounds that it was a foreign creation and alleged that the Bloc was directly supported and financed by the Italians. The Unionist Party rejected all allegations that the Moslems were badly treated by the Ethiopian Government and maintained that all groups of the population in Ethiopia were accorded equal treatment, which would also be the case in Eritrea after reunion with Ethiopia. The Unionist Party rejected the criticism that it supported terrorism and stated that accusations to that effect were only put forward by the Independence Bloc and its sympathizers in order to conceal their own weakness and lack of support from the population. It did not admit that the economic work of the Italians had been intended to benefit the Eritrean population as such and was opposed to allowing the Italians to exercise any influence or take part in the administration of the country; they and the half-castes would be protected under a democratic constitution, based on international law and human rights, provided that they obeyed the laws of the country and wished to do good for the whole of the country and not merely for themselves.

110. The Unionist Party, in claiming the reunion of the whole territory of Eritrea with Ethiopia, originally rejected the claims of the Moslem League of the Western Province for partition, considering this party only to consist of a few chiefs dependent on the British Administration and in the belief that the Unionists themselves were in the majority in the Western Province. At a later stage, 58/ the Unionist Party informed the Commission that, while not departing from its basic desire for reunion of Eritrea with Ethiopia, it might be that one solution for the whole country would not be considered workable at the forthcoming meeting of the General Assembly. Having also taken note of a recent change of views in the Western Province, the Unionist Party, therefore, indicated that, if the majority of the inhabitants of the Western Province were found to oppose reunion, it would not oppose a separate solution for that Division, provided that the remainder of Eritrea were then unconditionally joined with Ethiopia. It was stated that this decision had been taken by the leaders of the Party, as they were entitled to do in an emergency and since a basic change of policy was not at issue. 59/ The Keren branch, however, protested to the Commission against the action of the party headquarters. 60/ An agreement was reached at the same time between the parties favouring conditional union with Ethiopia and the Moslem League of the Western Province, 61/ that neither group would oppose the respective solutions advocated by the other in the event of partition being decided upon by the United Nations.

111. *The Independent Eritrea United to Ethiopia Party* 62/ expressed the same desires as the Unionist Party, except that it was prepared to agree to independence, provided that union with Ethiopia would subsequently be possible. This party, which claimed its main support in Keren and the neighboring districts of the Western Province, stated that it had broken away from the Independence Bloc and from the Independent Eritrea Party because of the Italian interference with the policy of the Bloc.

112. The Liberal Unionist Party, 63/ which claimed its main support in Eastern Eritrea, desired union with Ethiopia on certain conditions designed to preserve the use of Eritrean languages and to safeguard the customs of the country. The members of this Party had originally adhered to the Liberal Progressive Party but had broken away after the latter had joined the Independence Bloc. They stated that they were now opposed to the Bloc because of it Italian affiliations, which clearly showed that the Italians intended to regain control over Eritrea through the Bloc. Representatives of the party had visited Addis Ababa and had received satisfactory assurances from the Ethiopian Government as to the realization of the conditions they wanted as the basis for the union of the two countries. The Party did not want the Italians or the Italo-Eritrean half-castes to have any part in the political life of the country but stated that they would be free to remain in Eritrea "as workers".

113. The Independent Moslem League, 64/ which claimed its main support in Massawa and the eastern lowlands, desired union with Ethiopia under conditions designed to preserve the rights of Moslems and especially assuring equal treatment of Moslems and Copts, recognition of all Moslem institutions and recognition of the Arabic language which should be taught side by side with the official language of Ethiopia. The majority of the members of the party had belonged to the Moslem League, but it was stated that they had broken away when the League joined the Independence Bloc. Representatives

---

57/ A/AC.34/SR.17.
58/ A/AC.34/R.151.
59/ A/AC.34/SR.42.
60/ A/AC.34/R.170.
61/ A/AC.34/R.168.
62/ A/AC.34/SR.14.
63/ A/AC.34/SR.23/Part I.
64/ A/AC.34/SR.24, A/AC.34/SR.25.

of the Independent Moslem League had been to Addis Ababa and stated that they had received satisfactory assurances as to the fulfilment of the conditions they put forward for the union of Eritrea to Ethiopia. This party, too, considered that real independence for Eritrea could be obtained only in union with Ethiopia. It felt that the Italians in Eritrea would be humanely treated by the Ethiopian Government, in the same way as their compatriots now residing in Ethiopia, but refused to state the views of the party as such, declaring that the Italians had their own country, as the Eritreans had theirs.

The Independence Bloc and allied parties

114. *The Independence Bloc* 65/ desired immediate independence for the whole of Eritrea, and that a constituent assembly should determine the form of government. It was claimed that the Bloc and its affiliated parties were supported by the vast majority of the population, who opposed union with Ethiopia, the partition of Eritrea or any form of trusteeship. The Eritrean people were considered fully able to rule themselves. The representatives of the Bloc expressed strong opposition towards the claims of Ethiopia, maintaining that Eritrea had never formed a real part of the Ethiopian Empire, that there were no real racial links between the two countries, and that even the Province of Tigrai had been annexed to Ethiopia against the will of its inhabitants. The Ethiopian Government was accused of supporting terrorist activities in order to prevent the free expression of public opinion particularly in the highlands. Moslems were said to be ill-treated in Ethiopia, and the Ethiopian Government was said to be unable to manage its own affairs. The British Administration was criticized on the basis of allegations that it supported plans for the partition of Eritrea, favoured the Unionists and did not seriously try to prevent terrorism. The Bloc dismissed the claims of the Unionist Party because it considered it to be in the minority, which compelled it to resort to terrorism. The claims of the Moslem League of the Western Province were opposed by the Bloc on the grounds that that party was composed only of chiefs in the pay of the British Administration and because it aimed at the partition of the territory, which was against the wishes of the whole population. The attitude of the Bloc towards the Italians in Eritrea was that they would be treated according to international law and enjoy the same position as other foreign communities. Because of the ties of blood relationship which many Italians had with Eritreans, they would be welcome to stay in the territory.

115. The views of the Bloc were supported in separate statements by the representatives of the *Independent Eritrea Party* 66/ and the *Veterans' Association.* 67/

116. *The New Eritrea Party* supported the declarations of the Independence Bloc, 68/ but was also prepared to accept United Nations trusteeship should immediate independence prove impracticable. The spokesmen of this group made strong accusations against the Unionists for resorting to terrorism in order to prevent opponents from expressing their opinions, and accused the British Administration of seeking to influence the political opinions of the people. The Party was of the opinion that the Italians, whose exodus would spell economic disaster, should remain in Eritrea in accordance with provisions to be inserted in the future Eritrean constitution.

117. The Intellectual Association of Eritreans, 69/ which did not claim to be a mass movement, supported the policy of the Independence Bloc. The group would not object to union with Ethiopia if it were approved by a majority in the Eritrean Parliament after independence had first been gained.

118. *The Italo-Eritrean Association*, to which the Commission gave three hearings, 70/ supported the main statements of the Bloc. The Association, which claimed the support of Italians and many half-castes, desired immediate independence for Eritrea, with a United Nations trusteeship for an interim period if the United Nations so decided. Free harbour zones at Massawa and Assab were proposed in order to afford Ethiopia an outlet to the sea. As noted earlier in this memorandum, the spokesmen of the Association stressed the economic inter-dependence of the different regions of Eritrea, the important role the Italo-Eritreans were called to play in the evolution of the country and ways and means of making it self-supporting. They averred that annexation to or federation with Ethiopia would be a retrograde step for Eritrea, which had higher social, economic and administrative standards. It was said that agreement had been reached with the other parties of the Bloc that the social and economic rights of Italians and Italo-Eritreans would be safeguarded if independence were granted. They asked that if independence were rejected and another solution, which was not desired, were decided upon, the United Nations should properly safeguard the position of the Italians in Eritrea so that they could remain in the country and freely carry on their activities which were indispensable to the life of the country.

119. The claim for the independence of Eritrea was further supported by the C.R.I.E., 71/ *The Representative Committee of Italians in Eritrea*, on behalf of the 20,000

65/ A/AC.34/SR.12.
66/ A/AC.34/SR.13.
67/ A/AC.34/SR.19.
68/ Ibid.
69/ A/AC.34/SR.22.
70/ A/AC.34/SR.15; A/AC.34/SR.16/Part I, A/AC.34/SR.26
71/ A/AC.34/SR.15, A/AC.34/SR.34/Part I, A/AC.34/SR.41.

Italians then residing in the territory. Should immediate independence not be granted, the Committee considered Italian trusteeship as most appropriate, or alternatively a United Nations trusteeship with wide Italian participation. The statements of the Committee also paid attention to considerations of an economic nature, relating to the inter-dependence of the different parts of Eritrea and explaining how the country could be made self-supporting. The Committee indicated that if the majority of the people after receiving independence wished to join Ethiopia, the Italian group would follow the decision, but did not believe that a majority would be obtained. In view of the prevailing insecurity in Eritrea, which the British Administration was alleged to be unable or unwilling to combat, the C.R.I.E. submitted a request to the Commission, for transmission to the United Nations, that the present Administration not be allowed to remain in the territory any longer.

120. *The Eritrean Chamber of Commerce* submitted several papers of an economic nature, to which reference has been made earlier in this memorandum, in support of its view that Eritrea should not be partitioned and that, if properly administered, it could in a very short time become a self-supporting country.

Moslem League of the Western Province

121. *The Moslem League of the Western Province* claimed to represent the majority of the population of that area, who were stated to be opposed both to union with Ethiopia or with the Sudan. It therefore pleaded for a separate solution for the Western Province. It desired British administration for the area for a period of ten years and subsequent independence. It also requested the establishment of a legislative assembly for the Western Province. In advocating partition, the spokesmen of the party declared that they were speaking only for the Western Province and that the population of the other parts of Eritrea must be left to take their own decision as to their future.

The party had broken away from the Moslem League because of alleged affiliations of the latter with the Italians, and because the League had abandoned its original programme, which was to promote proposals for independence after a preparatory period of British trusteeship.

D. *Hearings of the local population*

122. During extensive travels throughout Eritrea, the Commission visited thirty-seven centres and held sixty-four hearings at which the views of political groups of the local population were heard. On the recommendation of the Administration, and in order to avoid clashes and disorder, the procedure followed by the Commission and its field groups was to hold meetings at separate places in the different centres with the local groups representing the main trends of political opinion. In this way two meetings were held at each centre in the highlands and in the eastern lowlands, where the main division was between the parties favouring union with Ethiopia on the one hand, and the parties favouring immediate independence on the other. In the Western Province separate meetings were also held for the supporters of the Moslem League of the Western Province.

123. The spokesmen of the different groups appearing at the field hearings were heard in their capacity as representatives of the local branches of the respective political parties and only exceptionally were hearings accorded to individuals, local chiefs or other persons connected with the Administration. In the main it can be said that the local spokesmen who appeared at the field hearings merely repeated the view expressed to the Commission in Asmara by the political parties to which they belonged; often party leaders and some mobile supporters preceded the Commission in order to be present at these meetings. The procedure followed by the Commission thus differed from that of the Four-Power Commission which had heard representatives of each village, family or tribal unit and so assist in establishing the real numerical support of the political parties.

124. The attendance at the meetings gave a certain indication of the relative strength of the different parties. The impressions gained in this way broadly confirm the claims of the Unionist Party and allied groups that they have the support of a large majority of the people of the highlands in the Hamasien, Akkele Guzai and Serae Divisions. The Unionist meetings in this area drew large numbers while those of the Independence Bloc were small, and sometimes none appeared. The representatives of the Bloc nevertheless claimed to have the real support of the inhabitants and attributed the absence of large numbers of people at their meetings to terrorist activities on the part of the "Shifta" gangs, which they alleged were organized from Ethiopia and helped by the Unionists, and to the seasonal absence of the people for grazing purposes.

125. Throughout the Red Sea Division by far the largest attendances were at the meetings of supporters of the Independence Bloc, mostly represented by adherents of the Moslem League. The Unionist Party and the Independent Moslem League, however, also assembled considerable numbers of people, except at Assab. At the end of the Commission's work at Asmara, claims were made by representatives of certain nomadic tribes in the southern Danakil region that the hearings at Assab and Zula had been called without sufficient warning to these tribes, who had therefore been unable to appear in support of the Independent Moslem League.

126. In the Western Province the Unionist Party seemed to have its main support at Keren and in the immediate neighbouring districts; Unionist meetings in other parts of the Province only showed negligible attendances. The Independence Bloc and the Moslem League of the Western Province were able to muster considerable numbers of supporters at hearings also in the more remote parts of the area, the meetings of the Bloc assembling the largest crowds everywhere in this Division.

E. *Membership and support of the political parties*

127. The information gathered by the Commission and the claims put forward by representatives of the various groups do not provide a basis for an evaluation of the precise number of supporters of the different political parties. Both at the hearings at Asmara and during the field hearings the representatives of all parties made the most exaggerated statements as to the number of their members and supporters. The number of supporters, claimed by the different parties both in the territory as a whole as well as in the different districts, were often considerably in excess of the total population as estimated by the British Administration. Large discrepancies could also be noted between the figures given by the central organizations of the parties at Asmara, and the figures indicated by the local representatives at the field hearings. A tabulation of figures of membership and supporters, claimed by the various political parties in Eritrea at the hearings at Asmara and at the field hearings, shows that the parties claimed to have the support of more than 3.5 million people, while the total population of Eritrea is estimated at not much more than one million. The Unionist Party and allied parties claimed about 1.3 million, while the Independence Bloc claimed more than 2 million supporters. The Moslem League of the Western Province was more modest in claiming the support of about 215,000 people out of the total population of the Western Province estimated at about 360,000. These exaggerated claims were made more conspicuous by the fact that the various parties were unable to give exact information as to how they arrived at them and usually admitted that the number of actually registered members was small as compared with the number of supporters, which included women and children.

128. An approximate general evaluation of the relative strength of the various political parties can, therefore, not be based on the claims put forward by the parties themselves, but must be made on all available evidence and sources of information, including the direct observation which the members of the Commission were able to make during the field trips in the territory.

129. In this connexion account also has to be taken of the extent to which extraneous factors may have influenced the formation and expression of the political wishes of the people of Eritrea: As noted in the earlier summary of the views of the political parties, the pro-Unionist group has indicted the Independence Bloc as being the product of Italian intervention, and not the result of spontaneous growth. Again, the Moslem League of the Western Province alleged, and on occasion produced witnesses to testify, that food, clothing and funds were distributed by the Bloc to draw adherents. On the other hand, there is the counter-charge by the Bloc against the pro-Unionist parties, that they accepted assistance from Ethiopia and that terrorist practices and the sanctions of the Coptic Church were employed to swell the Unionist ranks and stifle their opponents.

130. There is little doubt that such extraneous influences have been at work. But there is a strong tendency to exaggerate them, and to take refuge behind them in weak situations. No reliable proof ever was adduced, and the Abuna Marcos, head of the Eritrean Coptic Church, consistently denied, that non-Unionist Copts had been forcibly enrolled by threats of excommunication. The two priests who alleged discrimination for political reasons admitted their participation in theological disputes of long standing. The Coptic Church certainly wields considerable influence, but it must not be overlooked that the Unionist movement in the highlands has many of the characteristics of an expanding popular movement. Operating with simple and easily understandable slogans, it reflects the fact that the Tigrinya-speaking Copts undoubtedly consider themselves as Ethiopians. The salute "Ethiopia!" not only resounded at their meetings but met the Commission all along the highways in southern Eritrea, whether from a few tiny children on a hill-top, casual passers-by or village communities massed along the roadside. Such results cannot be produced by transporting large bodies of adherents from one place to another.

It was confirmed by Administration officials that "Shifta" bands have sought to influence political dissidents in some highland districts, but it also is a fact that the bulk of the terrorist outrages in Eritrea have mainly been directed against individual Italians. Moreover, weak attendances at Bloc meetings were too often attributed to terrorism, or to absence on nomadic grazing, when other meetings were well attended, for the excuses to be convincing. In one case, 72/ a solitary witness of the party of the Bloc tried to explain the absence of his numerous supporters by producing a typewritten declaration to the effect that he had himself walked throughout the night to elude his pursuers and reach the meeting, only to admit in an unguarded moment that the letter had been typed before he set out on the journey.

72/ A/AC.34/R.87, questions (c) and (d).

On the other hand, as far as the Independence Bloc is concerned, its close association with Italian political interests is apparent from its composition. After the field group hearing at Mansura, the distribution of food by officials of the Bloc to those who had attended the meeting was actually witnessed. There also is no question that, in the case of the Moslem League, by far the strongest party in the Bloc, religious sentiment has been a powerful aid to unifying political sentiment. However, at most Independence Bloc meetings real enthusiasm was encountered and this invalidates any charge that the Bloc is entirely a creation, and under the direction, of the Italians and does not represent a substantial trend of opinion.

131. It therefore cannot be said that, on account of extraneous influences or propaganda dodges, the Commission's field hearings failed in their purpose of affording a reasonable indication of the views held by the people of Eritrea on the different solutions which have been proposed for the country and which have to quite an extent penetrated their political perception. It would, however, be proper to recognize that, whatever the means which might be employed, it is impossible to gauge accurately the permanence and exact strength of the political persuasions of the people of Eritrea. This is because of the primitive character of Eritrean society, the large-scale illiteracy of the people and the obvious limitations of the political parties as shown by their unblushing claims to many more supporters than there are people and their naive approach to the practical aspects of government.

F. *Summary finding on the wishes of the people*

132. The hearings have shown that, in the three administrative divisions of the highlands, the bulk of the Christian Coptic population strongly favours the reunion of Eritrea with Ethiopia. In addition, a not inconsiderable number of Moslems there support the claim for union, and this is not unexpected in view of the close association of interests with their Coptic neighbours. The Unionist and allied parties have strong support also around Keren and a noticeable adherence through the Independent Moslem League on the eastern slopes and the area around Massawa. The support of these Moslems for the proposal of union with Ethiopia certainly cannot be explained away by such arguments as a reference to the instance where fifteen Copts attended a meeting of the Commission dressed as Moslems. In view of the overwhelming support enjoyed by the pro-Unionist parties in the highlands, and to a lesser extent also in the other areas mentioned, it is not unlikely that a majority of the Eritreans favour political association with Ethiopia. In the circumstances obtaining in Eritrea, however, accurate figures cannot be compiled.

133. On the other hand, there are large groups who oppose the movement for union with Ethiopia, mainly among the Moslems in the Western Province and in the Red Sea Division, including the Danakil desert. Generally, few Copts appeared at hearings of the Independence Bloc, except one whole village group in the Akkele Guzai, whose chief is the President of the Bloc, and another group in the Serae headed by a chief of the same family. With the defection of the Moslem League of the Western Province from the Bloc, there is little doubt that the supporters of the proposal that an independent Eritrean State be created immediately today represent a definite minority of the Eritrean population.

134. Both the pro-Unionist and pro-Independence groups, who together make up a large majority of the population, reject the partition of Eritrea in principle. Attention has already been drawn to the declaration of the pro-Unionist group of parties that a separate solution would be accepted for the Western Province, if the United Nations should decide on a dual solution and a majority in the Western Province want it. The Moslem League of the Western Province asked for such a dual solution but it did not appear that its adherents were in the majority.

135. The alternative possibility of trusteeship was put by the Commission at all hearings. The Unionist Party, however, insisted on reunion as the only solution and said it would accept no other. The Moslem League in turn requested an independent Eritrea, and declined to express views on trusteeship in the event of the United Nations not acceding to independence. The Representative Committee of Italians in Eritrea intimated that, in the contingency mentioned, Italian trusteeship (which Italy itself no longer supports) would be preferred, failing which direct United Nations trusteeship should be applied. It was definitely established that most of the indigenous population completely reject Italian trusteeship. Indeed, there is a large measure of agreement amongst all parties that there should be no participation by the local Italian population in the future government of Eritrea, no exception being made for Italians born in Eritrea or for Italo-Eritrean half-castes.

IV. The views of interested governments

Ethiopia

136. The Ethiopian Government, in its declaration to the Commission, requested the incorporation of the whole of Eritrea into Ethiopia, but said that it would respect the desires of the people of the Western Province for a separate solution for that territory, if a clear majority there want it.

137. The Ethiopian Government referred to the joint history of the present-day Eritrea and Ethiopia. It stated that 3,000 to 4,000 years ago the Hamitic and Semitic immigrants into Ethiopia settled in the Tigrai first, that Eritrea has formed a part of the Tigrai, and that the rulers of that area owed allegiance to the Ethiopian sovereign; hence natural and historical bonds of ethnic and social affinities have always existed between Eritreans and Ethiopians, and their language, customs, art and religion are identical. The Ethiopian Government furthermore asserted that there is an overwhelming support, on the part of 75 per cent of the Eritrean people, for union with Ethiopia. Allegations that pressure has been brought to bear to that end by the Ethiopian Government and the Patriarch of the Coptic Church were rejected, as also that "Shifta" terrorists have been condoned by that Government. The Ethiopian Government, on the other hand, insisted that Italy had expended large sums to influence the views of the Eritrean people in favour of so-called independence. In further support of the proposal for incorporation, the Ethiopian Government drew attention to the economic dependence of Eritrea on Ethiopia in the following respects: Eritrean imports are double its exports; a balance is obtained, and the ports of Massawa and Assab can provide a livelihood, only with the help of earnings on Ethiopian transit trade, even though the bulk of Ethiopian foreign trade still passes through Djibouti. Ethiopia is the main source of Eritrea's food imports. Finally, some 90 per cent of the Eritrean people depend directly on Ethiopian pasture lands. In these circumstances, the Ethiopian Government has rejected the validity of proposals "to subject the population of Eritrea to facing the rigours of an artificial independent existence". It declared that Italy is attempting to regain control over the territory of Eritrea "through a formula that at the same time flies in the face of clear economic facts, the wishes of the population, the political possibilities, and the national security of Ethiopia". The statement of the Ethiopian Government added that "Ethiopia will no longer supinely tolerate through this patent disguise of a so-called Italian independence of Eritrea, any such threat to our existence". The Ethiopian Government also rejected the accusations of discrimination against Moslems. It pointed out that one-fourth of the inhabitants of Ethiopia are Moslem, but that on the other hand one-third of its higher government officials, 17 per cent of the elementary school children in Ethiopia, and 22 per cent of the Ethiopian students studying abroad with government financial assistance, are Moslem. As far as the Italian minority is concerned, the Ethiopian Government drew attention to the presence of thousands of Italians in Ethiopia, who have themselves sought permission to stay rather than return to Italy.

138. In carrying out its responsibilities, the Commission was instructed by the General Assembly, *inter alia*, to take into account the rights and claims of Ethiopia based on geographical, historical, ethnic or economic reasons, including in particular its legitimate need for adequate access to the sea. That the Eritrean highlands geographically form part of the Tigrai plateau is evident from any map, and there is no doubt that historical and ethnical bonds exist between the populations of the two areas. These features are present in a lesser degree in other parts of Eritrea. Economically, Eritrea is without doubt closely dependent on Ethiopia. The reverse is also true because of the location of Eritrea between Ethiopia and the Red Sea. Direct access to the sea is, therefore, of considerable economic significance to Ethiopia and of vital strategic importance to her as well. Geographically, the excellent deep-water harbour of Massawa is the natural outlet from, and point of supply to, northern Ethiopia, which includes the Tigrai and Gondar. Assab is the nearest port to the Wollo Province, around Dessie. The railway from Djibouti in turn provides the shortest coastal link with Addis Ababa. At present Ethiopian imports and exports go over the following routes:

Tonnage of Ethiopian imports and exports (1948)

By railroad to Djibouti	180,000
By road to or via Eritrea	39,000
By Bahr River to Sudan	4,000
Via British Somaliland	20,000
Unknown	37,000

139. It is seen, therefore, that the needs of Ethiopia are so intertwined with the future of Eritrea that, in devising a plan for the well-being of the latter, justice demands that suitable provision should be made for the interests of the former.

Egypt

140. The Government of Egypt has confirmed its announcement, made at the Conference of the Deputies of Foreign Ministers at London on 29 July 1948, that it supports the unanimous wishes of the Eritrean people that their country's unity should be safeguarded. At the same time, the Government of Egypt reserved its right to express at a later stage its point of view on the final disposal of Eritrea, as it would be premature to anticipate the results of the Commission's work.

141. However, the Government of Egypt indicated that if the Commission were to confirm the conclusions previously arrived at by the Four-Power Commission of

Investigation, as to the desire of the Eritrean population to ensure the country's unity, the point of view of the Government of Egypt would remain unchanged. If, on the other hand, the United Nations Commission for Eritrea should reach different conclusions owing to new data, or an unforeseeable reversal of opinion ascertained in the course of investigation, the Egyptian Government would then duly reconsider the question in the light of those new facts and its own historical rights.

France

142. In the communication transmitted to the Commission, the French Government stated that it relied entirely upon the Commission to proceed within the framework of its terms of reference, taking into account the conditions at present obtaining. The Government of France, however, referred to the statements made by its representatives at the third and fourth sessions of the General Assembly, to the effect that the territory of Eritrea was heterogeneous in its population and that Ethiopia was entitled to compensation for the past and to guarantees for the future. It also stressed the desire to conform to the wishes of the indigenous inhabitants, including the Italian minority.

143. The French Government also pointed to its statement in the Political Committee on 1 October 1949, to the effect that any constructive decision should receive the agreement of both Ethiopian and Italian Governments so as to prepare for their future collaboration. Such collaboration would in the opinion of the French Government ensure peace and security and the development of prosperity in that part of the world.

144. Finally, the French Government considered that the necessary measures should be taken to provide adequate guarantees for foreign interests and property.

Italy

145. The Italian Foreign Minister, Count Sforza, informed the Commission verbally that the Italian Government no longer advocated or desired Italian trusteeship over Eritrea. In the note presented by that Government, it was indicated that Italy was deeply interested not only in the welfare of the Italians and their descendants who, having dedicated their activity to Eritrea, are bound to that country, but also in the welfare of the Native population. The Italian Government recognized the right of Eritreans to have their wishes respected and considered that the basic criterion to be adopted in the disposal of Eritrea is respect for the wishes, rights and interests of the population, including the Italians in Eritrea. It was of the opinion that there is no reason why Eritrea should be delayed on its road to independence, if independence corresponds to the historical conditions and the interests of the country, and it saw no reason to believe that if independence were granted it would be against the interests of Ethiopia; it stated that the solution of the Eritrean problem must be accompanied by the protection of the legitimate interests if Eritrea and Ethiopia, the chief common interest of both being to live in peace together and to co-operate fruitfully to mutual advantage. The Italian Government considered that the characteristics and structure of Eritrea are such as to make a strong argument for the maintenance of its unity. It stated that the various parts of Eritrea constitute complementary elements which give to the whole a large measure of economic and financial self-sufficiency. The Italian Government also emphasized that Eritreans, though divided by race and religion, have in the past lived peacefully side by side, and that they still know how to live together profitably in a community which includes them all and which is based on collaboration and peace.

146. The Italian Government denied that any part of Eritrea occupied by Italy was taken from Ethiopia. It stated that Danakil, where Italy first established itself, was occupied after agreements with the local sheiks; that the northernmost part, including Massawa and the Dahlak Islands, was part of the Ottoman Empire; that the western lowlands were acquired by Italy by a tripartite agreement between Italy, Great Britain and Ethiopia in 1903; and that the highlands were not considered as an integral part of the Ethiopian Empire inasmuch as King Menelik of Ethiopia invited the Italians to occupy the district of Asmara, while the highland zones south of Asmara were recognized as part of Eritrea by the Italo-Ethiopian treaty of 1900.

United Kingdom

147. The Government of the United Kingdom reiterated the view previously expressed at the General Assembly, that the Red Sea Province, including Massawa, and the Hamasien, Akkele Guzai and Serae Divisions should be incorporated in Ethiopia subject to safeguards for the Italian and other minorities, including appropriate municipal charters for the city of Asmara and the port of Massawa. The United Kingdom Government did not put forward detailed proposals to safeguard minorities and for municipal charters but stated that if the idea were accepted in principle, the details could be worked out. In proposing the inclusion of Massawa in the area to be ceded to Ethiopia, it pointed out that this is the natural port of the plateau and could not be separated from it or from Asmara without grave economic disruption. It supported the incorporation of the port of Assab and the Danakil coast because of the absence of lateral communication with the rest of Eritrea and the close racial,

geographical, and linguistic affinities of this region to the adjacent Danakil areas of Ethiopia.

148. As regards the Western Province, the United Kingdom Government did not consider that the inhabitants should be incorporated in Ethiopia contrary to their expressed wishes, nor that the Province could justifiably be placed under a separate trusteeship looking to its future existence as a separate State. It, therefore, supported its incorporation in the adjacent Sudan, as being the best solution on ethnic, geographic and religious grounds.

149. The Government of the United Kingdom was firmly of opinion that the establishment of an independent Eritrean State is not a practicable solution. It stated that the territory is not and never has been economically viable and that it possesses neither the national, religious, racial, linguistic, nor geographical unity which would be prerequisites of such a State.

The Government stated that it could not support any proposal involving the return of an Italian Administration to Eritrea in any form.

150. The United Kingdom Government expressed its opposition to trusteeship, either for a definite or an indefinite period, and stated that on account of the facts given above trusteeship could have no aim or purpose since the inhabitants of Eritrea could not, in the foreseeable future, be in a position to take over their own government from a Trustee Power. It stated through its representative that it would not accept the responsibilities of trusteeship for the whole or any part of the territory.

V. Peace and security in East Africa

151. The Commission has been directed to take particular account of the following factors in examining the problem of the disposal of Eritrea:
 (a) The wishes of the inhabitants of Eritrea;
 (b) The best means of promoting their welfare;
 (c) The capacity of the people for self-government;
 (d) The rights and claims of Ethiopia;
 (e) The interests of peace and security in East Africa.

The facts pertaining to the first four items have already been set out in this memorandum. The interests of peace and security in East Africa remain to be considered.

152. Eritrea is a very rugged and broken country, and this fact has throughout made adequate policing difficult and costly. Strategically, the external defence of Eritrea is rendered complicated by her long coastline and flat coastal plain and by the absence of natural frontier barriers in the interior. Whether or not peace and security could be maintained in such conditions would, however, be influenced less by pure strategic considerations than by the ability of the territory to meet the costs of policing and defence, by the degree of internal unity or dissension and by the political relationships with neighbouring countries.

153. There is an acute internal political division amongst the people of Eritrea on the basic question of the future of the country. This division of opinion has recently led to an outbreak of political violence between groups of Moslems and Copts in Asmara, while "Shifta" bands have over a period committed sporadic outrages in various parts of the territory. The security position in Eritrea is, therefore, perilous. The fact must be faced, moreover, that the movement for union with Ethiopia has many of the characteristics of a popular movement, and it is more than likely that outright frustration of these wishes would make the position of internal security in Eritrea untenable. Nor would it in that event be unrealistic to expect assistance for the unionist groups from Ethiopia, in view of that country's own espousal of the same cause.

154. It has, in addition, been demonstrated that Eritrea is not economically viable and lacks the resources and financial means to become such in the foreseeable future. In such circumstances and in view of the acute internal political division and state of tension in Eritrea, the conclusion is ineluctable that the creation of a separate Eritrean State entirely on its own would contain all the elements necessary seriously to prejudice the interests of peace and security in East Africa, now and in the future.

PART II. PROPOSALS FOR THE SOLUTION OF THE PROBLEM OF ERITREA

VI. General conclusions

155. A fair and lasting solution for the problem of Eritrea must be realistic and take into account all the salient facts of the case. They were, therefore, examined in detail in part I of this memorandum.

156. Attention is, firstly, drawn to the fact that Eritrea is a poor country, without any prospects of progressing as a separate economic entity, and dependent in most vital respects on Ethiopia's rich farming resources and transit trade. In the view of the delegations of Burma, Norway and the Union of South Africa, these facts preclude a solution which has as its aim the creation of an entirely separate Eritrean State, whether in the immediate future or after an interval of international trusteeship.

157. Secondly, attention is drawn to the expressed political wishes of the people. With the defection of the Moslem League of the Western Province from the Independence Bloc, the protagonists of an independent Eritrean State, who were probably close on half the total population before, are now in a definite minority. On the

other hand, it is not unlikely that an over-all majority of the total Eritrean population favour reunion with Ethiopia, in view of the support for this course by the overwhelming mass of Christian Copts and by sizeable numbers of Moslems living next to them in the highlands and in the Red Sea Division.

158. Thirdly, attention is drawn to the legitimate aspirations of Ethiopia for access to the sea, both on economic and security grounds, and for the reintegration of the Eritrean people, many of whom have the most intimate bonds with the people of northern Ethiopia.

159. The close affinities between large sections of the Eritrean and Ethiopian peoples, the strong demand for reunion by probably the majority of Eritreans, the common strategic interests of the two countries and the fact that Eritrea lacks the resources to protect herself, have convinced the delegations of Burma, Norway and the Union of South Africa that, in the interests of peace and security in East Africa and of the welfare of the Eritrean people, the best solution for Eritrea must be based on close political association with Ethiopia. Economic and financial association also is a sine qua non in view of the dependence of Eritrea on the rich Ethiopian hinterland and of Ethiopia on the transport and harbour facilities of Eritrea, and in view of Eritrea's poor resources, weak finances and inability to maintain itself without aid from a strong partner.

160. It is appreciated that a solution, based on the principle of economic and political association with Ethiopia, may not at the moment command general support in Eritrea, where passions have been inflamed by political propaganda and the resort to violence by irresponsible elements. These activities do not, however, reflect the true feelings of the people. Although Eritrea's boundaries are the product of colonial expansion in the 1880's, so that it is neither a geographical unit nor an economic whole, a common past and seventy years of common rule have had potent unifying effects not only between the diverse peoples of Eritrea but also in their relations with the Italian settlers; such amity cannot readily be destroyed and there is no doubt that resort to violence is repugnant to the deep-rooted desire of all sections in Eritrea to continue to live in peace side by side. The delegations of Burma, Norway and the Union of South Africa, in condemning the resort to murder and violence by irresponsible elements, must emphasize that they believe this in large part to be a direct consequence of the unfortunate delay in settling the future of the country. They truly fear that the situation would, perhaps irretrievably, go from bad to worse unless a final settlement is effected soon.

161. In view of this paramount need for an early and final solution, the delegation of the Union of South Africa has decided to relinquish the suggestion it made to the Commission during the general debate. It then proposed that the highlands and Red Sea Division be placed under Ethiopian trusteeship with a view to eventual self-government as a federal part of Ethiopia, and that British Administration be temporarily continued in the Western Province until the people there are able to make up their minds between joining either Ethiopia or the Sudan since an independent State in the Western Province would be fantastic. The course suggested would, however, involve a further period of suspense before a permanent settlement of the problem could be effected, and in order to avoid this the delegation of the Union of South Africa has decided to join with the delegation of Burma and support its federal solution which would permanently and effectively meet the exigencies of the case.

162. The delegation of Norway, like the delegations of Burma and the Union of South Africa, subscribes to the principle of political and economic association between Eritrea and Ethiopia, but differs from these delegations in regard to the precise formula to be applied to that end. The delegations of Burma and the Union of South Africa, therefore, submit their joint recommendations below, and these are followed by separate recommendations by the delegation of Norway.

VII. Proposals by the delegations of Burma and the Union of South Africa

163. In the course of investigations, it soon became apparent that the crux of the problem in Eritrea is the conflict of two ardent forms of nationalism, namely, the desire of the Unionist groups to join Ethiopia and the striving of the Independence Bloc for an independent Eritrean State. These respective claims have the stamp of validity and they have been steadfastly put forward by these two political groups. As these claims are irreconcilable, it is impossible fully to satisfy the demands of either group without causing a grave miscarriage of justice to the other. A fair but effective compromise is, therefore, necessary.

164. For the reasons stated in conjunction with the delegation of Norway, the delegations of Burma and the Union of South Africa are convinced that a solution for Eritrea must be based on close political and complete economic association with Ethiopia. On the other hand, the delegations of Burma and the Union of South Africa are emphatic that such a solution should be designed so as also to satisfy to a material extent the political sensibilities of the Moslem population of Eritrea, who on the whole are afraid to join Ethiopia, and to safeguard the position of the Italian settlers and Italo-Eritrean half-castes who have a permanent stake in the country.

165. The delegations of Burma and South Africa are not satisfied that the rights and interests of the large Moslem community would be fully safeguarded in every respect, and if they were that the general body of Moslems would believe it, if Eritrea were to be incorporated outright into Ethiopia, as the Unionists desire. The two delegations consider, however, that the overriding aims of the political and economic association between Eritrean and Ethiopia and of effective safeguards for the rights and interests of the Moslems and the Italian and other minorities could be achieved by means of a federation of Eritrea and Ethiopia. Such a federation should take place on terms compatible with the self-respect and domestic autonomy of both countries and provide for joint responsibility and collective action in such fields as defence, external affairs, taxation, finance, inter-State commerce and communications. A customs union and a general rule of non-discrimination would also be prerequisites.

166. A federal plan of this nature received considerable attention in Sub-Committee 17 of the First Committee of the General Assembly, and the Ethiopian delegation then indicated to the Political Committee 73/ that it did not reject it in principle. In the opinion of the delegations of Burma and the Union of South Africa a federal solution would answer the two most vital issues of the Eritrean problem, to which all other considerations are subordinate, namely, (a) the wishes and welfare of the people of Eritrea and (b) the maintenance of peace and security in East Africa. For such a plan recognizes the inalienable right of the people of Eritrea to fashion their own destiny, in conjunction with their federal partner on certain common problems, without the wishes and aspirations of either of the two main sections of the people of Eritrea being subordinated to those of the other. This is as it should be, since the two main religious and linguistic groups of the territory have in the past shown striking proof of their ability to co-operate with each other, and the delegations of Burma and the Union of South Africa are convinced, notwithstanding the vicissitudes of Eritrean politics, that the people can and will collaborate to serve the interests of their common land in the future, when a final decision to institute federation is given by the General Assembly. This desire to continue to live side by side is strongly evidenced by the reluctance of all groups and parties in Eritrea to assent to the partition of the country. Although the Unionist and allied parties and the Moslem League of the Western Province recently accepted partition on a conditional basis, this took place as a direct alternative to completely abandoning their respective points of view, without a possible synthesis and compromise to safeguard the rights of all groups having been considered. The federal plan put forward by the delegations of Burma and the Union of South Africa accordingly seeks to preserve the unity of Eritrea, thus encouraging her people to pattern their loyalty and patriotism to one single design and to find expression for their energy and skill in a united Eritrea within the framework of a federal constitution.

167. By this means recognition will, therefore, be accorded at one and the same time to the twin facts that Eritrea is the common motherland of the highland Copts and lowland Moslems and has close historical, ethnical and social associations with Ethiopia. In that way alone can peace and security be preserved in this part of East Africa. By strengthening the existing close economic ties between Eritrea and Ethiopia, the welfare of the people of Eritrea will, moreover, be actively promoted and Ethiopia's legitimate claim for adequate access to the sea satisfied.

168. The joint review by the delegations of Burma, Norway and the Union of South Africa has shown to what considerable extent the level of Eritrean economy is dependent on the technical proficiency and managerial activities of the Italian settlers. To a lesser extent this is also true of other foreign communities, but they are smaller and it is an advantage that many urban Eritreans understand the Italian language, while many Italians are conversant with the vernacular and customs of the indigenous people. The continuance of Italian enterprise in Eritrea is vital also for the further development of the territory, and the delegations of Burma and the Union of South Africa, therefore, consider that the personal and property rights of the Italian and other foreign communities in Eritrea should be safeguarded in the federal constitution. In order to be fully effective, the delegations urge that, on the suggestion of the General Assembly, this question should form the subject of friendly discussion and agreement between the Governments of Italy and Ethiopia. In view of the declarations of these two Governments to the Commission there is every reason to believe that a harmonious understanding would be welcomed by both. This is highly necessary. Without Italian technical guidance, Eritrea would sustain a serious economic setback, and that would be the very negation of the upliftment programmes of the United Nations and its specialized agencies.

169. The proposal for federation by the delegations of Burma and South Africa, therefore, holds tangible promises for the future. This cannot be said in respect of two other solutions which are widely canvassed. The total integration or incorporation of Eritrea into Ethiopia would arouse popular Moslem antagonism and might lead to internal strife with possible external intervention.

73/ A/C.1/W.8/Add.2, page 140.

The immediate or future independence of Eritrea, without close political association with Ethiopia, must result in the economic disruption of Eritrea and in political upheaval on the part of the Coptic population. Nor have the people of Eritrea developed a sufficient capacity for self-government to stand on their own. In federation with Ethiopia, the administrative and financial burdens of government would, however, be shared on important questions of mutual concern to the two countries.

170. The delegations of Burma and the Union of South Africa accordingly submit to the General Assembly the following proposals, which accord with the Commission's mandate and would make it possible to settle the urgent problem of Eritrea in a manner which would be both fair and effective:

(a) Eritrea to be constituted a self-governing unit of a federation of which the other member shall be Ethiopia, under the sovereignty of the Ethiopian crown;

(b) Each member shall possess local legislative and executive autonomy, but full authority shall be vested in the federal government with regard to such matters as defence, external affairs, taxation, finance, inter-State commerce and communications;

(c) A customs union between the two members shall be obligatory;

(d) A common citizenship shall prevail throughout the federation. No discrimination shall be practised as regards religious, personal, civic or property rights and equal rights and privileges shall be guaranteed in the constitution for all minorities;

(e) The federation shall be established following a transitional period not exceeding three years. During this period the current affairs of the territory shall continue to be conducted by the present Administration, subject to the understanding that residents of Eritrea shall be inducted in office as much as possible, and that the General Assembly shall appoint an advisory council consisting of the United Kingdom, Ethiopia and Egypt to arrange for the transfer of power to the people of Eritrea and, in conjunction with the Government of Ethiopia and an elective assembly of Eritreans to be established for the purpose, to ensure the formulation of the federal constitution;

(f) The establishment of the Federation of Eritrea and Ethiopia shall be declared by the General Assembly of the United Nations as soon as its advisory council certifies that the federal constitution has been adopted by the Government of Ethiopia and the Eritrean Assembly.

Suggestions by the delegation of Burma

171. The delegation of Burma is in agreement with the delegation of the Union of South Africa that the General Assembly should cause the details of the proposed federal plan to be worked out. For the guidance of the Assembly, the delegation of Burma submits the following detailed provisions which, it suggests, might find a suitable place in the federal plan and constitution:

(i) The governmental structure of the two States of Ethiopia and Eritrea shall be federal and shall consist of a federal government and governments of Ethiopia and Eritrea, with the Emperor of Ethiopia as the constitutional Head.

(ii) Among the organs of government there shall be an executive body, a federal body and a federal court;

(iii) The federal legislative body shall be composed of two chambers;

(iv) Election to its first chamber shall be on the basis of proportional representation of the population as a whole;

(v) Election to its second chamber shall be on the basis of equal representation of the Ethiopian and Eritrean people;

(vi) The federal legislative body shall be empowered to legislate on all matters entrusted to the federal government;

(vii) Legislation shall be enacted when approved by a majority of votes in both chambers of the federal legislative body;

(viii) Full authority shall be vested in the federal government with regard to defence, external affairs, taxation, finance, and inter-State commerce and communications;

(ix) The executive branch of the federal government shall be responsible to the federal legislative body;

(x) The federal court shall be the final court of appeal with regard to constitutional matters;

(xi) The members of the federal court shall be appointed by the Emperor with the approval of both chambers of the federal legislative body;

(xii) All decisions of the federal court are final;

(xiii) There shall be but one citizenship throughout the federation;

(xiv) The constitution shall guarantee equal rights and privileges for all minorities, irrespective of race or religion;

(xv) The two States of Ethiopia and Eritrea shall enjoy full powers of local self-government in all matters other than defence, external affairs, finance and inter-State commerce and communications and shall pass such local laws and regulations as may be desirable, subject only to the provisions of the federal constitution.

VIII. Proposals by the delegation of Norway

172. The delegation of Norway subscribes to the factual review elaborated in agreement with the delegations of Burma and of the Union of South Africa and to

its ample demonstration of the necessity for the political association of Eritrea with Ethiopia. The delegation of Norway, after close examination of all sides of the problem, finds, however, that such association would be best secured, to the mutual benefit of both countries, by their complete and immediate reunion.

173. We are fully satisfied that the overwhelming majority of the people of Eritrea are in favour of such a reunion. It is true that different views have been expressed by the spokesmen or leaders of groups or parties who proclaim a desire that Eritrea obtain autonomy as an independent State. Apart from the absolute impossibility of checking the figures given by the various groups as to the number of their adherents, we find it more important to consider the fact that the people especially of the highlands always considered themselves as Ethiopians, and that before 1946 no political division existed in the country. Except for the Unionists, who in 1941 under the name "Patriotic Association for the Union of Eritrea with Ethiopia" had already manifested their views, the opposition parties did not appear until 1946 and 1947; they were obviously born out of the political possibilities presented by the discord between the Powers about the future of Eritrea, and were created by a handful of ambitious Eritreans, partly former officials in Italian service, who by uniting in their groups the apparently greater part of the Moslem population have undeniably succeeded in giving to the newborn political activity an aspect of religious differences. Not only did no political division exist before 1946, but there had, indeed, never before existed any political feeling at all; except for the popular movement which, after the liberation of the country in 1941, sprang from the then awakened national consciousness of the Eritrean people and tended quite naturally towards reunion with the country they felt they belonged to. Nor did there ever exist any hostile religious feelings. The townspeople as well as the rural population, Moslem and Christian, lived in perfect harmony, the rural dwellers, regardless of their different creeds or tribal customs, being fully occupied with their tasks of cultivation and grazing, as indeed they are until this day in Eritrea and—what is worth mentioning—also in Ethiopia. It can therefore safely be said, we think, that the situation which has now been created is to a great extent artificial; it is not founded on serious political considerations, but is partly the result of a confusion in the mind of the primitive masses who are supposed to support the independent movement as to the true meaning of the word "independence" in opposition to the word "union".

174. We feel convinced that if Eritrea and Ethiopia, after their liberation from Italian domination in 1941, had been united together, such a union would have met with no opposition. We believe that this solution, for what had since become the problem of Eritrea, would still respond to the wishes of the people as dictated by their real interests.

175. On account of the economic interdependence of the two countries, which embraces all fields of their activities, and because of the similarity in the natural conditions of both countries, the union of Eritrea to Ethiopia would secure to the Eritrean people, nomadic or settled, the undisturbed continuation of their customary livelihood. Moreover, and this is not of least importance, the possibilities would thereby be created for progress and development along lines consistent with their traditions and economic realities, by the mutual effort of the Eritrean and Ethiopian peoples, who are so closely related and whose contacts are so congenial. That would mean, in our opinion, the welfare of all the inhabitants of Eritrea.

176. Having regard to the fact that the Eritreans are so far removed from the stage where they could govern themselves, that, regardless of the number of the claimants, the claim for independence has to be dismissed, we consider the reintegration of Eritrea into Ethiopia as the only rational and satisfactory solution. In principle this solution should apply to the whole territory of Eritrea. It seems to us impossible to give way to the separatist wishes of that part of the population of the Western Province which, in refusing union either with Ethiopia or Sudan, aims at the setting up in this area of a separate independent State. This can only be characterized as a utopian and unrealistic dream. In case it should be found, however, that the opposition of the Western Province presents an obstacle to the union of Eritrea with Ethiopia, we would not be opposed to its provisional exemption from such a union, nor to its continued administration by the British Government for the period required to give the people of the Western Province the opportunity of deciding in fuller knowledge which of their two neighbouring countries they wish to join. It should be noted in this connexion that if, in determining the future status of Eritrea, the Western Province were excluded, the adherents to the Independence Bloc in the rest of the country would find themselves reduced to a trifling minority compared to the numerical strength of the Unionists, since the parties opposing union with Ethiopia have most of their adherents in the Western Province.

177. The reunion of Eritrea to the "mother country" would, in our opinion, offer the best guarantees for the peaceful existence of Eritrea's inhabitants, native or foreign, and give them the best conditions of security. On the other hand, it is certainly to be feared that an independent Eritrea, poor as it would be and helplessly ex-

posed to interference from many sides, would soon become the scene of serious discord and internal strife.

178. We do not share the apprehensions which have been expressed by certain groups of the population, and especially by some political groups of the population, and especially by some political groups of Italians, with regard to possible discrimination which could be expected from the government of a united Eritrea and Ethiopia. No other foreign communities voiced such fears, and there is no reason to believe that Italian residents in Eritrea would be prevented from carrying on their trade or industry, which is so important for the economy of the country, any less freely than do thousands of Italians until this day in Ethiopia itself. Taking into account the repeated declarations made by the Government of Ethiopia that it is fully prepared to respect and maintain the rights of all minorities, we do not consider it necessary to try to establish any system of special safeguards or guarantees of such rights. On the contrary, we believe that stipulations of that nature might only create new possibilities for dissension and so imperil the position of the minorities they were meant to protect.

179. As for the external peace and security of this part of Africa, it is evident and needless to demonstrate that this could not possibly be better secured than by the unification of the economic and defensive resources of both these territories in the hands of one Government, which would be in a position to impose respect for its rights.

180. The claims of Ethiopia, so clearly expressed at many previous occasions and lately revived with ample justification before the Commission, should not be confused with an imperialistic attempt towards colonial expansion. They are based as much on geographical, economic and ethnic reasons as they have their background in the history of Ethiopia and of the disputed territory which now forms Eritrea. There is no need to go into the remote history of this subject, and it is sufficient to recall the events through which Italy came to Eritrea. In 1869 it acquired a strip of coast near Assab; in 1885, it occupied Massawa, till then held by the Egyptians on a kind of lease from the Ethiopian Emperor; next came the Italian defeat in 1887, when the garrison at Dogali, near Massawa, was destroyed by the Emperor's Governor of Eritrea; further battles and treaties finally led up to the Italo-Eritrean Treaty of 1900, by which the Ethiopian Government ceded the southern part of Eritrea of toady to Italy. These facts prove the exercise by Ethiopia of its sovereignty over the Eritrean territory right down to the Red Sea, and offer ample justification for the historical claim for its reintegration.

181. The return of Eritrea does not, therefore, mean its submission to the domination of an alien Power; reunited to Ethiopia, Eritrea would be rejoining the independent Ethiopian Empire, remaining as independent as Ethiopia itself, and participating in the Government with equal rights and responsibilities. The proposal to reunite Eritrea to Ethiopia is not a new one. It has always been in the centre of the discussions at the United Nations General Assembly, now favoured by various Governments and then again abandoned. We believe that any further attempts to by-pass this solution, e.g., by introducing any form of trusteeship with a view to later independence which materially would prove impossible, would only be an expedient causing useless postponement of a final solution. The same would be true of proposals to establish a trusteeship over Eritrea with the view of future self-government in federation with Ethiopia. Both these solutions imply the perpetuation of an Eritrean State as a separate entity, although there is no doubt that within its present borders it is not in a position of ever becoming a viable State. Eritrea was an artificial creation by the Italians, and the first thing they did when they occupied Ethiopia was to split up Eritrea and to link certain parts of it with the neighbouring Ethiopian province. To establish Eritrea as an entity, either independently or as a self-governing federal Province, would make it impossible to effect the necessary adjustments in its administration.

182. We further believe that, in order to ensure a harmonious development, it must be left to the Ethiopian State to adopt the constitutional provisions which would be best suited to conditions in this part of Africa. To impose obligations on Ethiopia to organize its relation with Eritrea on the basis of a federative status, without any knowledge as to whether this would be the best constitutional solution, could easily lead to future conflict and unrest, and in the end endanger the peace of East Africa. It must here be stressed that the suspense in which the establishment of the status of Eritrea is being held, and would continue to be held under trusteeship, seriously hampers its normal life and gravely endangers the security of its people. It is therefore imperative that a final and definite decision be taken now. The immediate reunion of the two countries would end this highly dangerous state of affairs and, in our opinion, it offers the only realistic and rational solution of the problem, conforming to the wishes of the people, securing their welfare, and serving the interests of peace and security in this part of the world.

183. The delegation of Norway, therefore, proposes that the whole territory of Eritrea be reunited to Ethiopia, it being understood that, in the conditions and for the purposes set forth earlier, the Western Province could provisionally and for a limited period of time be left under the present British Administration.

MEMORANDUM 74/ SUBMITTED BY THE DELEGATIONS OF GUATEMALA AND PAKISTAN 75/

General political situation in Eritrea

184. Before reaching Eritrea the Commission had learnt from various sources that the political situation in the country was tense and that several bombing incidents and murders had taken place during the previous year or two.

185. During its stay at Asmara the Commission learnt with regret of several murders, road hold-ups, arson and other violent crimes in which the victims were mostly either Italian colonists or supporters of the Independence Bloc. The attempted assassination of Italians and others continued throughout the period of the Commission's stay in Eritrea, and, according to information received at Geneva, the situation remained the same even after its departure.

Disorders at Asmara on 21 to 23 February 1950

186. On 21 February the Commission heard with dismay that large-scale rioting between Copts and Muslims had started in the town of Asmara, the immediate cause of which was the throwing of a bomb near the headquarters of the Unionist Party, at the funeral procession of a Muslim who was opposed to Unionists and who had been murdered the previous day by a gang of "Shifta." 76/, 77/ The consequence was three days of bloody rioting in which about fifty persons lost their lives and a large number were wounded.

Wishes and welfare of the population

187. The Commission found the following organized parties, representative of three different policies with regard to the future of Eritrea:

(a) *Parties advocating independence for the whole territory:*

Muslim League
Liberal Progressive Party
New Eritrea Party
Italo-Eritrean Association
Veterans Association
Intellectual Party
National Party
Independent Eritrean Party

(b) *Parties advocating union of the territory with Ethiopia:*

Unionist Party
Liberal Unionist Party
Independent Eritrea united to Ethiopia Party
Independent Muslim League (of Massawa)

(c) Party advocating trusteeship by the United Kingdom for the Western Province prior to independence:

Muslim League of the Western Province

188. The parties wanting independence of the territory have grouped themselves into what they call the "Independence Bloc", although they continue to maintain their original identity.

189. It is extremely difficult to ascertain the exact numerical strength of the different political parties. Their leaders and spokesmen always gave evidently exaggerated figures to the Commission. This was carried to such an extent that, if the figures supplied to the Commission were added up, the total would be several times larger than the whole population of the territory.

190. The Commission held hearings at numerous places in Eritrea in order to ascertain the wishes of the population with regard to the future of the country. These hearings took place in specially arranged settings, the groups being separated from each other by several kilometres, and in such a way that the Commission could not announce its arrival sufficiently in advance. Generally, the same people, including spokesmen of different groups, were constantly seen at the different places. It was noticed at our field hearings that the representatives who came to make statements repeated the same answers to questions put to them and gave the impression that they had been carefully rehearsed. Whenever questions were put to persons in the crowd, the answers were confused and unintelligible. It was evident at the hearings held in the highlands, where the bulk of the adherents of the Unionist Party are found, that the organization of those

---

74/ Original: English-Spanish

75/ The notes appearing at the foot of the pages in the name of one delegation are the responsibility of that delegation. It should be understood that the other delegation subscribing to the memorandum does not necessarily share those points of view. In drafting this memorandum we have avoided repeating information appearing in the report of the Four-Power Commission.

76/ "Shifta" means political terrorists in Eritrea.

77/ *The delegation of Pakistan wishes to add the following*: Information received from the British Administration from time to time was that the "Shifta" bands mainly attacked those persons who were opposed to union with Ethiopia. It was common knowledge in Eritrea that these gangs withdrew from Eritrea into Ethiopia whenever they were pursued by forces of law and order and that the Tigré Province was used by them for rest and perhaps sanctuary, The British Administration was good enough to make available to the members of the Commission, for their information, secret reports relating to the activities of the gangs. These reports, which could not be made public, showed clearly that many of the gangs came from Ethiopia into Eritrea and that, if some of their members were wounded, they were treated in the hospitals in Ethiopia. A formidable list of political outrages was presented to the Commission by Mr. Ibrahim Sultan, Secretary-General of the Independence Bloc. The Commission was not informed of any steps having been taken by the Ethiopian Government for the Suppression of these gangs in their territory. The statement of the Foreign Minister of Ethiopia mentions that terrorism will increase if the problem is not solved in accordance with the will of what he considers to be the "majority".

present was semi-military. Quite a number of them wore uniforms and distinctive marks, notwithstanding an order from the British Administration prohibiting the use of uniforms on such occasions. It was apparent that the Unionist cause enjoyed the favour of the Administering Authority in that region.

191. The influence of religion is a preponderant factor in the development of political trends in Eritrea. In that connexion, the Commission was able to verify what had already been observed by the Four-Power Commission, which visited the country in 1947. 78/ The religious beliefs of the inhabitants is closely connected with their political adherence, which mainly accounts for the fact that the majority of the Christian Copts advocate the annexation of the territory to Ethiopia. With regard to the influence of the Coptic Church in favour of annexation, it is important to point out that the Coptic Church of Eritrea depends hierarchically upon Ethiopia. The Commission was informed about interference by religious authorities of that Church in favour of annexation and of the ideas of the Unionist Party. It also heard complaints about threats and reprisals by the leaders of the Coptic Church of Eritrea against those who opposed annexation.

192. The Commission heard allegations to the effect that several Copts had been excommunicated because they did not hold the same political views as those of the Unionist Party. At nearly all the gatherings of the Unionist Party a large number of priests were seen with church emblems, and it was obvious that the clergy was using its influence over the laity. At some places priests and monks complained that they had been threatened or actually excommunicated by the Abuna of the Coptic Church for refusing to support the Unionist Party.

193. Terrorism, which has developed in Eritrea in the form of a system to support a particular policy, is another important factor leading to the grouping of the inhabitants into political parties. Some people who were opposed to the annexation of the territory of Eritrea have been subjected by terrorists to attacks on their person and property. Others, out of fear, have been compelled to follow the parties which advocate annexation. Prominent leaders of political parties favouring independence have been attacked, such as the President of the Independent Eritrea Party, Mr. Woldemariam, on whose life four attempts have been made. Such criminal practices make it difficult to ascertain even approximately the true desire of those who now declare themselves in favour of annexation, as it cannot be said that, in every case, the spontaneity of their political affiliation is guaranteed.

194. In these conditions, the political conviction of many of the inhabitants who support the Unionist cause cannot but be viewed with doubt. This is even more understandable if one takes into account the scant knowledge of political questions by the majority of the inhabitants, which is natural in a country that has been administered as a colony and where, up to recent times, a number of them were still serfs.

195. The Commission questioned the representatives of the various groups, both in Asmara and at many other places in Eritrea, for which it had to travel thousands of kilometres. It endeavoured, within the limit of its possibilities, to ascertain the wishes of the inhabitants with regard to the following fundamental matters:

(a) Independence of the territory;
(b) Trusteeship of the territory;
(c) Annexation of the whole territory to Ethiopia;
(d) Partition of the territory and annexation of the eastern part of Ethiopia and the Western Province to the Anglo-Egyptian Sudan.

196. The great majority of the inhabitants of the eastern and western lowlands, and groups of varying importance in the plateau, were in favour of immediate independence. When they were questioned as to which Administering Authority they would prefer if it were considered that the country was not ready for independence and it were decided to place the territory under the Trusteeship System, the majority expressed the desire that the United Nations be directly entrusted with the administration of the territory.

197. The case for annexation of Eritrea to Ethiopia found strong support in the provinces of the plateau, where, judging by the demonstrations, a considerable majority favours that solution. Opposition to partition of the territory, such as the annexation of the highlands and the Red Sea Division to Ethiopia and the Western Province to the Anglo-Egyptian Sudan, was almost unanimous. One political party, the Muslim League of the Western Province, advocated trusteeship by the United Kingdom for that province, with a view to independence. Even the groups which formed this League expressed their opposition to the annexation of the Western Province to the Sudan.

198. All observations lead to the conclusion that it is necessary to maintain the unity of the territory. The highlands and the lowlands, linked by railroad, a good highway system, and other means of communication, are complementary to each other. The idea of annexing the provinces of Hamasien, Akele Guzai, Serae and the Red Sea Division to Ethiopia and the Western Province to the Sudan has been put forward. We do not find any reasons which would justify the partition of Eritrea. This solution is contrary to the expressed wishes of the inhabitants, would do harm to the economy and the prosperity of the territory, and does not conform to the Charter of the

---

78/ Report of the Four-Power Commission, paragraph 39, page 96.

United Nations. In our opinion, separation of the Western Province from the rest of Eritrea will mean the fragmentation of the Muslim population and will not be in the interests of the country. We should point out that, in accordance with this solution, as proposed, it is desired to annex to Ethiopia the province covering that part of the coast line of the Red Sea, where strong resistance and even hostility towards that country prevails among the great majority of the inhabitants. In order to achieve the wellbeing of the population of Eritrea, the unity of the territory must be maintained. The solution to the problem of the disposal of Eritrea must therefore be a single one and must apply to the whole country.

199. The Muslim League of the Western Province, whose importance, even in the only province in which it exists, is relatively small, declared itself in favour of placing the Western Province under United Nations trusteeship, irrespective of the solution applied to the remainder of the country. A separate Western Province will have no means of communication with the sea, as the only railway line and the main road which connect it with the port of Massawa pass through the highlands. Such a proposition would not be to the benefit of the territory, and it would clearly be against the desires of the great majority of the population of the whole territory in general, and of that province in particular.

200. Several parties have declared themselves in favour of the annexation of Eritrea to Ethiopia. The Unionist Party is the most important of this group. 79/

201. We have already mentioned the participation of the Coptic Church in favour of annexation, as well as the part played by terrorism in support of that policy.

202. The population of the plateau has a certain affinity with one of the Ethiopian provinces, namely, the Tigré Province. In that part of Eritrea, as in Tigré, the Tigrinya language is spoken, but this affinity between a part of Ethiopia and a part of Eritrea is not sufficient to justify the absorption of Eritrea by Ethiopia. This language, on the other hand, is not spoken throughout Eritrea, nor is it spoken throughout Ethiopia. Neither is it the official language of that country. No important and general affinity exists between Ethiopia and Eritrea. On the contrary, the inhabitants bear resentment and hostility towards Ethiopia.

203. The economic, ethnic, historical and security reasons, 80/ together with others advanced in favour of annexation, are not sufficient for us to recommend this solution to the United Nations, nor are we convinced that the majority of the population wishes it, or that this would be the best course for promoting the welfare of the inhabitants.

204. In our tour throughout Eritrea, we saw that a large number of people were opposed to the annexation of the territory to Ethiopia and in favour of independence. We were impressed by the way in which these people behaved, as well as by the courage and firmness with which they expressed their views, notwithstanding the risks to which they often exposed themselves. There can be no doubt that, in the eastern and western lowlands, the great majority of the population is in favour of independence and is strongly opposed to any idea of annexation or partition of the territory. All over the country we met groups that were in favour of independence, particularly among the Muslims, but it is evident that their greatest strength is in the lowlands. 81/

205. All peoples have the right to be free. The Eritreans have the right to independence, since a majority of the population claims it and there are no juridical reasons justifying any other procedure. Under present conditions there is nothing to justify a different solution for this territory. Independence does not exclude subsequent decisions taken in a democratic way by the people of Eritrea to link their country in the form of confederation or federation, or even of unconditional union with Ethiopia, when it happened to be the unmistakable wish of the people, should the occasion arise. But that is not the case at present and it is not possible to tie the fate of one country to that of another in advance and irrevocably, when a large part of the population rejects that solution and demands independence. 82/

79/ *The delegation of Pakistan wishes to add the following*: The Secretary-General of the Unionist Party, Mr. Tedla Bairu, admitted that the figures which he had supplied relating to the supporters of his party were inaccurate and that the Muslim population of the western lowlands had ceased to support union with Ethiopia. With regard to the eastern lowlands, he preferred not to give a categorical reply until the question had been studied further by his party. Our delegation took care to find out the extent of the Muslim following of this party. From what we observed in the field trips, we noticed that, in all the big gatherings which the party presented to us in the highlands, the Muslims were very few. In the lowlands, at the Unionist gatherings, the total number never exceeded a handful of persons and even among them Muslims were conspicuous by their small number. In order to dupe the Commission, the party resorted to many malpractices. One such which came to light was through the arrest of some Coptic Christian supporters of the Unionist Party disguised as Muslims. At some other places representatives who came to support the Unionist cause were found to be bogus. The Commission received numerous complaints of impersonation by Copts as Muslims at Unionist gatherings.

80/ See paragraphs 213-218; 252-258.

81/ *The delegation of Pakistan wishes to add the following*: The numerical strength of the population as given is not exact. The figures supplied by the British Administration show that nearly half the population of Eritrea is Muslim and a little under half is Coptic—the difference between the two being a few thousands. These population figures, however, are not based on any census and cannot be regarded as entirely accurate. The Muslim League claims that the total Muslim population of Eritrea is 70 per cent and that even in the highlands they are equal in number to the Copts.

82/ To the question whether they would be prepared to submit to a test of opinion by a democratic method, such as by setting up a constituent assembly elected by a wide franchise which would have the power and authority of declining for union with Ethiopia or remaining independent, the supporters of the Independence Bloc welcomed it, whereas the Unionist Party demurred.

206. We observed that, while Eritrea possesses trained people, it does not have a sufficient number of them to assume the government of the territory immediately. A period of time is necessary for the political, economic, social and educational development of the inhabitants, and to ensure the tranquillity of the territory before they are able to take over the government.

207. For cases such as this, the United Nations Charter has provided the Trusteeship System. In Article 81, it establishes that the authority which exercises the administration of a Trusteeship Territory may be one or more States or the Organization itself. The Independence Bloc generally agreed to a limited period of direct United Nations trusteeship. It objected in general to a single Power trusteeship. The Unionist group demanded immediate union with Ethiopia and therefore the question of trusteeship does not arise in that case.

208. Taking into account the difficulties which exist in the designation of one State or a group of States in the particular case of Eritrea, we are of the opinion that the most appropriate course would be for the United Nations to take direct charge of the administration.

The Italian minority

209. We were impressed by the work which the Italians have done and are doing in the territory. The wonderful road system, railway, port facilities and all other kinds of public works are essentially the result of Italian technical skill and enterprise. The industries of importance in the territory, such as the match factory, button factories, glass works, sisal products, brewery, chinaware factory, and electric works belong to and are run by Italians.

210. The Italian agricultural and dairy farming concessions are a model of industry and efficiency in a backward territory.

211. The mines, some of which have had to be abandoned on account of lawlessness, are worked under the direction of Italian engineers. In all these activities, considerable native labour is employed. The towns of Asmara and, to some extent, Massawa, can be described as Italian towns and without the Italian population they are liable to crumble and come to an end. The Commission witnessed the sad state of the town of Decamere, which now appears completely deserted after the departure of a large number of its Italian residents.

212. In order to keep alive the economic life of the principal towns and of Eritrea as a whole, the continuing participation by Italians and half-castes is essential. Many of the former were born in Eritrea and know no other home. They are entitled to protection, which should be of a kind of which they could feel confident. They feel that, in an independent Eritrea, they will be able to live in peace and prosperity. Therefore, from the point of view of this very important minority also, independence is the best possible solution for Eritrea. They are confident that Eritrea can be economically a self-supporting country within a few years, and that partition will do it great harm.

Peace and security in East Africa

213. The terms of reference of resolution 289 (IV) of the General Assembly instruct the Commission for Eritrea to take into consideration the interests of peace and security in East Africa in studying the problem.

214. It has often been repeated that Ethiopia needs the control of Eritrean territory for reasons of security against possible aggression from outside. Such a possibility does not exist. The surrounding countries, such as the Anglo-Egyptian Sudan, the countries on the other side of the Red Sea, and the neighbouring colonial territories administered by France and the United Kingdom, as well as former Italian Somaliland, which is now under the International Trusteeship System of the United Nations, do not present any danger to the peace of Ethiopia, nor, in general, to the peace and security of that area of the world.

215. Trusteeship by the United Nations over Eritrea would be the best guarantee of internal peace and security in that territory and of international peace and security in East Africa. The main groups would live in peace side by side, as they have been living for centuries. In Eritrea, under trusteeship or independence, the minorities are confident that they also would have security. Within the framework of a union of Eritrea with Ethiopia the Muslim majority and the Italian minority feel that they could never be happy. The Muslims and Italians have expressed their views in no uncertain terms. 83/

216. An independent Eritrea—which can never become a military stronghold—could never constitute a threat to Ethiopia.

217. Against a hypothetical future aggression on the part of a great military Power, alien to Africa, there is the international guarantee by the United Nations. If, by any unhappy chance, that guarantee should become ineffective, the control of the territory of Eritrea would not save Ethiopia nor safeguard it against an aggression of that type.

218. On the contrary, the annexation of Eritrea, in part or in whole, to Ethiopia, or the annexation of a part of Eritrea to the Sudan against the will of a large portion of the Eritrean population, would create constant internal

---

83/ *Note by the delegation of Pakistan*: The apprehensions of the Muslim population of Eritrea are justified by the conditions prevailing in Ethiopia up to the present time.

friction, giving rise inter alia to police measures of repression and to political persecutions which could jeopardize the internal tranquillity of Ethiopia and peace and security in that part of the world.

Economic situation in Eritrea

219. The economic capacity of Eritrea and its possibilities of development have been one of the most discussed points and have, at the same time, served as a political instrument for the support of one or another policy in favour of a given solution of the problem.

220. Thus, those who support the Unionist cause have passionately exaggerated the bad situation, in order to arrive at the conclusion that the territory cannot at present and will never be able to become self-supporting from the economic point of view. On the other hand, those who support the principle of independence have also exaggerated the future possibilities of Eritrea and have asserted, also passionately, that the country will be able to achieve complete economic independence in a short period.

221. Both views are exaggerated and both are erroneous.

222. There is, however, one undeniable fact: that, at present, there hardly exists a country in the world which could be said to be economically independent. The idea of economic interdependence has already replaced the old concept of self-sufficiency.

223. On the other hand, it is very difficult, and would be erroneous, to judge the economic capacity of Eritrea in the light of the present situation only, without taking into consideration the fact that the existing circumstances are abnormal.

224. When the Second World War started, a flourishing economy had already been initiated in Eritrea with the development of important agricultural, industrial and mining activities. Even if it is true that the war produced other industries in the economic life of Eritrea, it also obstructed the progressive course of the methodical development which had been initiated. To this circumstance could be added another no less important. During the last decade nothing has been done towards the economic improvement of the territory, whereas much has been done to the contrary. It may be pointed out, by way of example, that prosperous enterprises, such as the cultivation of cotton, have been abandoned; the more important gold mines have been closed, destroyed, or dismantled; the free development of the growing of tobacco and other plants has been handicapped. All this has been due to administrative action, to which must unfortunately be added some other decisive factors, such as: (a) the uncertainty regarding the future disposal of the territory; (b) political agitation bearing on the same subject; (c) terroristic activities and the complete lack of security for life and property, which have brought about the abandonment of important agricultural and industrial activities, handicapped transport, and caused unrest throughout the country; (d) the continuous exodus of Italians, which has been, in the main, due to (c) above.

225. Among the abandoned agricultural farms, it is enough to mention those of coffee which, in 1940, promised to meet the local requirements within a short time. The present harvest is less than one-third of that of 1940, not to speak of the abandoned young plants which, today, could be in full production.

226. It is also important to mention, as a further factor, that the complete lack of bank credits for agriculture, manufacturing and trade has greatly hindered the economic development of the territory. The role that credit plays at present in the economic life of any country, including the more advanced ones, is well known.

227. It should also be considered that, since the present Administering Power in Eritrea is interested in a certain political solution of the problem and hopes that at least a part of that territory may be added to its possessions, it should not be surprising that far from improving the existing conditions, that Power is not even concerned about their deterioration, for the more that Eritrean economy suffers, the more probabilities there would be for that Power to carry out its political plans.

228. Any evaluation that may be made of the present Eritrean economy, that did not take into account the circumstances and factors briefly outlined above, would give an erroneous picture of the situation and would lead to an estimation, also erroneous, of the future possibilities.

229. Most of the information on the economic situation of the territory received by the Commission emanates from the British Administration and obviously tends to support the political position of the British Government with regard to the problem.

230. In the present abnormal circumstances, the economic situation of Eritrea is not only bad but deteriorates from day to day. This situation is not capable of change so long as the problem of the disposal of Eritrea remains unsolved.

231. It is true that climatic conditions of the territory are not the most favourable for easy large-scale agricultural development. Rainfall is comparatively scanty and in some areas is insufficient for farming. There is no river that flows continuously, with the exception of the Setit—which in places serves as the frontier between Eritrea and Ethiopia. However, the land is not bad generally speaking, and, in view of the topography of the country, the possibility of storing rain water for irrigation is very considerable and could be carried out compara-

tively economically. Irrigation by canals would also be possible, using the water of numerous seasonal streams—a system which was begun before the Second World War, with satisfactory results.

232. Thus, though it is not possible to increase the rainfall in a short period of time so long as gradual and extensive plans of re-afforestation are not carried out, it is at least possible and relatively easy, through the increased storage of rain water for irrigation and the use of the seasonal running streams to the same end, to increase progressively the percentage of cultivated lands, not only for solving the deficit in the production of grains (one-sixth of the consumption), but even for maintaining some reserves for export.

233. The main agricultural products of Eritrea are grain, vegetable-fibres, coffee, tobacco, cotton, citrus fruits, tropical fruits, and others. This is one of the few places in the world where the dum palm exists, the nut of which is used for the manufacture of buttons, alcohol, and oil for soap and cattle fodder. The skin of the nut contains tannin in industrial quantities and the shell is used as fuel. From the palm leaves are obtained fibres of excellent quality for marine ropes, and raw material for the manufacture of paper.

234. Cattle breeding is a considerable source of wealth in Eritrea on account of the dairy and meat products and the industry and export of skins. This important item in the economy of the territory is also affected by the insufficient rainfall of the country. The cattle are forced to migrate twice a year for pasture. Any measure taken towards storing rain water would alleviate the situation, with consequent progress for this important industry, which, moreover, is a truly popular source of wealth, since cattle breeding is not concentrated in big farms, but is the patrimony of the individual Eritrean.

235. The agricultural production statistics are incomplete and insufficient and have not the real value which is generally attached to statistics, since the present conditions are not normal, as has already been pointed out.

236. As regards the mineral wealth of Eritrea, one principal fact should be emphasized: there is not sufficient information to form an idea of its extent, quality and value.

237. The fact best known concerning mining is that numerous deposits of gold exist both in the highlands and the lowlands. In 1940, the output, which was beginning to reach a steady level, amounted to 17,000 ounces, with great probabilities of increase. The main mines were destroyed, closed or dismantled and during several years there was no yield. The gold mines have also been greatly affected by terroristic activities and the lack of security in the country. In 1949, the production was only 2,800 ounces.

238. It is also known that there are deposits of iron, copper, nickel, mica, asbestos and other minerals. Traces of manganese, titanium, magnesium and chromium have been found, but the available information, in general, is extremely deficient. In some cases, it has been said that either the material is not of good quality, as for example, nickel, or that its location is difficult of access.

239. There are also deposits of salts of sodium and potassium, of kaolin and feldspar, which are used in local manufactures. There is a great deal of marble, and, although it seems that there is no coal, lignite of low quality has been found.

240. It is also known that, during the last years of the Italian régime, drillings were made to locate oil in the Dahlak Islands off Massawa, but, due to the war, those prospectings were not completed, and no report is available regarding the results. On the other hand, the existence of sediments of the Miocene Age on the coast north of Massawa has been confirmed, but no drillings have been made.

241. While it cannot be said that Eritrea is very rich in minerals, neither can it be said that it is poor. Knowledge about mining in Eritrea and the information available on which to base a judgement are extremely deficient. It is a fact, however, that mining is practically an unexplored field.

242. Eritrea has several hundred kilometres of coast and an important archipelago in the Red Sea—one of the richest seas in the world. The fishing industry and the exploitation, in general, of the marine wealth offer a very ample and promising field for the economy of Eritrea. There are already some industries, such as fish meal, oils, sea-shell products, mother-of-pearl, snails, coral and pearl, with immense possibilities of development.

243. Geographically, Eritrea includes two completely different regions: the highlands of Hamasien, Serae and Akele Guzai and the western and eastern lowlands. Both regions are complementary to each other economically by the diversity of their animal, vegetable and mineral products, by the interchange of industrial raw materials, by the differences of climate and season and by the facilities afforded by one to the other for the seasonal migration of cattle. It should also be pointed out that both regions are linked by excellent highways and railways.

244. Eritrea has a considerable number of industries whose importance is based mainly on the good quality of their products. The industries in Eritrea vary greatly, as can be judged by the following: chemical products, preserved meats, butter, cheese, fish, fish meal, beer, wines, liquors, alcohol, glassware, chinaware and porcelain, matches, paper, medicinal and pharmaceutical products, leather goods, dum-palm and mother-of-pearl

buttons, vegetable fibres (sisal and dum-palm), essential oils and shark oils, skins and leather, and gum arabic. The majority of these products are exported. There are also other products for local consumption, such as soap, perfume, cigarettes, and cement products.

245. Most of these industries use local raw materials. There are other industries, merely for processing, which employ mainly imported raw materials, such as wheat-flour, whose exportation reached more than a million kilogrammes in 1948, with a value of more than £76,000.

246. Eritrean industries are not artificial, as they have, on occasion, been characterized, nor do they depend mainly on cheap labour. They are well established and their products, on account of their quality, are well received in the neighbouring markets, such as Ethiopia, Sudan and the countries on the other side of the Red Sea. Many of their products, such as buttons, vegetable fibres, and fish meal, go to European markets. Another industry is that of salt, which has a good market in the Far East, mainly in India and Japan.

247. There is no reason to doubt the success, development and increase of these industries in the future. On the contrary, if they have been able to subsist through the difficult conditions of recent years, it can be logically inferred that they will subsist and develop better in the future, when the conditions of unrest and abnormalcy, pointed out above, disappear.

248. Another industry worthy of mention, on account of its public value and its contribution to many aspects of the economic life of Eritrea, is the electric power industry. Considerable efforts have been made to develop hydro-electric power and there are plans already prepared, the implementation of which was prevented by the war and subsequent conditions, for its expansion to the point where it would be possible to dispense with electricity produced by imported fuels.

249. There is no reason to suppose that foreign markets may be closed to Eritrean products in the future, since the latter are of good quality and some of them, such as buttons and fibres, do not encounter strong competition. Moreover, it could not be said that Eritrea itself is a small or poor market for its own products. In the same measure as the Eritrean people (more than one million) are able to raise their standard of living, their consumption capacity will increase accordingly, particularly with regard to products such as matches, foodstuffs, edible oils and soap. There is no reason to say that the match industry will not be able to subsist because it depends on euphorbia wood, the consumption of which contributes to the deforestation of the country, since the wood used for boxes and sticks can be replaced by cardboard, the manufacture of which is easy and for which there is in the territory adequate raw material. The sticks can also be substituted by cotton fibres coated with paraffin.

250. As has already been indicated elsewhere, Eritrea has an excellent system of communications. Transportation is also, at the present time, affected by the abnormal conditions under which the country suffers and to which reference was made at the beginning of this chapter.

251. The railway has an annual deficit of approximately £25,000, despite the fact that its use is compulsory for most goods traffic and that the use of motor trucks has been prohibited alongside the railways. This deficit, however, is also largely due to the abnormal situation and to the fact that many of the economic activities of the country are paralysed.

252. An important factor in the economy of Eritrea is the transit of goods to and from Ethiopia through Eritrean ports and territory.

253. There is no doubt that there exists a strong community of economic interests between Eritrea and Ethiopia, not only on account of the need of the latter to use Eritrean ports for its foreign trade and the gains which accrue to Eritrea by this transit, but also on account of the markets mutually afforded for their various products. At present, Ethiopia supplies most of the grain deficiencies in Eritrea (one-sixth of the consumption) and, in turn, imports several products manufactured in Eritrea. On the other hand, several Eritrean industries—certain vegetable oil factories, for example—utilize Ethiopian raw materials. Eritrea also carries on certain import and re-export business in some products of Ethiopia and of the Arabian peninsula, after certain processing in Eritrea.

254. These economic ties deserve the greatest consideration and merit the conclusion of appropriate agreements which would facilitate close co-operation and would tend eventually towards a very advantageous economic union for both countries.

255. It should be pointed out that external trade to and from Ethiopia cannot be exclusively channelled through only one of the Eritrean ports. Products to and from the northern region of Ethiopia naturally pass through the port of Massawa, while products to and from Addis Ababa and the central and southern regions of Ethiopia pass through the ports of Djibouti, in French Somaliland, and Assab in Eritrea. The port of Assab is, therefore, the most suitable one for external trade from the Ethiopian region of Dessie.

256. The transit trade of the Eritrean ports is much greater than the Eritrean trade of those ports.

257. In considering these circumstances, the advantageous geographical position of Eritrea, from the

commercial point of view, should be taken into account. In the neighbourhood of important commercial centres such as Port Sudan, Djibouti, Aden, Hodeida and Jeddah, Eritrea has within reach very important maritime routes, such as those uniting the Indian Ocean and the Far Eastern countries with the Mediterranean Sea and the European countries through the Red Sea. Its two ports have good anchorage, size and facilities sufficient for a prominent commercial position, both with regard to the maritime routes themselves and access to and from the rich lands of the interior.

258. This privileged position could be better taken advantage of for the economic development of Eritrea through the establishment of free zones in the ports of Massawa and Assab, which, besides attracting great quantities of merchandise to such ports, would enormously facilitate an extensive commercial exchange and, in a very special way, the external trade of Ethiopia.

259. As is the case in all countries under colonial régime, Eritrea has a decided disequilibrium in her balance of trade. Her exports reach an average of £1,600,000, while her imports exceed £3,000,000. It should be remembered that these figures correspond to the present abnormal period in which, for example, Eritrea, while able to produce enough coffee for its own consumption and even for export of a certain amount, is importing 500 tons annually at a value of £75,000. It should also be remembered that, due to that colonial policy, its imports are subject to special controls and it cannot freely negotiate for the imports of its requirements in the most favourable markets, but only in those which the authorities permit. These are seldom the least expensive or the nearest.

260. The Eritrean Chamber of Commerce has explained that the deficit in the balance of trade is smaller than it seems to be, since important invisible revenue items have not been taken into consideration, and points out the following as concrete instances: (a) revenue derived from transit trade (£25,500); (b) revenue derived from land transportation (£34,000); (c) sea cargo and passenger fares (£27,000); (d) transport insurance policies taken out in Eritrea (£5,000); (e) air cargo (£12,187); (f) tourist trade, including movement of foreigners (£20,000); (g) payment for servicing ships and planes (£12,225). To these revenues should be added the remittances made to their families by Eritrean workers living outside the territory. Consequently, the Eritrean Chamber of Commerce reaches the conclusion that there are a number of invisible revenues, to the extent of approximately £140,000, which should be deducted from the deficit in the balance of trade.

261. It is necessary to stress also that this deficit in the balance of trade, as well as that which at present exists in the budget, which will be dealt with below, is due also in part to the following factors: (a) the complete lack of bank credit for agriculture, industry and trade; (b) the inadequate system of taxation in force; (c) the customs system in force, which is also inadequate and antiquated and tends to direct the trade to and from specific countries; (d) the lack of proper organization in the ports, which would expedite the traffic of goods and the increase in their volume; (e) the policy of transport, designed only to solve the problem of the operation of the railways; (f) the impossibility of negotiating commercial treaties with other countries at present. In this regard, one cannot fail to note another important factor relating to the imports of foreign products, equal and often inferior in quality to the products of Eritrea. For example, we ourselves saw in the territory matches imported from India and the Union of South Africa, and butter imported from Australia.

262. The budget of revenue and of administrative expenditure has also, as in almost all colonial territories, a substantial deficit—around £400,000 in the current budget—which itself hardly amounts to a total of £2,800,000. It should be emphasized that the greater part of the Eritrean budget is allocated to Police and Prisons to the amount of almost £400,000, while Education receives only £107,000 and Agriculture hardly £56,000. This fact is the more significant because, in spite of the amount allocated to the police service, the Administering Authority has not been capable of maintaining order and security in the territory.

263. The budget deficit, however, will easily disappear with the return to the country of normal conditions and, above all, tranquillity. The normal increase of economic activities will itself balance the budget deficit, mainly through a more careful and less expensive administration than the colonial one, a more just revision of taxes, a more economic and effective system for their collection, the suppression of arbitrary exemptions, such as the one at present applied to officials of the Administration who pay taxes in London and not in Eritrea, in spite of the fact that they receive salaries paid out of the meagre budget of the territory.

264. Finally, Eritrea would be able to maintain, in normal conditions, an economic position which would allow it to live and progress with dignity, to balance its trade and not only to eliminate the budget deficits of the previous years, but even to increase its income in such a way as to be able to take care of the urgent and pressing requirements of its population, in social, educational and agricultural matters and gradually to undertake the work of progress and betterment in all aspects of the life of the Eritrean community, with the technical assistance which

could be provided by the specialized agencies of the United Nations.

Conclusions

265. We believe the best solution for the future of Eritrea to be independence. But, at the same time, we are of the opinion that independence cannot be made effective immediately. Therefore, the welfare of Eritrea can best be promoted by placing the territory under direct trusteeship by the United Nations for a maximum period of ten year, at the end of which it should become completely independent.

266. The Charter of the United Nations provides that territories of certain categories, which include those detached from enemy States as a result of the Second World War, are to be treated as Trust Territories with the objective of their progressive development towards self-government or independence.

267. Therefore, we recommend to the General Assembly:

(1) That Eritrea, within its present boundaries, shall be an independent sovereign State.

(2) That this independence shall become effective at the end of a period of ten years from the date on which the General Assembly approves this recommendation.

(3) That, during the period mentioned in paragraph 2, Eritrea shall be placed under the International Trusteeship System, with the United Nations itself as the Administering Authority.

(4) That the Administrator who exercises authority on behalf of the United Nations be appointed by the General Assembly and be assisted and advised by an advisory council composed of representatives of the following States:

United States of America (in view of its contribution to the programme for the development of underdeveloped areas and its interest in the future of dependent territories);

Ethiopia and Italy (in view of their well-known interests);

A Muslim country (in view of the proportion of the Muslim population and to ensure geographical distribution);

A Latin-American country (in view of the principle of geographical distribution and of Latin America's interest in the fate of dependent territories).

That, to ensure the representation of the population, a representative of the Coptic Christians, a representative of the Muslims and a representative of the minorities be included in the advisory council.

(5) That economic agreements be concluded between Eritrea and Ethiopia for the primary purpose of facilitating trade and the transit of goods, and with a view to an eventual economic union.

(6) That free zones be established in the ports of Massawa and Assab to facilitate the exchange of goods and the movement of shipping, taking advantage of the special conditions of the two ports and their strategic geographical position.

(7) That, with a view to promoting the integral development of the country, the United Nations send a mission of experts from the various specialized agencies in order to make appropriate studies for the development of the country on a technical basis.

(8) That the present administering Power, on the appointment of the United Nations Administrator, shall initiate immediately all necessary steps for transfer of power to him.

It is further considered opportune to recommend:

(a) That the United Nations Educational, Scientific and Cultural Organization study the advisability of establishing a university with its centre at Asmara, making use of its suitable position, for the benefit not only of Eritrea but also of the neighbouring countries, which do not possess centres of higher education.

(b) That, on receipt of the report of the mission of experts recommended above, appropriate steps be taken for financing the programmes suggested for the development of Eritrea, in accordance with that missions's recommendations.

...

Document 5

Report of the Interim Committee of the General Assembly (excerpt)

A/1388, 1950

...

II. Work of the Interim Committee

A. *Consideration of the report of the United Nations Commission for Eritrea*

7. The report of the United Nations Commission for Eritrea was presented to the Interim Committee at its 39th meeting held on 13 July 1950 by Mr. Mian Ziaud-Din (Pakistan), Rapporteur of the Commission.

8. At the same meeting, the Committee was informed by the Secretary-General of the desire of the Italian Government to participate in the discussions of the Committee on the question of Eritrea, and decided to invite the representative designated by the Italian Government to attend the meetings of the Committee for that purpose. His Excellency, Mr. Giuseppe Brusasca, Under-Secretary of States for Foreign Affairs of Italy, thereafter took part in the discussions of the Committee on this subject.

9. Debate on the report of the Commission for Eritrea took place during the 40th, 41st, 42nd, and 44th meetings, held during the period from 14 to 31 July 1950.

10. At the 45th meeting held on 15 September, the Chairman summarized the situation with respect to the report of the Commission for Eritrea in the following statement to the Interim Committee:

> "The trend of the speeches in the Interim Committee, since it started the examination of the report of the Commission for Eritrea and the evident drive of all the delegations to reach a solution on a basis of compromise, encouraged me, as I expressed in our last meeting, to explore every means of reconciling the conflicting interests which have hitherto prevented any decision being reached regarding the future status of Eritrea.
>
> "Confidential discussions, initiated jointly by the United States and United Kingdom delegations, has taken place with the representatives of the interested delegations in an endeavour to find suitable grounds for a satisfactory formula. The unremitting efforts made by these two delegations resulted in considerable progress being made in establishing principles on which such a formula could be built.
>
> "As Chairman of the Interim Committee, I had been kept confidentially informed of the steps which were being taken as discussion proceeded and I, myself, later participated in them. When the proper moment arrived, I assumed the responsibility, again on a strictly informal basis, of taking them further. In this, Ambassador Padilla Nervo of Mexico joined, in a personal capacity, in order to widen the scope of the discussion. The formula which resulted from these strenuous efforts to seek a compromise that might lead to the solution of this complex and difficult problem appears to those who took part in the conversations under my direction as a carefully balanced formula capable of meeting the widely divergent views. It affords a common denominator to the opposing interests. It takes into consideration the positive and constructive elements contained in the report of the Commission for Eritrea and the trend of the debate in the Interim Committee. It agrees with the directives established by the Treaty of Peace and with the principles of the United Nations Charter. It respects the best interests of the inhabitants of Eritrea and affords an adequate protection to the foreigners resident therein. It recognizes the fundamental needs of Ethiopia as expressed in the discussions which have taken place in the General Assembly. Although that formula does not give entire satisfaction to all interests involved, as least it can be said that it affords a useful basis for further discussion in the General Assembly in view of finding a solution for the Eritrean question.
>
> "Considerations which were alien to the principles involved in the solution of this problem did not permit us to recommend to the Interim Committee the formula which arose from the consultations carried on under my direction. I regret that the Interim Committee has not now the necessary time to proceed with its endeavours in order to make a set of recommendations to the General Assembly on the question of Eritrea. Much of our time was consumed in the process of consultation to arrive at a formula capable of reconciling so many divergent views, and which could obtain the necessary majority. Our inability, despite our best efforts, to succeed in reaching a consensus of opinion among a substantial number of delegations, must not however cause us to lose heart. Our strivings have not been in vain.

No striving when sincere can ever be in vain. The results of our efforts might again be taken up and carried further by the General Assembly.

"The Interim Committee did a good job. The general debate which took place here contained a wealth of wise suggestions which most surely will be greatly helpful to the General Assembly when it tackles again a settlement of this difficult problem. The question of the future destination of Eritrea was entrusted to the General Assembly for a solution, and the General Assembly cannot rest at ease before it settles that question in accordance with the principles of the Charter and to the advantage of the people of Eritrea.

"In view of the extremely short time which remains before the opening of the General Assembly session, I suggest that the best course for us to follow is to request our Rapporteur to make his report to the General Assembly incorporating in it this statement of the Chairman."

11. The Interim Committee concurred in the suggestion of the Chairman.

...

Document 6

General Assembly resolution concerning the report of the United Nations Commission for Eritrea and the report of the Interim Committee of the General Assembly

A/RES/390 (V), 2 December 1950

A

Whereas by paragraph 3 of Annex XI to the Treaty of Peace with Italy, 1947, the Powers concerned have agreed to accept the recommendation of the General Assembly on the disposal of the former Italian colonies in Africa and to take appropriate measures for giving effect to it,

Whereas by paragraph 2 of the aforesaid Annex XI such disposal is to be made in the light of the wishes and welfare of the inhabitants and the interests of peace and security, taking into consideration the views of interested governments,

Now therefore

The General Assembly, in the light of the reports 1/ of the United Nations Commission for Eritrea and of the Interim Committee, and

Taking into consideration

(a) The wishes and welfare of the inhabitants of Eritrea, including the views of the various racial, religious and political groups of the provinces of the territory and the capacity of the people for self-government,

(b) The interests of peace and security in East Africa,

(c) The rights and claims of Ethiopia based on geographical, historical, ethnic or economic reasons, including in particular Ethiopia's legitimate need for adequate access to the sea,

Taking into account the importance of assuring the continuing collaboration of the foreign communities in the economic development of Eritrea,

Recognizing that the disposal of Eritrea should be based on its close political and economic association with Ethiopia, and

Desiring that this association assure to the inhabitants of Eritrea the fullest respect and safeguards for their institutions, traditions, religions and languages, as well as the widest possible measure of self-government, while at the same time respecting the Constitution, institutions, traditions and the international status and identity of the Empire of Ethiopia,

A. *Recommends that*:

1. Eritrea shall constitute an autonomous unit federated with Ethiopia under the sovereignty of the Ethiopian Crown.

2. The Eritrean Government shall possess legislative, executive and judicial powers in the field of domestic affairs.

3. The jurisdiction of the Federal Government shall extend to the following matters: defence, foreign affairs, currency and finance, foreign and interstate commerce and external and interstate communications, including ports. The Federal Government shall have the power to maintain the integrity of the Federation, and shall have the right to impose uniform taxes throughout the Federation to meet the expenses of federal functions and services, it being understood that the assessment and the collection of such taxes in Eritrea are to be delegated to

---

1/ See *Official Records of the General Assembly, Fifth Session, Supplements, Nos. 8 and 14.*

the Eritrean Government, and provided that Eritrea shall bear only its just and equitable share of these expenses. The jurisdiction of the Eritrean Government shall extend to all matters not vested in the Federal Government, including the power to maintain the internal police, to levy taxes to meet the expenses of domestic functions and services, and to adopt its own budget.

4. The area of the Federation shall constitute a single area for customs purposes, and there shall be no barriers to the free movement of goods and persons within the area. Customs duties on goods entering or leaving the Federation which have their final destination or origin in Eritrea shall be assigned to Eritrea.

5. An Imperial Federal Council composed of equal numbers of Ethiopian and Eritrean representatives shall meet at least once a year and shall advise upon the common affairs of the Federation referred to in paragraph 3 above. The citizens of Eritrea shall participate in the executive and judicial branches, and shall be represented in the legislative branch, of the Federal Government, in accordance with law and in the proportion that the population of Eritrea bears to the population of the Federation.

6. A single nationality shall prevail throughout the Federation:

(a) All inhabitants of Eritrea, except persons possessing foreign nationality, shall be nationals of the Federation;

(b) All inhabitants born in Eritrea and having at least one indigenous parent or grandparent shall also be nationals of the Federation. Such persons, if in possession of a foreign nationality, shall, within six months of the coming into force of the Eritrean Constitution, be free to opt to renounce the nationality of the Federation and retain such foreign nationality. In the event that they do not so opt, they shall thereupon lose such foreign nationality;

(c) The qualifications of persons acquiring the nationality of the Federation under sub-paragraphs (a) and (b) above for exercising their rights as citizens of Eritrea shall be determined by the Constitution and laws of Eritrea;

(d) All persons possessing foreign nationality who have resided in Eritrea for ten years prior to the date of the adoption of the present resolution shall have the right, without further requirements of residence, to apply for the nationality of the Federation in accordance with federal laws. Such persons who do not thus acquire the nationality of the Federation shall be permitted to reside in and engage in peaceful and lawful pursuits in Eritrea;

The rights and interests of foreign nationals resident in Eritrea shall be guaranteed in accordance with the provisions of paragraph 7.

7. The Federal Government, as well as Eritrea, shall ensure to residents in Eritrea, without distinction of nationality, race, sex, language or religion, the enjoyment of human rights and fundamental liberties, including the following:

(a) The right to equality before the law. No discrimination shall be made against foreign enterprises in existence in Eritrea engaged in industrial, commercial, agricultural, artisan, educational or charitable activities, nor against banking institutions and insurance companies operating in Eritrea;

(b) The right to life, liberty and security of person;

(c) The right to own and dispose of property. No one shall be deprived of property, including contractual rights, without due process of law and without payment of just and effective compensation;

(d) The right to freedom of opinion and expression and the right of adopting and practising any creed or religion;

(e) The right to education;

(f) The right to freedom of peaceful assembly and association;

(g) The right to inviolability of correspondence and domicile, subject to the requirements of the law;

(h) The right to exercise any profession subject to the requirements of the law;

(i) No one shall be subject to arrest or detention without an order of a competent authority, except in case of flagrant and serious violation of the law in force. No one shall be deported except in accordance with the law;

(j) The right to a fair and equitable trial, the right of petition to the Emperor and the right of appeal to the Emperor for commutation of death sentences;

(k) Retroactivity of penal law shall be excluded;

The respect for the rights and freedoms of others and the requirements of public order and the general welfare alone will justify any limitations to the above rights.

8. Paragraphs 1 to 7 inclusive of the present resolution shall constitute the Federal Act which shall be submitted to the Emperor of Ethiopia for ratification.

9. There shall be a transition period which shall not extend beyond 15 September 1952, during which the Eritrean Government will be organized and the Eritrean Constitution prepared and put into effect.

10. There shall be a United Nations Commissioner in Eritrea appointed by the General Assembly. The Commissioner will be assisted by experts appointed by the Secretary-General of the United Nations.

11. During the transition period, the present administering Power shall continue to conduct the affairs of Eritrea. It shall, in consultation with the United Nations Commissioner, prepare as rapidly as possible the organization of an Eritrean administration, induct Eritre-

ans into all levels of the administration, and make arrangements for and convoke a representative assembly of Eritreans chosen by the people. It may, in agreement with the Commissioner, negotiate on behalf of the Eritreans a temporary customs union with Ethiopia to be put into effect as soon as practicable.

12. The United Nations Commissioner shall, in consultation with the administering Power, the Government of Ethiopia, and the inhabitants of Eritrea, prepare a draft of the Eritrean Constitution to be submitted to the Eritrean Assembly and shall advise and assist the Eritrean Assembly in its consideration of the Constitution. The Constitution of Eritrea shall be based on the principles of democratic government, shall include the guarantees contained in paragraph 7 of the Federal Act, shall be consistent with the provisions of the Federal Act, and shall contain provisions adopting and ratifying the Federal Act on behalf of the people of Eritrea.

13. The Federal Act and the Constitution of Eritrea shall enter into effect following ratification of the Federal Act by the Emperor of Ethiopia and following approval by the Commissioner, adoption by the Eritrean Assembly and ratification by the Emperor of Ethiopia of the Eritrean Constitution.

14. Arrangements shall be made by the Government of the United Kingdom of Great Britain and Northern Ireland as the administering Power for the transfer of power to the appropriate authorities. The transfer of power shall take place as soon as the Eritrean Constitution and the Federal Act enter into effect, in accordance with the provisions of paragraph 13 above.

15. The United Nations Commissioner shall maintain his headquarters in Eritrea until the transfer of power has been completed, and shall make appropriate reports to the General Assembly of the United Nations concerning the discharge of his functions. The Commissioner may consult with the Interim Committee of the General Assembly with respect to the discharge of his functions in the light of developments and within the terms of the present resolution. When the transfer of authority has been completed, he shall so report to the General Assembly and submit to it the text of the Eritrean Constitution;

B. *Authorizes* the Secretary-General, in accordance with established practice:

1. To arrange for the payment of an appropriate remuneration to the United Nations Commissioner;

2. To provide the United Nations Commissioner with such experts, staff and facilities as the Secretary-General may consider necessary to carry out the terms of the present resolution.

316th plenary meeting,
2 December 1950

B

The General Assembly, to assist it in making the appointment of the United Nations Commissioner in Eritrea,

Decides that a Committee composed of the President of the General Assembly, two of the Vice-Presidents (Australia and Venezuela), the Chairman of the Fourth Committee and the Chairman of the Ad Hoc Political Committee shall nominate a candidate or, if no agreement can be reached, two or three candidates, for the post of United Nations Commissioner in Eritrea.

316th plenary meeting,
2 December 1950

Document 7

Progress report of the United Nations Commissioner in Eritrea during the year 1951 (excerpt)

A/1959, 16 November 1951

Chapter I
Historical background, terms of reference and appointment of the United Nations Commissioner in Eritrea

Section 1. Historical background

1. Following the occupation of Eritrea by the Allied Armed Forces and in conformity with Article 10 of the Conditions of Armistice signed by Italy on 3 September 1943, with Article 23.2 of the Peace Treaty with Italy and with paragraph 11 of United Nations General Assembly resolution 390 A (V), Section A, Eritrea has been under United Kingdom administration since 1941.

2. Under Article 23.3, of the Peace Treaty with Italy, bearing the date of 10 February 1947, the Governments of the Union of Soviet Socialist Republics, the United Kingdom of Great Britain and Northern Ireland, the United States of America and France were to determine jointly, within one year from the coming into force of the Treaty, the final disposal of Italy's territorial possessions in Africa, including Eritrea, to which Italy, under Article 23.1, renounced all rights and title.

3. The Four-Power Commission of Investigation for the former Italian Colonies stayed in Eritrea from 12 November 1947 to 3 January 1948. In view of the Council of Foreign Ministers not having reached any agreement upon the expiry of the period set out in Article 23.3, the following provision of Annex XI to the Peace Treaty came into effect:

> "If with respect to any of these territories the Four Powers are unable to agree upon their disposal within one year from the coming into force of the Treaty of Peace with Italy, the matter shall be referred to the General Assembly of the United Nations for a recommendation, and the Four Powers agree to accept the recommendation and to take appropriate measures for giving effect to it."

4. The question of the disposal of the former Italian colonies was considered at the second part of the third regular session of the General Assembly by the First Committee, but the General Assembly rejected a resolution recommended by it providing, *inter alia*, that Eritrea, except for the Western Province, be incorporated into Ethiopia, and decided to postpone further consideration of the question. At the fourth regular session, the General Assembly adopted resolution 289 (IV), establishing the United Nations Commission for Eritrea to consist of representatives of Burma, Guatemala, Norway, Pakistan and the Union of South Africa, "to ascertain more fully the wishes and the best means of promoting the welfare of the inhabitants of Eritrea, to examine the question of the disposal of Eritrea and to prepare a report for the General Assembly, together with such proposal, or proposals as it may deem appropriate for the solution of the problem of Eritrea".

5. The United Nations Commission for Eritrea held plenary, sub-commission and working group meetings in Eritrea from 14 February to 6 April 1950, and in conformity with its terms of reference, obtained information from the Administering Power and from representatives of the population of the territory including minority groups. The Commission also consulted the Governments of Egypt, Ethiopia, France, Italy and the United Kingdom and drafted its report in Geneva, where it sat between 25 April and 8 June 1950.

6. The report of the United Nations Commission for Eritrea (Official Records of the General Assembly, fifth session, Supplement No. 8 (A/1285)) included a "Memorandum submitted by the delegations of Burma, Norway and the Union of South Africa" and a "Memorandum submitted by the delegations of Guatemala and Pakistan". The various solutions advocated in the two memoranda were as follows:

(a) *The delegations of Burma and the Union of South Africa*

A federation of Eritrea and Ethiopia "on terms compatible with the self-respect and domestic autonomy of both countries" and providing for a "joint responsibility and collective action in such fields as defence, external affairs, taxation, finance, inter-state commerce and communications. A customs union and a general rule of non-discrimination would also be prerequisite."

(b) *The delegation of Norway*

Reunion of the whole territory of Eritrea to Ethiopia, it being understood that, in certain conditions and for certain purposes, the Western Province could provisionally and for a limited period of time be left under the present British Administration.

(c) *The delegations of Guatemala and Pakistan*

Direct trusteeship by the United Nations for a maximum period of ten years, at the end of which Eritrea should become completely independent. During the period of trusteeship there should be an Administrator appointed by the General Assembly and advised by a council composed of representatives of the United States of America, Ethiopia, Italy, a Moslem and a Latin-American country and a representative of the Coptic Christians, of the Moslems and of the minorities; economic agreements to be concluded between Eritrea and Ethiopia, with a view to an eventual economic union; free zones in the ports of Massawa and Assab; the United Nations to send a mission of experts from the various specialized agencies, on the report of which appropriate steps should be taken to finance the programme suggested for the development of Eritrea, and finally a study by UNESCO of the advisability of establishing a university with its centre at Asmara.

7. Pursuant to section C, paragraph 4, of resolution 289 (IV), the Interim Committee of the General Assembly considered the report of the Commission for Eritrea during its 40th, 41st, 42nd and 44th meetings, and at the 45th meeting it concurred in the suggestion of the Chairman to incorporate in the report to the General Assembly a statement by the Chairman of the Interim Committee. In this statement (A/1388) (Official Records of the General Assembly, fifth session, Supplement No. 14, p.2), the Chairman referred to confidential discussions with the representatives of the interested delegations, which had been initiated jointly by the representatives of the United Kingdom and United States of America, and in which the Chairman of the Interim Committee and Mr. Padilla

Nervo (Mexico) had later participated. It was further stated that, although the resulting formula afforded "a useful basis for further discussion in the General Assembly," considerations "alien to the principles involved in the solution of this problem" did not permit those participating in the discussions to recommend the formula to the Interim Committee.

8. The reports of the United Nations Commission for Eritrea and the Interim Committee of the General Assembly were considered at the fifth regular session by the *Ad Hoc* Political Committee. A draft resolution sponsored by Bolivia, Brazil, Burma, Canada, Denmark, Ecuador, Greece, Liberia, Mexico, Panama, Paraguay, Peru, Turkey and the United States of America (A/AC.38/L.37 and Corr.1) was introduced by the representatives of the United States at the 48th meeting and approved by the *Ad Hoc* Political Committee at its 56th meeting, by 38 votes to 14, with 8 abstentions (A/1561). Further, the *Ad Hoc* Political Committee at its 64th meeting approved, by 28 votes to 4, with 4 abstentions, a second draft resolution relating to the appointment of the United Nations Commissioner in Eritrea (A/1561/Add.1). The General Assembly, at its 316th meeting held on 2 December 1950, adopted the first resolution submitted by the *Ad Hoc* Political Committee in its report (A/1561), by 14 votes to 10, with 4 abstentions. Further the General Assembly, at the same meeting, adopted, with a drafting change, by 45 votes to 5, with 6 abstentions, the second draft resolution submitted by the *Ad Hoc* Political Committee in its additional report (A/1561/Add.1).

...

Section 3. Appointment of the United Nations Commissioner in Eritrea

10. By virtue of resolution 390 B (V) of 2 December 1950, 1/ a Committee, established by the General Assembly to nominate a candidate or candidates for the office of the United Nations Commissioner in Eritrea, agreed to nominate the following candidates:

Mr. Victor Hoo (Assistant Secretary-General);

Justice Aung Khine (Burma);

Mr. Eduardo Anze Matienzo (Bolivia).

The General Assembly, at its 325th plenary meeting on 14 December 1950, elected by secret ballot Mr. Eduardo Anze Matierzo to the office of United Nations Commissioner in Eritrea.

Chapter II
Activities of the Commissioner

Section 1. Preliminary discussions with the Governments of the United Kingdom, Italy and Ethiopia

11. (a) *The United Kingdom*

Following on an invitation received from the Government of the United Kingdom before leaving the United Nations Headquarters in New York, the Commissioner visited London on his journey to Eritrea in the last days of January 1951. There he had informal talks with officials of the British Foreign Office covering all matters of mutual concern in the implementation of the United Nations resolution. The Commissioner was given assurance of the determination of the United Kingdom Government to carry out to the letter its obligations under the United Nations resolution and hopes were expressed that there would be the closest co-operation between the Commissioner and the Administering Authority.

12. (b) *Italy*

Continuing his journey to Eritrea, the Commissioner accepted an invitation from the Italian Government to stop in Rome for informal talks with members of the Government. In the course of the talks he was given full assurance of the desire of the Italian Government to collaborate with him in the fulfilment of his mission.

13. (c) *Ethiopia*

Shortly after his arrival in Eritrea, the Commissioner flew to Addis Ababa to pay a courtesy visit to His Imperial Majesty the Emperor of Ethiopia, and the Ethiopian Government. The Commissioner was received in audience by his Imperial Majesty and had unofficial conversations with members of the Ethiopian Government. Friendly expressions of a desire to collaborate in the implementation of the United Nations resolution were exchanged, and on his return to Asmara, the Commissioner informed the Eritrean Press that he felt that he had reached full agreement with the authorities in Addis Ababa on broad lines of policy and objectives. He added that he was relying on the understanding and co-operation of the Ethiopian Government for the success of his mission.

1/ The text of the resolution reads as follows:
"The General Assembly, to assist it in making the appointment of the United Nations Commissioner in Eritrea,

"Decides that a Committee composed of the President of the General Assembly, two of the Vice-Presidents (Australia and Venezuela), the Chairman of the Fourth Committee and the Chairman of the Ad Hoc Political Committee shall nominate a candidate or, if no agreement can be reached, two or three candidates for the post of United Nations Commissioner in Eritrea."

Section 2. Statement by the Commissioner on his arrival in Eritrea

14. On 9 February 1951, the day of his arrival in Eritrea, the Commissioner held a conference and other personalities and members of the Press attended. At the opening of the conference, the Commissioner made the following statement, which was subsequently conveyed to the inhabitants of Eritrea through the Press and other means of communication:

"(1) Inhabitants of Eritrea:

"I feel deeply moved on setting foot on Eritrean soil, where I am going to live among you, working with you and your leaders and learning to know you during the coming momentous months when your country is to be led along the path to local self-government, within a federation with your neighbour, Ethiopia.

"(2) I have been sent here to represent the United Nations, an organization of sixty nations, large and small, which was established towards the end of the Second World War in order to maintain peace, and so safeguard the welfare of the peoples of the world. This organization has for some time been trying to find a satisfactory solution for the future of Eritrea, taking into account all your problems, your history and traditions and your wishes. It has been a source of inspiration to me to find these countries, most of which have no direct interest in the future of Eritrea, striving in the spirit of the United Nations Charter to find a solution which would give satisfaction to all parties. The solution which has now been adopted is a middle-of-the-road plan which should give satisfaction not only to those who want to be united with Ethiopia, but to those who want Eritrea to be independent.

"(3) I am deeply conscious of the honour done to me by the General Assembly of the United Nations, and of the heavy responsibility it has laid on me in electing me as United Nations Commissioner in Eritrea. It gives me great satisfaction to take part in such a constructive task, the implementation of which will, I hope, bring happiness, stability and freedom to the people of Eritrea. I am also very happy that the plan will give satisfaction to Ethiopia in recognizing her claims for an outlet to the sea, and the historical ties and traditions binding Ethiopia and Eritrea. May it bring about one great country in Africa, in which all the inhabitants will have equal right to live peacefully and to receive legal protection.

"(4) My principal task will be to draft a constitution for Eritrea and to assist and advise you in adopting its provisions. I cannot help you, however, towards this goal of brotherhood unless you are all prepared, irrespective of party or creed, to help me in this important work. To carry this out successfully the first condition is that strife must disappear and that you all accept peacefully and with single-hearted co-operation this decision of the United Nations, which is in keeping with the high principles of the United Nations Charter. These same principles have inspired all the decisions of the United Nations, and, indeed, they have guided the Members of the United Nations in finding what is considered as a fair and just solution for the future of your country. It has been recommended by a majority of nations, both large ones and small ones—such as my own country, Bolivia—that Eritrea and Ethiopia shall become a federation under the sovereignty of the Ethiopian Crown, with Eritrea constituting an autonomous unit.

"(5) You now have new hopes for the future on which to build. This new spirit has been already shown in the discussions at Lake Success, when all the interested countries showed a remarkable spirit of compromise, and gave assurances that they would carry out the plan adopted and aid the United Nations Commissioner. In these discussions the General Assembly was deeply impressed with the sincerity and tenor of the statement made by the Ethiopian Foreign Minister. He stated before the assembled United Nations that, while feeling that the recommendations would not entirely satisfy the hopes of the Eritrean population or the claims of Ethiopia, his country would respect them and would loyally exert all its efforts to bring about their implementation. He also stated that the Ethiopian Government had deeply at heart the interests and the welfare of the population of Eritrea; that Moslems in Eritrea could be assured of the fullest respect for their rights and privileges and would receive equal opportunities for posts in Ethiopia and Eritrea; that no bitterness or discrimination would be shown towards any political group in Eritrea; that Italians would not be treated as former enemies, but as friends, and, in fact, that all Eritreans, irrespective of their former political attitude, would be brothers with the Ethiopian people, thus bringing to an end a long epoch of exile and sufferings.

"(6) I was also impressed with the statement by the representative of the British Government, who pledged his Government to do its best to carry out the General Assembly's recommendations for a Federation between Ethiopia and Eritrea. I have since received in London the renewed assurances of the British Government that it will do its utmost to support me in my task and to carry out the United Nations decision. I should like to emphasize at this point that the British, who liberated your territory in the Second World War, have borne the burden of administering Eritrea for the last ten years. With their traditional high sense of duty and responsibility they have carried this out constructively and have laid the foundations on which Eritrea could develop politically.

"(7) In this respect I can also say the same thing of the Italian Government. Not only did its representatives make sincere statements at Lake Success, showing its willingness loyally to abide by the United Nations decision, but I have received renewed personal assurances from the Italian Government in Rome in recent days. I fully realize that the existence of the Italian population in Eritrea has been and will be one of the important factors in the progress and development of Eritrea under federation.

"(8) In my concern for the future well-being of Eritrea, I visited Washington before leaving for Asmara, and was very happy to find that the United States Government had very much at heart the welfare of Eritrea. The United States is ready to help the Eritrean people with economic and technical assistance within the framework of President Truman's plan, known as Point Four, which is designed to help the under-developed countries. I can also say that the Secretary-General of the United Nations is prepared to help by providing all the staff I need to assist me. He has also given me assurances that his staff of technical assistants are ready to assist in the progress of Eritrea. I am very hopeful that all these offers, given in the spirit of co-operation, will help to build a new political entity in Africa.

"(9) I will try now to explain to you more clearly what the resolution adopted by the General Assembly means to your territory. Eritrea will have a government of its own which will possess legislative, executive and judicial powers in internal and domestic affairs. The jurisdiction of the Federal Government, in which Eritreans will be included, will extend to defence of the whole territory, to foreign affairs, currency and finance, foreign and interstate commerce and communications both external and interstate, including ports. All these matters are clearly set out in a Federal Act which has been drawn up and recommended by the United Nations, and which will be submitted to the Emperor of Ethiopia for ratification. The Act will ensure to residents in Eritrea, without distinction of nationality, race, sex, language or religion, the enjoyment of human rights and fundamental liberties. In plainer terms, this means that all of you who inhabit Eritrea will have the right to live freely and peacefully, to own property, to hold your own opinions, to follow your own religion, to receive education and to have the right of fair trial, with the right of petition to the Emperor.

"(10) The first step towards this goal will be the formation of a representative Eritrean assembly. The British Administration, which will continue to conduct the affairs of Eritrea while the plans of which I have told you are being put into effect, will, in consultation with me, organize as early as possible an Eritrean public administration in which Eritreans will serve at all levels.

"(11) *Inhabitants of Eritrea*, the United Nations has set you an example of conciliation and compromise. It is for you now, in that same spirit, to grasp firmly this opportunity and, setting aside your personal views and differences to join together in the single purpose of serving your country during this momentous period, when the foundations are to be laid for an Eritrean Administration in federation with Ethiopia.

"(12) In conclusion, I can warmly assure you that I shall not spare myself in labouring to bring about the successful conclusion of the responsible task laid on me by the United Nations. I am here as your friend to help you, and my door will always be open to you. I appeal to you all to assist me and the British Administration by exercising restraint, peacefulness, loyalty and brotherly love, so that the interests of you all, of your country and of Ethiopia may be served, and the wishes of the United Nations fulfilled."

Section 3. Initial visits of the Commission to various parts of Eritrea

15. The Commissioner, shortly after his arrival in Eritrea on 9 February, 1951, embarked upon a series of personal visits to various towns and villages in the territory. The visits extended over a period of eleven weeks, from 28 February to 12 May 1951, inclusive.

16. The purpose of such visits was twofold. In the first place they were designed to give the Commissioner a first-hand impression of the inhabitants, their way of life, the character of the country and its agricultural and other resources, while at the same time, the Commis-

sioner would learn something of the problems of the inhabitants, their hopes and their aspirations. In the second place, the visits would give the inhabitants an opportunity to meet the Commissioner and express their views concerning the plan for Federation as well as permit the Commissioner to explain in some detail the background of the General Assembly's recommendation for federation, the nature of his task and the future status of Eritrea federated with Ethiopia under the sovereignty of the Ethiopian Crown.

17. With the assistance of the British Administration, the Commissioner, accompanied by members of his staff, visited almost all the principal centres of population as well as numerous towns and villages. 2/ He talked with district and tribal chiefs, village elders, religious and political personalities, peasants, artisans, and representatives of minority groups. He visited agricultural concessions, mining properties, factories, schools, hospitals and public works, and was made acquainted with the administrative, legislative and judicial machinery of government. He also visited the port of Assab, approximately two hours by air from Asmara.

18. All political groups and indeed, all sections of the population with which the Commissioner came into contact, voiced their approval and acceptance of the General Assembly's resolution of 2 December 1950, 3/ and the Commissioner was given assurances of their support in the discharge of his responsibilities. In turn, he urged them to work together in a spirit of harmony and co-operation so that the terms of the General Assembly's resolution would be carried out during the transition period with a minimum of friction.

19. In spite of the acceptance of the idea of federation, however, the Commissioner had an impression of pessimism among the population, which he ascribed to the lack of security in the territory. He also had the feeling that a number of people did not fully believe in the federal solution or in the possibility of its being carried through. On all possible occasions, therefore, he attempted to instill a spirit of optimism and self-confidence into the population.

...

Chapter III
Developments in Eritrea

Section 1. Security: The shifta problem

150. The problem of organized banditry and terrorism carried out by *shifta* in Eritrea on a wide scale until very recently was one which the Administration had the greatest difficulty in meeting.

151. During recent years, *shifta* activity progressively increased in scope and intensity to such an extent that lives and property in unguarded areas became endangered and the economic life of the country suffered in consequence. *Shifta* activity took the form of terrorism and banditry, the latter directed against Europeans as well as against the indigenous inhabitants. It was also introduced into communal warfare and inter-tribal raids.

The general security situation

152. Opinion was widely shared that final agreement on the plan for federation would result in the restoration of more normal conditions and thereby reduce, if not eliminate entirely, the *shifta* menace. Unfortunately, this expectation was not realized during the first part of 1951. Apart from communal and tribunal disputes in which the *shifta* appeared to have taken an active part, organized banditry and terrorism against peaceful elements of the population perpetrated by *shifta* gangs increased in intensity and over a wide area of the country. *Shifta* activity took the form of armed hold-ups of trains, buses and individuals, the theft and destruction of cattle and other property, raids on concessions and attacks on villages, police posts and motor convoys, resulting in the killing and wounding of a considerable number of innocent civilians, police and military personnel. Free movement outside Asmara and other towns was consequently restricted by the authorities and normal economic and social intercourse severely curtailed.

Action by the United Nations Commissioner

153. Since his arrival in Eritrea, the United Nations Commissioner has been deeply concerned with the problem. While realizing that under the terms of the United Nations resolution he had no direct responsibility for security in the country, he felt entitled, nevertheless, to take cognizance of the situation. In his initial visits to various parts of Eritrea, he had urged all sections of the population to work toward a common goal in a spirit of understanding and co-operation and to assist the British Administration and himself wholeheartedly in carrying out their respective tasks. In that connexion, he deplored *shifta* terrorism and expressed his earnest desire to see security re-established throughout the country in order that plans for federation could be carried out unimpeded by strife and bloodshed.

154. On 31 March 1951, the Commissioner addressed a communication to the Chief Administrator, in which he declared his preoccupation with the problem and offered the moral weight of the United Nations in dealing with what he considered to be a grave emergency. He believed that the activities of *shifta* were having a

---

2/ A schedule of visits is contained in Annex 1 [not reproduced here].
3/ A/AC.44/R.2, R.3, R.4, R.5, R.8, R.9, R.14.

detrimental effect on public opinion at a time when it was important to ensure a feeling of security and confidence among the inhabitants in order to implement properly the provisions of the United Nations resolution of 2 December 1950. He agreed that one approach to the problem would be the institution of an amnesty programme combined with a vigorous policy of carrying out sentences against *shifta*. 4/

155. At a press conference held in Asmara on 4 April 1951, the Commissioner condemned the activities of *shifta* against lives and property in Eritrea and reiterated the views which he had communicated to the Chief Administrator in his letter of 31 March 1951. 5/ The Commissioner also became deeply interested in the methods pursued by the British Administration in combating *shifta* terrorism and on two occasions (19-20 April 1951), on an invitation from the Administration, the Commissioner, accompanied by the Special Advisor to the Chief Administrator, journeyed to a number of remote localities in small observation planes in order to inspect police field force posts and discuss the situation with the officers in charge.

156. In spite of the Administration's earnest efforts to combat banditry and terrorism, the situation in the view of the Commissioner showed no appreciable improvement during the ensuing month. Consequently, on the eve of inaugurating consultations with the inhabitants concerning the preparation of a draft of the Eritrean constitution, on 1 May 1951, he announced that he felt compelled to postpone consultations because of the condition of insecurity which continued to exist throughout the territory. In making this announcement he voiced the following views:

"I do not believe it advisable, from the psychological point of view, to begin these consultations at a time when the population, which desires peace and security above all else, is in danger. Furthermore, I do not think it proper that I should travel about the country, flying the flag of the United Nations, over roads stained with the blood of people attacked by the terrorists. While I know there are cases where the United Nations flag has had to be flown over roads stained with blood, it has been as a symbol of the United Nations stand against aggression and in the protection of human rights. Finally, my conscience will not allow me to travel at present throughout the territory with an armed escort, while the inhabitants whom I desire to meet will run the risk of ambushes and attacks from *shifta* when coming to meet me.

"I want you to know that this decision does not in any way constitute a cessation but only a postponement of the consultations with the inhabitants; the staff of the United Nations will continue with the complicated task of the preparatory work. I may, however, in the meantime, consult members of the population who will not incur any risks by having to travel long distances for this purpose.

"I have the profound hope that this delay in my work will only be of short duration, and that soon the situation will have improved sufficiently to permit me to meet the inhabitants of Eritrea in an atmosphere of optimism and security; such improvement will be the harbinger of a happy future for this country. 6/

157. In a letter dated 21 May 1951, addressed to the Commissioner, the Chief Administrator made the following observations concerning the Commissioner's statement of 1 May 1951:

"On my return to Eritrea my attention has been drawn to your statement to the press on 1st May last regarding the effect of banditry on the populace.

"I appreciate that your motive, as you explained in a subsequent speech, was to make a moral protest against the prevailing lawlessness in Eritrea. But your statement might, I suggest, give a reader, and particularly a reader outside Eritrea, the impression that the lives and property of the population at large are endangered and that the people you wish to consult in accordance with the United Nations resolution are threatened with intimidation by violence for political reasons.

"It is regrettably true that banditry has continued in spite of the United Nations resolution of December 1950 but it is generally considered to have lost the political complexion formerly attributed to it. On the contrary, the political parties which were formerly in bitter opposition presented an agreed and joint address at your recent meetings in Asmara.

"The evidence available to the British Administration does not lead me to believe that persons you have consulted have been subject to intimidation nor that those you may wish to meet are endangered for political reasons. In the three months which have elapsed since the United Nations Commissioner arrived in Eritrea, two persons have lost their lives while travelling on the main roads. The remaining fatal civilian casualties, some sixty in number, occurred in tribal and communal affrays and acts of

---
4/ The full text of the communication is contained in Annex 10.
5/ A/AC.44/R.7.
6/ Annex 11.

armed brigandage. The highway robberies which have occurred were indiscriminate acts for reasons of gain and had no apparent political complexion.

"I do not wish to suggest that this letter should be communicated to the press or otherwise published but I should be grateful if you would give it the same distribution in official circles as was given to your statement. Its contents are not intended to influence your own conclusions but only to record the opinion of the British Administration in pursuance of the full, frank and close consultations which we mutually maintain in all aspects of our joint task." 7/

158. The Commissioner, in a communication dated 24 May 1951, addressed to the Chief Administrator, replied in the following terms:

"I have the honour to acknowledge the receipt of your letter of 21 May 1951, concerning my statement to the Press on 1st May 1951, regarding the effect of banditry on the population of Eritrea.

"While I am still concerned about the gravity of the problems of banditry and public security in this country, I have taken note of the optimistic picture which you have presented in your letter:

"I am particularly pleased to have received your Excellency's communication on this important subject at a moment when His Britannic Majesty's Government has approved a measure which I am sure will contribute to the pacification of this country, and in whose execution I am prepared to assist to the extent of my abilities.

"I am happy to inform you that, in accordance with the wish expressed in your letter, I am making the necessary arrangements so that it may have the same distribution in official circles as was given to my statement, in order that the opinion of the British Administration may be placed on record." 8/

159. By letter of 26 July 1951, the Chief Administrator replied to the Commissioner as follows:

"I have refrained until now from acknowledging the receipt of your letter of the 24th May, regarding the effect of banditry on the population of Eritrea, because I wished, before doing so, to be in a position to gauge the effect of the measures the British Administration has been taking to suppress banditry since your letter was written. I am glad to say that they have met with considerable success.

"With respect, I would suggest to Your Excellency that I drew no optimistic picture of banditry or public security in my letter of 21st May 1951. The letter simply explained that, in my view, the persons whom you had consulted in Eritrea had not been subjected to political intimidation from bandits, and that those whom you wished to meet were not in danger of politically inspired attacks by bandits because they were coming to meet you for your consultations. I felt it necessary to do this because your public statement on the 1st May might give the impression that such political intimidation was rife."

160. By letter of September 1951, the Commissioner informed the Chief Administrator that in his statement of May 1951 announcing the postponement of consultations with the inhabitants, he had not intended to imply that persons who came to consult him were in danger for political reasons. His main concern was that conditions of insecurity in the territory had led to pessimism and fear, and therefore he had considered it inadvisable to initiate consultations in such an atmosphere as prevailed at that time.

Measures taken by the British Administration to combat shifta *activity: proclamation of a general amnesty and other security measures*

161. The British Administration, meanwhile, had had under consideration for some time a plan for granting a general amnesty to all *shifta* in respect of their past lawless activities, linked with vigorous measures to be taken against *shifta* who failed to surrender or who committed offences following the proclamation of a general amnesty. Such a plan for combating *shifta* activity was favoured by important groups among the inhabitants. Furthermore, it was held to be in keeping with local traditions and historical precedents, although a conditional amnesty in the past, while inducing large numbers to surrender, had not brought about the elimination of *shifta* bands.

162. On 19 June 1951, the Chief Administrator proclaimed a General Amnesty which carried the following provisions:

"GENERAL ASSEMBLY

"In view of the United Nations resolution concerning the Federation of Ethiopia and Eritrea and in view of the necessity for creating an atmosphere of peace and tranquillity in which to give effect to this resolution, His Majesty's Government have approved the granting of a General Amnesty in the following terms to all *shiftas* in respect of their past activities as *shiftas*.

7/ Annex 12.
8/ Annex 12.

"No action will be taken by the police or by the courts against any *shifta* in respect of his past activities as a *shifta* if he presents himself to a competent official of the Administration within one month after the date of this Notice and had not committed any offence after the terms of this Amnesty have received general publicity. The *shiftas* who so present themselves to the authorities will be required to hand over their arms.

"The most rigorous action will be taken against *shiftas* who do not avail themselves of this Amnesty, or who commit offences after this Notice has received general publicity.

"If this offer of Amnesty is successful in bringing about a cessation of *shifta* activities, a Commission will be set up to advise the Chief Administration regarding the review of sentences on *shiftas* now in prison which have been imposed on them in respect of offences committed by them as *shiftas*, and the extension to such *shiftas* of the benefits of this Amnesty.

"The Administration expects those who take advantage of this General Amnesty to return to their families and resume their normal peaceful occupations. Should circumstances make this impossible in all cases temporary provision will be made for their subsistence by public works and other means.

"Disputes and feuds which have been created during the period of *shifta* activities will be settled, as far as possible, by customary methods of conciliation and compensation.

"Detailed instructions to give effect to the above will be issued to officers of the Administration and by other means." 9/

163. This proclamation was accompanied by a "Notice to the Public" which stated that "His Excellency the Chief Administrator in proclaiming the general amnesty published to-day wishes it to be known that H.M.G. are desirous of bringing peace to Eritrea by traditional methods of clemency and pardon. He has been guided in recommending this course by the advice he has received from almost every organ of public opinion in the country and all sections of the people, as well as the expressed desire of His Imperial Majesty the Emperor of Ethiopia that peace should be restored to Eritrea by traditional and merciful means. The opposite course would entail further hardship to the guilty and innocent alike. He therefore now appeals to the people of Eritrea to extend the same measure of forgiveness for the injuries they have suffered from those to whom the Administration is now offering clemency. He calls upon all the people, including the injured and those who have caused their injuries, to co-operate with the Administration in making the amnesty offered by H.M.G. the means of restoring peace. He also expects the people of Eritrea to co-operate with the Administration for the prevention of further crimes by refusing help of any kind to those who remain *shifta* and for helping the Administration to capture those who commit criminal acts hereafter." 10/

164. In order to deal more effectively with the security situation in Eritrea and to implement that section of the General Amnesty proclamation providing for rigorous action against *shifta* who failed to surrender or who committed offences following the proclamation announcement, the Chief Administrator, in a proclamation issued a few days before the General Amnesty, i.e. on 14 June 1951, established special courts to deal with armed bands or persons who sheltered or assisted armed bands. In addition, the proclamation provided for communal responsibility according to which collective fines could be imposed on a community if there was reason to believe that offences had been committed within the community area. Community bonds could also be demanded in order to secure public order. 11/ A number of *shifta*, who subsequently committed offences employing threats of armed force, were tried and convicted under the provisions of the proclamation and executed by hanging.

Steps taken by the Commissioner following the proclamation of a General Amnesty

165. Simultaneously with the proclamation of a General Amnesty by the British Administration, the United Nations Commissioner made the following announcement:

"I have been informed by the Chief Administrator that His Britannic Majesty's Government has approved the granting of a general amnesty to all *shifta*, irrespective of their past activities. As I have already stated publicly on many occasions, in my capacity of United Nations Commissioner in Eritrea, I have been, and am, deeply concerned about the *shifta* outrages on human life and property and *shifta* terrorism which has seriously affected the economic activities of Eritrea and divided its people amongst themselves, causing strife and bloodshed between them at a time when, under the auspices of the United Nations, a dramatic evolution in Eritrean history is in the course of preparation. As I have said before, the General Assembly resolution on the future of Eritrea, which is destined to conciliate the

---

9/ Annex 13.
10/ Ibid.
11/ The full text of proclamation No. 104 is contained in A/AC.44/L.1.

aspirations of the people of Eritrea and to provide peace and progress in this part of Africa must, before it can be realized, have the solid support of all Eritreans, united in faith, in the achievement of a common destiny.

"I have made every effort to understand the genesis of the problem and to acquaint myself with the thoughts of the leaders of Eritrean public opinion and I am in complete agreement with His Britannic Majesty's Government in affirming that almost all organs of public opinion and almost all sections of the population are united in recommending the re-establishment of peace in Eritrea through traditional methods of clemency and mercy. Nevertheless, the adoption of these methods pre-supposes unanimity and solidarity in reaching these high objectives, and must not in any event be allowed to lead to anarchy and disturbances.

"I consider that the duty given to me by the General Assembly of the United Nations—that of preparing a constitution and assisting and advising in its consideration—is not merely an academic exercise but a matter of political importance. This political mission must have the backing of the people of Eritrea, acting together in the interests of liberty and order, free from fear, and protected by principles established by a civilized world for the preservation of human life and property. In this spirit and to this end, I, the United Nations Commissioner in Eritrea, believe it my duty strongly to support the measures of clemency and mercy granted by His Britannic Majesty's Government for the purpose of restoring an atmosphere of peace and tranquillity in which to give effect to the resolution of the United Nations concerning the federation of Eritrea and Ethiopia.

"I hope that in such an atmosphere it will be possible to lay the foundations on which the Eritrean constitution must be based, and I sincerely hope, therefore, that the objectives behind these constructive measures will be fully realized. To this end I offer the moral weight of the United Nations and invoke the principles of the Charter in making a strong appeal to *shifta* to take advantage of the general amnesty and to become loyal and peaceful citizens of their country, playing their part and shouldering responsibility in the development of their common future. I also call upon the inhabitants of Eritrea to cooperate with the British Administration in putting into effect this great enterprise which I hope will open up a new era of peace in Eritrea." 12/

166. At a conference held in Asmara on 29 June 1951 at which prominent personalities and members of the Press were present, the Commissioner announced his intention to proceed with his plan for consulting the inhabitants of Eritrea concerning the preparation of a draft of the Eritrean constitution.

Results of the General Amnesty and the present security situation

167. On 21 July 1951, the British Administration issued the following communication:

"On 19th June 1951, the Chief Administrator of Eritrea published a notice approving an amnesty to all bandits who surrendered with their arms within a month. At the same time a new public security proclamation was promulgated giving the Chief Administrator greater powers for the repression and prevention of banditry.

"As a result of tribal and inter-communal strife in which armed bandits were participating an area in Eastern Eritrea was put under military authority on 23 June. Police action against recalcitrant bandits was taken throughout the country.

"During the period of the amnesty 1,086 13/ bandits have surrendered and 93 arrests were made under the public security proclamation. Measures have also been taken by the British Administration to assist the return of the surrendered bandits to normal life and to settle outstanding tribal and individual feuds. Measures are being taken for the apprehension of bandits who have not surrendered and the prevention of banditry in the future."

168. In addition to those *shifta* who surrendered to the British Administration, many crossed the border in order to surrender to the Ethiopian authorities in accordance with an arrangement between the two administrations. The majority of known *shifta* leaders have surrendered, either to the British Administration or to the Ethiopian authorities, and the number at present at large is considered to be negligible.

169. The success of the general amnesty programme and the new security measures put into effect may be gauged by the fact that the movement of all road transport throughout Eritrea, with two minor exceptions, 14/ was finally decontrolled as of 3 August 1951, and rail transport now proceeds unescorted by police.

12/ A/AC.44/L.1.
13/ The final number of surrenders, including many allowed after 19 July 1951, amounted to 1,330.
14/ From Adi Quala to the Ethiopian border, a distance of 18 miles, and from Senafe to the Ethiopian border, a distance of 16 miles.

The number of *shifta* incidents since the termination of the period of amnesty have been insignificant, consisting principally of cattle thefts and individual hold-ups involving the stealing of small amounts of money and clothing. Active communal and tribal disputes have also diminished in number and in importance.

170. However, since the beginning of October there has been some evidence of new *shifta* activity. As a result the Chief Administrator, on 11 October 1951, issued the following warning to all heads of Districts, Tribes and Villages:

> "During the past month there has been peace in Eritrea to an extent that the country has not known for a long time. Ninety-nine persons out of every hundred in the country are thankful for this. But the hundredth man still thinks that he can make an easy living by being a *shifta* and committing crimes of violence and intimidation. Recently there have been signs that *shifta* may again become active and I wish it to be known that the strong measures taken in the past against the *shifta* and those who help them will continue. If necessary they will be made stronger still.
>
> "*Shifta* cannot operate in Eritrea without the knowledge and help of the people. Many people have contributed to the restoring of security by resisting the *shifta* and helping the forces of law and order. I again call on all law-abiding people to prevent the *shifta* from causing further trouble. It is entirely to their advantage that they should do so because otherwise they may suffer more from the security measures of the Administration than from the *shifta*.
>
> "The *shifta* now in action are few in number: are the people of Eritrea going to allow themselves to be intimidated by them?"

171. This notice was widely distributed in leaflet form throughout the territory and also published in the local Press.

172. Despite these few recent instances of *shifta* activity which, it is hoped, will be successfully checked, the measures taken by the British Administration to combat *shifta* terrorism have brought about the desired results, namely, the restoration of normal conditions throughout the greater part of the territory, wherein security of life and property are now reasonably well assured. The continued maintenance of security depends largely upon the effectiveness of punitive measures for combating banditry and terrorism, upon the effectiveness of rehabilitation schemes for returning *shifta* to a normal mode of life, and upon the continued co-operation of the inhabitants with the authorities to the extent that *shifta* are given no form of assistance.

Section 2. The political situation

Political trends up to 2 December 1950

173. Prior to the adoption of the General Assembly's resolution of 2 December 1950 the groupings and major policies of the political parties in Eritrea were briefly as follows:

174. The Unionist Party, concentrated predominantly in the highlands, advocated the unconditional union of Eritrea with Ethiopia. The Liberal Unionist Party and the Independent Eritrea United to Ethiopia Party, both having a relatively small following, supported conditional union with Ethiopia, while the Independent Moslem League, with headquarters in Massawa, also supported union with Ethiopia under conditions designed to protect Moslem interests. The Independent Moslem League derived its chief support from among the Moslems of the Red Sea and Hamasien.

175. The independent Bloc was formed in 1949 by coalition of the Moslem League in Eritrea, the Liberal Progressive Party, the Nationalist Party of Massawa, the New Eritrea Party, the Italo-Eritrean Association and the Veterans Association. The Bloc was joined later by two new organizations, the Independent Eritrea Party and the Intellectual Association of Eritreans. All of these parties, united as a bloc, demanded immediate independence for Eritrea.

176. Finally, the Moslem League of the Western Province advocated a separate solution for the Western Province, namely, a ten-year trusteeship under British Administration followed by independence, leaving the rest of the territory to decide its future for itself. Qualified support was belatedly received from the Unionist and allied parties, which signified that if the majority of the inhabitants of the Western Province opposed union with Ethiopia, they would agree to a separate solution for the Western Province, provided that the rest of the territory were united with Ethiopia.

The situation subsequent to 2 December 1950

177. It is unnecessary in this brief review of the political situation to enter into details regarding the views of the political parties on constitutional questions, since these are covered fully in the section devoted to consultations with the inhabitants (chapter II, section 6(d)). It will be sufficient to refer to the main political developments which have taken place up to the time of completion of this report.

178. Pursuant to adoption of the General Assembly's resolution of 2 December 1950 and to the appointment of the United Nations Commissioner in Eritrea, a "Peace Congress" was held in Asmara on 31 December

1950, on which occasion a communiqué was jointly issued by all Eritrean political parties as follows:

"All political parties of Eritrea, in view of the necessity to bring about general pacification, in the light of what has been decided on the future political status of Eritrea, have decided:

"(1) To respect in all its parts the decision to federate Eritrea with Ethiopia in conformity with the principles, the intentions and the recommendations approved by the General Assembly, and its practical implementations;

"(2) To give the best possible co-operation to the Commissioner of the United Nations with a view to drafting the constitution of Eritrea;

"(3) To facilitate the task of the British Administration with regard to the maintenance of public order and to co-operate with it to this end;

"(4) To pledge themselves that all united forces of the Eritreans will be mobilised to ensure, at the earliest possible date, the progress and prosperity of the Eritrean people."

179. Further, it was announced on 16 February 1951 15/ that a General Assembly of the "Patriotic Association, Union of Eritrea with Ethiopia" (the Unionist Party) held at Asmara on 14 February, had unanimously approved a motion expressing *inter alia* the Party's "firm intention" "fully to implement the decision of the General Assembly" and to this end to work in a spirit of harmony and goodwill with the British Administration and the United Nations Commissioner.

180. In a letter dated 17 February 1951, addressed to the United Nations Commissioner and published in "Il Quotidiano Eritrea" on 22 February 1951, it was pointed out that the "Eritrean Bloc for Independence", at a meeting of the component parties held at Decamere on 28 December 1950, had decided *inter alia* "to change its name to the 'Eritrean Democratic Front' in order to adapt it to the new situation", to respect and implement the decision to federate Eritrea with Ethiopia in conformity with the principles, intentions and recommendations approved by the General Assembly of the United Nations, if all the other interested parties did the same, and to collaborate fully with the Commissioner and the British Administration.

181. The Moslem League of the Western Province was also prepared to respect the plan for federation, although it subsequently advocated the regional division of Eritrea into two areas, one Christian and the other Moslem.

182. On being invited to formal consultations at the Palace, Asmara, on 7 July 1951, the Unionist Party, by letter dated 7 July 1951, suggested that "to avoid...polemics", the Commissioner should "consult the political parties and the leaders of the political parties locally, through their representatives and spokesmen, by going, as...you did in the past, to the various districts of Eritrea, where the political groups will make known their views." It was further stated that once the consultations with the people were finished, the "heads and leaders" of the Unionist Party would make known their views on all problems.

183. The United Nations Commissioner, by letter dated 13 July 1951, accepted the procedure suggested so far as the Unionist Party was concerned.

184. A schism within the ranks of the Unionist Party, Massawa branch, took place in July and dissidents claiming to represent the Unionist Party in Massawa visited the Commissioner in Asmara, on 21 July 1951 16/ in order to express their views on constitutional issues, views which differed substantially from those expressed by Unionist Party representatives elsewhere.

185. By letter of 19 July 1951, the President of the Red Sea Province branch of the Unionist Party in Massawa informed the Commissioner that the dissident group referred to above represented no-one but themselves.

186. In April 1951 the National Party of Massawa, up to that time a member of the Eritrean Democratic Front, announced that it no longer associated itself with the Front, and shortly thereafter entered into a working partnership with the Independent Moslem League and the Moslem League of the Western Province.

187. These three parties, during the Commissioner's formal consultations at Asmara with the political parties, submitted identical documents asking for the establishment of two separate administrations in Eritrea, respectively based on the predominantly Moslem-(Western and Eastern lowlands)-and Coptic-(the Highlands) areas.

188. However, on being confronted with the "cantonisation" plan 17/ by the Moslem League of the Western Province, the Commissioner, at the 10th meeting, stated that he did not feel able to take it seriously into consideration since the United Nations resolution was based on the fact that Eritrea would be an autonomous unit and the proposal appeared, therefore, to be against the spirit of the resolution. 18/

15/ "Il Quotidiano Eritrea", Asmara, 16 February 1951
16/ A/AC.44/R.31
17/ A/AC.44/R.22
18/ A/AC.44/SR.10, pp.2 and 3

189. Following the Commissioner's disagreement with this scheme, the Moslem parties appeared to change their position. As a result, the Moslem League of the Western Province, although still advocating two separate Assemblies for the Christians and Moslems, concentrated on such constitutional issues as the Emperor's representative, the Eritrean flag and Eritrea's languages. Since these topics assumed religious or symbolic significance and involved no subject on which supporters of the country's unity differed, a new political alignment became noticeable during the Commissioner's formal consultations in the Western Province.

190. In contrast with past political differences between the Eritrean Democratic Front end and, in particular, the Moslem League on the one hand and the Moslem League of the Western Province on the other, virtual identity of respective views on the main constitutional issues brought about outward signs of mutual agreement.

191. At the 48th meeting, held at Keren, a statement was handed to the Commissioner which, it was pointed out, "contained the views of the Eritrean Democratic Front, the Moslem League in Eritrea, and the Moslem League of the Western Province and which showed that they were not divided".19/

192. Again at the same meeting, a representative stressed the identity of the tenets of the Moslem League of the Western Province with the Eritrean Democratic Front's views on language, the flag and the Emperor's representative. 20/ While the analysis of replies given during the consultations will be found in another section, it should be noted that such claims as Friday observance or the assignment of Moslem officials to predominantly Moslem areas, lent themselves to a manifestation of Moslem solidarity.

193. It is to be noted, however, that wide differences on constitutional issues continue to be evident between the Unionist and allied parties on the one hand and the predominantly Moslem parties on the other. At this stage the situation belies the expressions of unity and faithful adherence to the provisions of the resolution made at the "Peace Congress" in Asmara on 31 December 1950 and on subsequent occasions before the Commissioner.

194. The Commissioner has viewed this development with considerable misgiving. At a press conference held at the Palace, Asmara, on 17 October 1951, the Commissioner expressed himself in the following terms:

"Although various political parties appeared to be determined to maintain their former differences of view and have not shown the expected spirit of conciliation, the inhabitants whom the Commissioner met during the course of his consultations displayed a spirit of brotherhood and tolerance and helped to establish his great faith and hope in the future destiny of the country. It is in this spirit that the Commissioner has found a renewed stimulus which enables him to carry on his work with a feeling of optimism, of faith in the resolution of the United Nations, and with confidence in the future of Eritrea. 21/

"Confident that existing differences offer no serious basis of disagreement which cannot be settled by conciliation and collaboration, I do not consider it necessary to ask the General Assembly of the United Nations to re-examine the question of Eritrea. It is, however, my intention to present a progress report for circulation among the Member nations of the United Nations at the coming meeting of the Assembly to be held in Paris."

(*Signed*) Eduardo ANZE MATIENZO
United Nations Commissioner in Eritrea

Supplementary paragraphs to the progress report

195. Subsequent to the completion on 24 October 1951 of the progress report of the United Nations Commissioner in Eritrea, the Commissioner held in Asmara one formal meeting on 31 October 1951 with the Administering Authority, represented by the Chief Administrator, Eritrea and the Special Adviser, and two formal meetings on 25 October and 6 November 1951 respectively, with the Government of Ethiopia, represented by the Vice Minister of Foreign Affairs, His Excellency Ato Zaude Gabre Heywot, on the subject of the draft Eritrean constitution.

Consultation with the Administering Authority

196. On 31 October 1951, the Commissioner had a formal meeting 22/ with the Administering Authority when he gave the Chief Administrator and the Special Adviser an account of his impressions of the consultations which he had recently concluded with the inhabitants of Eritrea on the subject of the draft constitution and discussed ways of resolving the controversies which had arisen over such questions as the flag, the official languages and the representatives of the Emperor.

197. He also briefly outlined provisional ideas for the establishment of a number of organs or councils to deal with certain specific matters, ideas which would be further explored with the group of legal experts in Geneva. The Chief Administrator was in general agreement

---

19/ A/AC.44/SR.48, p.3
20/ A/AC.44/SR.48, p.4
21/ Full text in Annex 7 (b) [not reproduced here].
22/ A/AC.44/SR 71.

with the Commissioner's plans but stated that he would like to give further thought to the matters raised.

Consultations with the Government of Ethiopia

198. At a meeting 23/ on 25 October 1951 with the Vice Minister of Foreign Affairs, Mr. Zaude Gabre Heywot, the Commissioner, with the purpose of making his position on certain controversial matters clear to the Government of Ethiopia, presented his point of view on the legal, political and psychological aspects of the General Assembly's resolution. The Commissioner stressed the fact that in the implementation of the resolution, he intended to abide by the letter and spirit of its provisions, taking into account, however, the realities of the problem as well as the interests and responsibilities of the Government of His Imperial Majesty.

199. At a meeting 24/ with the Commissioner on 6 November 1951, Mr. Zaude Gabre Heywot, Ethiopian Vice Minister of Foreign Affairs, replied to some of the points raised by the Commissioner in his expose of 25 October 1951. The Vice Minister of Foreign Affairs again re-affirmed the position of the Government of Ethiopia concerning the necessity for a strong link between the Ethiopian Crown and the Eritrean executive and expressed the readiness of the Government of Ethiopia to co-operate fully at all times with the Commissioner in the execution of his task.

[Note: Annexes 1-13 and Addendum A/1959/Add.1 of 20 December 1951, concerning further consultations and statements of the United Nations Commissioner, are not reproduced here.]

23/ A/AC.44/SR 70.
24/ A/AC.44/SR 72.

Document 8

General Assembly resolution on economic and financial provisions relating to Eritrea

A/RES/530 (VI), 29 January 1952

Whereas, in accordance with the provisions of article 23 and paragraph 3 of annex XI of the Treaty of Peace with Italy,1/ the question of the disposal of the former Italian colonies was submitted on 15 September 1948 to the General Assembly by the Governments of France, the Union of Soviet Socialist Republics, the United Kingdom of Great Britain and Northern Ireland and the United States of America,

Whereas, by virtue of the above-mentioned provisions, the four Powers have agreed to accept the recommendation of the General Assembly and to take appropriate measures for giving effect to it,

Whereas the General Assembly, by resolution 390 A (V) of 2 December 1950, recommended that Eritrea be constituted an autonomous unit federated with Ethiopia under the sovereignty of the Ethiopian Crown not later than 15 September 1952, and laid down the necessary provisions for effecting the federation of Eritrea with Ethiopia, and left for settlement by the United Nations only the problem referred to in paragraph 19 of annex XIV of the Treaty of Peace with Italy, while taking into account, *inter alia*, the importance of assuring the continuing collaboration of the foreign communities in the economic development of Eritrea,

Whereas paragraph 19 of annex XIV of the Treaty of Peace with Italy, which contains the economic and financial provisions relating to ceded territories, states that "The provisions of this Annex shall not apply to the former Italian Colonies. The economic and financial provisions to be applied therein will form part of the arrangements for the final disposal of these territories pursuant to article 23 of the present Treaty",

Whereas it is desirable that the economic and financial provisions relating to Eritrea should be determined before Eritrea is constituted an autonomous unit federated with Ethiopia under the sovereignty of the Ethiopian Crown in order that they may be applied as soon as possible,

The General Assembly
Approves the following articles:

Article I

1. Subject to the provisions of paragraphs 4 and 5 of this article Eritrea 2/ shall receive, without payment, the movable and immovable property located in Eritrea

1/ See *Treaty Series. Treaties and international agreements registered or filed and recorded with the Secretariat of the United Nations*, volume 49, 1950 I, No. 747.

2/ The term "Eritrea" as used in the present resolution is to be interpreted in conformity with paragraph 3 of resolution 390 (V) where the jurisdiction and responsibilities of the Federal Government and the Eritrean Government are set out.

owned by the Italian State, either in its own name or in the name of the Italian administration in Eritrea, and such property shall be transferred to Eritrea not later than the effective date of the final transfer of power from the Administering Power to the appropriate authorities referred to in paragraph 14 of resolution 390 (V) of the General Assembly of the United Nations.

2. The property referred to in paragraph 1 shall be taken as comprising:

(a) The public property of the State (*demanio publico*);

(b) The inalienable property of the State (*patrimonio indisponibile*);

(c) The property of the Fascist Party and its organizations as listed in article 10 of the Italian Royal Decree No. 513 of 28 April 1938;

(d) The alienable property of the State (*patrimonio disponibile*);

(e) The property belonging to the autonomous agencies (*aziende autonome*) of the State which are:

Ferrovie dell 'Eritrea
Azienda Speciale Approvigionamenti
Azienda Miniere Africa Orientale (AMAO)
Azienda Autonoma Strade Statali (AASS);

(f) The rights of the Italian State in the form of shares and similar rights in the capital of institutions, companies and associations of a public character which have their *siège social* in Eritrea. Where the operations of such institutions, companies and associations extend to Italy or to countries other than Eritrea, Eritrea shall receive only those rights of the Italian State or the Italian administration of Eritrea which appertain to the operations in Eritrea. In cases where the Italian State or the Italian administration of Eritrea exercised only managerial control over such institutions, companies and associations, Eritrea shall have no claim to any rights in those institutions, companies and associations.

3. Properties, institutions, companies and associations referred to in paragraph 2 of this article shall be transferred as they stand at the date of transfer and Eritrea will take over all commitments and liabilities outstanding at that date in connexion with those concerns.

4. Italy shall retain the ownership of the following property listed in paragraph 2 of this article, that is to say:

(a) The immovable property necessary for the functioning of Italian government representation in Eritrea; 3/

(b) The immovable and movable property as at the date of the present resolution used for the functioning of the schools and hospitals of the Italian community in Eritrea.

5. The following property listed in paragraph 2 of this article, that is to say, buildings used for worship (including the land on which they are built and their appurtenances) shall be transferred by Italy to the religious communities concerned.

6. Italian cemeteries, monuments and ossuaries in Eritrea shall be respected. Arrangements for their preservation and maintenance shall be made between Italy and, after Eritrea becomes an autonomous unit federated with Ethiopia, the appropriate authority under the Federal Act.

7. Subject to the provisions of paragraphs 4, 5 and 6 of this article, nothing in paragraph 1 of this article shall be taken as in any way restricting the right of the Administering Power to make, during the period of its administration, such dispositions of property referred to in paragraph 2 of this article, whether limited to that period or otherwise, as may be required by law or may be appropriate for the good government of the territory, or may be necessary for the implementation of the present resolution.

Article II

1. Subject to the provisions of this article, the Administering Power shall continue to have the custody of all public archives and documents located in Eritrea which relate to administrative or technical matters in Eritrea or to property which is to be transferred by Italy under article I of the present resolution or are otherwise required in connexion with the administration of the territory.

2. Italy shall hand over to the Administering Power, on request, the originals or copies of any such public archives or documents located in Italy.

3. The Administering Power shall hand over to Italy, on request, the originals or copies of any such public archives or documents located in Eritrea which are of interest to Italy or concern Italian nationals or juridical persons, especially those who or which have transferred or hereafter transfer their residence to Italy.

4. The rights and obligations of the Administering Power under the preceding provisions of this article shall, when Eritrea is constituted an autonomous unit federated with Ethiopia, devolve upon the appropriate authority under the Federal Act to which the Administering Power shall hand over such public archives and documents as have been received from Italy.

5. The handing over of the above-mentioned archives and documents or copies thereof shall be exempt

---

3/ The nature of Italian Government representation remains for settlement between the future Federal Government and the Italian Government in accordance with international law and practice.

from payment of dues and taxes, and the cost of transport thereof shall be borne by the government requesting them.

Article III

The Italian social insurance organizations now operating in Eritrea shall remain wholly responsible for fulfilling all their respective obligations towards insured persons as is provided for under present social insurance legislation, and the present legal rights and obligations of the said organizations shall be respected. These obligations may be extended to include other categories of insured persons by agreement between the appropriate authority under the Federal Act and the said organizations.

Article IV

1. Italy shall continue to be liable for the payment of civil and military pensions or other retirement benefits earned as at the date of coming into force of the Treaty of Peace with Italy and owed by it at that date.

2. The amount of these pensions or retirement benefits shall be determined in accordance with the law which was in force in Eritrea immediately prior to the cessation of Italian administration of the territory and shall be paid directly by Italy to the persons entitled in the currency in which they were earned.

Article V

Eritrea shall be exempt from the payment of any portion of the Italian public debt.

Article VI

Italy shall return to their owners, in the shortest possible time, all ships in its possession or that of its nationals or juridical persons which are proved to have been the property of its former Eritrean subjects or to have been registered in Eritrea, except in cases in which the ships have been acquired in good faith.

Article VII

1. The property, rights and interests of Italian nationals, including Italian juridical persons, in Eritrea shall, provided they have been acquired in accordance with the laws prevailing at the time of acquisition, be respected. They shall not be treated less favourably than the property, rights and interests of other foreign nationals, including foreign juridical persons.

2. Italian nationals in Eritrea who have left or who leave Eritrea to settle elsewhere shall be permitted freely to sell their movable and immovable property, realize and dispose of their assets and, after settlement of any debts and taxes due from them in Eritrea, transfer their movable property and the funds they possess, including the proceeds of the above-mentioned transactions, unless such property or funds were unlawfully acquired. Such transfers of property or funds shall not be subject to any export duty.

The procedure for the transfer from Eritrea of such property or funds and the times within which they may be transferred shall be determined by agreement between the Administering Power, or after Eritrea becomes an autonomous unit federated with Ethiopia the appropriate authority under the Federal Act, on the one hand, and Italy on the other hand. No such agreement shall be restrict the right of transfer provided for in the paragraph above.

3. Companies incorporated under Italian law and having their *siège social* in Italy shall be dealt with under the provisions of paragraph 2 above.

Companies incorporated under Italian law and having their *siège social* in Eritrea and which wish to remove their *siège social* elsewhere shall likewise be dealt with under the provisions of paragraph 2 above, provided that more than 50 per cent of the capital of the company is owned by persons usually resident outside Eritrea and provided also that the greater part of the activity of the company is carried on outside Eritrea.

4. The property, rights and interests in Italy of former Italian nationals belonging to Eritrea and of companies previously incorporated under Italian law and having their *siège social* in Eritrea shall be respected by Italy to the same extent as the property, rights and interests of foreign nationals and of foreign companies generally.

Such persons and companies are authorized to effect the transfer and liquidation of their property, rights and interests under the same conditions as may be established under paragraph 2 above.

5. Debts owed by persons in Italy to persons in Eritrea or by persons in Eritrea to persons in Italy shall not be affected by the transfer of sovereignty. The Administering Power, Italy and, after Eritrea becomes an autonomous unit federated with Ethiopia, the appropriate authority under the Federal Act, shall facilitate the settlement of such obligations. As used in this paragraph the term "persons" includes juridical persons.

Article VIII

1. Property, rights and interests in Eritrea which, as a result of the war, are still subject to measures of seizure, compulsory administration or sequestration, shall be restored to their owners.

2. Nothing in this article shall apply to any compulsory acquisition or requisition by the Administering

Power for public purposes in Eritrea which is valid under the civil law of Eritrea.

Article IX

1. The former Italian nationals belonging to Eritrea shall continue to enjoy all the rights in industrial, literary and artistic property in Italy to which they were entitled under the legislation in force at the time of the coming into force of the Treaty of Peace.

2. Until the relevant international conventions are applicable to Eritrea the rights in industrial, literary and artistic property which existed in Eritrea under Italian law shall remain in force for the period for which they would have remained in force under that law.

Article X

1. In this article:

(a) "Concession" means a grant by the former Italian administration or by the Administering Power or by a municipal authority of the enjoyment in Eritrea of specific rights and assets in exchange for specific obligations undertaken by the concessionaire with regard to the use and improvement of such assets, such grant being made in accordance with the laws, regulations and rules in force in Eritrea at the time of such grant;

(b) "Contract in the nature of a concession" means a lease for a period of years by the former Italian administration or by the Administering Power or by a municipal authority of land in Eritrea by the terms of which lease the tenant undertakes obligations similar to those of a concessionaire in the case of a concession, such lease not being made under any specific law, regulation or rule containing provisions for such leases.

2. Concessions granted during the period of the former Italian administration shall be recognized as valid for all purposes and shall be respected accordingly.

3. Where a concessionaire satisfies the appropriate authorities that a document of title perfecting his concession should have been issued to him but, owing to conditions created by the state of war or to *force majeure*, was not so issued, and that his concession, if it had been perfected by the issue of the document, would not be liable to revocation, the appropriate authorities shall issue a document of title to the concessionaire which shall have the same validity as the document which should have been issued originally.

4. Where the period of lease, in the case of a contract in the nature of a concession granted during the period of the former Italian administration, has expired during the period of administration by the Administering Power and has been renewed on a temporary basis by the Administering Power, or where any lease of such nature has been initially granted by the Administering Power, such Power may, if satisfied that the tenant has fulfilled the obligations undertaken by him and that it is in the interests of the economy of Eritrea so to do, grant to the tenant a concession for such period as is appropriate having regard to the nature of the land in question.

5. A concession or contract in the nature of a concession granted during the period of the former Italian administration shall not be liable to revocation by reason of the failure by the concessionaire or tenant to fulfil any obligation of the concession or contract if the appropriate authorities are satisfied that such failure was due solely to conditions created by the state of war or to *force majeure*.

6. Where a concessionaire or tenant satisfies the appropriate authorities that any document of title evidencing his concession or contract in the nature of a concession has been lost or destroyed and the appropriate authorities are able to ascertain the terms of the document and are satisfied that the concession or contract in the nature of a concession is not liable to revocation, they shall issue to the concessionaire or tenant a new document of title which shall have the same validity as the one which has been lost or destroyed.

Article XI

1. A United Nations Tribunal shall be set up, composed of three persons selected by the Secretary-General for their legal qualifications from the nationals of three different States not directly interested. All or any of such persons may be members of the Tribunal provided for in article X of resolution 388 (V) of the General Assembly of the United Nations. The Tribunal, whose decisions shall be based on law, shall have the two following functions:

(a) It shall give to Italy and the Administering Power, or when Eritrea becomes an autonomous unit federated with Ethiopia the appropriate authority under the Federal Act, upon request by any of those authorities, such instructions as may be required for the purpose of giving effect to the present resolution;

(b) It shall decide all disputes arising between the said authorities concerning the interpretation and application of the present resolution. The Tribunal shall be seized of any such disputes upon the unilateral request of any of those authorities.

2. The Tribunal shall have exclusive competence on matters falling within its functions in accordance with paragraph 1 of this article. In the event of any matter in dispute being referred to the Tribunal, any action pending in civil courts shall be suspended.

3. Italy, the Administering Power and, when Eritrea becomes an autonomous unit federated with

Ethiopia the appropriate authority under the Federal Act, shall supply the Tribunal as soon as possible with all the information and assistance it may need for the performance of its functions.

4. The seat of the Tribunal shall be in Eritrea. The Tribunal shall determine its own procedure. All requests referred to in paragraph 1 of this article shall be presented to the Tribunal not later than 31 December 1953 and the Tribunal shall pronounce its decision on each such request within a delay not exceeding two years from the date of its presentation to the Tribunal. As soon as its decisions have been pronounced on all such requests pursuant to the foregoing, the Tribunal shall terminate. It shall afford to the interested parties an opportunity to present their views, and shall be entitled to request information and evidence which it may require from any authority or person whom it considers to be in a position to furnish it. In the absence of unanimity the Tribunal shall take decisions by a majority vote. Its decisions shall be final and binding.

*366th plenary meeting,
29 January 1952*

Document 9

Final report of the United Nations Commissioner in Eritrea (excerpt)

A/2188, 17 October 1952

I have the honour to transmit herewith the final report on my mission for consideration by the General Assembly at its seventh regular session.

The report is submitted in accordance with paragraph 15 of resolution 390 A (V) of 2 December 1950, 1/ which lays down that the United Nations Commissioner shall make appropriate reports to the General Assembly of the United Nations concerning the discharge of his functions and that when the transfer of authority has been completed, he shall so report to the General Assembly and submit to it the text of the Eritrean Constitution.

This report, which contains a general account of the mission's work, supplements the report submitted to the General Assembly at its sixth regular session in documents A/1959 and A/1959/Add.1. Since the latter report was submitted, the following general developments have taken place.

The main item of the Commissioner's terms of reference under the resolution was the preparation of a draft Constitution to be submitted to a representative assembly of Eritreans chosen by the people.

After discussing the interpretation of the terms of resolution 390 A (V) with a panel of legal consultants, a first draft Constitution was drawn up at Geneva. In a revised form, it was then transmitted to the Administering Authority and to the Government of Ethiopia, as provided in the resolution.

The consultations took the form of veritable negotiations and resulted in the drafting of a text which was acceptable to the parties concerned. That text was submitted to the Eritrean Assembly elected by the people and convened and arranged through the good offices of the Administering Authority in accordance with the provisions of paragraph 11 of the resolution.

Some amendments were made to the draft constitution and the final text as a whole was adopted unanimously by the Eritrean Assembly on 10 July 1952. The Constitution was approved by the Commissioner on 6 August 1952 and ratified by the Emperor on 11 August 1952. It could not enter into force, however, until ratification of the Federal Act, which took place on 11 September 1952 in Addis Ababa.

Thus all the action provided for in the General Assembly resolution with respect to the Constitution has been carried out and the attached report gives a detailed account of all the relevant events; it also contains, in annex, the final text of the Constitution.

The other terms of reference under which the Commissioner was acting, not in these instances personally and in consultation with other authorities, but as an authority consulted by the Administering Authority, are also dealt with in the report.

I should like to say how much I appreciated the consistently co-operative spirit of the Administering Power and Administering Authority and to emphasize the cordial relations which prevailed throughout the consultations with the Ethiopian Government and the parties concerned. I should also like to mention the high quality of the work accomplished by the Assembly and the conciliatory spirit shown by the representatives and by the people. I also wish to thank you most warmly for your co-operation and unstinted assistance and for the competence and hard work of the members of the United Nations Secretariat whom you assigned to help me in the

---
1/ The text of United Nations General Assembly Resolution 390 A (V) is annexed to the report. [The resolution is reproduced here as Document 6.]

performance of my mission, and to pay a tribute to the learning of the legal experts who assisted me in the drafting the Constitution.

I have the honour to be, Sir...

E. ANZE MATIENZO
United Nations Commissioner
in Eritrea

INTRODUCTION

Section 1: Historical and Political

1. The General Assembly of the United Nations, at its fifth regular session, recommended that Eritrea should constitute an autonomous unit federated with Ethiopia under the sovereignty of the Ethiopian Crown. The relevant resolution, 390 A (V), of 2 December 1950, the text of which is annexed to the present report, was the culmination of four years' endeavour by the Council of the Foreign Ministers, the Paris Conference and, finally, the United Nations, to decide on the disposal of this former Italian colony, administered by the United Kingdom since 1941.

2. Eritrea lies between the Red Sea to the east, the Sudan to the north and west and Ethiopia to the south, and has an area of 117,248 sq. km. (45,800 sq. miles). From Massawa on the Red Sea to the frontier town of Sabderat in the west, the distance is almost the same as from the Sudanese frontier in the north to the Setit and Mareb rivers in the south (about 500 km). But the Red Sea Division is wedged between Ethiopia and the coast from north-west to south-east, having a length of some 600 km. and a breadth of a little more than 100 km. at certain points.

3. Although there are no accurate census figures, the British Administration estimated the population at about one million. It is made up of Christians and Moslems in roughly equal numbers, the plateau being inhabited mainly by Christians and the lowlands by Moslems.

4. The populations of the plateau (the Hamasien, Serae and Akele Guzi divisions), as well as of the "Abyssinian Districts" of the Keren region, all have practically the same social structure. The basic unit is the village community made up of kinship groups of families, among which only the settlers and their families have rights in the surrounding lands. The villages were administered in the past by a chief, assisted by elders.

5. The nomad tribes of the north and west (Sahel, Beni Amer, Mensa, etc.) comprise nobles and serfs who owed them services and tribute now for the most part abolished; class distinctions have not completely disappeared, however.

6. Thirdly, the Red Sea coast area is inhabited by the Danakils, the semi-nomadic Saho-speaking tribes and the Samhar people. Under Italian rule, tribal chieftains were added to the democratically-organized kinship groups, which had their own chiefs.

7. Finally, the peoples of the south-west (Baria and Kunama) living in semi-permanent villages, are organized in family and tribal groups, each family group having its council of elders.

8. Among the foreign communities, whose economic activity is important to the country, the Italian, Arab, Indian, Greek, Jewish and Sudanese have official organizations. The largest communities are the Italian, numbering approximately 17,000, and those coming originally from Asia, mainly Arab and Indian.

9. The Italian Administration, facilitated by the acquisition of the Bay of Assab by the Rubattino Company, began with the foundation of the colony of Eritrea (January 1890). The Italian population in Eritrea, besides being large in number, has played a big part in the development of the country (communications network, ports, town planning) and in its progress in agriculture (concessions) and industry. The Italian Administration ended in 1941 with the entry of the Allied armed forces.

10. It is at this time, in 1941, that the Unionist Party claims to have begun its activities, though pointing out that a "movement" for union with Ethiopia had long existed in Eritrea. The Four Power Commission of Investigation, however, referring to the actual founding of the party, set the date at 1946. 2/ The party's aim was unconditional union with Ethiopia.

11. Towards the end of 1946, a Moslem League of Eritrea was founded at Keren, in the Western Province; it demanded the independence of Eritrea or, if that were not considered possible, "an international trusteeship for ten years with internal independence under the control of the British Government". 3/ In 1949, this Moslem League joined with a number of less important parties to form an Independence Bloc, and changed its programme, demanding immediate independence for Eritrea.

12. Finally, the Moslem League of the Western Province, consisting of former members of the Moslem League of Eritrea and founded at the beginning of 1950, advocated a separate solution for the Western Province, namely, a period of British Administration followed by independence, the rest of the territory to be left free to decide its own future.

13. Since the Council of Foreign Ministers had not been able to reach agreement in spite of the dispatch of a Commission of Enquiry (November 1947 to January

---

2/ Four Powers Commission of Investigation for the former Italian colonies, vol. I, *Report on Eritrea*, p. 13.
3/ *Ibid*, vol. I, app. 20, p. 3.

1948), the question was submitted to the United Nations General Assembly, in accordance with annex XI, paragraph 3 of the Treaty of Peace with Italy which states:

> "If with respect to any of the these territories the Four Powers are unable to agree upon their disposal within one year from the coming into force of the Treaty of Peace with Italy, the matter shall be referred to the General Assembly of the United Nations for a recommendation, and the Four Powers agree to accept the recommendation and to take appropriate measures for giving effect to it."

14. At its third regular session, the General Assembly, after discussion, postponed the question of the disposal of the former Italian colonies until the fourth regular session.

15. The United Nations Commission for Eritrea, established at the fourth regular session by resolution 289 A (IV), Section C, of 21 November 1949, to "ascertain all the relevant facts" and submit proposals "appropriate for the solution of the problem of Eritrea", concentrated its attention on the two following factors:

(1) The rights and claims of Ethiopia based on geographical, historical, ethnic or economic reasons;

(2) The need to find an acceptable compromise between the solutions recommended by the population, which ranged from independence to union with Ethiopia. 4/

16. The solution of Federation, adopted by the General Assembly by 46 votes to 10, with 4 abstentions, (resolution 390 A (V)), on the basis of proposals by the representatives of Burma and the Union of South Africa on the United Nations Commission for Eritrea, and of a draft resolution submitted by a number of delegations, 5/ took into account the wishes and welfare of the inhabitants of Eritrea, the interests of peace and security in East Africa and the rights and claims of Ethiopia. It was essentially a middle-of-the-road formula, and the Commissioner, having acquainted himself with the facts in Eritrea, stated on many occasions that in his view it appeared to be the best possible "compromise". 6/

Section 2: Resolutions 390 A (V) and 390 B (V) of the General Assembly of the United Nations. Terms of Reference and Election of the United Nations Commissioner in Eritrea

17. The text of resolution 390 A (V) of 2 December 1950, the first seven paragraphs of which form the Federal Act, is reproduced as annex I to the present report.

18. Paragraph 10 of the resolution provided for the appointment by the General Assembly of a United Nations Commissioner in Eritrea. By resolution 390 B (V), adopted at the same meeting on 2 December 1950, it was decided to establish a Committee to assist in making the appointment. When the report of the Committee was received, the General Assembly, at its 325th plenary meeting on 14 December 1950, by secret ballot elected Mr. Eduardo Anze Matienzo to the office of United Nations Commissioner in Eritrea. 7/

19. The duties of the Commissioner and the powers conferred upon him were set out in paragraphs 12, 13 and 15 of section A of the resolution. Thanks to the co-operation and goodwill which he received from the other interested parties and from the Eritreans themselves, the Commissioner did not find it necessary to exercise the power of consultation with the Interim Committee conferred by paragraph 15 of the resolution.

20. The main duties and powers of the Commissioner are summarized below in chronological order (subject to overlapping) and in order in which they are dealt with in this report.

(1) The duty, in consultation with:

(a) The Administering Authority;

(b) The Government of Ethiopia; and

(c) The inhabitants of Eritrea,

of preparing a draft of the Eritrean Constitution which shall:

(a) Be based on the principles of democratic government;

(b) Include the guarantees contained in paragraph 7 of the Federal Act; and

(c) Contain provisions adopting and ratifying the Federal Act on behalf of the people of Eritrea.

(2) The duty of submitting the draft Constitution to the Eritrean Assembly.

(3) The duty of advising and assisting the Eritrean Assembly in its consideration of the draft Constitution.

(4) The power and, if in the Commissioner's opinion it conformed to the principles of the resolution, the duty of approving the Constitution as adopted by the Eritrean Assembly.

(5) The duty of making appropriate reports to the General Assembly of the United Nations concerning the discharge of his functions and, having maintained his headquarters in Eritrea until the transfer of power had been completed; the duty of so reporting to the General Assembly and submitting to it the text of the Eritrean Constitution.

4/ Report of the United Nations Commission for Eritrea, *Official Records of the General Assembly, Fifth Session, Supplement No. 8* (A/1285).

5/ Bolivia, Brazil, Burma, Canada, Denmark, Ecuador, Greece, Liberia, Mexico, Panama, Paraguay, Peru, Turkey, United States of America (A/AC.38/L.37 and Corr. 1.).

6/ See document A/AC.44/R.55, p. 4.

7/ *Official Records of the General Assembly, Fifth Session, Supplement No. 8* (A/1285).

21. Moreover, under the provisions of paragraph 11, the Administering Authority was required to consult the United Nations Commissioner on certain matters assigned to it, namely the organization of an Eritrean administration, the induction of Eritreans into all levels of the administration and the convocation of a representative assembly of Eritreans chosen by the people. The Administering Authority was also authorized, in agreement with the Commissioner, to negotiate on behalf of the Eritreans a temporary customs union with Ethiopia.

22. The Government of the United Kingdom of Great Britain and Northern Ireland was responsible for the transfer of power to the appropriate authorities as soon as the Eritrean Constitution and the Federal Act had entered into effect. Although not required to do so, the Administration consulted or notified the Commissioner informally at each stage of its preparations for the transfer of power. 8/

23. The difficulty of the Commissioner's task is evident from a glance at the legal framework of the resolution and the circumstances in which he was called upon to act.

24. So far as the legal framework is concerned, it may be said that the United Nations General Assembly, in its resolution A (V), not only drafted the Federal Act, but laid down the principles on which the Constitution of Eritrea was to be based.

25. Within this framework, the Commissioner was himself a "subsidiary organ" of the United Nations, for the resolution made no provision for him to have a council. His mandate was of a dual nature. In the first place, he was required to act as counsel by preparing a draft Constitution, in the consideration of which he was to advise and assist the Eritrean Assembly. Secondly, the resolution gave him real powers of decision, since he was called upon to agree to any negotiation of a temporary customs union between Eritrea and Ethiopia, and to approve the Constitution of Eritrea.

26. To confer power on a United Nations Commissioner to take decisions concerning the preparation of a constitution for a political unit is a new departure.

27. The legal questions to be settled were complex:

(1) First, the Commissioner had the duty of preparing legal texts compatible with the principles and rules formally laid down by the General Assembly of the United Nations, in conformity with the wishes of the inhabitants and—since it was for the Emperor to approve the Constitution by ratification—acceptable to the Ethiopian Government. Moreover, provision for consultation with the Administering Authority was expressly made in the resolution of 2 December 1950.

(2) Secondly—a new departure in constitutional history—the Commissioner had to prepare a Constitution for an autonomous unit—Eritrea—which was a member of a Federation whose organs had not yet been fully created. The Federal Act, incorporated in the resolution of 2 December 1950, determined only the principles of the future Federation; the resolution did not stipulate how they should be put into effect by creating the necessary organs, as it did in the case of the Eritrean Constitution.

28. Beside these legal features of the resolution there was also an extremely complicated de facto situation, hardly susceptible of rapid change owing to the traditions and rights established or perpetuated during the successive phases of the country's history.

29. The main task of the United Nations Commissioner in Eritrea was the preparation of a constitution which in conformity with resolution 390 A (V) would firmly establish for the future the foundations of autonomy for Eritrea federated with Ethiopia under the sovereignty of the Ethiopian Crown.

30. In accordance with paragraph 15 of the resolution, which provided that the Commissioner should make appropriate reports to the General Assembly concerning the discharge of his functions, the Commissioner submitted a Progress Report 9/ to the General Assembly at its fifth regular session.

31. The present report covers the whole of his mission and describes first the work leading up to the entry into effect of the Constitution and the enactment of the organic laws:

Chapter I. Preparatory work and consultations for the preparation of a draft Constitution.

Chapter II. Drafting of the Constitution.

Chapter III. Convening by the Administering Authority of a representative Assembly of Eritreans chosen by the people.

Chapter IV. Submission of the draft Constitution to the Eritrean Assembly. Discussions. Adoption of the amended text.

Chapter V. Approval of the Constitution by the Commissioner. Ratification of the Constitution and of the Federal Act by the Emperor of Ethiopia.

Chapter VI. Characteristic features and the legal basis of the Eritrean Constitution of 10 July 1952.

Chapter VII. Organic laws complementary to the Constitution.

32. Furthermore, in accordance with paragraph 11 of the resolution, the Administering Authority consulted

---

8/ The steps taken by the Administering Authority to implement the provisions of the resolution concerning it are the subject of a separate report to the General Assembly on the administration of Eritrea from December 1950 to September 1952 submitted by the Administering Authority and reproduced as a United Nations document (A/2233).
9/ A/1959 and Add.1.

the Commissioner on matters coming within its competence. These consultations form the subject of:

Chapter VIII. Consultations with regard to a temporary customs union and the organization of an Eritrean Administration.

33. In accordance with paragraph 15 of the resolution, the Commissioner maintained his headquarters at Asmara until 15 September 1952, the date on which the transfer of power took place.

34. Paragraph 15 also required the Commissioner to submit the text of the Eritrean Constitution to the General Assembly. The final chapters therefore deal with the following matters:

Chapter IX. Transfer of power.

Chapter X. Submission of the Eritrean Constitution to the General Assembly of the United Nations.

There is also a concluding chapter containing general observations.

...

CHAPTER III
CONVENING BY THE ADMINISTERING AUTHORITY OF A REPRESENTATIVE ASSEMBLY OF ERITREANS CHOSEN BY THE PEOPLE

Section 1. Arrangements for the elections

406. One of the tasks which the British Administration was required to carry out in consultation with the United Nations Commissioner was to "make arrangements for and convoke a representative assembly of Eritreans chosen by the people" (resolution 390 (V), paragraph 11).

407. In accordance with its mandate, the British Administration, by Proclamation No. 121, dated 28 January 1952, adopted the procedure which, taking into account local conditions—social, geographical and political—as well as the time and means available to the officials responsible for the arrangements, it considered most appropriate. In a letter to the British Administration dated 4 February 1952, the Commissioner stated that the proclamation "shows great experience of the problem and a deep knowledge of the traditions of the country".

408. Direct elections, in a single stage, by secret ballot, were held in the towns of Asmara and Massawa only. In all other constituencies the elections were carried out in two stages, in the following way:

(1) The various districts (settled population) or tribes (nomads) elected delegates to the electoral colleges. Generally speaking, this first stage was conducted in accordance with local custom;

(2) At the second stage, the electoral college elected the members of the Assembly by secret ballot.

409. The participation of Eritreans in the primary stage in the case of indirect elections was governed, however, not by custom, but by rules established for the purpose. The qualifications required, the same as in the case of the direct elections, were as follows:

A person shall be qualified to vote if he:

1. Is an inhabitant of Eritrea; and
2. Is not a person who possesses foreign nationality and who is not descended from a parent or grandparent wholly of blood indigenous to Eritrea; and
3. Is a male; and
4. Is not less than 21 years of age; and
5. Has been ordinarily resident in the constituency for a period of not less than one year; and
6. Is of sound mind; and
7. Is not serving a term of imprisonment.

410. With regard to eligibility for election to the Assembly, the first three conditions laid down for the electorate were repeated in Proclamation No. 121; certain other requirements, such as those of age (30 instead of 21 years) and residence (not less than two years in the constituency during the last ten years), were raised; conditions were added which disqualified undischarged bankrupts or persons whose property was subject to certain measures or who were party to a subsisting contract with the Administration (unless they had disclosed the existence and nature of such contract); as regards officials employed by the Administration, they could apply for a leave of absence without pay for the purpose of furthering their candidature.

Section 2. Election and composition of the Eritrean Assembly

411. The various Eritrean parties had been founded and, prior to the United Nations resolution of 2 December 1950, had pursued their activities along the lines of the different solution proposed for the future of Eritrea.

412. As soon as he arrived in Eritrea, the Commissioner was obliged to emphasize the fact that from the day on which the United Nations General Assembly had adopted the recommendation regarding Federation the problem had completely changed in character. The various parties, in their replies to the Commissioner's questions on the Constitution were, no doubt, still able to attempt to steer the Federation towards a pattern differing as little as possible from their previous ideas. The very fact, however, that during the official consultations with the Commissioner the political parties were under the necessity of stating their views on the basic aspects of the Constitution gave the electorate, in full knowledge of the facts, freedom of choice among the views of the candi-

dates from the different parties. It seems certain, moreover, that the actual influence of the political parties as such was considerably stronger in the direct than in the indirect ballot constituencies, for in the latter a number of traditional considerations played a part.

413. It seems clear that, although the way in which the Administration had divided up the territory into electoral constituencies aroused some protests, mainly from the Moslems, in most cases it was impossible to please everyone. For instance, whereas the towns in the Western Province which asked to be represented in the Assembly had far too small a population—less than 9,000 in Keren and less than 6,000 in Agordat and Tessenei, the proportion having been fixed at one representative for about 15,000 people—the complaints about tribal grouping in the constituencies generally arose because the population had different views on the subject of division. In those circumstances, any concession to one point of view would have aroused discontent among those of the opposite opinion.

414. In other cases, the claims of the Moslems raised a question of principle. In point of fact the Moslems who are geographically dispersed throughout the Hamasien and Serae divisions—unlike the Christians of the Western Province who are centred in the "Abyssinian districts"—could not have voluntarily accepted a representative except on the basis of religion, which would have been anomalous in the system of territorial constituencies adopted.

415. Taking into account the fact that there were two ballots, the direct elections on 25 and 26 March 1952, and the second stage of the indirect elections on 26 March 1952, produced, in so far as it has been possible to determine precisely the political complexion of those elected, the following results:

Unionists and Liberal Unionists	32
Democratic and Independent Front (Moslem League and other parties of the Front)	18
Moslem League of the Western Province	14
National Party	1
Independent Moslem League	1
Total	66

416. In addition, a representative from the Democratic Front and a member of the Moslem League of the Western Province were elected by second ballot (indirect election) on 12 May 1952, thus amending the foregoing figures to nineteen for the Democratic Front and fifteen for the Moslem League of the Western Province.

Section 3. Preliminary proceedings of the Assembly

417. At the first meeting of the Eritrean Assembly, which was inaugurated with due ceremony on 28 April 1952, the Chief Administrator in his opening address, stated that the convocation of the Assembly by the British Administration marked the beginning of democratic institutions in Eritrea as well as a step towards the Federation of Eritrea and Ethiopia under the sovereignty of the Ethiopian Crown. He referred to the sympathy with which the Government of the United Kingdom and the British people were following this process of development and trusted that the Assembly would discharge its task speedily so that the transfer of power could take place not later than 15 September 1952.

418. The Commissioner then made a statement in which he paid tribute to the successful holding of the elections rendered possible by the co-operative spirit displayed by the Eritrean people and the organizing ability of the British Administration. That comment was equally true of the indirect elections, but the way in which the population had adapted itself to the entirely new method of direct and secret ballot was naturally even more remarkable than the normal working of the traditional tribal and district meetings.

419. Contrasting the atmosphere of peace and brotherly feeling with the unhappy days of banditry and tribal feuds, the Commissioner exhorted the members to prove themselves worthy of the sense of responsibility and patriotism already shown by their electors.

420. He stated that the draft Constitution he would shortly be submitting to the Assembly was based strictly on the principles of the resolution, the interests of the parties concerned and the wishes of the Eritrean people. Nevertheless, since the General Assembly had adopted a compromise solution, party strife in the Assembly would be all the more dangerous, for it might destroy the balance set up by the resolution of 2 December 1950.

421. In conclusion, the Commissioner stressed the fact that Eritrea was fortunate in acquiring at the same time autonomy and a Constitution based on democratic principles. He pointed out, however, that the belief of the people in their institutions was an indispensable factor for the success of an undertaking in which, in accordance with his mandate from the General Assembly, he would do his utmost to co-operate.

422. Finally, the Representative of the Emperor of Ethiopia, bringing to the Assembly the good wishes of the Emperor, emphasized the importance and urgency of the task to be carried out. There had been a long period of waiting before it had been possible, thanks to the efforts of Ethiopia, the United Kingdom, the United States and many other Members of the United Nations, to bring about a settlement of the Eritrean question, on the basis

of the aspirations of the inhabitants of Eritrea and the principle of close association with Ethiopia.

423. The Emperor was convinced of the sincerity and perspicacity with which the Commissioner had applied himself to drafting a Constitution, and of the need for the Assembly to succeed quickly in its task, since the future of the population, as well as peace and security in East Africa, depended upon it. The Emperor therefore exhorted the members of the Assembly to set aside all party strife, and assured Eritreans that he would regard them as his sons just as he did their Ethiopian brothers.

424. On 29 April 1952, 10/ by secret ballot, the Assembly elected Ato Tedla Bairu as President—by 49 votes to 11, with 2 abstentions, and 4 spoiled papers—and Sheikh Ali Mohamed Mussa Redai as Vice-President by 48 votes to 17 with one abstention.

425. The two who were elected had, in common, youth—both being under 40 years of age—and a knowledge of languages; they also represented different religions, the President being a Christian and the Vice-President a Moslem. A spirit of mutual tolerance among Eritreans was thus evident, which augured well for the subsequent work of the Assembly.

426. The Assembly had before it draft Standing Orders drawn up by the British Administration. The draft, while stating that the proceedings of the Assembly would be conducted in English, Arabic and Tigrinya (article 9) made provision in the same article for members to speak in Italian if they wished, in which case the speech would be interpreted into the other languages of the Assembly. The latter provision was rejected by the Assembly which, on 30 April 1952, 11/ adopted the draft Standing Orders without further amendment by 56 votes to none, with 9 abstentions.

...

Chapter VI
Characteristic Features and Legal Basis of the Eritrean Constitution of 10 July 1952

Section 1. Provisions of the Eritrean Constitution deriving from the establishment of the Federation

A. *Approval and ratification of the Federal Act*

506. Since Eritrea forms part of a Federation, the legal basis of the Eritrean Constitution must first be considered within the framework of that Federation.

507. Under the terms of paragraph 12 of the resolution of the General Assembly of the United Nations, the Constitution of Eritrea must contain provisions adopting and ratifying the Federal Act on behalf of the people of Eritrea. Under the terms of paragraph 8 of the resolution, the Federal Act must also be submitted to the Emperor of Ethiopia for ratification. Thus the two parties are invited to adhere to the Federation of their own free will.

508. The conditions laid down in the resolution have been duly fulfilled, since the Assembly, by unanimously adopting article 1 of the Eritrean Constitution—by which the Federal Act is adopted and ratified—has confirmed the adherence to the principle of federation noted by the Commissioner during his consultations throughout the country.

B. *Status of Eritrea*

509. The Federal Act establishes the main elements of the Federal Constitution. These are as follows:

(1) The organs of the Federation, which comprise the Emperor of Ethiopia, the Imperial Federal Council, and the Federal executive, legislative and judicial branches (paragraphs 1 and 5);

(2) The respective jurisdictions of the Federation and of Eritrea (paragraphs 2, 3 and 4);

(3) The nationality of the Federation (paragraph 6).

510. Implementation measures are clearly essential to complete the structure of the Federation. They must provide, in particular, for the appointment of the Imperial Federal Council and the establishment of the Federal executive and legislative branches. Just before the transfer of powers, the Federal Government was represented solely by the Emperor of Ethiopia, who is the sovereign of the Federation. It was the duty of the Emperor to enact the constitutional and other laws required to supplement the main foundations and establish the Federal institutions in accordance with the provisions of the Federal Act. 12/

511. In view of their importance for Eritrea, the provisions of the Federal Act establishing federal institutions, defining the jurisdiction of Eritrea and determining its financial obligations and rights have been incorporated in the Constitution.

512. Thus the constitutional status of Eritrea within the Federation is restated in articles 3, 4 and 5 of the Constitution which reproduce paragraphs 1, 2 and 3 of the Federal Act almost word for word.

513. The list of matters within the jurisdiction of Eritrea given in article 5, paragraph 2 of the Constitution, is not exhaustive. It is clearly stated in paragraph 1 of that article that the jurisdiction of Eritrea extends to all matters not reserved to the Federal Government.

514. Article 6 of the Constitution reproduces the provisions of paragraphs 3 and 4 of the Federal Act. It is

---

10/ A/AC.44/R.112.
11/ A/AC.44/R.114.
12/ These implementation measures have been initiated. They were announced by the Emperor in his speech on the ratification of the Federal Act, cf. chapter V, paragraph 497.

obvious that the effect of these provisions can in no way be modified by their incorporation in the Constitution of Eritrea. Article 6 of the Constitution should be interpreted in the same way as the corresponding provisions of the Federal Act.

515. Nevertheless the Federation certainly does not possess a unilateral power of decision as regards the application of these provisions and the matter was raised during the discussions of the Representative Assembly. Any difficulties which may arise in this connexion will have to be settled by a federal tribunal appointed for the purpose by the Federal Government and consisting of both Ethiopian and Eritrean judges.

516. Finally, the provisions of paragraph 5 of the Federal Act are incorporated in article 7 of the Constitution. Article 7, paragraph 2, merely reproduces the second part of paragraph 5 of the Federal Act. Paragraph 1 of this article supplements the first part of paragraph 5 by stipulating that Eritrean representatives in the Imperial Federal Council shall be appointed by the Chief Executive with the approval of the Assembly. The supplementary provision does not encroach upon federal powers. It is natural for the Eritrean representatives in the Imperial Federal Council to be appointed by a procedure fixed by Eritrean law. 13/

517. It is not unusual for provisions laid down in the Constitution of a Federal State to be incorporated in the Constitution of a member State. Many examples are to be found in the constitutions of the member States of the American Union. 14/

518. During its discussions, the Representative Assembly even considered the possibility of including all the provisions of the Federal Act in the Constitution. 15/ All the provisions of the Federal Act, in fact, are to be found in the Constitution whether the actual wording of the Federal Act has been reproduced or its substance retained. Under one form or another these provisions are therefor binding on Eritrea, Ethiopia and the Federation simultaneously.

C. *Federal nationality and Eritrean citizenship*

519. Article 8 of the Constitution refers to the provisions of paragraph 6 of the Federal Act concerning nationality in the Federation. It recognizes the existence of a single nationality throughout the Federation. The regulations of nationality rights is clearly a function of the Federal legislature.

520. Article 8 of the Constitution also refers to the Eritrean citizenship expressly mentioned in paragraph 6 (c) of the Federal Act. It leaves the conditions for acquiring Eritrean citizenship to be fixed by law.

521. Federations frequently recognize citizenship of their member States, apart from the nationality of the Federation. This is true for instance of Switzerland. 16/ Conditions for the acquisition of such citizenship are laid down sometimes in the Constitution, sometimes by law and sometimes by the Constitution and the laws giving effect to it. 17/ In the organic law which amplifies clauses of the Constitution relating to the election of the Assembly, Eritrean citizens are defined as follows: "Any person who has acquired Federal nationality in Eritrea under the provisions of paragraph 6 of the Federal Act or who has acquired Eritrean citizenship under any other law for the time being in force".

522. Article 9 of the Constitution of Eritrea provides that on the basis of reciprocity, Federal nationals who are not Eritrean citizens shall enjoy the same rights as Eritreans. The two paragraphs of article 9 are complementary, not contradictory. The exercise of political rights in Eritrea by nationals of the Federation and by Eritreans is governed by the Constitution and the laws in force.

523. The equality of rights thus accorded in Eritrea to nationals of the Federation is subject to the grant, in Ethiopia, of the same privileges to nationals of the Federation who are not Ethiopian citizens. This is the sense of the reciprocity clause.

524. Similar provisions are to be found in most Federal Constitutions. 18/ The only difference is that the reciprocity clause is not included; it is not required, since the provisions of a federal constitution are equally applicable to all member groups, and reciprocity is thus compulsory. But since the Constitution of Eritrea is not law in the other part of the Federation, it is understandable that the reciprocity clause in article 9 had to be included. It guards against any violation of equality of rights to the detriment of Eritrean citizens. Moreover in the absence of any provision in the Federal Act, the provisions of

---

13/ A/AC.44/SC.1/R.1, page 26.

14/ Thus, article VI, 2 of the Federal Constitution is reproduced in whole or in part in the constitutions of Arizona (II,3), California (I,3), Georgia (XII,1), Idaho (I,3), Maryland (2), New Mexico (I,1), Oklahoma (I,1), South Dakota (VII,27), Utah (I,3), West Virginia (I,1), Washington State (I,2), Wyoming (I,2), Amendment X to the Federal Constitution is reproduced in the constitutions of Maryland (3), New Hampshire (I,7), and West Virginia. The provisions of amendment XIV (I) to the Federal Constitution are to be found in the constitutions of nearly all the States.

15/ A/AC.44/R.56, page 3.

16/ Constitution of Switzerland, Article 43 of paragraph 1.

17/ The Constitution of the Canton of Appenzell, Switzerland, provides at the end of article 4 that "Detailed provisions for acquiring the status of citizen of the Canton shall be fixed by law". Cf. Constitution of Geneva, articles 18-20.

18/ Article IV, section 2, paragraph 1 of the United States Constitution provides that: "The Citizens of each State shall be entitled to all Privileges and Immunities of Citizens in the several States". Article 43 of the Constitution of Switzerland provides that: "A Swiss national having an established domicile shall, in the place of such domicile, enjoy full rights as a citizen of the Canton and as a burgess of the commune". Article 45 guarantees the right to establish domicile.

article 9 could not have been unilaterally enacted as Federal law without the agreement of Eritrea. This agreement is given by the Constitution.

525. The reciprocity clause establishes equality of treatment of nationals of the Federation, whether they are resident in Eritrea or in Ethiopia. It does not require persons possessing federal nationality to be guaranteed the same rights in both parts of the Federation. It provides that equality of treatment shall be reciprocal and this is sufficient. 19/

D. *Representation of the Emperor of Ethiopia in Eritrea*

526. Article 10 of the Constitution provides that there shall be a representative in Eritrea of the Emperor of Ethiopia. The legal justification and effect of such representation must now be considered.

527. The problem was to give the Emperor's Representative constitutional status by including this office in the Eritrean constitutional system without impairing the autonomy of Eritrea, and thus to establish a link between the Crown, at the head of the Federation, and the democratic institutions of Eritrea. On this, as on various other questions, the Federal Act contains no express provision. The Federation it establishes is, however, a monarchy under the sovereignty of the Ethiopian Crown.

528. In federal monarchies, the Sovereign and the Crown are the symbol of federation. They are represented in the different parts of the federation. 20/

529. In his capacity as Sovereign of the Federation, the Emperor may constitutionally instal a representative in Eritrea with the duty of co-ordinating 21/ Federal services in that country, providing liaison with the Eritrean Government and receiving the petitions to the Emperor provided for in paragraph 7 (i) of the Federal Act. Such an appointment would be compatible with the provisions of the Federal Act and would in no way encroach on Eritrean jurisdiction.

530. Thus, there was no legal reason why provisions concerning the representation of the Emperor should not be included in the Eritrean Constitution, provided that the autonomy of Eritrea and the democratic character of its institutions were not directly or indirectly impaired. It will be observed that as regards Eritrean affairs the functions assigned to the Emperor's Representative by the articles of chapter II are purely formal.

531. Article 10 does not prescribe the procedure for appointing the Emperor's Representative. This appointment rests with the Emperor; but the usual practice would be for the Imperial Government unofficially to consult the Chief of the Eritrean Executive. 22/

532. Articles 12 and 72 of the Constitution concerning the investiture and swearing-in of the Chief Executive, article 73 concerning the swearing-in of Secretaries of Executive Departments, article 13 concerning the speech from the throne and the opening and closing of sessions of the Assembly and articles 15 and 58 concerning the promulgation of legislation assign only formal duties to the Emperor's Representative.

533. The Emperor's Representative invests the Chief Executive, but plays no part in his appointment. The Chief Executive is elected by the Assembly, and it is the duty of the President of the Assembly to proclaim the election of the candidate obtaining the necessary number of votes, in accordance with article 68 of the Constitution. The President of the Assembly will officially inform the Emperor's Representative of the name of the candidate elected. The Emperor's Representative is obliged to carry out the investiture but has no right to supervise or investigate the election of the Chief Executive. Under the terms of article 12 of the Constitution, the investiture is a mere formality. It marks the formal assumption of office by the Chief Executive.

534. The same legal interpretation should be placed upon the swearing-in prescribed in articles 12, 72 and 73 of the Constitution. The wording of the oath is prescribed in the Eritrean Constitution. The oath is sworn to the Assembly before the Emperor's Representative. The latter cannot, by his abstention, prevent the Chief Executive or the Secretaries of Executive Departments from taking office.

535. The speech from the throne provided for in article 13 of the Constitution enables the Emperor, through his Representative, to deal with affairs of common interest to the Federation and to Eritrea. The speech may not deal with the domestic affairs or internal policy of Eritrea and may not be followed by any discussion or vote of the Assembly, whether favourable or unfavour-

---

19/ This is the interpretation placed upon article IV, section 2, paragraph 1 of the Constitution by the Supreme Court of the United States. (See W. W. Willoughby. *The Constitutional Law of the United States*, New York, 1929, Vol. I, section 160, page 287.)

20/ This is true of the Federal States of the Commonwealth (Canada and Australia). There are representatives of the Crown in the Provinces of Canada and in the member states: Constitution of Canada (British North American Act of 1867 and subsequent amendments), articles 58 to 60; Constitution of the Commonwealth of Australia (article 110) and Constitutions of the various member states.

21/ The appointment of co-ordinators for federal services in the member states, i.e., of true representatives of the President, has often been considered in a republican federal State such as the United States of America. The constitutional nature of such an appointment has never been called in question. Moreover, the President of the United States takes precedence at official ceremonies of member states.

22/ With regard to the States of the Commonwealth, the Imperial Conference of 1930 (Cmd. 3717, HMSO, London, 1930) stated that: "The parties interested in the appointment of a Governor-General of a Dominion are His Majesty the King, whose representative he his, and the Dominion concerned".

able. The speech does not bind the Chief Executive or the Eritrean Assembly in any way. 23/

536. Promulgation by the Emperor's Representative, as provided in article 15 and article 58, paragraphs 4 and 5, of legislation adopted by the Assembly, is a mere formality. The Emperor's Representative is required to promulgate such legislation within the time limits prescribed in the above-mentioned provisions.

537. In order that a law may not be prevented from coming into effect by failure to promulgate, the Constitution provides (article 58, paragraph 6) that if it is not promulgated within the time limit laid down, a law shall come into effect after publication by the Chief Executive. 24/

538. Article 14 and article 58, paragraphs 2 and 3 of the Constitution give the Emperor's Representative the right to request that legislation adopted by the Assembly be reconsidered.

539. This provision does not give the Emperor's Representative the power to intervene in the domestic affairs of Eritrea. It establishes a political procedure for settling conflicts of jurisdiction which may arise between the Federation and Eritrea.

540. The Constitution of Eritrea provides certain safeguards for this procedure. A request for reconsideration is only admissible if it relates to a law which "encroaches upon Federal jurisdiction, or involves the international responsibility of the Federation". The reasons for the request must be stated and it must be transmitted to the Chief Executive within twenty days after the voting of the law by the Assembly.

541. During its second debate, the Assembly must consider whether the law complained of is in conformity with the Federal Act or not. It merely verifies the constitutionality of the law adopted, taking the observations of the Emperor's Representative into consideration.

542. This procedure is clearly incomplete and limited. It only applies to Eritrean and not to Federal laws. It does not necessarily result in a final decision on the constitutionality of the law complained of, for the Assembly can nevertheless proceed to adopt the law alleged to be unconstitutional by a two-thirds majority vote.

543. The existence of the Imperial Federal Council will allow the representatives of Eritrea to express their opinion on federal laws which they might regard as encroaching on Eritrean jurisdiction.

544. The existence of this procedure does not, however, remove the need to establish appeal procedure with the necessary safeguards.

545. These safeguards can only be provided by the setting up of an impartial Supreme Court with powers to settle conflicts of jurisdiction between the Federation and Eritrea in the final instance. 25/

E. *Ratification by the Emperor of Ethiopia of amendments which might be made to the Constitution*

546. Article 93, paragraph 3 of the Constitution provides that any amendments thereto will enter into effect after ratification by the Emperor of Ethiopia. The resolution of the United Nations General Assembly provides (paragraph 13) that the Constitution of Eritrea shall enter into effect following ratification of the Federal Act and the Constitution by the Emperor of Ethiopia. The Constitution follows up this provision by giving permanence to the intervention of the Sovereign of the Federation.

547. From a strictly legal standpoint the intervention of the Emperor of Ethiopia appeared essential. The Constitution could not enter into force without ratification by the Emperor. His ratification was given to a particular text and any modification or amendment of that text must therefore be ratified by him. This is the application of a traditional principle of law, namely the principle of the converse act or identity of procedure. 26/ Against this principle of the converse act it could, however, be objected that ratification by the Emperor of Ethiopia is not prescribed in the Federal Act. Such ratification is required by the General Assembly's resolution, together with approval by the United Nations Commis-

---

23/ It would be in conformity with parliamentary practice for the speech from the throne to be communicated in advance to the President of the Assembly and to the Chief Executive.

24/ It is the duty of the Chief Executive to publish any laws not promulgated by the Emperor's Representative within the constitutional time limit. Failure to discharge this duty would be a serious violation of the Constitution coming within the scope of article 75 concerning removal from office of the Chief Executive.

25/ Report of the Panel of Legal Consultants, A/AC.44/SC.1/R.1. Generally speaking, comparative constitutional law shows that the constitutionality of laws is tested both by court procedure and by political machinery. The President of the United States of America who, under article I, section 7, paragraph 2 of the Constitution, has power to ask for reconsideration of laws adopted by Congress, makes frequent use of this power to return, for reconsideration, laws he considers to be unconstitutional. President Taft's message to Congress on 28 February 1913, alleging the unconstitutional nature of the Webb-Kenyon Act concerning the transportation of spirituous liquors in inter-State commerce, clearly showed up the effect of this political safeguard as compared with judicial safeguards. (W. W. Willoughby, *The Constitutional Law of the United States*, Vol. 2, page 974). Under article 36, paragraph 2 of the Constitution, the President of the French Republic, acting on the advice of the President of the Council, may ask Parliament to reconsider a law. This procedure also enables him to request the Assemblies to reconsider laws regarded as unconstitutional (Message of 1 August, 1949, J.O.R.F. Deb. Parl. Ass. Nat., 14 October 1949). Under the Constitution of the USSR, the constitutionality of laws of the Federated Republics is tested by political procedure; authority for this purpose is vested in the Supreme Soviet of the Union by article 14(d) of the Constitution of 1936.

26/ The same legal principle was applied by the Panel of Legal Consultants when considering amendment of the Federal Act. The principle is defined by Professor Ch. Rousseau as follows: "Rules of law, whether derived from treaties or laws, remain legally binding so long as they have not been duly abrogated by the procedure used for their formulation" (*Principes généraux du Droit international public*, Vol. I., No. 234).

sioner, as a condition for the entry into force of the new Constitution. It is not prescribed for the future.

548. The main legal basis of article 93, paragraph 3, of the Constitution is to be found in the practice of Federal States. The Constitutions of the member States are directly or indirectly subject to examination by the federal State. The purpose of such examination is to ensure that local constitutions respect the principles laid down in the Federal Constitution. 27/

549. Thus the provision contained in article 93, paragraph 3, might appear in the Federal Constitutional Laws enacted to implement the Federal Act. In order to avoid any difficulty of interpretation, however, it seemed advisable to insert this provision in the Constitution as well. The Assembly supported this view unanimously, except for four abstentions. 28/

550. Ratification of amendments to the Constitution by the Emperor of Ethiopia is all the more necessary because paragraph 7 of the Federal Act requires the Federal Government to ensure respect for human rights and fundamental liberties in Eritrea. The Federal Government must therefore be in a position to prevent suppression or restriction of these rights and freedoms by the Eritrean Constitution.

551. The purpose of federal ratification, however, defines its scope. Refusal of ratification will only be possible in respect of amendments at variance with the provisions of the Federal Act, and in such a case ratification must be refused.

Section 2. Provisions of the Eritrean Constitution concerning human rights and fundamental freedoms

552. Paragraph 7 of the Federal Act contains a declaration of the human rights and fundamental freedoms established in Eritrea. These rights and freedoms must be guaranteed by the Federal Government.

553. These guarantees appear in paragraph 7 in a twofold form. First, the general principle of respect for human rights and fundamental freedoms is laid down. Secondly, these rights and freedoms are enumerated in a non-restrictive list. Article 22 of the Constitution reproduces paragraph 7 of the Federal Act in full and the succeeding articles explain and amplify its provisions.

554. In principle, these provisions concerning fundamental rights and freedoms guaranteed by the Federal Act and the Eritrean Constitution, have the force of imperative legal rules with immediate effect, applicable by the Supreme Court. By way of exception certain provisions of paragraph 7 of the Federal Act and chapter IV of the Eritrean Constitution must be put into effect by legislation before they can be applied. Examples are paragraph 7 (e) of the Federal Act, articles 22 (e) and 31, paragraph 1, of the Constitution concerning the right to education and freedom to teach and article 33, paragraph 1 of the Constitution concerning the protection of working conditions. 29/ It will be for the judicial branch to recognize any such exceptional cases.

555. The fundamental rights and freedoms directly guaranteed by the Constitution may be amplified and defined by ordinary laws. The final sub-paragraph of paragraph 7 of the Federal Act lays down that no limitations may be applied to these rights unless they are justified by respect for the rights and freedoms of others or by the requirements of public order and the general welfare. This provision is reproduced in article 34 of the Constitution, which stipulates, in a second paragraph, that the law may in no case impede the normal enjoyment of fundamental rights and liberties. Finally, article 77 of the Constitution prohibits legislation by the Chief Executive in this field, in which the Assembly has sole competence.

556. Thus the Constitution provides for the protection of rights and freedoms. In case the other organs of the State, the Assembly and the Executive, should fail in their duties, it gives the Supreme Court the means of exercising effective control over legislation concerning these rights. For it affirms that liberty is the rule; any restrictive provision of the law must be justified, must come within the scope of the exceptions expressly prescribed and may not suppress the rights guaranteed. The judicial branch is therefore made the guardian of individual rights and fundamental freedom. It can only perform this task if it is completely independent, as prescribed in

---

27/ Article 6 of the Federal Constitution of Switzerland provides that:
"The Cantons must request the Confederation to guarantee their Constitutions".
The Constitution of the USSR provides as follows:
"Article 14. The jurisdiction of the Union of Soviet Socialist Republics, as represented by its higher organs of State power and organs of State administration, embraces: (d) Control over the observance of the Constitution of the USSR and ensuring conformity of the Constitutions of the Republics of the Union with the Constitution of the USSR.
"Article 16. Each Republic of the Union has its own Constitution, which takes account of the specific features of the Republic and is drawn up in full conformity with the Constitution of the USSR."
Article IV, section 4, of the Constitution of the United States of America provides that:
"The United States shall guarantee to every State in this Union a Republican Form of Government".
The Constitution of Libya contains the following provision:
"Article 177. Each province shall formulate its own Organic Law provided that its provisions are not contrary to the provisions of this Constitution."
All these provisions are designed to ensure conformity of the Constitutions of member States with the Federal Constitution.
28/ A/AC.44/R.136, page 2.
29/ Such provisions may be compared with certain constitutional texts in force which are recognized as guiding principles in social policy: Constitution of Ireland, article 45; Constitution of India, part IV.

article 86, paragraph 3, of the Constitution. The function thus assigned to the judicial branch is in conformity with constitutional practice in many modern States. 30/

557. It will also be the duty of the Federal Government to ensure that Eritrean laws respect human rights and fundamental freedoms. This duty is expressly laid upon it by paragraph 7 of the Federal Act. Among the means by which the Federal Government may discharge this duty is the power given to the Emperor's Representative to request reconsideration of Eritrean laws. 31/

558. If the Federal Government should fail to provide the guarantees prescribed in paragraph 7, the Federation may be held responsible internationally.

559. The content and sources of the rights and freedoms guaranteed have already been analysed. It is sufficient to point out that the Universal Declaration of Human Rights is the direct source of the corresponding articles of the Federal Act and the Eritrean Constitution. 32/

560. From a legal standpoint, it is necessary to consider what persons enjoy these rights and freedoms. Paragraph 7 of the Federal Act begins as follows: "The Federal Government, as well as Eritrea, shall ensure to residents in Eritrea..." 33/ In principal Human Rights are guaranteed to all persons in Eritrea. In certain respects, however, the status of persons who reside in Eritrea differs from that of those who are merely transients. Certain restrictions may be applied to the latter in keeping with a practice which is widespread in democratic States especially as regards public freedoms.

561. Article 36 of the Constitution provides that nationals of the Federation as well as foreign nationals shall have the right to respect for their personal status. This provision was particularly necessary in a country embracing communities with wide social and religious differences. It applies the principles laid down in the last paragraph of the preamble to the United Nations General Assembly's resolution and guarantees respect for the traditions and religions of the inhabitants. 34/ Moreover, article 36 of the Eritrean Constitution permits the development of personal status.

562. With regard to foreign nationals, the terms of the article imply that their own national law will be applied to their personal status. This rule is recognized by the private international law of many modern States and is traditionally accepted in Ethiopia. 35/

Section 3. Provisions of the Eritrean Constitution embodying the principles of democratic government

563. The United Nations General Assembly's resolution instructs the Commissioner that "the Constitution of Eritrea shall be based on the principles of democratic government" (paragraph 12).

564. The classical forms of democratic government are direct government, semi-direct government and representative government. The first two forms obviously had to be rejected in Eritrea as far as the central government is concerned. Representative democracy requires all political institutions to be directly or indirectly based on election by the people, i.e., on the franchise. It requires that the franchise shall not be limited for reasons of birth, means or education. These fundamental requirements may be satisfied, from a legal standpoint, by a wide variety of political systems, the commonest of which are the parliamentary system, the presidential and directorial systems and the intermediate types partaking of both these systems. 36/

565. In the present instance, the choice was suggested by the social structure of the country. The aim was to establish stable government institutions exercising mutual restraint on one another and based on a free vote. A parliamentary system without deep historical roots dangerously weakens the executive power. A presidential system in a new democracy might facilitate autocratic schemes. The Constitution adopted in Eritrea endeavours, as far as legal technique permits, to avoid both these dangers. It establishes a what may be called a semi-presidential system.

566. The Eritrean Constitution creates a strong Executive having wide powers, but elected for a fixed term by the Assembly. It strengthens the electorate, and hence the Assembly, by entrusting the supervision of electoral rolls and proceedings to an organ independent of the Executive, namely the Electoral High Commission. It limits the powers of the Executive by placing the Civil

---

30/ Examples are provided by the United States of America, Eire, Canada, Australia, India, many South American Republics, Italy and Switzerland (Cantonal legislation). Moreover, in countries where it is left mainly to the ordinary law to define the scope of liberties, the judicial branch always plays an important part in protecting individual liberties against arbitrary regulations and acts of the executive authorities.

31/ Articles 14 and 58 of the Constitution.

32/ See Chapter IV, section 3 of this report.

33/ The French translation states: "à toutes les personnes qui résident en Erythrie".

34/ The Declaration of Constitutional Principles adopted by the United Nations General Assembly for Somaliland lays down a similar rule. Article 9, paragraph 1 guarantees to the inhabitants: "The preservation of their personal and successional status with due regard to its evolutionary development." (A/1294) Similarly, article 192 of the Constitution of Libya provides that: "The State shall guarantee respect for the systems of personal status of non-Moslems." (A/C.32/Council/R.174).

35/ M. Marein, General Adviser to the Imperial Ethiopian Government: The Judicial System and the Laws of Ethiopia (Rotterdam, 1951) pp. 113-114, 116-117, 119-121.

36/ English writers use the terms parliamentary (or executive) government and non-parliamentary (or fixed) government.

Service and the corps of public officials under the authority of an independent Civil Service Commission.

567. The analysis of the provisions of the Constitution concerning government organs and functions will show how the desired balance between the powers has been achieved.

A. *The electorate*

568. Under the Eritrean Constitution the composition and organization of the electorate and electoral proceedings are outside the control of the Executive.

569. The composition of the electorate is based on the principle of universal suffrage. Under the terms of article 20 of the Constitution all men are entitled to vote provided that they possess Eritrean citizenship, have attained the age of twenty-one years and are under no legal disability. 37/ The only limitation of the principle of universal suffrage is the exclusion of women from the electorate, but this merely means that it is not yet possible in Eritrea to achieve the common ideal proclaimed by the Universal Declaration of Human Rights.

570. The independence of the electorate and the effectiveness of its action depend to a large extent on a complete and accurate census of all voters.

571. In order to ensure that the electoral rolls are accurately drawn up, the Constitution establishes, in article 45, an Electoral High Commission consisting of three persons appointed by the Supreme Court. This method of appointment ensures its independence and impartiality, thus providing the electorate with all the desirable guarantees; the High Commission is responsible not only for compiling the electoral rolls, but also for supervising all electoral proceedings and for preventing or putting a stop to irregularities.

572. The whole machinery of the electoral system is described in chapter VII on the organic laws, in the analysis of the Electoral Act. 38/

B. *Representative organs*

573. The Constitution establishes two organs representing the Eritrean people at different stages, the Assembly and the Chief Executive. The Assembly, which is elected by the electorate, in turn elects the Chief Executive.

(1) The Assembly

574. The Constitution establishes a uni-cameral system (article 39). There are many reasons for this choice. 39/ On financial grounds it was necessary to avoid overloading the political structure of a country with limited resources. It was advisable to take account of the number of qualified persons available to perform parliamentary, governmental and administrative duties. 40/

575. Articles 42, 53-55 and 70 define the status of members of the Assembly.

576. In accordance with a traditional constitutional rule, eligibility to the Assembly presupposes firstly qualification for being registered as a member of the electorate. Such qualification is sufficient without inscription on an electoral roll. In other words the Constitution requires possession of the right to vote but not its exercise. In addition to possession of the right to vote there are other conditions (article 42). The age for eligibility is fixed at 30 years; officials of the Eritrean or Federal Government are not eligible unless they have resigned at the time of presenting their candidature; candidates for election to the Assembly must prove that they have been resident in Eritrea for three years and have resided in their constituency for two years during the last ten years. Members of the Assembly are eligible for re-election (article 47, paragraph 2).

577. The incompatibility of the office of a public official with membership of the Assembly is especially important in Eritrea, where it is necessary to protect from political influences the new corps of officials on whose integrity and efficiency the sound administration of the autonomous unit will depend.

578. The meaning of the term "official" will have to be accurately defined by law. The Constitution refers, in principle, to persons having the status of public official and coming under the authority of the Civil Service Commission provided for in article 82. 41/

579. The Chief Executive and the Secretaries of Executive Departments are also officials of the Eritrean Government. They are ineligible unless they have resigned at the time of presenting their candidature. Ineligibility of the Chief Executive and the Secretaries of Executive Departments and the incompatibility of their functions with membership of the Assembly also follow from articles 69 (1), 70 and 75 of the Constitution. The Chief Executive and Secretaries of Executive Departments are not responsible to the Assembly. Hence parliamentary status and discipline could not be applied to them. Their functions are therefore incompatible with membership of the Assembly.

37/ The Commissioner, in collaboration with the British Administration, has prepared a draft electoral law which defines such disabilities. See chapter VII, section 3 C (b) below.

38/ The draft Organic Law jointly prepared by the Commissioner and the British Administration laid down conditions for establishing and revising the electoral rolls, the rules applicable to electoral proceedings and the legislative, administrative and judicial powers of the Electoral High Commission.

39/ See above, chapter I, section 2.C and D.2, (d)(1).

40/ A/AC.44/R.69 page 3 and R.70.

41/ This principle is followed in the organic law drafted jointly by the Commissioner and the British Administration. See chapter VII, section 3 G below.

580. Again, other grounds of incompatibility may be established by law.

581. The Constitution confers on members of the Assembly those immunities (irresponsibility and inviolability) that are essential to the free exercise of their functions (article 54). It ensures their material independence by according them a renumeration fixed by law (article 55).

582. The Constitution fixes the term of office of the Assembly at four years (article 47, paragraph 1). But the Assembly does not sit continuously during that period. The provisions governing its sessions are laid down in the Constitution (articles 48, 49, paragraph 4, and 78, paragraph 3).

583. In accordance with regular constitutional practice, the Assembly is granted wide powers of self-organization. These powers it exercises in adopting its own rules of procedure (article 51). The Constitution merely stipulates that a quorum shall comprise two-thirds of the members of the Assembly (article 50). It provides for the election of officers at the opening of the first regular session of each year (article 52) and grants such officers the right, when the Assembly is not in session, to raise the immunity of members of the Assembly (article 54, paragraph 2, second sub-paragraph).

584. Article 60, paragraph 1, refers to a Finance Committee. In addition, the Constitution implicitly contemplates the creation of other committees by empowering the Chief Executive, whose right of access to the Assembly is recognized, to be represented in the Assembly and its Committees by the Secretaries of Executive Departments (article 76, paragraph 7). These provisions, in conjunction with the Chief Executive's right to intervene during debates and again before the closure, limit the Assembly's powers of self-organization.

(2) The Chief Executive

585. The executive power is vested in a single person, the Chief Executive (article 67). The Constitution rules out the collegial or directorial system. Such is the contemporary tendency. Even in parliamentary governments the reins of government are left more and more in the hands of the Prime Minister or the President of the Council. His ministers are associates, not equals.

586. The Chief Executive is assisted by Secretaries of Executive Departments.

587. The appointment of the Chief Executive rests with the Assembly. He is appointed by election at the opening of each new legislature (article 68, paragraph 3). The intention in making the duration of the legislature and the term of office of the Chief Executive identical was to establish a constant link of mutual confidence between the two powers.

588. Eritrean citizens having attained the age of thirty-five years and in possession of their political rights are eligible for the office of Chief Executive (article 68, paragraph 2). 42/ Members of the Assembly, public officials and judges are eligible. But in the event of a candidate who performs one of these functions being elected to the office of Chief Executive he must choose between his new and his former post, the office of Chief Executive being incompatible with any other public office or legislative function.

589. The election procedure is governed by article 68, paragraph 1 of the Constitution. Election is by secret ballot, a two-thirds majority of the votes cast being required. Votes must be cast by at least two-thirds of the members of the Assembly in office, that is to say, the constitutional quorum (article 50). If no candidate obtains the required majority at the first ballot, another ballot is held among all the candidates, except the candidate receiving the least number of votes, and so on until a candidate obtains the required majority.

590. It should be pointed out that the Constitution does not forbid the introduction of new candidates after each ballot. But if any such new candidate receives the least number of votes he is eliminated from the next ballot. No candidate thus eliminated can stand again, at least not in the next ballot. 43/

591. The Constitution provides no solution should this procedure fail after several ballots. The Chief Executive can be elected only by a two-thirds majority; a simple majority was regarded as insufficient by the constituent Assembly, which has thus made it necessary for future Eritrean Assemblies to display a spirit of conciliation and compromise. 44/ But if no candidate obtains the constitutional majority the Chief Executive in office will retain his post provisionally.

592. Should the office of Chief Executive fall vacant during the term of office of a legislature, a new election is held by the same procedure. This election must be held within fifteen days of the office falling vacant (article 68, paragraph 4, and article 75, paragraph 3).

42/ The Chief Executive is eligible for re-election (article 68, paragraph 5).
43/ This question should be carefully settled, within the framework of the constitutional provisions, in the Assembly's rules of procedure.
44/ This system is not exceptional. It is found in parliamentary constitutions. The appointment of the President of the Council in France requires an absolute majority of the members comprising the Assembly (article 45 of the French Constitution). A similar system is applied, under the Italian Constitution, for the election of the President of the Republic (article 83). The Basic Law of Western Germany for the election of the Chancellor (article 63) and the Korean Constitution for the election of the President of the Republic (article 53) provide that a simple majority shall finally suffice, if no candidate would otherwise be elected.

593. The designation of an acting Chief Executive lies with the Chief Executive in office, who designates one of the Secretaries of Executive Departments to act for him if he is temporarily prevented from discharging his duties or if his post falls vacant, until such time as a new Chief Executive is elected (article 71). The Chief Executive has practically a free choice. He has merely to give the person he selects a post as Secretary of an Executive Department, if he does not already hold one. But it is essential that such designation should take place as soon as the Chief Executive has been elected. Furthermore, the Chief Executive may modify his choice at any time during his period of office. 45/

594. The Chief Executive may cease to hold his office for various reasons.

595. The Chief Executive's term of office normally comes to an end on the election of a new Chief Executive, which takes place, in accordance with the Constitution, at the opening of each new legislature (article 66, paragraph 3). It may also be terminated during the legislature by the death, resignation or removal from office of the Chief Executive. The exceptional procedure governing removal from office is described in detail in article 75 of the Constitution. It is based on the classic traditional provisions with regard to disqualification. The Assembly may only decide to impeach the Chief Executive before the Supreme Court by a two-thirds majority of its members.

596. On the other hand, the Assembly may in no case dismiss the Chief Executive. The latter is not responsible to the Assembly. He is independent of the Assembly throughout the whole of his term of office. In other words, in relation to the Assembly he is in the same position as members of the Assembly in relation to the electorate. The Chief Executive represents the Assembly as the latter represents the electorate. This situation is characteristic of a non-parliamentary system.

597. The Constitution defines the organizational principles of the Executive. It leaves to the law the task of applying these principles. 46/

598. The Secretaries of Executive Departments are appointed and dismissed by the Chief Executive. They assist, and are responsible to, him (article 69). They may be periodically convened in council by the Chief Executive. This council has no power of decision (article 74).

C. *Legislative functions and constituent power*

(1) Functions of the Assembly

599. The Assembly votes the laws (article 56). It constitutes the supreme legislative authority. The procedure for the drafting and adoption of laws is laid down in the Assembly's rules of procedure (article 57, paragraph 2). Nevertheless, the Constitution provides that the initiative in submitting laws lies with the individual members of the Assembly and the Chief Executive (article 57, paragraph 1).

600. The laws adopted by the Assembly are immediately transmitted by the President of the Assembly to the Chief Executive. The date on which a law is voted is of considerable importance, since it initiates a period of twenty days within which the Emperor's Representative may, on the grounds already stated, request reconsideration of the law and the Chief Executive himself may also request reconsideration (article 58, paragraphs 3 and 4). This right conferred on the Chief Executive is met with in other Constitutions. 47/

601. Where no request for consideration has been submitted before the expiry of this time-limit of twenty days, the law must be promulgated and published in accordance with the procedure set forth in article 58, paragraphs 4, 5 and 6, and article 76, paragraph 5. The same applies where, after reconsideration has been requested, the law has been adopted by the Assembly by a two-thirds majority.

602. The law which has been promulgated and published may be challenged as unconstitutional before the Supreme Court (article 90, paragraph 3). Should the law conflict with the Constitution, the latter shall prevail.

603. Among the legislative functions of the Assembly, special mention must be made of its competence in budgetary matters. The Constitution of Eritrea lays down principles and rules governing the drafting and adoption of the budget, its implementation and the supervision of its implementation. Provision is made for laws to be enacted embodying those principles and rules. 48/

604. In accordance with a practice constantly encountered in comparative budgetary law, the budget is drafted by the government (article 59). The Chief Executive's draft budget is examined by the Assembly Finance Committee, a general debate on it being held in the Assembly, at the beginning of the second regular session (article 60, paragraphs 1 and 2). Following this general debate, the Chief Executive must submit to the Assembly a revised draft budget including any suggestions made by it which he may see fit to incorporate. It thus rests with

---

45/ The acting Chief Executive, on assuming office after the resignation or death of the Chief Executive, must also designate an acting Chief Executive.

46/ Thus article 69, paragraph 4, leaves the number and functions of Secretaries of Executive Departments to be prescribed by law. The Commissioner has prepared a draft law on this point in conjunction with the British Administration. See chapter VII, section 3 B below.

47/ For example, in varying forms, in the Constitutions of Czechoslovakia (article 58 and 59), Finland (article 19), France (article 36), Iceland (article 26), Italy (article 74), Norway (articles 78 and 79) and the United States of America (article 7, section F).

48/ The organic law on the Budget drafted jointly by the Commissioner and the British Administration is examined in chapter VII, section 3 D of this report.

the Assembly to adopt suggested amendments to the budget, in the form of resolutions, during the debate. At this stage in the debate, the Assembly may propose to the Chief Executive that the expenditure estimates in the draft budget be either reduced or increased, subject in the latter case to the stipulation regarding the balancing of income and expenditure contained in article 60, paragraph 3, which will be considered later.

605. During the second phase, the Assembly takes a decision on the various items of the revised budget (article 60, paragraph 3). In other words, it votes appropriations for each Executive Department in turn.

606. It may reduce the expenditure estimates, except those included in the budget to cover national debt payments.

607. It may not increase the expenditure estimates in the draft budget without the consent of the Chief Executive and unless it votes an equivalent increase in the revenue estimates. On this particular point, then, the right of amendment of members of the Assembly is limited. The expenditure estimates submitted by the Executive represent a maximum, and the Assembly is thus invited to play the role of moderator in public expenditure (article 60, paragraph 3 (a)). Similar provisions are to be found in a number of Constitutions. 49/

608. The budget must be adopted before the beginning of the financial year; otherwise, the Constitution stipulates that the draft budget, amended by the Chief Executive, "shall be deemed to be adopted" (article 60, paragraph 4). The object of this provision is to prevent governmental action being paralysed for lack of funds through delay by the Assembly in voting the budget. It is thus incumbent on the Assembly to carry out its examination of the budget promptly enough to forestall adoption of the Chief Executive's draft budget by tacit consent. 50/

609. When the delay in adopting the budget is due to the failure of the Chief Executive to observe the time-limit laid down in the Constitution 51/ for submission of the draft budget, adoption by tacit consent is ruled out. In such a case, if the budget has not been adopted before the beginning of the financial year, the Chief Executive must request the Assembly to grant him, by extension of the previous budget, provisional appropriations for a limited period (e.g., one month).

610. The estimates for the expenses of the Assembly must be included in the budget. In accordance with parliamentary usage, proposals for such expenditure must be drafted by a committee of the Assembly and handed by the President of that body to the Chief Executive for inclusion in his draft budget. 52/

611. The Executive is responsible for implementation of the budget. Taxes may be levied only under the conditions fixed by the Assembly. Appropriations may not be exceeded or diverted from the purpose assigned to them in the budget law (article 61).

612. To enable the Executive to meet urgent expenditure, the Constitution authorizes the Assembly to include in the budget a special credit not to exceed 10 per cent of the total expenditure estimates authorized by the budget law (article 63).

613. In case of emergency, entailing commitments in excess of this special credit, it would be possible for the Chief Executive to submit a supplementary draft budget to the Assembly.

614. In addition to the control exercised by the Executive's finance and accounting services, a check on the implementation of the budget is kept by an Auditor-General elected by the Assembly (article 64 of the Constitution).

615. Final approval of the accounts for each financial year is given by the Assembly on the basis of a report submitted by the Chief Executive with the assistance of the Auditor-General (article 64, paragraphs 1 and 3).

616. Apart from its functions in the sphere of ordinary legislation, the Assembly has constituent power, since this is not vested in an ad hoc body, such as an Assembly elected for the purpose. The Constitution confers on the Eritrean Legislative Assembly the power to amend the Constitution, but the manner in which this action can be taken differs from ordinary legislative procedure.

617. The initiative as regards amendments to the Constitution lies with the Chief Executive and the members of the Assembly. A proposed amendment emanating from the members of the Assembly is inadmissible unless submitted by at least one quarter of the actual number of members (article 92, paragraph 1).

618. The proposed amendment cannot be discussed by the Assembly until twenty days at least after it has been submitted. This time allowed for reflection is designed to obviate the adoption of any amendment under pressure of extraneous circumstances.

619. Amendment procedure varies according to the majority obtained by the proposal in the Assembly.

49/ Western Germany (article 113); Bavaria (article 78); Rhineland-Palatinate (article 118); France (article 17); Ireland (article 17, para. 1); the Sarre (article 110).

50/ A number of Constitutions provide for an analogous system, in the same eventuality, in the form of a prolongation of the previous year's budget; Western Germany (article 11); Bavaria (article 78(4)); Rhineland-Palatinate (article 116, last paragraph); Saxony (article 81); Denmark (article 47, second paragraph); the Sarre (article 107).

51/ The draft budget must be submitted to the Assembly at least one month before the opening of the second regular session of the Assembly (article 59, para. 1), and the revised draft budget within ten days following the closure of the debate in the Assembly.

52/ The rules of procedure of the Assembly will have to lay down the conditions under which this section of the budget must be drafted.

620. If the Assembly adopts the proposal by a majority of three-quarters of the members in office, this decision is final and the proposed amendment is approved.

621. If an amendment is approved by an absolute majority of the members in office or by a majority of two-thirds of the members present and voting, it must be debated again.

622. This second debate can only take place after the next legislature has been elected. Thus the amendment is indirectly put to the electorate. 53/

623. The maximum period that may elapse between the two debates is slightly over four years if the amendment is first adopted at the beginning of a legislative period, and the minimum period a few months if it is first adopted at the end of a legislative period.

624. The majorities required are the same for the second vote as for the first (article 93, paragraph 2).

625. A similar revision procedure is to be found in many Constitutions. In view of the fact that a single Assembly has power to carry out revision, the conditions laid down in the Eritrean Constitution are not excessive. 54/ The Eritrean Assembly did not by any means consider the revision procedure laid down in the Commissioner's Draft to be too inflexible, but would have preferred to see amendment of the Constitution made more difficult.

626. In exercising its power to revise the Constitution, the Assembly may not amend the Federal Act. This restriction is stated in article 91, paragraph 1.

627. Moreover, article 16 of the Constitution may be amended (article 91, paragraph 2). This provision gives the authority of constitutional law to the rule laid down in the United Nations resolution (paragraph 12): "the Constitution of Eritrea shall be based on the principles of democratic government".

(2) Powers of the Chief Executive

628. The Constitution confers wide powers on the Chief Executive in the matter of legislation and issuing of regulations. 55/ In the first place, the Chief Executive is empowered to issue the regulations required to implement the laws (article 76, paragraphs 2 and 8). Secondly, the Chief Executive is authorized to fill in any gaps in the laws in force (article 77). This power can be exercised only in the interval between sessions of the Assembly. The Chief Executive must submit any orders thus issued to the Assembly, which may repeal them. Such orders may not relate to any of the matters dealt with in chapter IV of part I of the Constitution, and must be compatible with the Constitution and the laws in force.

629. Finally, articles 78 and 79 of the Constitution endow the Chief Executive with emergency legislative powers, subject to supervision by the Assembly.

D. *Powers of the Executive*

630. The Constitution makes the Chief Executive responsible for the direction of the administrative departments and public services (article 76). He also possesses power of decision, within the limits set by the Constitution and the laws of the Assembly.

631. However, to prevent the Chief Executive from having unlimited powers, the Civil Service is placed under the authority of an independent Commission (article 82). This Commission is under the chairmanship of the Chief Executive or his representative, but its composition and the conditions under which it is to function are determined by law. The Civil Service Commission is responsible for the appointment, promotion, transfer and discharge of officials and for taking disciplinary action. Such a system, which tends to discourage favouritism and

---

53/ In some Constitutions it is expressly provided that Assemblies undertaking to amend the Constitution must be re-elected. After the elections, a final decision on the proposed revision is taken. (Constitution of Belgium, article 131; Constitution of the Netherlands, article 204; Constitution of Denmark, article 94; Constitution of Norway, article 119; Constitution of Colombia, article 190). The Constitution of Honduras lays down procedure similar to that adopted for Eritrea in this instance (article 200).

54/ The basic law in Western Germany requires a two-thirds majority of both Assemblies for revision (article 79); the Constitution of Bavaria requires a two-thirds majority of the members of the Diet and a public referendum (article 75); the Constitutions of the Rhineland-Palatinate (article 129) and of Saxony (article 96) require either a two-thirds majority of the members of the Assembly or a public referendum; the Constitution of France requires, first, the adoption of a resolution by an absolute majority of the members of the National Assembly, then the adoption of a bill to revise the Constitution either by a two-thirds majority of the National Assembly, or by a three-fifths majority of both Assemblies or by a simple majority, in which case revision must be approved by a public referendum (article 90); the Italian Constitution requires a two-thirds majority of the members in office in both Chambers, failing which there may be a referendum; the Hungarian Constitution requires a two-thirds majority of the National Assembly (article 15-III); the Constitution of Norway requires a two-thirds majority of the Storthing (article 119); the "Little Constitution" of Poland requires a majority of two-thirds of the statutory number of deputies; the Constitution of the Sarre requires a majority of three-quarters of the statutory number of members of the Assembly (article 103); the Constitution of Czechoslovakia requires a majority of three-fifths of the total number of deputies (article 54, paragraph 2); the Constitution of Turkey requires that a proposal for revision be submitted by at least one-third of the members of the Assembly and adopted by two-thirds of the members (article 102); the Constitution of the USSR requires a two-thirds majority vote in each Chamber of the Supreme Soviet. In the member States of the American Union a simple majority of members in each Chamber is sometimes required for the adoption of amendments (23 States); sometimes a majority of two-thirds is required (18 States) and sometimes a majority of three-fifths (7 states); in some States the amendment must be adopted again by a second legislature (14 States). Subject to approval by the States in certain cases, the Constitution of India requires a two-thirds majority in both Houses of Parliament, comprising at least half the members (article 368); the Constitution of Ceylon requires a majority of two-thirds of the members of the House of Representatives (article 29, paragraph 4). In most South American States more than a simple majority is also required for revision of the Constitution (cf. Bolivia, article 174; Brazil, article 217; Chile, article 108; Cuba, articles 285-286; El Salvador, article 171; Guatemala, article 206; Honduras, article 200; Mexico, article 135; Paraguay, article 94; Uruguay, article 281; Venezuela, article 248).

55/ The extension of the powers of the Executive with regard to legislation and issuing of regulations is a characteristic feature of the contemporary period.

the creation of a group of hangers-on, has been adopted by the legislation of a number of countries. 56/

632. Moreover, although the Assembly may not interfere in the exercise of executive functions, it enjoys the right of supervision under the Constitution. In accordance with article 66, it may submit questions orally or in writing and ask for a debate on the Government's policy.

633. In a semi-presidential system such as that adopted for the Constitution of Eritrea, relations between the Executive and the Assembly should naturally be strictly defined. Failure to include provisions to that end, or the introduction of different provisions, would have transformed the semi-presidential system into a parliamentary one. The limited intercourse provided for under article 66 of the Constitution is, however, sufficient to keep the Chief Executive in touch with public opinion and to enable the pressure of the latter to be adequately felt.

Section 4. The Judiciary

634. Article 85 of the Constitution of Eritrea provides that judicial power shall be exercised by a Supreme Court and by other courts which will apply the various systems of law in force in Eritrea. Article 86 provides that the judiciary shall be completely independent and free from all political influence and from any pressure or intervention on the part of the Assembly or the Executive.

635. The judges are appointed by the Chief Executive on the recommendation of the President of the Assembly to whom a list of at least three candidates for appointment must be supplied by a Committee composed of the President of the Supreme Court and two judges chosen by the members of the Supreme Court and of the court or courts immediately inferior thereto. The judges are appointed for a period of seven years, which term may be renewed.

636. It was left to the law to establish the status of the judges and the organization of the courts. A description of the measures taken in this law to ensure the independence of the judiciary, in accordance with the provisions of the Constitution, is given in chapter VII of this report.

637. Apart from its jurisdiction as a court of last resort, the Supreme Court has exclusive jurisdiction in the following matters forming an integral part of the Constitution on which action may be required to ensure the observance and application of its provisions:

(1) Disputes concerning the constitutionality of laws and orders;

(2) Conflicts of jurisdiction between Eritrean courts;

(3) Actions based on administrative acts brought against the Government of Eritrea or the public services, unless special courts have been established by law to try such cases;

(4) Criminal and disciplinary responsibility of judges; and

(5) Trial of the Chief Executive when impeached by the Assembly under article 75 of the Constitution.

Section 5. The Advisory Council of Eritrea

638. The Advisory Council of Eritrea, established by article 84 of the Constitution, is an institution designed to enable the necessary plans to be drawn up for economic and social progress in Eritrea, and to endow the country with the technical, economic, administrative and social resources commensurate with its new status.

639. By the very establishment of this Advisory Council, the Constitution of Eritrea stresses the importance of such problems for the country's future. 57/

640. It lays the foundations and formulates the guiding principles of an essential institution which it will be the task of the Assembly and the Chief Executive to organize, maintain and develop.

641. An organic law 58/ has been drawn up by the Commissioner, in collaboration with the British Administration, to develop the principles laid down by the Constitution and to indicate the manner in which the Advisory Council shall function. The main features of this law are described in chapter VII, section 3 of this report.

Section 6. Transitional provisions

642. Article 96 of the Constitution stipulates that the laws and regulations in force shall remain in force so long as they have not been repealed or amended—provided they do not conflict with the Constitution. A similar provision is to be found in a number of other constitutions. It embodies an indisputable principle of law. 59/

643. Article 99 extends the term of office of the Assembly responsible for adopting the Constitution of Eritrea. The Commissioner had proposed that the extension should not exceed two years. The Assembly, however, was of the opinion that this period would not be sufficient to enable it to establish the constitutional institutions and to examine and adopt the essential organic

---

56/ For instance, in the United States of America, the Republic of India and Ceylon.

57/ The Advisory Council of Eritrea may be compared to the economic councils set up, either under the constitution or by law, in many countries during the last thirty years. The Advisory Council of Eritrea, like these economic councils, is not a political organ but a technical adviser to the public authorities.

58/ A/AC.44/L.16

59/ Cf. the Constitution of Ireland (article 73); Constitution of Korea (article 100); Draft Constitution of Israel (article 77), Constitution of Libya (article 210).

laws. It decided that, in view of Eritrea's special position, a period of at least four years would be necessary.

644. The other transitional provisions (articles 97 and 98) concern the Administering Authority in Eritrea, their object being to facilitate the transfer of the power vested in that Authority under paragraph 14 of the resolution of the United Nations General Assembly.

...

CHAPTER IX
THE TRANSFER OF POWER

760. Paragraph 15 of the resolution of the United Nations General Assembly states that: "The United Nations Commissioner shall maintain his headquarters in Eritrea until the transfer of power has been completed", and upon completion "he shall so report to the General Assembly".

761. The opinions expressed during the discussions by several delegations and the traditions of the United Nations General Assembly, born of the experience of previous missions, showed that in the matter of the transfer of power the Commissioner was to be regarded more or less as an "observer".

762. Owing to some nervousness among certain sections of the population during the transition period, on 27 August 1952 the Commissioner issued a Press release covering the following main points:

(1) The transfer of services had been the subject of discussions between the Commissioner and the Chief Administrator, the Eritrean authorities and members of the representative Assembly, and Ethiopian and Italian officials;

(2) During these conversations, the Commissioner had made clear that the terms of the resolution laid upon him no direct responsibility with regard to federal matters or the transfer of power;

(3) Nevertheless, in so far as the application of paragraph 15 of the resolution was concerned, it was his duty, in his capacity as United Nations observer, to report to the General Assembly on the whole operation;

(4) The Federation, in the form recommended by the General Assembly and accepted by the Eritrean population, struck a balance between the Federal Government and the autonomous unit of Eritrea. It was the duty of all interested parties to co-operate in a spirit of mutual understanding in setting up this equilibrium, the possibility of which was clearly brought out by paragraphs 3 and 5 of the United Nations resolution in which the division of responsibility between the Federal Government and the Government of Eritrea was precisely defined, and which also provided for Eritrean participation in the setting up of an Imperial Federal Council and in the Federal Government;

(5) Recent conversations which the Commissioner had had gave evidence that all parties were equally animated by a spirit of goodwill.

763. This Press release undoubtedly had a soothing effect on those sections of opinion which were the most apprehensive, and the feeling of confidence was strengthened by the statement made by the Chief Administrator to the Eritrean Assembly on 4 September 1952.

764. The following are the main points of this statement:

(1) The British Administration was bound by the resolutions of 2 December 1950 and 29 January 1952, and had to take steps to set up the Federation and create federal services.

(2) It was the duty of the Administering Authority to decide which among the present public services in Eritrea should become federal and which should remain Eritrean. Although this decision lay with the United Kingdom Government, the United Nations Commissioner and the Government of Ethiopia had been consulted.

(3) The resolution of 29 January 1952 provided for the transfer of State property, with certain exceptions, by the British Administration to Eritrea, "Eritrea" being defined in the resolution as being either the Federal Government or the Government of Eritrea, according to the nature of the jurisdiction and responsibilities vested in the respective governments by the resolution of 2 December 1950.

(4) The provisions for the transfer made due allowance for the legitimate needs of the Federal and Eritrean authorities. The transfer was merely the transmission of a right of occupation and possession and of an administrative responsibility; there was no implication of right of ownership so called. That was a matter to be settled between the Federal Government and the Government of Eritrea after the setting up of the Federation.

(5) The Chief Administrator then gave particulars of the services already transferred to the Federal Authorities and emphasized the fact that the admission of the autonomous unit into a Federation with a sovereign State which was a Member of the United Nations had brought considerable benefit to Eritrea, and that in return the Federal Government was entitled to enjoy every facility in Eritrea to enable it to cope with the responsibilities devolving upon it under the resolution of 2 December 1950.

765. Moreover, the statement of the Emperor of Ethiopia on Eritrean participation in the machinery of federal government, made at the time of ratification of the Federal Act, 60/ strengthened the favourable psychological effect already produced by the assurances of the Commissioner and Chief Administrator.

60/ Chapter V of the present report, paragraph 497 [not reproduced here].

766. The ceremony of the transfer of power, held at 4.45 p.m. on 15 September 1952 at Government House, thus took place in an atmosphere of confidence.

767. After the signing of the Termination of Powers Proclamation by the Chief Administrator, copies were presented to the Emperor's representatives, to the Chief Executive of the Government of Eritrea and to the United Nations Commissioner.

768. After this ceremony, the Chief Administrator thanked all those who had assisted him in his work, and especially the United Nations Commissioner. He also offered his best wishes to the successors of the British Administration in Eritrea.

769. The following is the text of the Proclamation: 61/

TERMINATION OF POWERS PROCLAMATION (No. 136, 1952) BY THE BRITISH ADMINISTRATION, ERITREA

Whereas by a resolution of the General Assembly of the United Nations dated 2 December, 1950, Eritrea shall constitute an autonomous unit federated with Ethiopia under the sovereignty of the Ethiopian Crown as therein provided:

And whereas it is provided by the Eritrean (Termination of Administration) Order, 1952, that the Authority of Her Majesty in Eritrea shall determine as from such date as shall for the purpose of enabling the Federal Act and the Constitution of Eritrea to enter into effect be proclaimed therein by the Chief Administrator:

And whereas by the said resolution of 2 December, 1950, it is provided that the jurisdiction of the Federal Government in Eritrea shall extend to certain matters and that the jurisdiction of Eritrean Government shall extend to all other matters:

And whereas by the said resolution of 2 December, 1950, it is provided that the Administering Power shall make arrangements for the transfer of power to the appropriate authorities:

And whereas by a resolution of the United Nations dated 29 January, 1952, it is provided that Eritrea (which term for the purposes of the resolution is said to be interpreted in conformity with paragraph 3 of the said resolution of 2 December, 1950), shall receive without payment certain movable and immovable property located in Eritrea owned by the Italian State either in its own name or in the name of the Italian Administration in Eritrea and that such property shall be transferred to Eritrea not later than the effective date of the final transfer of power from the Administering Power to the appropriate Authorities:

Now therefore, I, Duncan Cameron CUMMING, Companion of the Most Honourable Order of the Bath, Commander of Most Excellent Order of the British Empire, Chief Administrator of Eritrea, hereby proclaim as follows:

1. To the intent that Eritrea shall become an autonomous unit in the manner provided in the Resolution of the United Nations dated 2 December, 1950, and in order that the Federal Act and the Constitution of Eritrea shall enter into effect the authority of Her Majesty in Eritrea shall determine.

2. The powers and jurisdiction of the Administering Power are hereby transferred to the Federal Government and the Eritrean Government.

3. The property set out in the First Schedule hereto is hereby transferred to the Federal Government and the property set out in the Second Schedule hereto is hereby transferred to the Eritrean Government.

4. This Proclamation may be cited as the Termination of Powers Proclamation, 1952, and shall come into force at midnight on 15/16 September, 1952.

770. Thanks to the spirit of collaboration shown by the interested parties directly responsible, the Commissioner was thus able not only to take cognizance of the transfer of power but also, through the information with which he had been spontaneously provided, to testify to the faithful application, both of the spirit and of the letter of the resolution.

771. In concluding this chapter, mention must be made of the telegram sent by the Secretary-General of the United Nations to the Commissioner on the occasion of the transfer of power, which reads as follows:

"Please express to representatives of United Kingdom as Administering Power and to appropriate Federal and Eritrean Authorities my deep gratification on occasion transfer of power in Eritrea in compliance decisions of General Assembly within specified time limits *stop* This historic step has been made possible by the co-operation and high sense of responsibility of all the parties concerned working with the United Nations towards a common objective *stop* Please extend my congratulations to the

---

61/ As regards the plans drawn up for the transfer dealt with in the resolution, see the Administering Authority's Report (document A/2233).

Eritrean people on this achievement which your own devoted service in Eritrea has so greatly contributed to bring about *stop*

TRYGVE LIE
Secretary-General"

772. The Commissioner communicated the contents of this message to the Chief Administrator, to the Emperor's Representative, and to the Chief Executive of the Government of Eritrea.

CHAPTER X
SUBMISSION OF THE ERITREAN CONSTITUTION TO THE GENERAL ASSEMBLY

773. With the completion of the transfer of power, the Commissioner, acting under paragraph 15 of the resolution, submits to the General Assembly the text of the Eritrean Constitution. The document as approved by the Commissioner, adopted by the Eritrean Assembly and ratified by the Emperor of Ethiopia, constitutes annex II of the present report.

CONCLUSIONS

774. With the ratification of the Federal Act by the Emperor of Ethiopia on 11 September 1952, and the promulgation of the Termination of Powers Proclamation by the Administering Power on 15 September 1952, the General Assembly's resolution of 2 December 1950 was put into effect and the task entrusted to the Commissioner completed.

775. The foundations of the Federation of Ethiopia and of the autonomous unit of Eritrea have thus been laid. So far as Eritrea is concerned, the Constitution approved by the Commissioner, adopted by the Assembly and ratified by the Emperor, completes the structure. That Constitution, together with the organic laws passed by the Eritrean Assembly, faithfully reflects not only the letter, but also the spirit of the resolution; so far as any document can, it gives Eritrea a fair and promising start in its existence as an autonomous unit within the Federation. Much more than a mere document will be required, however, to ensure life and continuity for the institutions thus created. The Federation and Eritrea will have to learn to live side by side, each respecting the proper sphere of activity and jurisdiction of the other. As the first Panel of Legal Consultants pointed out, "the régime prescribed in the General Assembly's resolution ... can only operate satisfactorily if Ethiopia accepts it freely and without any unexpressed reservation, and intends to apply it in good faith".

776. My conversations with His Majesty the Emperor of Ethiopia have convinced me that such good faith exists and that it is the Emperor's sincere desire that the Federal Act should be implemented in accordance with both the letter and spirit of the resolution.

777. On the Eritrean side, the discussions I held with the people from the outset, and the spirit in which the Eritrean Representative Assembly adopted the Constitution have convinced me that there is a genuine readiness for full co-operation with the federal authorities and a real respect for the unity of the Federation under the sovereignty of the Emperor.

778. The procedure for setting up the necessary organs of the Federal Government is laid down in the resolution, except for the means whereby, if mediation fails, conflicts of jurisdiction can be satisfactorily settled by a tribunal whose impartiality is manifest in its proceedings and composition. For this purpose, a joint act by the two legislatures will be required; it is to be hoped that, with the goodwill of both parties, this final guarantee of faithful implementation of the resolution will soon be provided.

...

II. Constitution of Eritrea

(TEXT OF THE CONSTITUTION AS ADOPTED BY THE ERITREAN ASSEMBLY ON 10 JULY 1952)

...

PREAMBLE

In the name of Almighty God,
Trusting that He may grant Eritrea peace, concord and prosperity,
And that the Federation of Eritrea and Ethiopia may be harmonious and fruitful,

We, the Eritrean Assembly, acting on behalf of the Eritrean people,

Grateful to the United Nations for recommending that Eritrea shall constitute an autonomous unit federated with Ethiopia under the sovereignty of the Ethiopian Crown and that its Constitution be based on the principles of democratic government,

Desirous of satisfying the wishes and ensuring the welfare of the inhabitants of Eritrea by close and economic association with Ethiopia and by respecting the rights and safeguarding the institutions, traditions, religions and languages of all the elements of the population.

Resolved to prevent any discrimination and to ensure, under a régime of freedom and equality, the brotherly collaboration of the various races and religions in Eritrea, and to promote economic and social progress,

Trusting fully in God, the Master of the Universe.
Do hereby adopt this Constitution as the Constitution of Eritrea.

PART I. GENERAL

Article 1
Adoption and ratification of the Federal Act

1. The Eritrean people, through their representatives, hereby adopt and ratify the Federal Act approved on 2 December 1950 by the General Assembly of the United Nations.

2. They undertake to observe faithfully the provisions of the said Act.

CHAPTER I. STATUS OF ERITREA

Article 2
Territory of Eritrea

The territory of Eritrea, including the islands, is that of the former Italian colony of Eritrea.

Article 3
Autonomy and federation

Eritrea shall constitute an autonomous unit federated with Ethiopia under the sovereignty of the Ethiopian Crown.

Article 4
Legislative, executive and judicial powers

The Government of Eritrea shall exercise legislative, executive and judicial powers with respect to matters within its jurisdiction.

Article 5
Matters coming within the jurisdiction of Eritrea

1. The jurisdiction of the Government of Eritrea shall extend to all matters not vested in the Federal Government by the Federal Act.

2. This jurisdiction shall include:

(a) The various branches of law (criminal law, civil law, commercial law, etc.);

(b) The organization of the public services;

(c) Internal police;

(d) Health;

(e) Education;

(f) Public assistance and social security;

(g) Protection of labour;

(h) Exploitation of natural resources and regulation of industry, internal commerce, trades and professions;

(i) Agriculture;

(j) Internal communications;

(k) The public utility services which are peculiar to Eritrea;

(l) The Eritrean budget and the establishment and collection of taxes designed to meet the expenses of Eritrean public functions and services.

Article 6
Contribution by Eritrea to the expenses of the Federal Government

1. Eritrea shall bear its just and equitable share of the expenses of Federal functions and services.

Assessment and levying of Federal taxes

2. The Government of Eritrea shall assess and levy in Eritrea, by delegation from the Federal Government, such taxes as are established to that end for the benefit of the whole of the Federation.

Revenue from customs duties

3. Within the revenue which accrues to Eritrea shall be included the customs duties on goods entering or leaving the Federation which have their final destination or origin in Eritrea, in accordance with the provisions of paragraph 4 of the resolution of 2 December 1950 of the General Assembly of the United Nations.

Article 7
Representation of Eritrea in the Imperial Federal Council

1. The Eritrean representatives in the Imperial Federal Council, composed of equal numbers of Ethiopians and Eritreans, shall be appointed by the Chief Executive with the approval of the Assembly. They shall be formally invested in office by the Emperor.

Participation of Eritreans in the Federal Government

2. Eritreans shall participate in the executive and judicial branches and shall be represented in the legislative branch, of the Federal Government, in accordance with law and in the proportion that the population of Eritrea bears to the population of the Federation.

Article 8
Eritrean citizenship

Persons who have acquired Federal nationality in Eritrea under the Federal Act (Section A, paragraph 6 of the General Assembly Resolution 390 A (V)) and have been granted Eritrean citizenship in accordance with the laws of Eritrea shall be citizens of Eritrea.

Article 9
Rights of Federal nationals who are not Eritrean citizens

1. On the basis of reciprocity, Federal nationals who are not Eritrean citizens shall enjoy the same rights as Eritreans.

2. Federal nationals shall enjoy political rights in accordance with the Eritrean Constitution and laws on the basis of reciprocity.

CHAPTER II. REPRESENTATION OF THE EMPEROR IN ERITREA

Article 10
The Emperor has a representative in Eritrea

There shall be a representative in Eritrea of His Imperial Majesty, the Emperor of Ethiopia, Sovereign of the Federation.

Article 11
Rank of the Representative of the Emperor

The Representative of the Emperor shall, on all occasions, have the place of precedence at official ceremonies in Eritrea.

Article 12
Administering of the oath of office to the Chief Executive before the Representative of the Emperor. Formal investment of the Chief Executive in office

The Chief Executive, elected by the Assembly in accordance with Article 68, shall take the oath of office in accordance with the provisions of Article 72. The Representative of the Emperor, having noted that the Chief Executive has been elected by the Assembly, shall formally invest him in office in the name of the Emperor, Sovereign of the Federation.

Article 13
Opening and closing of sessions of the Assembly

At the opening and closing of sessions of the Assembly, the Representative of the Emperor may deliver the speech from the throne in which he will deal with affairs of common interest to the Federation and to Eritrea.

Article 14
Transmission of legislation to the representative of the Emperor

1. When draft legislation has been voted by the Assembly, the Chief Executive will transmit it immediately to the Representative of the Emperor.
2. If the Representative of the Emperor considers that draft legislation voted by the Assembly encroaches upon Federal jurisdiction, or that it involves the international responsibility of the Federation, he may transmit a request to the Chief Executive within twenty days after the vote by the Assembly for reconsideration of the draft legislation by the Assembly, indicating his reasons for doing so.

Article 15
Promulgation of legislation

The Representative of the Emperor will promulgate legislation in the manner laid down in Article 58.

CHAPTER III DEMOCRATIC GOVERNMENT IN ERITREA

Article 16
The principles of democratic government

The Constitution of Eritrea is based on the principles of democratic government.

Article 17
Respect for human rights

The Constitutional guarantees to all persons the enjoyment of human rights and fundamental freedoms.

Article 18
Organs of government are provided for by the people and shall act in the interests of the people

1. All organs of government are provided for by the people. They are chosen by means of periodic, free and fair elections, directly and indirectly.
2. The organs of government shall act in the interests of the people.

Article 19
Rule of law

1. The organs of government and public officials shall have no further powers than those conferred on them by the Constitution and by the laws and regulations which give effect thereto.
2. Neither a group of the people nor an individual shall arbitrarily assume the exercise of any political power or of administrative functions.
3. Public officials shall perform their duties in strict conformity with the law and solely in the public interest.
4. Public officials shall be personally answerable for any unlawful acts or abuses they may commit.

Article 20
Franchise

The electorate shall consist of those persons possessing Eritrean citizenship who:
(a) Are of male sex;
(b) Have attained the age of twenty-one years;
(c) Are under no legal disability as defined by the law; and
(d) Have been resident for one year preceding the election in the constituency where they shall vote.

Article 21
Federal flag

1. The Federal flag shall be respected in Eritrea.

Flag, seal and arms of Eritrea

2. There shall be a flag, seal and arms of Eritrea, details of which shall be decided upon by law.

CHAPTER IV. HUMAN RIGHTS AND FUNDAMENTAL FREEDOMS

Section I. Provisions reproduced from the Federal Act

Article 22
Provisions reproduced from the Federal Act

The following provisions of paragraph 7 of the Federal Act shall be an integral part of the Constitution of Eritrea:

"The Federal Government, as well as Eritrea, shall ensure to residents in Eritrea, without distinction of nationality, race, sex, language or religion, the enjoyment of human rights and fundamental liberties, including the following:

"(a) The right to equality before the law. No discrimination shall be made against foreign enterprises in existence in Eritrea engaged in industrial, commercial, agricultural, artisan, educational or charitable activities nor against banking institutions and insurance companies operating in Eritrea;

"(b) The right to life, liberty and security of person;

"(c) The right to own and dispose of property. No one shall be deprived of property, including contractual rights, without due process of law and without payment of just and effective compensation;

"(d) The right to freedom of opinion and expression and the right of adopting and practising any creed or religion;

"(e) The right to education;

"(f) The right to freedom of peaceful assembly and association;

"(g) The right to inviolability of correspondence and domicile subject to the requirements of the law;

"(h) The right to exercise any profession subject to the requirements of the law;

"(i) No one shall be subject to arrest or detention without an order of a competent authority, except in case of flagrant and serious violation of the law in force. No one shall be deported except in accordance with the law;

"(j) The right to a fair and equitable trial, the right of petition to the Emperor and the right of appeal to the Emperor for commutation of death sentences;

"(k) Retroactivity of penal law shall be excluded."

Section II. Other provisions

Article 23
Freedom and equality before the law. Everyone is a person before the law

All persons are born free and are equal before the law without distinction of nationality, race, sex or religion and, as such shall enjoy civil rights and shall be subject to duties and obligations.

Article 24
Prohibition of torture and certain punishments

No one shall be subject to torture or to cruel, inhuman or degrading treatment or punishment.

Article 25
Right to freedom of movement

Everyone resident in Eritrea has the right to freedom of movement and to the choice of place of residence in Eritrea subject to the provisions of Article 34.

Article 26
Freedom of conscience and religion

The right to freedom of conscience and religion shall include the right of everyone, either alone or in community with others and in public or private, to manifest his religion or belief in teaching, practice, worship and observance.

Article 27
No discrimination to the detriment of any religion

No economic, financial or political measure of a discriminatory nature shall be taken to the detriment of any religion practised in Eritrea.

Article 28
Recognition of religious bodies as persons before the law

Religious bodies of all kinds and religious orders shall be recognized as possessing juristic personality.

Consequently, any religious denomination or any group of citizens belonging to such denomination shall be entitled:

(a) To establish and maintain institutions for religious, educational and charitable purposes;
(b) To conduct its own affairs in matters of religion;
(c) To possess and acquire movable and immovable property;
(d) To administer its property and to enter into contracts.

Article 29
Religious instruction and worship in public schools

No pupil attending a public school shall be required to take part in any religious instruction at such school or attend any religious service at such school.

Article 30
Freedom to express opinions

Everyone resident in Eritrea shall have the right to express his opinion through any medium whatever (Press, speech, etc.) and to learn the opinions expressed by others.

Article 31
Right to education and freedom to teach

1. Everyone resident in Eritrea shall have the right to education. The Government shall make every effort to establish schools and to train teachers.
2. The Government shall encourage private persons and private associations and institutions, regardless of race, nationality, religion, sex or language, to open schools, provided that they give proof of the required standards of morality and competence.
3. The instruction in the schools shall conform to the spirit of the Constitution.

Article 32
Associations and companies

1. Everyone resident in Eritrea shall have the right to form associations or companies for lawful purposes.
2. Companies or associations shall enjoy fundamental freedoms in so far as their nature permits.
3. Such companies or associations shall be regarded as persons before the law.

Article 33
Protection of working conditions

1. Everyone resident in Eritrea, regardless of nationality, race, sex, or religion, shall have the right to opportunity of work, to equal pay for equal work, to regular holidays with pay, to payment of dependency allowances, to compensation for illness and accidents incurred through work and to a decent and healthy standard of life.

Trade unions
2. Everyone resident in Eritrea shall have the right to form and to join trade unions for the protection of his interests.

Article 34
Control by law of the enjoyment of human rights and fundamental freedoms

1. The provisions in the last sub-paragraph of paragraph 7 of the Federal Act apply to the whole of Chapter IV of Part I of the Constitution. This sub-paragraph reads as follows:

"The respect for the rights and freedoms of others and the requirements of public order and the general welfare alone will justify any limitations to the above rights."

2. In applying the aforementioned provisions, the enjoyment of human rights and fundamental freedoms may be regulated by law provided that such regulation does not impede their normal enjoyment.

Article 35
Duties of individuals

Everyone shall have the duty to respect the Constitution and the laws, and to serve the community.

CHAPTER V. SPECIAL RIGHTS OF THE VARIOUS POPULATION GROUPS IN ERITREA

Article 36
Property rights

Nationals of the Federation, including those covered by sub-paragraphs (b) and (d) of paragraph 6 of the Federal Act, as well as foreign nationals, shall have the right to respect for their customs and their own legislation governing personal status and legal capacity, the law of the family and the law of succession.

Article 37
Property rights

Property rights and rights of real nature, including those on State lands, established by custom or law and exercised on Eritrea by the tribes, the various population groups and by natural or legal persons, shall not be impaired by any law of a discriminatory nature.

Article 38
Languages

1. Tigrinya and Arabic shall be the official languages of Eritrea.
2. In accordance with established practice in Eritrea, the languages spoken and written by the various

population groups shall be permitted to be used in dealing with the public authorities, as well as for religious or educational purposes and for all forms of expression of ideas.

PART II. THE ASSEMBLY

CHAPTER I. COMPOSITION AND ELECTION OF THE ASSEMBLY

Article 39
Creation of an Assembly representing the Eritrean people

1. Legislative power shall be exercised by an Assembly representing the Eritrean people.
2. Members of the Assembly shall represent the Eritrean people as a whole, and not only the constituency in which they are elected.

Article 40
Number of members of the Assembly

1. The Assembly shall be composed of not less than fifty and not more then seventy members.
2. Within the limits prescribed in the preceding paragraph, the number of members shall be fixed by law.

Article 41
Constituencies

1. The territory of Eritrea shall be divided into electoral constituencies, each electing one representative.
2. These constituencies shall be established in such a way that they will be approximately equal in population. The boundaries of the constituencies shall be fixed by law.

Article 42
Eligibility

All members of the electorate shall be eligible for election to the Assembly provided that:
(a) They have reached the age of thirty;
(b) They have been resident in Eritrea for three years and have been resided in the constituency for two years during the last ten years;
(c) They are not disqualified for any reason laid down by law; and
(d) They are not officials of the Eritrean or Federal Governments, unless they have resigned at the time of presenting their candidature.

Article 43
The two voting systems

1. The members of the Assembly shall be elected either by direct or indirect ballot.

2. The system of voting to be used in any given constituency shall be laid down by law.
3. Voting by direct ballot shall be personal, equal and secret.

For this purpose, a roll of qualified voters shall be drawn up, and revised from time to time.

The system for establishing electoral rolls shall be fixed by law.

4. The first stage of voting by indirect ballot shall be conducted in accordance with local custom. At the second stage, voting shall be personal, equal and secret.

Article 44
Election by direct ballot and election at second stage in the case of indirect ballot

1. If a candidate for the Assembly obtains an absolute majority of the votes cast he shall be declared elected.
2. If no candidate obtains an absolute majority, as defined in paragraph 1, a second ballot shall be held, and the candidate who then obtains the greatest number of votes shall be declared elected.

Article 45
Electoral High Commission

1. An electoral High Commission consisting of three persons appointed by the Supreme Court established under Article 85 shall be responsible for supervising all electoral proceedings (including the compiling of electoral rolls), and for preventing or putting a stop to irregularities.
2. The High Commission shall appoint, in each constituency, from among the electors of that constituency, a representative to act under its authority.
3. The said representative shall be assisted by an advisory election committee, consisting of members chosen by him from among the electors of that constituency.

As soon as an election period has been declared open in accordance with the law every candidate shall be entitled to be represented on the committee.

4. The implementation of the present article shall be prescribed by law.

Article 46
Disputed elections to the Assembly

1. At the opening of the session following an election, the Assembly shall confirm its members. All members whose elections are unchallenged shall be confirmed simultaneously.
2. In any case where an election is challenged, the Assembly shall decide, by a two-thirds majority of the members present, whether the challenged election is valid, provided that such two-thirds majority shall be not less than one half of the members of the Assembly in office.

3. In the event of a member's election not being confirmed, he may, within three days following the adoption of the decision by the Assembly, appeal to the Supreme Court established under Article 85, but shall not take his seat until the Supreme Court has given its decision.

Article 47
Term of the Assembly

1. The Assembly shall be elected for a term of four years.
2. Members shall be eligible for re-election.
3. If there is a vacancy during the term of an Assembly, a by-election shall take place. No by-election can, however, take place within six months of the election of a new Assembly.

CHAPTER II. SESSIONS AND MEETINGS

Article 48
Regular sessions

1. The Assembly shall hold two regular sessions each year.
2. The Assembly shall meet in regular session on a date to be specified by law.
This session shall continue for at least one month.
3. The opening date of the second regular session shall be fixed by the Chief Executive after consulting the President of the Assembly.
This second session shall be devoted primarily to voting the budget and the Assembly shall consider no other matter until the budget has been voted. The session shall not close until the budget has been voted as prescribed in Article 60.
4. The closing date of regular sessions shall be fixed by the Chief Executive after consulting the President of the Assembly.
5. With the consent of the President of the Assembly, the Chief Executive may suspend a session for a period not exceeding twenty days.

Article 49
Special sessions

1. The Chief Executive may convene the Assembly to a special session.
2. The Chief Executive shall convene the Assembly to a special session whenever a written request is submitted by not less than one-third of the members.
3. When the Assembly is convened to a special session by the Chief Executive on his own initiative, only the questions set forth in the notice convening the Assembly shall be discussed. The Chief Executive shall fix the closing date of the session.

4. When the Assembly is convened to a special session at the request of not less than one-third of its members, it shall determine its own agenda. The Chief Executive shall fix the closing date of the session in agreement with the President of the Assembly.

Article 50
Quorum

Two thirds of the members of the Assembly shall compose a quorum.

Article 51
Rules of procedure

The Assembly shall adopt its own rules of procedure.

Article 52
Officers of the Assembly

The Assembly shall elect its officers at the opening of the first regular session of each year or at the beginning of a new Legislature. The officers shall consist of a President, a Vice-President and, if the Assembly so desires, other officers.

CHAPTER III. STATUS OF MEMBERS OF THE ASSEMBLY

Article 53
Swearing-in of members

Before taking up their duties, members of the Assembly who have not served in the previous Legislature shall take, in accordance with the faith and the customary practice of the individual concerned, the following oath before the President of the Assembly:

"I undertake before Almighty God" (or an invocation conforming to the faith and the customary practice of the member of the Assembly concerned) "to respect the Federation under the sovereignty of the Imperial Crown, loyally to serve Eritrea, to defend its Constitution and its laws, to seek no personal advantage from my office, and to perform all my duties conscientiously."

Article 54
Parliamentary immunity

1. Members of the Assembly shall not be liable to prosecution for opinions expressed or votes cast by them in performance of their duties.
2. Members of the Assembly shall not be arrested or prosecuted without the authorization of the Assembly; save that in case of flagrant delict they may be arrested, but the prosecution, even in this case, shall be authorized by the Assembly.

When the Assembly is not in session, such authorization may be given by its officers. The Assembly may subsequently decide that proceedings shall be discontinued.

Article 55
Remuneration of members of the Assembly

1. Members of the Assembly shall receive a remuneration fixed by law.

2. No increase of remuneration shall take effect until the term of office of the Assembly voting it has expired.

CHAPTER IV. POWERS OF THE ASSEMBLY

Article 56
General powers of the Assembly

The Assembly shall vote the laws and the budget, elect the Chief Executive and supervise the activities of the Executive.

Section I. Legislative functions

Article 57
Drafting and adoption of legislation

1. Draft legislation may be introduced into the Assembly by members of the Assembly or submitted to the Assembly by the Chief Executive.

2. Such legislation shall be considered, discussed and put to the vote as provided in the Assembly's rules of procedure.

Article 58
Request for a reconsideration

1. Draft legislation adopted by the Assembly shall be immediately transmitted by the President of the Assembly to the Chief Executive.

Approval of legislation by the Chief Executive

2. The Chief Executive will transmit it as soon as received to the Representative of the Emperor who may request, in accordance with the provisions of Article 14, that it be reconsidered by the Assembly.

Publication

3. If the Representative of the Emperor, exercising the prerogatives for which provision is made under Article 14, has transmitted a request to the Chief Executive for reconsideration, giving his reasons for doing so, the Assembly must take a further vote. The draft legislation must obtain a two-thirds majority vote to be adopted.

4. If the draft legislation has been adopted after reconsideration, as provided in the preceding paragraph, or if the Representative of the Emperor has not exercised his prerogatives under Article 14, the Chief Executive must within twenty days after the vote taken by the Assembly, either approve the draft legislation and transmit it to the Representative of the Emperor for promulgation within five days of its receipt, or return it to the Assembly with his comments.

5. If the Chief Executive shall have returned the draft legislation to the Assembly, the Assembly shall reconsider the draft legislation and take a further vote on it. If the draft legislation is then adopted by a two-thirds majority, the Chief Executive shall transmit it to the Representative of the Emperor for promulgation within five days of its receipt.

6. All draft legislation adopted in accordance with the provisions of this article but not promulgated within the time limit laid down in paragraphs 4 and 5 of this Article, shall come into effect after publication by the Chief Executive.

Section II. Budget

Article 59
Submission of the draft budget by the Chief Executive

1. At least one month before the opening of the second regular session of the Assembly, the Chief Executive shall submit a draft budget for the next financial year.

2. The draft budget shall cover the whole of the revenue and expenditures of the Government of Eritrea for the next financial year.

Article 60
Examination and adoption of the budget by the Assembly

1. During the month preceding the second regular session of the Assembly, the Assembly Finance Committee shall examine the draft budget submitted by the Executive and report to the Assembly.

2. A general debate on the draft budget shall be held at the beginning of the second regular session of the Assembly.

Within ten days following the closure of the debate, the Executive shall submit a revised draft budget including the amendments it may decide to make to its first draft as a result of the observations made by the Assembly.

3. The Assembly shall then proceed to examine the various items of the budget:

(a) It shall first adopt the expenditure estimates, with or without amendments, only the total estimate for each Executive Department being put to the vote.

The Assembly may not increase the estimates proposed in the draft budget unless increase is balanced by corresponding estimates of revenue and has received the consent of the Executive.

(b) The Assembly shall then adopt, with or without amendments, the revenue estimates chapter by chapter, each of which shall be put to the vote separately.

4. The complete budget shall be adopted before the beginning of the financial year; otherwise, the amended draft budget submitted by the Executive as provided in paragraph 2 above shall be deemed to be adopted, provided the Executive has itself observed the time-limit laid down in Article 59 and in the present article.

Article 61
All taxation and expenditure must be authorized by law

No tax shall be levied and no expenditure shall be incurred unless authorized by law.

Article 62
Form of the budget

A law shall be enacted governing the form in which the budget is to be submitted and voted on each year.

Article 63
Credit for urgent expenditure

1. When voting the budget, the Assembly shall include a credit for urgent expenditure.

2. The amount of this credit shall not exceed 10 per cent of the expenditure estimates.

3. At the beginning of the following session of the Assembly, the Chief Executive shall report on the use he has made of this credit. The Assembly shall take a vote on this report.

Article 64
Accounts for past financial years

1. Within eighteen months following the close of each financial year, the Executive shall submit the accounts to the Assembly for approval.

2. An Auditor-General, independent of the Executive, shall be elected by the Assembly.

3. The principal function of the Auditor-General shall be to examine the annual accounts, and to make a report to the Assembly containing his observations on them at the time of their presentation to the Assembly.

4. The method of election and the matters within the competence of the Auditor-General shall be established by law.

Section III. Election and supervision of the Executive

Article 65
Election of the Chief Executive

The Assembly shall elect the Chief Executive as provided in Article 68.

Article 66
Supervision of the Executive by the Assembly

1. Members of the Assembly may submit questions in writing or short questions orally to the Executive, which shall reply.

2. At the request of ten members of the Assembly, a debate may be held on the Executive's policy.

The Executive shall be entitled to intervene both in the course of the debate and before its closure.

PART III. THE EXECUTIVE

CHAPTER I. COMPOSITION AND APPOINTMENT

Article 67
Composition of the Executive

The Executive shall consist of a Chief Executive assisted by Secretaries of Executive Departments.

Article 68
Election of the Chief Executive

1. The Chief Executive shall be elected by the Assembly by secret ballot; if a candidate obtains two thirds of the votes he shall be declared elected. If no candidate obtains the requisite number of votes the candidate receiving the least number of votes shall be removed from the list and the Assembly shall vote again on the remainder repeating the process if necessary until a candidate obtains the required number of votes.

2. Only Eritrean citizens having attained the age of thirty-five years and in possession of their political rights shall be eligible for office of the Chief Executive.

3. The Assembly shall elect a Chief Executive at the opening of each new legislature.

4. In case of death or resignation of the Chief Executive, the Assembly shall elect a successor within fifteen days. If the Assembly is not in session, the President of the Assembly shall convene it to a special session.

The newly elected Chief Executive shall remain in office until the expiry of his predecessor's term.

5. The Chief Executive shall be eligible for re-election.

Article 69
Appointment of Secretaries of Executive Departments

1. The Chief Executive shall have power to appoint and dismiss Secretaries of Executive Departments, who shall be responsible to him.

2. Only persons qualified to be members of the Eritrean electorate shall be eligible to hold office as Secretaries of Executive Departments.

3. The Chief Executive shall select the Secretaries of Executive Departments in such a way as to ensure as far as possible a fair representation in his council of the

principal groups of the population and the various geographical areas of the territory.

4. The number and the functions of Secretaries of Executive Departments shall be prescribed by law.

Article 70
Incompatibility

The office of the Chief Executive or of Secretary of an Executive Department is incompatible with the holding of any other administrative or judicial office.

Article 71
Acting Chief Executive

The Chief Executive, on being elected, shall designate one of the Secretaries of Executive Departments to act for him if he is temporarily prevented from discharging his duties or, if his post fall vacant, until such time as a new Chief Executive is elected.

Article 72
Swearing-in of the Chief Executive

Before taking up his duties, the Chief Executive shall, according to his faith and customary practice, take the following oath in the Assembly before the Representative of the Emperor:

"I undertake before Almighty God" (or an invocation conforming to the faith and the customary practice of the Chief Executive) "to respect the Federation under the sovereignty of the Imperial Crown, loyally to serve Eritrea, to defend its Constitution and its laws, to seek the welfare of the Eritrean people in the unity of its inhabitants bound together by ties of brotherhood, whatever their race, religion or language, and to seek no personal advantage from office."

Article 73
Swearing-in of Secretaries of Executive Departments

Before taking up their duties, Secretaries of Executive Departments shall, according to their faith and their customary practices, take the following oath publicly in the Assembly before the Representative of the Emperor:

"I undertake before Almighty God" (or an invocation conforming to the faith and customary practice of the individual concerned) "loyally to respect the Federation under the Sovereignty of the Imperial Crown, loyally to serve Eritrea, to respect its Constitution and its laws, to seek no personal advantage from my office and to perform all my duties conscientiously."

Article 74
Council of the Executive

The Chief Executive shall from time to time summon a council of the Secretaries of Executive Departments. This Council shall advise the Chief Executive on matters of general policy and on any questions he may submit to it.

Article 75
Removal from office of the Chief Executive

1. The Chief Executive shall not be answerable for any act performed by him in the course of his duties except for a grave violation of the Constitution. He shall be answerable for failure to dismiss any Secretary of an Executive Department committing a grave violation of the Constitution.

2. In such circumstances, the Chief Executive may be impeached by a two-thirds majority of the members of the Assembly in office, and tried by the Supreme Court established under Article 85.

3. If the Supreme Court finds the charge to be proved, it shall order the removal from office of the Chief Executive. It may, furthermore, disqualify him from performing any executive function or legislative duty.

4. Removal from office shall be without prejudice to any proceedings which may be instituted if the acts committed by the Chief Executive constitute offences under criminal law.

CHAPTER II. POWERS OF THE EXECUTIVE

Article 76
Enumeration of powers

1. The Chief Executive shall ensure that the Constitution and the laws are enforced. He shall have responsibility for the direction of the Executive and Administrative Departments and public services. He shall be Chairman of the Civil Service Commission, for which provision is made in Article 82, and shall make appointments in accordance with the Constitution and the laws.

2. He shall be responsible for the internal police of Eritrea and, to this end, he shall issue regulations conforming to the Constitution and the laws to ensure the maintenance of public order and security.

3. He shall convene the sessions of the Assembly as provided in Articles 48 and 49 of the Constitution.

4. Each year, at the opening of the first regular session, he shall give an account to the Assembly of his conduct of affairs and report on the general situation of Eritrea.

5. He shall have the power to propose legislation. He may request the Assembly to reconsider draft legislation. He shall publish the laws after their promulgation or under the provisions of Article 58.

6. He shall submit to the Assembly a draft annual budget and the accounts for the preceding financial year, as provided in Articles 59, 60 and 64.

7. He shall have access to and the right of addressing the Assembly. He may be represented in the Assembly and its Committees by the Secretaries of Executive Departments.

8. He shall issue the regulations required to implement the laws.

9. He shall issue orders as provided in Article 77.

10. He may temporarily limit certain provisions of the Constitution as provided in Article 78.

11. He shall take the necessary measures for the suppression of brigandage, as provided in Article 79.

12. Official documents issued by the Chief Executive must be counter-signed by the Secretaries of Executive Departments concerned.

Article 77
Power of the Chief Executive to issue orders when the Assembly is not in session

1. In the interval between sessions of the Assembly, the Chief Executive shall have authority to issue, when necessary, orders governing any matter within the jurisdiction of the Government of Eritrea except matters dealt with in Chapter IV of Part I of the Constitution, provided that such orders are compatible with the Constitution and the laws in force.

2. Such orders shall be submitted to the Assembly which must approve or repeal them within a period of two months from the opening of the session following their promulgation.

3. Failing a decision by the Assembly within the above-mentioned period, orders issued by the Chief Executive shall be deemed to be confirmed.

Article 78
Limitation in time of emergency of certain constitutional provisions

1. In the event of a serious emergency which endangers public order and security, the Assembly may, on the proposal of the Chief Executive, adopt a law authorizing him to impose, under the conditions provided for in Article 34, temporary limitations on the rights set forth in Chapter IV of Part I of this Constitution.

2. The authorization thus given by law shall be valid for a maximum period of two months. If necessary, it may be renewed under the same conditions.

3. During the interval between sessions, the Chief Executive may, if it is urgently necessary, issue an order prescribing the measures referred to in paragraph 1.

In such cases, a special session of the Assembly shall be convened, as soon as possible and, at the latest, within twenty days following the promulgation of the order, to adopt a law approving, amending or repealing the said order.

Article 79
Suppression of brigandage

1. If public order and the security of persons and property in Eritrea are threatened by organized brigandage, the Chief Executive shall, after making a proclamation to the people, adopt the exceptional measures necessary to suppress such brigandage.

2. The Chief Executive shall inform the Assembly of the measures he has taken.

CHAPTER III. THE ADMINISTRATION

Article 80
Conditions of appointment of officials

Officials shall be chosen for their ability and character; considerations of race, sex, religion or political opinion shall not influence the choice either to their advantage or to their disadvantage.

Article 81
Status of officials

1. The general status of administrative officials shall be fixed by law.

2. The special status of the various categories of administrative officials shall be fixed by regulations.

Article 82
Civil Service Commission

1. A Civil Service Commission, under the chairmanship of the Chief Executive or his representative, shall be created.

2. This Commission shall be responsible for the appointment, promotion, transfer and discharge of officials, and for taking disciplinary action against them.

3. The composition of this Commission, the procedure for the appointment of its members, and the conditions under which it will function will be determined by law.

Article 83
Local communities

1. The Constitution recognizes the existence of local communities.

2. Municipalities shall be accorded the management of their own affairs.

3. Officials responsible for the administration of village and tribal communities shall be selected from persons of those local communities.

4. The conditions for the application of the preceding provisions may be determined by law.

PART IV. THE ADVISORY COUNCIL OF ERITREA

Article 84
Advisory Council of Eritrea

1. An Advisory Council of Eritrea is hereby established.

2. The function of the Council shall be to assist the Chief Executive and the Assembly, with a view to achieving economic and social progress in Eritrea. To this end it may:

(a) Draw up plans for the development of the country's resources and for the improvement of public health and hygiene;

(b) Put forward proposals concerning finance and the budget and the organization of the administration and the public services;

(c) Give advice on draft laws submitted to the Assembly;

(d) On the request of the Chief Executive or of the Assembly, prepare drafts of laws, regulations or orders.

3. The composition and organization of the Council shall be fixed by law.

PART V. THE JUDICIARY

SOLE CHAPTER

Article 85
Judicial power

Judicial power shall be exercised by a Supreme Court and by other courts which will apply the various systems of law in force in Eritrea. The organization of these courts shall be established by law.

Article 86
Qualifications required of judges

1. Judges shall be chosen from persons of the highest moral reputation and known to be well versed in the customs and legislation peculiar to the various systems of law which they are required to apply.

Oath

2. Before taking up office, judges shall, according to their faith and their customary practice, take the following oath:

"I swear before Almighty God" (or an invocation conforming to the faith and the customary practice of the judge concerned) "to be a faithful guardian of the law and to administer it impartially and independently in order to ensure that justice shall reign supreme in Eritrea."

Independence of the judiciary

3. The judiciary shall be independent and must be free from all political influence. The Assembly and the Executive shall not give orders or injunctions to the judges, nor shall they bring any pressure to bear on them.

Status of judges

4. The status of judges shall be established by law.

Article 87
Appointment of judges

1. Judges shall be appointed by the Chief Executive on the recommendation of the President of the Assembly who shall be supplied with a list of candidates by a Committee composed of the President of the Supreme Court and two judges chosen by the members of the Supreme Court and of the court or courts immediately inferior thereto.

2. The President of the Assembly shall recommend to the Chief Executive two candidates for each appointment.

3. The list of candidates drawn up by the committee provided for in paragraph 1 must include at least three names for each appointment.

Article 88
Responsibility of judges

The Supreme Court provided for in Article 85 shall have jurisdiction in respect of criminal or disciplinary responsibility of judges for acts in connexion with the discharge of their duties.

Article 89
Composition of the Supreme Court

1. The Supreme Court shall consist of not less than three and not more than seven judges. On the proposal of the Court, the number of judges may be decreased or increased by law.

2. Judges shall be appointed for a period of seven years, which period may be renewed.

Article 90
Jurisdiction of the Supreme Court

The Supreme Court shall have jurisdiction in the following matters:

(1) As a court of last resort with respect to appeals from final judgments on points of law, and also to the extent provided by law with respect to appeals both on questions of law and fact.

(2) Conflicts of jurisdiction between courts.

In the event of a question involving conflicting jurisdiction, proceedings shall be suspended and the issue shall be presented to the Supreme Court, which shall determine the competent jurisdiction.

(3) Disputes concerning the constitutionality of laws and orders.

If the constitutionality of a law or order is challenged before a Court, proceedings shall be suspended and the issue shall be presented to the Supreme Court, which shall decide whether such act is constitutional.

(4) Actions based on administrative acts brought against the Government of Eritrea or other public bodies, unless courts have been established by law to try such cases.

(5) Criminal and disciplinary responsibility of judges as provided in Article 88.

(6) Responsibility of the Chief Executive as provided in Article 75.

PART VI. AMENDMENT OF THE CONSTITUTION

SOLE CHAPTER

Article 91
Compliance with the Federal Act and the principles of democratic government

1. The Assembly may not, by means of an amendment, introduce into the Constitution any provision which would not be in conformity with the Federal Act.

2. Article 16 of the Constitution, by the terms of which the Constitution of Eritrea is based on the principles of democratic government, shall not be amended.

Article 92
Amendments to the Constitution

1. Any amendment to the Constitution must be submitted in writing either by the Chief Executive or by a number of members of the Assembly equal to one quarter of the actual number of members.

2. A period of twenty days must elapse between the submission of an amendment and the opening of the Assembly's discussion thereon.

Article 93
Conditions governing the adoption of amendments

1. If an amendment is approved by a majority of three quarters of the members of the Assembly in office, the amendment shall be declared adopted.

2. If an amendment is approved by two successive legislatures by a majority of two thirds of the members present and voting or by a majority of the members in office, the amendment shall be declared adopted.

Entry into effect of amendments

3. Any amendments to the Constitution adopted by the Assembly according to the provisions of the foregoing paragraphs will enter into effect after ratification by the Emperor, Sovereign of the Federation.

PART VII. TRANSITIONAL PROVISIONS

Article 94
Entry into force of the Constitution

1. This Constitution shall enter into effect following ratification of the Federal Act by the Emperor of Ethiopia, and following approval by the United Nations Commissioner, adoption by the Eritrean Assembly and ratification by the Emperor of Ethiopia of the Eritrean Constitution.

2. The Administering Authority shall continue to conduct the affairs of Eritrea until the transfer of power to the Government of Eritrea has taken place.

Article 95
Laws giving effect to the Constitution

1. Any laws giving effect to the present Constitution adopted by the Eritrean Assembly convened by the Administering Authority, shall enter into effect simultaneously with the Constitution.

2. Such laws shall conform strictly to the principles and provisions of the Constitution.

Article 96
Legislation remaining in force when the Constitution comes into effect

1. Laws and regulations which were in force on 1 April 1941, and have not since been repealed by the Administering Authority and the laws and regulations enacted by that Authority, shall remain in force so long as they have not been repealed and to the extent that they have not been amended.

2. In the event of conflict between such laws and regulations and this Constitution, the Constitution shall prevail in accordance with Article 90 (3).

Article 97
Respect for obligations contracted on behalf of Eritrea

1. Obligations of any kind contracted by the authorities administering Eritrea up to the date on which the Constitution enters into force shall remain valid for the Government of Eritrea and must be respected provided that such obligations relate to matters within the jurisdiction of Eritrea.

2. As from the date of the entry into force of the Constitution any undertaking regularly concluded by the Executive Committee established by the Administering Authority before the date of the entry into force of the Constitution shall remain valid and must be respected.

3. The provisions contained in paragraph 1 shall not apply to obligations terminated by the Peace Treaty with Italy of 10 February 1947 or by the Resolution adopted by the United Nations General Assembly on 29 January 1952.

Article 98
Retention of officials in office

Administrative officials and judicial officials whether Federal nationals or not, holding office when the Constitution enters into force, shall continue in office. They may be dismissed only on three months' notice.

Article 99
Term of the first Assembly

The Assembly responsible for adopting the Constitution shall exercise the powers of the Assembly as provided in the Constitution for a period of four years after the Constitution enters into force.

Document 10

Report of the Government of the United Kingdom concerning the administration of Eritrea for the period from December 1950 to September 1952 (excerpt)

A/2233, 27 October 1952

...

CHAPTER I
United Nations Resolution No. 390 (V) of 2nd December, 1950

Origin of the United Nations Resolution

1. The United Nations Resolution No. 390 (V) of 2nd December, 1950, contained the recommendations of the General Assembly for the final disposal of the former Italian colony of Eritrea and so propounded a solution for a matter which had remained in suspense since the entry into force, on 15th September, 1947, of the Treaty of Peace with Italy.

2. Article 23 of that Treaty, after recording the abandonment by Italy of all right and title to her former African colonies, stipulated in its third paragraph that the final disposal of these territories should be determined jointly by the Governments of the Soviet Union, the United Kingdom, the United States of America, and France, within one year from the date of coming into force of the Treaty. The following additional provision was appended as paragraph 3 of Annex XI:

> "If with respect to any of these territories the Four Powers are unable to agree upon their disposal within one year from the coming into force of the Treaty of Peace with Italy, the matter shall be referred to the General Assembly of the United Nations for a recommendation, and the Four Powers agree to accept the recommendation and to give effect to it."

3. After considerable enquiry and deliberation, which included the despatch to the territory of a fact-finding delegation, known as the Four-Power Commission of Investigation, the Governments concerned failed to reach agreement by the expiry of the term appointed. Accordingly, the Four Powers in a letter dated 15th September, 1948, referred the matter to the General Assembly of the United Nations for a recommendation.

4. By Resolution No. 289 A (IV) of 21st November, 1949, the General Assembly appointed a United Nations Commission for Eritrea composed of representatives of Burma, Guatemala, Norway, Pakistan and the Union of South Africa, the duties of which were to study and, by 15th June, 1950, to report on the problem of Eritrea, at the same time submitting a proposal or proposals appropriate for a solution of the problem. Having visited the territory and having consulted a number of interested Governments, the Commission on 8th June, 1950, approved a final report to the General Assembly which consisted of two separate and differing memoranda, furnished by the delegations of Burma, Norway and the Union of South Africa on the one hand and by the delegations of Guatemala and Pakistan on the other.

5. The submission of this report to the Interim Committee of the United Nations and later to the General Assembly at its Fifth Session gave rise to protracted discussion and negotiations which culminated, on 2nd December, 1950, in the adoption by 46 votes to 10 of Resolution No. 390 (V), the final implementation of which is the subject of this report. This Resolution provides for the federation of Eritrea and Ethiopia under the

sovereignty of the Ethiopian Crown, local powers being granted to the Eritrean State in the field of domestic affairs, whilst giving the proposed Federal Government jurisdiction over defence, foreign affairs, currency and finance, foreign and interstate commerce and external and interstate communications, including ports. The Resolution provided that a constitution for Eritrea was to be drafted by a Commissioner appointed by the United Nations and submitted to a representative assembly of Eritreans, chosen by the people, to be convoked by the British Administration in consultation with the Commissioner.

6. During the transition period of preparation for federation, not to extend beyond 15th September, 1952, the Administering Authority was to continue to conduct the affairs of the territory. A number of other important duties, which are the subject of the ensuing chapters of this report, including in particular the organisation of an Eritrean Administration and the eventual transfer of power to the appropriate successor authorities, were placed upon the shoulders of the Administering Authority. The text of the Resolution, the first seven paragraphs of which comprise the Federal Act, forms Annex A to this report [not reproduced here].

Nature of the United Nations Resolution

7. In the course of the enquiries and deliberations, in Eritrea and elsewhere, outlined above the future status of Eritrea had become the subject of widely differing views and aspirations. Appraisal of the question by the various parties engaged in its study, and the strong local feelings, had resulted in proposals for every conceivable form of settlement, ranging from full union with Ethiopia to outright independence through intervening graduations of trusteeship or temporary administration, including a demand for partition of the territory. These differing conceptions had by December 1950 been resolved for practical purposes, into the two clear-cut and opposing demands, for independence, immediate or ultimate, on the one hand and complete union with Ethiopia on the other. In face of this fundamental division, which rent Eritrea politically from the top to the bottom, it became clear that only a compromise between these two extremes had any chance of success.

8. The project of federal union with Ethiopia with domestic autonomy for Eritrea formulated after protracted and delicate negotiations was the inevitable product of this realisation. It was essentially a middle-way solution, and in this quality lay both its strength and weakness. It was a well balanced composium of those conflicting view-points which had hitherto resisted agreement, and it married the two fundamental principles of Ethiopian sovereignty and Eritrean autonomy. It had not been proposed by any political party in Eritrea and did not thereby invite opposition solely on that account from the others. Its successful application in the country for which it was designed therefore would be dependent upon the circumspection, tact and technical efficiency with which its aims were pursued in practice by the United Nations Commissioner and by the Administering Authority, severally and jointly, in the fulfilment of their respective tasks.

Special difficulties confronting the Administering Authority

9. The greatest handicap in giving full effect to the Resolution was the shortness of the time allowed in which to do it. The deadline of 15th September, 1952, by which federation had to be effective, provided only twenty months in which to carry out a task of some magnitude. The work of the Administration was overshadowed throughout by this knowledge.

10. Politically it was an encouraging sign that the adoption of the Resolution was at once greeted in Eritrea by public expressions of approval, one of them taking the character of a formal pledge of unity by the leaders of all political parties at a public meeting, and co-operation in making federation effective. However, in the circumstances prevailing at the time, such manifestations were little more than demonstrations of satisfaction at the attainment at long last of a firm decision, the full implications of which were not then apparent.

11. The conflict of view referred to in paragraph 7 above had deep roots in Eritrea. The twin theses of independence and union were the articles of faith of contending political parties and had sown bitter political and racial dissension among the population. The demand from the Western Province for separation from the rest of Eritrea was still strong and would not be lightly abandoned. There was therefore the danger that although the notion of federation, new in itself, which went some way to satisfy all parties, would be accepted in principle, the old controversy of independence versus union would continue to be fought out within its scope. Moreover, the years of uncertainty as to the country's political future had produced unrest and partisan animosities which could not be expected to give way immediately to national harmony. It was evident that both the Commissioner and the Administering Power would have to concentrate in the discharge of their duties upon abating the political temper in the country by showing that federation was not only a workable compromise but a desirable and practicable conception in its own right.

12. The British Administration of Eritrea therefore had to play its part in creating conditions of administrative stability and political calm in which national unity,

or at least genuine co-operation, could take shape and a reasoned and genuine acceptance of the solution come into being. This was a formidable task, but it has come about. In its achievement the warm and close relationship and understanding which have existed throughout between the British Administration and the United Nations Commissioner have been a potent factor. The nature and extent of this co-operation will be described in the succeeding chapters. The tolerance and good sense of the major political leaders, and of the Eritrean people themselves, have also been essential contributions. Valuable co-operation in matters affecting Italian interests was received from the representatives of the Italian Government throughout.

13. In addition to the above considerations the Resolution, in keeping with its compromise nature, necessarily left several provisions on matters of practical importance in an imprecise state, and the exact definition of these, particularly with regard to the allocation of responsibility between Eritrean and federal services, has been a source of some difficulty.

Specific duties laid upon the Administering Authority by the Resolution

14. As mentioned above, the Resolution clearly defined the respective functions during the transition period of the United Nations Commissioner and the Administering Authority respectively. Those of them that fell upon the British Administration are set out below, the paragraphs mentioned referring to the resolution itself:

(1) Conduct of the affairs of Eritrea (paragraph 11).

(2) Negotiation, if desirable, of a temporary Customs Union with Ethiopia (paragraph 11).

(3) Organisation of an Eritrean Administration (paragraph 11).

(4) Induction of Eritreans into all levels of the Administration (paragraph 11).

(5) Arrangements for and convocation of a representative assembly of Eritreans (paragraph 11).

(6) Arrangements for the transfer of powers to the appropriate authorities (paragraph 14).

Items (3), (4) and (5) above were to be done in consultation with the United Nations Commissioner.

15. The subsequent chapters of this report are devoted to an account of the way in which these responsibilities were fulfilled.

16. In addition to the above, paragraph 12 of the Resolution placed upon the United Nations Commissioner the duty to consult with the Administering Authority on the preparation of a draft of the Eritrean Constitution.

17. The organisation of the Eritrean "Government", as distinct from the Eritrean "Administration", was prescribed by paragraph 9 of the Resolution, but was not specifically made the responsibility of the Administering Authority although this coping stone naturally evolved during the progress of constitutional procedure.

18. By paragraph 11 of the Resolution the Administering Authority was given the power to negotiate, in agreement with the Commissioner, a temporary customs union with Ethiopia to be put into effect as soon as practicable. In the result this power was not exercised for reasons which will be explained later.

19. In general, therefore, the Resolution prescribed that, apart from the direct responsibility laid upon the Commissioner for the preparation and adoption of the Eritrean Constitution, the initiative in all other matters during the transition period rested upon the Administering Authority. Close co-operation between the two authorities was, however, imperative, and the helpful and friendly advice of the Commissioner and his staff was welcomed and was readily forthcoming at all stages and in all matters affecting the working out of the resolution.

...

CHAPTER VII

Consultations with the United Nations Commissioner and the Ethiopian Government on the draft Constitution

188. Prior to the arrival of the United Nations Commissioner in Eritrea he had been invited by Her Majesty's Government to visit London so as to provide an opportunity for a general and informal survey of the work which lay ahead in giving effect to the Resolution. These discussions traversed the whole field of the several and mutual responsibilities of the Commissioner and the Administering Authority and it was found possible to reach agreement on the general policy to be followed in fulfilling those responsibilities. From then on, close and friendly collaboration between the Commissioner and the British Administration, and a mutual exchange of information, was maintained in Eritrea on all matters arising out of the Resolution, the extent of which ranged far beyond the obligation for formal consultation established by the Resolution. This full co-operation and mutual understanding had pleasing and fruitful results.

189. The continuous contact thus achieved made it unnecessary to engage in a series of set meetings, but it was deemed wise for the purpose of record for two formal meetings, one on 27th June, 1951, and the other on 3rd November, 1951, to be held concerning the general outline of the Constitution and to permit of a general exchange of views upon the principles involved. The points discussed and the views expressed are contained in docu-

ments Nos. A/AC.44/L.6 and A/AC.44/SR.1 published by the Commissioner and as they, and the other negotiations on the subject, will be epitomised in the report to be submitted to the General Assembly by him there is no need to say more in this report other than that no important conflict of ideas arose. Later, as the draft Constitution took shape, the Administration was given ample opportunity to comment upon it and to suggest amendments to it. Views thus expressed were taken into full consideration by the United Nations Commissioner at all stages.

190. There is no provision in the Resolution for formal consultations between the Administering Authority and the Government of Ethiopia concerning the draft Constitution and none was held, but the uninterrupted liaison between the two authorities on the subject of the federal aspects of the Resolution enabled frequent unofficial conversations to take place both in Asmara and Addis Ababa on the subject of the drafting of the Constitution. These discussions, and the general liaison with the United Nations Commissioner mentioned above, were helpful in the process of reconciling some divergencies of view which had been revealed during the long consultations between the United Nations Commissioner and the Government of Ethiopia, and contributed towards the full agreement which was ultimately reached on all points.

191. The final draft text of the Constitution prepared by the United Nations Commissioner and presented to the Representative Assembly had therefore been the subject of close consultation between the Commissioner and the Administering Authority, as provided for in the Resolution, and it was presented by the Commissioner with the agreement and support of the British Administration.

...

CHAPTER XI

Final Preparations for the Transfer of Power

Federal Services

259. The massive preliminary work which the preceding chapters describe, and the successful completion of the Commissioner's labours in bringing into being an approved and ratified Constitution, had set the stage for the final transfer of powers to the successor authorities. In so far as the transfer of those responsibilities to the Federal Government was concerned, little more work remained to be accomplished. The necessary arrangements had been made in detail as already explained during the continuing series of technical discussions between the officials of the Administration and those sent from Addis Ababa for this purpose, on the basis of the transfer of the services as going concerns.

260. Practically the whole of the foreign and Eritrean staff employed in them were to be taken over by the federal authorities and suitable contracts for service were concluded between the latter and the key British officials whose retention was required and who were willing to stay.

261. The arrangements made provided for the transfer of all buildings, equipment and stores used by the services and the preparation of satisfactory inventories and transfer documents in respect of them. They enabled a satisfactory organisation to be set up so that the responsibility of administration and operation could pass with no break in continuity. The whole-hearted assistance and willing help extended by the Ethiopian Government and their officials throughout the transition period enabled these complicated questions to be settled in a manner satisfactory to all concerned.

Eritrean Government: Executive Committee

262. As a preliminary to the assumption of power by the Eritrean Government the work of the Executive Committee was vital. Under the able leadership of Sheikh Ali Mohammed Musa Radai, they devoted long hours and considerable concentration to the numerous and varied subjects which were referred to them for decision. Bearing in mind that the problems of government and administration with which they were called upon to deal were entirely new to most of them, considerable credit is due to them for the manner in which they handled their business. Detailed proposals for their examination were prepared by the Administration and responsible British officials attended their meetings, when required, to give explanations and guidance on technical matters.

263. Amongst the subjects which they successfully dealt with may be mentioned the following, which show the wide scope of their work:

(1) Calling for tenders and placing of contracts for the continuance of local supplies of petrol, oil and lubricants, of stores for the Medical, Police and Public Works Departments and for the supply of electric power and water.

(2) The detailed organisation of the District Administration (paragraph 121).

(3) The organic law on the functions of Government (paragraph 122).

(4) The complete establishment of staff, by grades, for all Departments of the Government, rates of pay, and the selection of officials to be retained for service (paragraph 141).

(5) The future organisation and maintenance of Government transport.

(6) The organisation and establishment of the Police Force and Prisons Service.

(7) The future of the Government Press and of the newspapers published by the British Information Services.

(8) The selection for employment and contracts for service of British staff whose services it was desired to retain (paragraph 144).

(9) Education policy.

(10) Formation of a separate Excise Department on its divorce from the Customs Department when the latter became a federal service.

(11) Conclusion of hiring agreements for private property still required by the Government (paragraph 91).

(12) The revision of the Judicial system in conformity with the Constitution (Chapter VIII).

(13) Procedure for the taking over of Government property on the transfer of power (paragraph 241).

(14) Draft budget estimates for the Eritrean Government for the period 11th September, 1952, to 10th September, 1953 (paragraph 75).

264. Some of the above items which have already been mentioned separately in this report were comprehensive in their scope, notably Nos. 2, 4, 6, 8, 12 and 14, and called for prolonged examination and deliberation. In all of the items, and many others not included in the above list, satisfactory interim decisions were taken which permitted the British Administration to complete the organisation of the Eritrean Administration and its plans for the transfer of power. Subjects on which they were not competent to take a final decision, some of which are not, in the interests of brevity, mentioned above, were referred to the Representative Assembly for action.

Organic Laws

265. The Eritrean Constitution, in order to be made effective, needed to be supplemented by certain laws, for which the Constitution provided, giving detailed application to some of the principles enshrined in it. Some of the laws were urgently necessary to enable the new Eritrean Government to function when the Constitution came into effect, and in particular:

(a) The Functions of Government Act (Article 69/4). (See paragraph 122.)

(b) The Administration of Justice Act (Article 61).

(c) The Budget Law (Article 64 (4)).

266. The following also called for by the Constitution, although of less pressing importance than the above, were also of an urgent nature:

(d) The Civil Service Act (Article 81).

(e) The Audit Act (Article 64 (4)).

(f) The Advisory Council Act (Article 84 (3)).

(g) The Electoral Act (Article 41).

267. Article 95 of the Constitution, which was especially drafted to deal with these "organic" laws, provided that laws giving effect to the Constitution adopted by the Eritrean Representative Assembly should enter into effect simultaneously with the Constitution. The reasons underlying this provision and the machinery for dealing with the laws had been agreed upon in discussion with the Commissioner, whose particular responsibility they were as being an essential projection of the Constitution itself. The Administration was closely concerned because the first named three at least were essential components of the fabric of the Eritrean Administration which it had to construct.

268. It was unavoidable for reasons which are given in Chapter VIII that item (b), which dealt with the Judicial régime, should be enacted and effective before the transfer of power. It was promulgated on 10th September, 1952, and entered into effect immediately.

269. Drafts of the other organic laws were prepared in agreement with the United Nations Commissioner, the bulk of the drafting, after the basic principles had been thrashed out in discussion, being undertaken by the Administration. They were drafted in strict conformity with the principles and provisions of the Constitution. An analysis of the laws themselves will be given in the report of the United Nations Commissioner, who himself addressed the Representative Assembly in general terms regarding them and the importance of their early enactment.

270. After the final drafts had received the approval of the Chief Administrator and the Commissioner they were submitted jointly on their behalf to the Executive Committee for examination, urgent approval and submission to the Assembly for adoption. Because of the pressure of work upon the Committee, the comprehensive nature of the laws, and the necessity of carefully translating them into Arabic and Tigrinya, only the most urgent of them, *i.e.*, the Eritrean Functions of Government Act, was actually adopted by the Assembly before, and thus became law when the Constitution came into force.

271. The remainder were however all transmitted by the Committee to the Assembly, which set up a special committee to examine them. There is every reason to suppose that they will become law without undue delay.

Revision of existing legislation

272. On 10th September, 1952, a Revision, Amendment, and Interpretation of Laws Proclamation was published which came into force at the same time as the Termination of Powers Proclamation. It was an important legal preliminary to the inception of the successor authorities and its objects were twofold:

(a) to repeal those laws relating to matters within the domestic jurisdiction of the Eritrean Government which either were unsuitable for continuance after the transfer of powers or would be inconsistent with the provisions of the Eritrean Constitution; and

(b) to amend provisions of such existing laws, which were otherwise suitable for continuance after the transfer of power, so to adapt them both to the conditions that would then prevail and to the provisions of the Eritrean Constitution.

273. This process of revision was considerably simplified and facilitated, firstly by the fact that the Administration of Justice Proclamation, which was published simultaneously, itself revised all the relevant laws relating to the Courts and the administration of justice in general; secondly, by the fact that in March 1949 a comprehensive revision and consolidation of the laws in force at that date had already been carried out.

274. Under the 1949 revision, all laws in force in Eritrea at the commencement of the occupation on 1st April, 1941, which had neither been suspended by, nor were inconsistent with, the provisions of any Proclamation issued by the British Administration were continued in force. In conjunction with the enactment in the proclamation now enacted of a provision corresponding to Section 38 of the English Interpretation Act, it was not found necessary to alter this provision of law.

275. A special committee was therefore appointed by the Administration, which worked through the whole of the existing British Proclamations, Regulations and Orders and decided on their continuance, amendment, or repeal in accordance with the above-mentioned objects.

276. The process of revision was simplified by the correspondence in function and powers of the Chief Executive, under the semi-presidential form of government established by the Eritrean Constitution, to those previously exercised by the Chief Administrator under the British Administration and by the Governor-General and Governor respectively under the former Italian Administration. Thus, with the conception of judicial and legal powers which were dealt with under the Administration of Justice Proclamation, and of a few minor matters, it was possible to provide that the powers and duties reserved in the existing legislation to the Chief Administrator as such, and as successor to the Governor-General and Governor in the former Italian Administration, should, after the transfer of power, be exercised by the Chief Executive. Powers and duties exercisable under the existing legislation by other authorities were transferred to the appropriate authority under the Eritrean Constitution or under the relevant organic laws, already referred to, supplementary to that Constitution.

277. In accordance with international practice the revision and amendment of the existing laws relating to matters within the jurisdiction, after the transfer of power, of the Federal Government were left to be dealt with by Federal laws.

Transfer of Power to the Successor Authorities and the departure of the British Administration

278. On the formal ratification of the Federal Act by the Emperor of Ethiopia on 11th September, the second period of grace, of four days, referred to in paragraph 243 above came into effect. The prepared scheme for the transfer of administration, of movable and immovable properties, and all other relevant responsibilities to the Federal Authorities and the Eritrean Government respectively, was put into effect immediately and the whole process was punctually completed without hitch.

279. The British officials who were not retained for service in Eritrea by the successor authorities were progressively withdrawn and repatriated, and the British military forces, which were replaced by a contingent of Federal troops who had arrived in their stead, left Eritrea, save for a small rear party to deal with the removal of British military transport and equipment, on 16th September.

280. On the evening of 15th September at a small formal ceremony attended by the Representative of the Emperor, the Chief Executive, Federal representatives, foreign representatives and senior officials of the Administration, the Chief Administrator signed the "Termination of Powers" proclamation (see Annex K [not reproduced here]), which ended British powers and responsibilities in Eritrea at midnight on 15th September, 1952. This was the date laid down in the United Nations Resolution by which it was to be accomplished.

281. At sunset an impressive and moving military ceremony was held, in the presence of representatives of all the authorities concerned in the implementation of the processes which have been described above, and of the largest crowd which had ever assembled in Asmara. The Federal flag was raised, and the British flag was lowered for the last time and handed over to the Chief Administrator for safe keeping. The tasks laid upon the Administering Authority had thus been fulfilled, and satisfactorily completed, within the time limit laid down by the United Nations: the federation was in being, the Eritrean Government was effectively organised and installed, the Federal Authorities had assumed their responsibilities and the powers were in the hands of the successor authorities.

282. Thus ended the period of eleven and a half years of British Administration in Eritrea, during which,

and not without credit, it had been the policy of Her Majesty's Government in the United Kingdom to administer the territory in the best interests of the country and of the people, whilst their political future was being decided and arranged.

283. The contents of this report explain how the comparatively short transition period was utilised. It remains only to add an expression of appreciation and gratitude for the unwavering co-operation and support of the distinguished Commissioner of the United Nations, the goodwill, help and friendship which at all times characterised the attitude towards the Administration of the Ethiopian Government, and the tolerance, good sense and statesmanship of the Eritrean leaders and the people whom they ably represent. The almost entire disappearance of the factional strife and political rivalry which had in the past marred the development and life of Eritrea was a heartening manifestation of a growing national harmony, the credit for which redounds almost entirely to the good sense of, and the innate desire for peace among, the Eritrean people themselves.

284. The federation and the new autonomous unit of Eritrea have thus taken shape in a gratifying atmosphere of friendship and goodwill which augurs well for the consolidation of the new arrangements in the testing days ahead.

Conclusion

285. The establishment of Eritrea as an autonomous unit federated with Ethiopia under the sovereignty of the Ethiopian Crown, and possessing legislative, executive and judicial powers in the field of domestic affairs, is a notable development and marks the beginning of a new era for the territory. Its newly-won possessions of a properly elected Government and legislature, an adequate administration, and a sound and workable Constitution, are valuable foundations on which, however, much careful building remains to be done.

286. The remarkable feature of the Eritrean settlement is that, in adopting and welcoming a compromise proposed from outside, the people have, at least for the present, bridged the racial and religious chasms which recently barred their progress. This is an achievement which all concerned must welcome and which we must hope will be preserved in the future.

287. Eritrea in itself remains economically and financially weak and has little prospect of becoming a viable State, but her integration with the Ethiopian Empire and the promise of financial assistance from that source should enable her eventually to improve her position.

288. The future of Eritrea will rest upon a sympathetic and ready understanding of her economic and political weakness, and upon the provision of wise guidance and material assistance by her larger and more happily endowed partner in the federation. The future of the federation will be affected by the degree of mutual respect between them for the rights, jurisdiction and traditions of each other. Her Majesty's Government in the United Kingdom share the belief of the United Nations Commissioner that federation has been entered into in the best of faith on both sides. They are conscious of the desire of His Imperial Majesty the Emperor of Ethiopia to bring peace and prosperity to his new people and to foreigners resident in the Empire, and of the intention of his Government scrupulously to observe the principles on which the new order has been constructed.

289. In severing their close connection with the Eritrean people over the past eleven and a half years Her Majesty's Government desire to end this report by wishing them success and happiness in the future in the new conditions in which they now find themselves.

Document 11

General Assembly resolution concerning the report of the United Nations Commissioner in Eritrea

A/RES/617 (VII), 17 December 1952

The General Assembly,

Recalling its resolution 390 A (V) of 2 December 1950, providing that Eritrea be constituted an autonomous unit federated with Ethiopia under the sovereignty of the Ethiopian Crown,

Having noted the adoption and ratification of the Eritrean Constitution and the ratification of the Federal Act embodying the provisions contained in paragraphs 1-7 inclusive of that resolution,

Having noted that the conditions laid down in paragraph 13 of resolution 390 A (V) of 2 December

1950 have been fulfilled, and that on 11 September 1952 the Federation of Eritrea with Ethiopia was proclaimed,

Noting further the final report 1/ of the United Nations Commissioner in Eritrea of 17 October 1952 and the report 2/ of the Administering Authority of 27 October 1952,

Noting with appreciation the part played by the United Nations Commissioner and the former Administering Authority in Eritrea in preparing Eritrea to take its place in the Federation,

Noting also with satisfaction the contribution made by Ethiopia to the establishment of the Federation and Ethiopia's expression of determination scrupulously to execute the provisions of the Federal Act,

1. *Welcomes* the establishment of the Federation of Eritrea with Ethiopia under the sovereignty of the Ethiopian Crown;

2. *Congratulates* the people and governmental authorities of the Federation for their effective and loyal fulfilment of resolution 390 A (V) of the General Assembly of 2 December 1950.

1/ See *Official Records of the General Assembly, Seventh Session, Supplement No. 15.*
2/ See document A/2233.

Document 12

Urgent appeal to the forty-sixth session of the Commission on Human Rights submitted by several non-governmental organizations

E/CN.4/1990/NGO/75, 7 March 1990

Question of the violation of human rights and fundamental freedoms in any part of the world, with particular reference to colonial and other dependent countries and territories

Written statement submitted by the following: World Confederation of Labour, a non-governmental organization in consultative status (category I), American Association of Jurists, Anti-Slavery Society, Arab Lawyers Union, Arab Organization for Human Rights, Human Rights Advocates, Human Rights Internet, International Association of Penal Law, International Association for the Defence of Religious Liberty, International Association of Educators for World Peace, International Commission of Jurists, International Commission of Health Professionals for Health and Human Rights, International Federation of Human Rights, International Fellowship of Reconciliation, International Organization for the Elimination of All Forms of Racial Discrimination, Pax Christi International, Pax Romana, Service for Peace and Justice in Latin America and the Union of Arab Jurists, non-governmental organizations in consultative status (category II), Centre Europe – Tiers Monde, Defence for Children International, International Federation of Rural Adult Catholic Movements, International League for the Rights and Liberation of Peoples, International Peace Bureau, International Pen and World Union for Progressive Judaism, non-governmental organizations on the Roster

The Secretary-General has received the following communication which is circulated in accordance with Economic and Social Council resolution 1296 (XLIV).

Urgent appeal to the forty-sixth session of the Commission on Human Rights

1. Eritrea was an Italian colony between 1889 and 1941 and was then placed under provisional British administration. In 1950, it was federated with Ethiopia on the basis of General Assembly resolution 390 (V) of 1950, contrary to the Charter of the United Nations and against the will of the Eritrean people.

2. It is an established fact that during the federation, the Ethiopian feudal rulers dismantled all democratic institutions. Among other things, they banned and abolished freedom of the press, association and trade unions and imposed Amharic, the Ethiopian language, to be the official language of Eritrea. Finally, they annexed Eritrea unilaterally and incorporated it into Ethiopia in 1962.

3. The United Nations, being the author and sole guarantor of the federation, remained silent and passive when the Ethiopian rulers violated the resolution despite the appeal and outcry of the Eritrean people.

4. During the last 29 years of conflict, the successive Ethiopian régimes have pursued a coercive policy to crush the struggle of the Eritrean people for its basic and legitimate right to self-determination.

5. In the process, they have committed colossal human rights violations, ranging from arbitrary arrests,

detention, torture, extrajudicial execution, blanket bombardment using napalm and cluster bombs, and the destruction of whole villages including churches, mosques, schools and farms. As a result, close to 900,000 people have taken refuge in foreign countries and tens of thousands have been internally displaced in their home land.

6. The Eritrean people are again confronted with the heavy burden and challenge not only of the on-going war but also of famine. Currently, there are 1.9 million people in need of urgent emergency food aid and a delay could bring about a catastrophic situation.

7. Therefore, we solemnly appeal to the Commission on Human Rights to remind the United Nations that it has the moral and legal responsibility to use its good offices to find a just and peaceful settlement to the Eritrea-Ethiopia conflict.

Document 13

Letter dated 13 December 1991 from the President of the Transitional Government of Ethiopia to the Secretary-General of the United Nations concerning the results of the Conference on Peace and Democracy held in Ethiopia in July 1991

A/C.3/47/5, Annex II, 29 October 1992

As Your Excellency is well aware, the transitional period in Ethiopia highlights the task of redressing the causes of the 30-year civil war in Eritrea and of establishing the basis of permanent peace and stability.

It is to be recalled that the Conference on Peace and Democracy in Ethiopia, held at Addis Ababa from 1 to 5 July 1991, adopted a Charter affirming that freedom, equal rights and self-determination of all peoples are the cardinal principles governing State affairs in the new Ethiopia. In the light of this, the Conference formally recognized that the people of Eritrea have the right to determine their own future by themselves, and accepted that the future status of Eritrea should be decided by the Eritrean people in a referendum to be conducted in the presence of international observers. The Provisional Government of Eritrea set up by the Eritrean People's Liberation Front (EPLF), on its part, decided to defer the referendum for two years which, we believe, contributes to the maintenance of peace and stability in our subregion. At the same time, agreement was reached on the modalities of the relationship between the Transitional Government of Ethiopia and the Provisional Government of Eritrea for the interim period.

Both the Transitional Government of Ethiopia and the Provisional Government of Eritrea have registered their commitment to respect the results of the referedum in Eritrea as the genuine choice of the people concerned, expressed in an exercise of self-determination.

The Transitional Government of Ethiopia, as an interested party in the outcome of the referedum, has the firm conviction that the referendum will be free and fair, and believes that the United Nations should play an active role in verifying that the referendum is, indeed, free and fair.

In this regard, the Transitional Government of Ethiopia wishes to bring to the attention of Your Excellency the need to initiate appropriate measures to enable the United Nations to play this role and make the necessary arrangements with the Provisional Government of Eritrea to facilitate the ways and means for United Nations supervision of the referendum. The Transitional Government of Ethiopia also wishes to point out that the time available for preparation in this regard is very short.

(*Signed*) Meles ZENAWI
President of the Transitional Government of Ethiopia

Document 14

Letter dated 15 January 1992 from the Secretary-General of the United Nations to the President of the Transitional Government of Ethiopia concerning United Nations involvement in the referendum process in Eritrea

Not issued as a United Nations document

I have the honour to refer to Your Excellency's letter dated 13 December 1991 addressed to my predecessor, Mr. Javier Pérez de Cuéllar, regarding United Nations involvement in the referendum to be held in Eritrea.

In this connection, I wish to inform your Excellency that the Secretariat is currently considering the appropriate role for the United Nations in the referendum with a view to facilitating the initiation of necessary measures by the United Nations. Under-Secretary-General James O. C. Jonah has had preliminary discussions on the matter with officials of your Government and those of the Provisional Government of Eritrea. We will continue these consultations in order to clarify further the role of the United Nations in the referendum and to help expedite the process.

Accept, Mr. President, the assurances of my highest consideration and my warmest regards.

(*Signed*) Boutros BOUTROS-GHALI

Document 15

Letter dated 19 February 1992 from the Secretary-General of the United Nations to the President of the Transitional Government of Ethiopia concerning United Nations involvement in the referendum process in Eritrea

Not issued as a United Nations document

I wish to refer to my letter of 15 January 1992 addressed to your Excellency regarding the request of your Government for United Nations involvement in the referendum to be held in Eritrea. I had informed your Excellency at that time that the Secretariat was considering the appropriate role for the United Nations in the referendum, and continuing its consultations with all concerned to seek further clarification on the matter. Following these consultations, I would like as the next step to bring to your attention certain considerations, including the options which could be pursued in regard to your request.

As your Excellency is aware, the involvement of the United Nations in national referenda depends on a number of prerequisites. Above all, there must be a clear mandate by the competent organ and an international dimension to the referendum. There must also be proper financing and the agreement of all concerned, in particular the country which represents in the United Nations the region where the referendum is to be held.

United Nations involvement in a referendum could include a broad range of tasks and responsibilities, from providing only technical assistance without assessment of the referendum process, to the organization and conduct of the entire referendum, including the drafting of laws and regulations.

Several other options fall in between those two categories. They include passive observation which will not involve investigation of complaints and public pronouncements; active observation which implies interaction with the electoral authorities and the public; observation with independent verification of the results; and organization of the electoral process in cooperation with the appropriate authorities.

All these options, which by no means are exhaustive, require the appropriate authorities to assume corresponding responsibilities—organizational, financial and otherwise—to augment the particular role that the United Nations may be called upon to undertake in the referendum.

The operation could be designed, in consultation with your Government, to fit the particular circumstances of the referendum. Such an approach would take into account your needs as assessed by your Government and the United Nations; the political and financial support of

Member States; the principles governing United Nations involvement in the referendum; and the commitment of the appropriate authorities to ensure a free and democratic referendum.

These and related issues need to be fully addressed in order to agree upon the appropriate role of the United Nations in the referendum in the context of the corresponding responsibilities and obligations that will be assumed by your Government and the Provisional Government of Eritrea. As stated earlier, the appropriate mandate authorizing United Nations involvement in the referendum would be required from the United Nations legislative organ concerned.

Under-Secretary-General James Jonah will be in Addis Ababa to represent me at the forthcoming session of the Council of Ministers of the Organization of African Unity. His presence in Addis Ababa will provide an opportunity to meet with representatives of your Government and those of the Provisional Government of Eritrea to exchange views on the options your Government might wish to pursue in cooperation with the United Nations for the organization and conduct of the referendum, and on the corresponding responsibilities that your Government might be expected to assume.

Detailed technical discussion could be arranged as a follow-up to Mr. Jonah's meetings with representatives of your Government and those of the Provisional Government of Eritrea.

Accept, Mr. President, the assurances of my highest consideration.

(*Signed*) Boutros BOUTROS-GHALI

Document 16

Eritrean Nationality Proclamation, issued on 6 April 1992 in Asmara

Not issued as a United Nations document

1. **Short Title**

This proclamation may be cited as "The Eritrean Nationality Proclamation No. 21/1992."

2. **Nationality by Birth**

    1. Any person born to a father or a mother of Eritrean origin in Eritrea or abroad is an Eritrean national by birth.

    2. A person who has "Eritrean origin" is any person who was resident in Eritrea in 1933.

    3. A person born in Eritrea to unknown parents shall be considered an Eritrean national by birth until proven otherwise.

    4. Any person who is an Eritrean by origin or by birth shall, upon application be given a certificate of nationality by the Department of Internal Affairs.

    5. Any person who is Eritrean by birth, resides abroad and possesses foreign nationality shall apply to the Department of Internal Affairs if he wishes to officially renounce his foreign nationality and acquire Eritrean nationality or wishes, after providing adequate justification, to have his Eritrean nationality accepted while maintaining his foreign nationality.

3. **Nationality by Naturalization (1934-1951)**

    1. Eritrean nationality is hereby granted to any person who is not of Eritrean origin and who entered, and resided in, Eritrea between the beginning of 1934 and the end of 1951, provided that he has not committed anti-people acts during the liberation struggle of the Eritrean people. He shall, upon application, be given a certificate of nationality by the Department of Internal Affairs, provided that he has not rejected Eritrean nationality. The provisions of article 2 (5) of this Proclamation shall apply when such a person possesses the nationality of another country.

    2. A person born to a person mentioned in sub-article 1 of this Article is Eritrean by birth. The Department of Internal Affairs shall, upon his application, issue him a certificate of nationality.

    3. The Department of Internal Affairs shall revoke the nationality of any person mentioned in sub-article 1 of this Article where it determines that he had acquired Eritrean nationality or the certificate of Eritrean nationality by fraud, deceit or concealment of decisive facts.

4. **Nationality by Naturalization (1952 and after)**

    1. Any person who is not of Eritrean origin and has entered, and resided in, Eritrea in 1952 or after shall apply for Eritrean nationality to the Secretary of Internal Affairs.

    2. The Secretary of Internal Affairs shall grant Nationality by Naturalization to the person mentioned in sub-article 1 of this Article provided that the person:

a. has entered Eritrea legally and has been domiciled in Eritrea for a period of ten (10) years before 1974 or has been domiciled in Eritrea for a period of twenty (20) years while making periodic visits abroad;

b. possesses high integrity and has not been convicted of any crime;

c. understands and speaks one of the languages of Eritrea;

d. is free of any of the mental or physical handicaps mentioned in Article 339-340 of the Transitory Civil Code of Eritrea, will not become a burden to Eritrean society and can provide for his own and his family's needs;

e. has renounced the nationality of another country, pursuant to the legislation of that country;

f. has decided to be permanently domiciled in Eritrea upon the granting of his Eritrean nationality;

g. has not committed anti-people acts during the liberation struggle of the Eritrean people.

3. A person shall be granted Eritrean Nationality by Naturalization and given a certificate of nationality pursuant to sub-article 2 of the Article only after he signs the oath of allegiance attached to, and is part of, this Proclamation before the Secretary of Internal Affairs or any other official designated by him. Eritrean nationality granted pursuant to Article 4 of this Proclamation shall be proclaimed in the Gazette of Eritrean Laws.

4. A person given a certificate of Eritrean nationality pursuant to sub-article 2 of this Article shall acquire the status of a Naturalized Eritrean national as of the date of receipt of the certificate.

5. The Secretary of Internal Affairs may cause the name any offspring on whose behalf an application has been made by a person responsible for him under the law and who has included in the certificate of nationality of the applying person. [sic] The minor offspring shall acquire the status of a naturalized national as of the date of the inclusion of his name.

6. Any person born to a naturalized Eritrean national pursuant to Article 4 of this Proclamation after the person has been granted the status of a Naturalized National becomes an Eritrean by birth.

5. **Nationality by Adoption**

The Secretary of Internal Affairs shall grant Eritrean Nationality by Naturalization and issue a certificate of nationality to a person adopted legally by, and upon the application of, an Eritrean national by birth or by naturalization or by the adopted person himself.

6. **Nationality by Marriage**

1. Any person of non-Eritrean origin who is legally married to an Eritrean national by birth or to a person granted Eritrean Nationality by Naturalization shall be granted Eritrean Nationality by Naturalization when such a person applies to the Secretary of Internal Affairs, provided the person:

a. has lived in Eritrea with the spouse for at least three (3) years;

b. has renounced his foreign nationality and is prepared to acquire Eritrean nationality; and

c. signs an oath of allegiance pursuant to Article 4(3).

2. A person who had been granted Eritrean nationality by reason of marriage shall be deprived of his nationality by the Secretary of Internal Affairs where such a person chooses to re-acquire his original nationality upon the death of the spouse or by divorce or when the marriage is declared null and void by a court of law.

7. **Time and Application Relative to the Exercise of Eritrean Nationality Rights**

A person granted Eritrean Nationality by Naturalization pursuant to Articles 4 to 6 of this Proclamation may, as of the date of the issuance to him of a certificate of Eritrean nationality, exercise the rights of an Eritrean national relative to the status of naturalization.

8. **Deprivation of Nationality**

1. A committee composed of the Secretaries of Justice, Internal Affairs and Public Administration may deprive of his nationality an Eritrean national by birth or an Eritrean granted Nationality by naturalization pursuant to Article 4 hereof, who has attained the age of eighteen and has capacity under the law where such a person:

a. voluntarily acquires a foreign nationality after the publication of this Proclamation; or

b. officially renounces his Eritrean nationality; or

c. signs an oath of allegiance of another country after the publication of this Proclamation; or

d. in violation of an explicit provision of Eritrean law, serves or continues to serve another country; or

e. is condemned for treason by a court of law.

2. A committee composed of the Secretaries of Justice, Internal Affairs and Public Administration may deprive of his nationality a person who has been granted Eritrean Nationality by Naturalization (Articles 4 to 6) where such a person:

a. acquires Eritrean nationality or a certificate of nationality by fraud, deceit or concealment of decisive facts; or

b. is confirmed, that he has, by illegally contacting external powers, committed acts which aided and abetted an enemy;

c. has committed treason outside Eritrea;

d. has been indicted for a crime and sentenced to more than five years imprisonment;

e. has committed any one of the acts enumerated in sub-article (1) hereof.

3. A person shall be deprived of his nationality pursuant to sub-articles (1) and (2) hereof only after the necessary investigation has been conducted and after such a person has been given an opportunity to defend himself.

9. Penalties

Whosoever:

1. intentionally and knowingly makes false statements, commits fraud or forges documents in matters relating to this Proclamation; or

2. attempts to use, or uses, the certificate of nationality of another person; or

3. permits another person to use his certificate of nationality; or

4. upon deprivation of his Eritrean nationality, refuses to return his certificate of nationality;

shall, upon conviction, be punished with imprisonment not exceeding three years, or a fine not exceeding Birr 5,000 or with both.

10. Powers to Issue Regulations

The Secretary of Internal Affairs is empowered to issue regulations to facilitate the implementation of the provisions of this Proclamation and in particular, to issue regulations relative to:

1. forms and registers designated to be used pursuant to the Proclamation;

2. the formalities and registration of the oath of allegiance to be performed pursuant to this Proclamation; and

3. the fees payable in relation to registration, statements to be issued, certificates to be given or the taking of an oath of allegiance, pursuant to this Proclamation.

11. Appeal

1. Any person who disagrees with the decision made by the Secretary of Internal Affairs regarding the application related to nationality or with a decision of the committee composed of the Secretaries of Justice, Internal Affairs and Public Administration regarding the deprivation of nationality, may appeal to the High Court, within one month after receipt of a written decision;

2. The decision of the High Court shall be final.

12. Repealed Laws

All hitherto enacted laws governing nationality have been repealed and replaced by this Proclamation.

13. Entry into Force

This Proclamation shall enter into force on the date of its publication in the Gazette of Eritrean Laws.

Done at Asmara, this 6th day of April, 1992,
The Provisional Government of Eritrea.

Document 17

Eritrean Referendum Proclamation, issued on 7 April 1992 in Asmara

Not issued as a United Nations document

PREAMBLE

Whereas the Eritrean people had to win a long and bitter war of liberation to assert their right to self-determination; and

Whereas the people and the Provisional Government of Eritrea have freely decided to delay for two (2) years the expression of this right to self-determination after which the results of an internationally-observed, free and fair referendum shall determine Eritrea's status in the comity of nations; and

Whereas during the two (2) years, it is fit and urgent for the people of Eritrea to freely and democratically decide whether or not they wish to become independent and thus conclusively determine Eritrea's status in the international community;

Now, therefore, it is hereby proclaimed as follows:

CHAPTER I — INTRODUCTORY

1. Short Title:

This Proclamation may be cited as the "Referendum Proclamation, No. 22/1992."

2. Definition:

In this Proclamation, unless the context otherwise requires:

(1) "Government" shall mean the Provisional Government of Eritrea;

(2) "Secretary General" shall mean the Secretary General of the Provisional Government of Eritrea;

(3) "Commission" shall mean the Referendum Commission established by the Provisional Government of Eritrea;

(4) "Commissioner" shall mean the Chairman of the Referendum Commission;

(5) "Identification Board" shall mean the board created by the Commission to issue a register of eligible voters;

(6) "Publicity and Information Board" shall mean the board created by the Commission to inform the Eritrean public about the meaning, purposes and process of the referendum and to widely publicize the referendum process;

(7) "Election Board" shall mean the board created by the Commission to conduct the balloting process of the referendum;

(8) "Administration Room" shall mean the room or section of a room in a polling station in which the process of identification of prospective voters shall take place and in which they shall await their turn to vote;

(9) "Ballot" shall mean a numbered slip attached to a counterfoil bearing the same number which shall be used for deposit in a ballot box in accordance with Article 35 hereof;

(10) "Tendered Ballot" shall mean a double envelope system which shall be used to resolve any doubts about a voter's registration or identity;

(11) "Association" shall mean any Eritrean group formed for the purpose of the referendum and registered in accordance with Article 30 hereof;

(12) "Electoral District" shall mean an electoral district established pursuant to Article 22 of this Proclamation;

(13) "Official" shall mean an official appointed pursuant to sub-paragraph 2 of Article 4;

(14) "Pollex Digital Imprint" shall mean the print made by placing ink on the upper part of the thumb, on the reverse side from the nail, and pressing the inked area onto paper;

(15) "Presiding Official" shall mean the official at each polling station designated pursuant to sub-paragraph 1 of Article 35 hereof to be in charge of that station;

(16) "To Publicize" shall mean to make known to the public by poster, newspaper, radio, television and all other available and appropriate means;

(17) "Registration Card" shall mean the card issued pursuant to sub-paragraph 2 (d) of Article 27 hereof to each person registered as voter;

(18) "Registration Office" shall mean a registration office established pursuant to sub-paragraph 1 of Article 26 hereof;

(19) "Registration Officer" shall mean the official designated pursuant to sub-paragraphs 1 and 2 of Article 25 hereof to be in charge of registration at a registration office;

(20) "Registration Period" shall mean the voter registration period established pursuant to Article 26 hereof;

(21) "Voting Booth" shall mean the room or section of a room in a polling station in which ballot boxes shall be placed and voters shall cast their votes;

(22) "Voting Register" shall mean a register of persons eligible to vote, prepared pursuant to Article 22 (2) hereof;

(23) "Waiting Space" shall mean an area sufficient to accommodate approximately ten (10) persons within the administration room and immediately adjacent to the voting booth, separated from the remainder of the administration room by a guard rail or guard rope, wherein persons to whom ballots have been issued shall await their turn to vote;

(24) "Referendum Court" shall mean the court established pursuant to Article 43 hereof.

CHAPTER II—GENERAL

3. The Referendum:

(1) A referendum on the future of Eritrea shall be held during, or before, the third week of April 1993.

(2) The Referendum Ballot shall be worded as follows: place an X or other mark in one box:

Do you approve Eritrea to become an independent, sovereign state?

Yes [ ]

No [ ]

(3) There shall be no other question or issue on the ballot. The ballot shall be printed in all Eritrean languages.

(4) The referendum must receive approval by the majority of the votes cast.

(5) The result of the referendum shall be put into effect immediately upon its announcement.

CHAPTER III—THE REFERENDUM COMMISSION

4. Establishment of the Commission:

(1) (a) There is hereby established a Referendum Commission. The Commission shall organize and conduct the referendum.

(b) The Commission shall have the necessary administrative structure to carry out the functions assigned to it by this proclamation and to carry out such other functions related to the referendum.

(2) The Commission shall consist of a Referendum Commissioner and four (4) Deputy Commissioners to be designated by the Secretary General.

(3) The Referendum Commission shall have:
(a) a Secretariat;
(b) an Identification Board;
(c) a Publicity and Information Board; and
(d) an Election Board.

(4) (a) The Commission may establish sub-commissions to undertake particular responsibilities and shall be assisted by a support group big enough to enable it to carry out its organizational and supervisory duties.

(b) The support group shall be seconded by the Government. The Commissioner shall define the duties of each sub-commission as well as units in the support group.

(c) The Commission shall be assisted by an independent jurist in the interpretation and application of this Proclamation.

5. Functions of the Commission:
(1) The Commission shall have the following main functions:
(a) guaranteeing a referendum that is free and fair;
(b) identification and registration of eligible voters;
(c) creation of the mechanism of the referendum;
(d) Publicizing the referendum and informing the voters.

(2) To this end, the Commission shall make arrangements to:
(a) guarantee the freedom of speech, assembly, movement and press for the purposes of the referendum;
(b) guarantee the security of the voters;
(c) publicize the referendum and encourage the free exchange of views;
(d) facilitate the return and vote of all eligible voters;
(e) promptly, adequately and fairly address all complaints regarding the identification and registration of voters, and the regulation, rules and instructions pertaining to the referendum as well as to the conduct of the referendum;
(f) make arrangements to ensure that law and order are maintained during the referendum campaign and voting.

6. Powers of the Referendum Commissioner:
(1) The Commissioner shall, subject to the supervision and control as provided in this Proclamation:
(a) have sole and exclusive responsibility over all matters relating to the referendum, including organization and conduct;

(b) promulgate the necessary rules and regulations, and issue the necessary instructions, to govern the organization and conduct of the referendum. The rules and regulations shall be designed so as to allow for a free and fair referendum;
(c) supervise the day-to-day planning of the referendum;
(d) establish the condition and modalities for the conduct of the referendum;
(e) ensure that all the provisions and guarantees of this proclamation are respected.

(2) To this end, the Commissioner shall, *inter alia*:
(a) set the starting date of the referendum;
(b) prepare the registers of voters;
(c) make arrangements for polling stations, ballot boxes and ballot forms, including outside Eritrea;
(d) supervise the manner and conduct of registration and voting. In particular, he shall, when he deems it necessary, set, for polling outside Eritrea, dates different from the date of the referendum voting conducted within Eritrea;
(e) create offices and appoint representatives abroad for the purpose of the referendum;
(f) issue directives governing the conduct of such polling stations;
(g) invite observers to observe the referendum process inside and outside Eritrea;
(h) set guidelines for the tallying of the voting and the issuance of the results thereof;
(i) address any petitions concerning the results of the voting.

(3) The Referendum Commissioner shall make arrangements for the maintenance of law and order during the entire referendum process. He shall, in particular, ensure that there is no resort to threats and intimidations or interference with the referendum process.

7. Organization of the Commission:
(1) The Commission shall establish sub-commissions and other branches in every province, district and sub-district in Eritrea.

(2) The Commission shall, where it deems it necessary, also establish other stations in other Eritrean locations as well as abroad to ensure the effective execution of its duties and to make the referendum process easily and readily accessible to all Eritreans.

(3) The Referendum Commissioner shall appoint all provincial and other referendum officials.

CHAPTER IV—ADMINISTRATION

8. Offices and Staff:
(1) There shall be a Secretariat of the Referendum Commission headed by a Deputy Commissioner. The

Deputy Commissioner shall be responsible for the administrative work of the Commission.

(2) Each sub-commission or branch at all administrative levels shall have such administrative offices and staff as are required to meet its needs and to perform its functions.

(3) The Referendum Commissioner shall, in consultation with concerned agencies of the Government, issue general instructions for the organization and staffing of these sub-commissions and branches. To this end, as and from the effective date of this Proclamation, all civil servants and other personnel entrusted with the performance of the activities of the Referendum Commission shall be transferred to and, for the duration of the referendum period, become the employees of the Commission.

(4) The Referendum Commissioner shall, within the framework of the general practice of the Government and/or the laws and regulations applicable to the civil service, determine the remuneration and travel allowances of the staff.

(5) The Referendum Commissioner shall, in consultation with concerned agencies of the Government, provide for appropriate in-service training of staff members.

(6) The Referendum Commissioner shall solicit for the necessary funds to cover expenses related to such training.

9. Budget:

(1) The cost of carrying out the referendum shall be borne by the Referendum Commission. The Referendum Commissioner shall prepare and publish estimates of all income and expenditure for the organization and supervision of the referendum.

(2) The budget shall constitute the legal basis for the administration of all income and expenditure and may include an appropriation to cover cases arising out of unforeseeable events.

(3) The Referendum Commissioner shall seek, and accept, internal and external grants and assistance as may be necessary to carry out the referendum, including from the Government and people of Eritrea.

(4) The Referendum Commissioner shall, no later than three (3) months following the end of the referendum, submit to the Auditor General of the Government the accounts of income and expenditure associated with the referendum.

10. Supervision and Control:

(1) Except as otherwise provided in this proclamation, or in other subsequent legislation, the Referendum Commissioner shall be responsible for the general supervision and control of the activities of all sub-commissions and branches at all levels.

He shall set the guidelines and establish the rules and regulations for the supervision and control of the activities of officials and employees of the commission and its branches.

(2) Deputy Commissioners concerned with the fields specified in sub-paragraph 3 of Article 4 hereof shall, within their respective areas, have the power to supervise and control the activities of the referendum process.

(3) The authorities specified in sub-paragraph 2 of this Article of the Proclamation shall ensure that:

(a) the sub-commissions and other branches perform their functions in accordance with the rules and regulations governing the referendum;

(b) actions of sub-commissions and branches shall not conflict with, or hinder the implementation of, the rules and regulations mentioned in sub-paragraph 3 (a);

(4) (a) The authorities specified in sub-paragraph 2 of this Article may, at any time, send officials to conduct an inspection of the activities of the sub-commissions or branches and may request reports from the head of the sub-commission or branch official or both; provided, however, that the Referendum Commissioner shall be informed of any inspection conducted by any other authority;

(b) the head of a sub-commission or a district official or both shall furnish all information and shall produce all such records and other information as may be requested by the authorities specified in sub-paragraphs 1 and 2 or persons designated by them to conduct an inspection;

(5) (a) Where the Referendum Commissioner determines that the head of a sub-commission or branch official is not performing his duties in accordance with the rules and regulations governing the referendum, he may order the concerned Deputy Commissioner specified in sub-paragraph 2 of this Article to have appropriate remedial measures and to make the sub-commission abandon certain activities within a specified period.

(b) Where appropriate, the Referendum Commissioner shall, prior to the issuance of any such order, give the concerned Deputy Commissioner the opportunity, within a specified period, to express his views and, where investigations have been carried out, to submit supplementary information and reports.

(c) Upon request by the Secretary General, the Referendum Commissioner shall conduct an appropriate investigation to determine whether the duties of any Board or sub-commission are being fulfilled in accordance with the rules and regulations governing the referendum.

CHAPTER V—OBSERVERS

11. Observers and their role:

(1) The Referendum Commissioner shall invite international and regional organizations as well as representatives of governments, other organizations and individuals to attend as observers the entire referendum process.

(2) All other interested international and regional organizations as well as governments may request the Referendum Commissioner to participate as observers. The Referendum Commissioner shall respond promptly to all such requests.

(3) Observers shall be allowed to follow the activities of the Commission, Boards and all sub-commissions and branches including, but not limited to, the identification and registration of voters as well as the actual voting, tallying and issuance of results.

(4) The Referendum Commissioner shall ensure that observers shall have free access to the Commission and Boards as well as to sub-commissions and branch offices at all levels. He shall further ensure that they receive all notices relative to dates and venues of identification, registration, and balloting as well as of appeals and objections thereon.

(5) Observers shall be allowed to register complaints with, or make observations to, the Referendum Commissioner in respect of any and all irregularities that they may observe or that may be brought to their attention. The Referendum Commissioner shall address such complaints and observations promptly.

CHAPTER VI—IDENTIFICATION OF VOTERS

12. Identification Board:

(1) There shall be established, as an integral part of the Referendum Commission, an Identification Board which shall assist the Referendum Commissioner in the fulfilment of his responsibilities in connection with the identification and registration of those eligible to vote in the referendum.

(2) The Identification Board shall be responsible for the establishment of provincial and district branches in Eritrea and other branches outside Eritrea.

13. Composition:

The Identification Board shall consist of a Deputy Commissioner, who shall become the Chairman, and other members appointed by the Referendum Commissioner with the prior approval of the Secretary General.

14. Duties:

The Identification Board shall be responsible for:

(1) verifying the identity and eligibility of the people of Eritrea, residing in Eritrea or abroad, who may wish to participate in the referendum;

(2) establishing registration districts into which the territory, refugee camps and other countries abroad shall be divided, to provide as accurate a basis as possible for computing the number of qualified voters in the referendum;

(3) establishing as precisely as possible, the number of Eritrean voters living both in Eritrea and abroad, including, in particular, those living in refugee camps outside Eritrea, with a view to identifying those who would be qualified to participate in the referendum;

(4) publishing the list prepared in Eritrea and abroad and making arrangements for challenges to the inclusion or exclusion of any person;

(5) submitting the results and conclusions of its work to the Referendum Commissioner who shall then authorize publication of the final list.

15. Expert Assistance:

The Identification Board shall be assisted by experts and village/community elders in the performance of its duties. These experts and elders shall be asked to make concrete suggestions on the best ways and means of identifying qualified participants.

16. Procedure:

(1) The Identification Board shall perform its functions in two (2) stages. In the first stage, the Board shall:

(a) create a committee of Eritrean experts recognized for their knowledge of Eritrean society;

(b) conduct an election whereby the population will elect village/community elders reputed for their knowledge of their localities.

In the second stage, it shall, with the help of the elders and experts, prepare a tentative roll of qualified voters.

17. Completion of work:

The Identification Board shall complete its work and submit its report to the Referendum Commissioner at least three (3) months before the beginning of the referendum voting.

CHAPTER VII—PUBLICITY AND INFORMATION

18. Establishment of a Publicity and Information Board:

(1) There shall be relevant publicity and information regarding the referendum process starting from the date of the publication of this Proclamation.

(2) There is hereby established a Publicity and Information Board composed of a Deputy Commissioner and three (3) distinguished Eritreans whose probity is recognized. They shall be appointed by the Referendum

Commissioner with the prior approval of the Secretary General. The Deputy Commissioner shall be the Chairman of the said Board.

(3) The Board shall conduct its activities until the end of the referendum.

(4) (a) The Board shall organize, supervise and oversee a publicity and information program on the referendum process;

(b) The purpose of the program shall be to inform the people of Eritrea about the meaning, purpose and process of the referendum and to widely publicize it.

(5) The Board shall:

(a) create any administrative structure and hire such staff as it may deem necessary within the bounds of its terms of reference as stated in sub-paragraph 4 of this Article or any subsequent, relevant legislation;

(b) prepare, in all Eritrean languages, copies of the proposition of the referendum as well as all explanatory materials;

(c) hold seminars, classes, film shows and exhibitions in all parts of Eritrea and abroad, particularly in refugee camps outside Eritrea:

(d) have any other functions that will help in the achievement of a free and fair referendum.

(6) The Chairman of the Publicity and Information Board shall submit periodic activity reports to the Referendum Commissioner.

CHAPTER VIII—THE ELECTION BOARD

19. Establishment of an Election Board:

There is hereby established an Election Board whose purpose is to conduct the balloting process of the referendum. The Board shall commence the performance of its duties at the beginning of the referendum.

20. Composition:

The Election Board shall consist of a Deputy Commissioner who shall be chairman of the Board and three (3) members appointed by the Referendum Commissioner with the prior approval of the Secretary General.

21. Duties:

(1) The Election Board shall be responsible for making arrangements for, and conducting the vote on, the referendum as provided in this Proclamation. In exercising its functions, the Election Board shall have the power and duty to make all relevant and necessary decisions and to take appropriate measures to enforce such decisions after prior consultation with the Referendum Commissioner and in accordance with the regulations governing the referendum. The Election Board shall transmit to the Referendum Commissioner the result of the referendum, who shall decide on the validity of the voting in the referendum, subject to appeal to the Referendum Court created for this purpose.

(2) The Referendum Commissioner shall issue regulations governing the performance of the functions of the Election Board.

CHAPTER IX—REGISTRATION OF VOTERS

22. Electoral Districts and Register of Voters:

(1) The Election Board shall be responsible for the creation of electoral districts in and outside Eritrea and for the establishment of a register of voters within each of these electoral districts.

(2) Voting registers shall be in such form as to provide for at least fifteen (15) columns of entries headed as follows:

(a) Serial number of registration;
(b) Date of registration;
(c) Full name of prospective voter;
(d) Name of paternal grandfather;
(e) Age;
(f) Place of registration;
(g) Period of residence at present location;
(h) Residences prior to present residence;
(i) Number of members of immediate family;
(j) Registration number;
(k) Signature or pollex digital imprint at time of registration;
(l) Signature or pollex digital imprint at time of voting;
(m) Three (3) unheaded columns for other entries.

23. Registration Centers:

(1) (a) There shall be registration centers in all electoral districts. In addition to stationary registration centers, there shall also be mobile registration teams covering relatively inaccessible places in the rural areas.

(b) There shall not be registration centers at any (i) police station, (ii) military base or (iii) residences of government officials or village elders.

(2) (a) There shall be a separate voting register, or registers as may be necessary, for each polling station in an electoral district. There shall also be a central register of voters comprising either a computerized list of voters or the duplicates of registration cards issued to all registered voters.

(b) Whenever possible, a computerized list of voters, by electoral district and in alphabetical order, shall be prepared on a weekly basis.

24. Persons Qualified for Registration:

Any person having Eritrean citizenship pursuant to Proclamation No. 21/1992 on the date of his application for registration and who was of the age of 18 years or older or would attain such age at any time during the registration period, and who further possessed an Identification Card issued by the Department of Internal Affairs, shall be qualified for registration.

25. Registration Officials:

(1) The Chairman of the Election Board shall ensure that only competent government employees of integrity who are regarded as impartial and in good social standing are appointed as district supervisors, district officers and registration team leaders.

(2) If, because of the unavailability of enough government employees, private individuals are to be appointed as registration officials, they shall be carefully screened before selection and their names and their addresses shall be published in advance.

(3) The Referendum Commissioner retains the right to withdraw any appointment made on the basis of sub-paragraphs (1) and (2) hereof if, in his view, such an appointment is not compatible with the holding of a free and fair referendum.

26. Time and Place for Registration:

(1) Any person who desires to be registered as a voter shall, during the registration period, present himself to the registration officer in the electoral district office of his residence. He shall present his identity card, issued by the Department of Internal Affairs at the time of his registration, and receive a voter registration card.

(2) The registration period shall be announced by the Referendum Commissioner. Registration shall end at least eight (8) weeks before the day of the voting.

(3) Registration offices shall be open continuously from 8 a.m. to 6 p.m. every day including holidays.

(4) After voting registers have been submitted to the Board, and before the beginning of elections, the Board shall compare the registers of the different polling and electoral districts and shall cancel the registration of, and strike out all entries pertaining to, any person who has been registered more than once in any one (1) voting register or in more than one (1) registration center.

(5) An alphabetical list of persons whose registration has been cancelled pursuant to sub-paragraph 4 of this article shall be prepared for each electoral district. The Board shall post such lists at the district office and shall publicize that such a list has been so posted.

27. Registration Procedure:

(1) When a person presents himself for registration, he must submit his Identity Card as proof that he meets the qualification set forth in Article 24 of this Proclamation;

(2) If a person is qualified to be registered in the electoral district where he has presented himself and it appears that he has not previously been registered, the registration officer shall:

(a) assign him to a polling station in his district;

(b) assign him a registration number;

(c) record in the voting register of the polling station to which the registration has been assigned:

(i) the appropriate information under the first ten(10) columns of entries as specified in Article 22 hereof;

(ii) the registrant's signature or pollex digital imprint;

(iii) any additional information relevant to registration;

(d) issue to the registrant a registration card bearing:

(i) the registrant's name;

(ii) his registration number;

(iii) the location and name or number of his polling station;

(iv) the name or number of the electoral district in which the registrant is registered to vote; and

(v) the signature of the registration officer.

28. Appeal Procedure:

(1) If a registration officer refuses to register any person as a voter, that person may appeal to the Board at any time up to four (4) weeks before the day of voting;

(2) The Board shall immediately inquire into the appeal. As part of its enquiry, it shall give the appellant a fair opportunity to be heard and to produce evidence in his favor;

(3) Subsequent to the completion of its enquiry, the Board shall, after consulting the Referendum Commissioner, prepare an order in writing either requiring the registration officer to register the appellant or denying the appeal;

(a) A Board order recognizing the right of the appellant to be registered shall be written in triplicate, two (2) of which shall be delivered to the appropriate registration officer and to the appellant while the third shall be retained by the Board;

(b) A Board decision rejecting an appeal shall be written in two (2) copies with one (1) copy delivered to the appellant and the other retained by the Board;

(c) When the appeal is rejected, the Board shall state clearly the facts and reasons for rejection;

(4) (a) When the appeal is rejected by the Board, the appellant may further appeal the decision to the

Referendum Court at any time up to two (2) weeks before the day of voting. A copy of the Board's decision shall accompany the appeal.

(5) If the Referendum Court reverses the order of the Board, it shall, not more than three (3) days after it makes its decision, and, in any case, no less than one (1) week before voting, prepare a written opinion stating the reasons for its decision. A copy of the opinion shall be delivered to the Referendum Commissioner, who shall, through the chairman of the Election Board, order the appropriate registration officer to register the appellant.

(6) Any Eritrean or group of Eritreans may appeal against the retention of names in the register of voters. The appeal procedure shall be as specified in paragraphs (1) to (5) hereof.

29. Submission of Voting Registers:

Immediately after the registration period terminates, each registration officer shall personally return to the Board, enclosed in a sealed container, the voting registers and remaining registration cards of his registration office.

CHAPTER X—REGISTRATION OF INDIVIDUALS AND ASSOCIATIONS

30. Petition for Registration:

(1) The Referendum Commissioner shall take all necessary measures to ensure that any Eritrean citizen, or association composed of Eritreans and residing in Eritrea and opposing Eritrean independence shall be able to express their views freely and without any restrictions; the Referendum Commissioner shall, in particular, guarantee the safety and freedom of all such individuals and associations.

(2) All such individuals and associations shall submit to the Commission applications using names, abbreviations and symbols proposed by themselves.

(3) Such individuals and associations may start to register as soon as the Referendum Commission is established but not later than four (4) weeks before the beginning of balloting.

(4) The names of such individuals and associations shall be published.

(5) All such individuals and associations shall strictly abide by the provisions of a code of conduct to be written by the Referendum Commissioner.

They shall undertake, at the time of registration, to accept the code of conduct. Contravention of the provisions of the code may result in warnings, suspension or cancellation of registration, depending on the gravity of the case as determined by the Referendum Commissioner.

CHAPTER XI—VOTING

31. Voting Day or Period:

(1) The referendum balloting shall begin six (6) months after the Identification Board submits its reports and its results shall be published within seventy-two (72) hours. Polling days shall be announced by the Referendum Commissioner.

(2) The referendum shall begin only after the Referendum Commissioner is satisfied that the process governing the referendum is equitable. The Referendum Commissioner shall have the authority to determine any circumstances requiring change in the dates.

32. Polling Stations:

(1) The Election Board shall establish as many polling stations as may be necessary for the speedy completion of the voting; provided, however, that in the area of every polling station there shall be a sufficient number of voters to maintain the secrecy of the ballots cast.

(2) Polling stations shall remain open from eight o'clock in the morning (8 a.m.) to six o'clock in the evening (6 p.m.).

(3) Throughout the period commencing three (3) days before the election and continuing until the removal of all ballot boxes upon completion of voting, every polling station shall be securely closed and guarded under lock and key at all hours when voting is not in progress. During such hours, entry into polling stations shall be strictly prohibited to all persons other than the Referendum Commissioner, Board members and authorized officials.

(4) Each polling station shall be so arranged as to permit a voter to cast his ballot in complete secrecy. It shall consist of an administration room and a voting booth which shall be so screened off or arranged that the activities in the voting booth shall be completely hidden from the view of persons in the administration room.

(5) The voting booth shall contain two ballot boxes—i.e. one each for or against the proposition in the referendum.

(6) (a) The administration room shall contain at least one (1) desk and two (2) chairs for the officials verifying registration, a trash can for destroyed registration cards and such other furniture as may be approved by the Board.

(b) A guard rail or rope shall be placed in the administration room near the entrance of the voting booth to provide enclosed waiting space accessible from the remainder of the administration room by a single entrance and exit.

33. Ballots and Ballot Boxes:

(1) The Election Board shall be responsible for providing to each of the polling stations such ballots, lists,

registers and other materials and equipment as may be necessary for the conduct of the balloting.

(2) A ballot shall consist of a numbered slip attached to a counterfoil bearing the same number. Ballots shall be numbered serially.

(3) Every ballot box shall be constructed with a single lid which can be opened and locked. Each lid shall contain an aperture sufficiently large to permit a ballot to be inserted into the box but not large enough to permit a ballot to be withdrawn from the box otherwise than by opening the lid.

(4) (a) Each ballot box shall be kept locked at all times except as authorized under this Proclamation. The aperture in each box shall be kept sealed at all times, except while voting is in progress.

(b) The seal of the aperture of a ballot box shall consist of a paper signed by at least two (2) officials and affixed to the box in such manner that no ballot may be inserted or withdrawn through the aperture without tearing the paper across all two (2) signatures.

34. Voting:

(1) Ballots shall be cast by voters individually in voting booths.

(2) The Election Board shall make the necessary arrangements to protect the secrecy of each ballot cast and to ensure that no voter votes more than once in any balloting.

(3) Voters are normally expected to cast ballots in the districts in which they have been registered; provided, however, that those who cannot do so because of special circumstances shall not be disenfranchised but shall be permitted to vote through tendered ballots.

(4) Voters about whose identity or registration there is doubt shall be requested to use tendered ballots.

(5) (a) The Election Board shall ensure that illiterate voters in need of assistance in marking their ballots in the voting booth are assisted by election officials. No other person shall be allowed to render such assistance.

(b) The assistance shall consist of only information regarding the manner of voting and the voter shall be alone in the voting booth.

(6) Observers shall observe all proceedings at polling stations. They shall not, however, attempt to influence or intimidate voters or breach the secrecy of the voting process.

(7) Ballots shall be deposited directly into the sealed ballot boxes described in Article 33 of this Proclamation.

35. Voting Procedure:

(1) Two (2) officials shall be assigned to each polling station. One of the officials shall have before him the appropriate voting register. The other official shall have the books of ballots. One of these officials shall be a Presiding Official.

(2) Each prospective voter shall present himself to the official having before him the voting register. The prospective voter shall clearly announce his name and shall present his registration card to the official. The official shall check the identity of the prospective voter by comparing the announced name with that stated on the registration card and by comparing the signature or pollex digital imprint thereon against that in the voting register at the registration number shown in the registration card. If there is any doubt as to the identity of the prospective voter the official may request the prospective voter to answer any inquiries relevant thereto. If the official deems it appropriate, he may request the prospective voter to place his signature or pollex digital imprint on a separate piece of paper and may compare same with the relevant signature or pollex digital imprint in the voting register.

(3) Where it appears that a prospective voter is duly registered to vote in the electoral district and has not previously voted in the election, he shall sign the voter register, if he has previously done so in registering as voter, or shall place therein his pollex digital imprint. Any previous signature, as contained in the register, shall be concealed from the prospective voter by an appropriate means until the completion of the second signature.

(4) Upon the satisfactory completion of the foregoing formalities, the registration card shall be handed to the second official. The second official shall tear the registration card into small pieces and deposit it in the trash can provided for this purpose. He shall then stamp on the top ballot in the counterfoil book before him the dated seal of the polling station. He shall then separate the ballot from the counterfoil and hand it to the voter.

(5) Upon receipt of a ballot, the voter shall immediately pass into the waiting space and shall await his turn to vote. Not more than ten (10) voters shall be within the waiting space at the same time. No person other than an official or a person holding a ballot issued to him shall be admitted to the waiting space.

(6) Voters shall enter the voting booth only one (1) at a time. No voter may remain in the voting booth for more than one (1) minute. No official or other person shall be present with a voter in the voting booth except

that two (2) officials may be present at a voter's request if he is unable to perform the act of voting by himself because of physical handicap. A voter shall vote by placing the ballot given to him in the ballot box bearing the symbol, if any, for or against the proposition.

(7) The voting booth shall be inspected by two (2) officials immediately after the exit of each voter therefrom in order to ascertain and correct any defacing of, or tampering with, the ballot boxes or the interior of the voting booth.

(8) At six o'clock in the evening (6:00 p.m.) the door to the polling stations shall be closed, and no more prospective voters shall thereafter be admitted into the station. Those persons who have at that time begun the formalities of identification or are within the waiting space shall be permitted to vote.

(9) At the end of each day's voting, the Presiding Official at each polling station shall, in the presence of the other official, seal all ballot boxes therein as provided in paragraph 4 of Article 33 of this Proclamation. The boxes shall remain sealed until the beginning of voting on the next day of voting when they shall be unsealed by the Presiding Official in the presence of the other official.

36. Denial of Vote:

(1) If a person has presented himself to vote at the wrong polling station, an official shall direct the person to the correct polling station as specified on the person's registration card; provided, however, that the provisions of paragraph 3 of Article 34 are duly respected.

(2) The official at a polling station shall not issue a ballot to any person whose identity has not been established or whose registration number, signature or pollex digital imprint does not correspond with that indicated in the voting register; provided, however, that the joint decision of the officials present at the polling station shall determine whether any person presenting a registration card shall be denied a ballot and such decision shall be recorded and signed by the officials on a form provided by the Board for this purpose. The Presiding Official shall have a casting vote. One (1) copy of the form, with the registration card in question affixed thereto, shall immediately be submitted to the Board, and one (1) copy of the form shall be given to the person who presented the card.

(3) In the event of a fraudulent act by a person who presents a registration card, election officials shall remand the person to the police for prosecution.

37. Responsibility of the Presiding Official:

(1) The Presiding Official at each polling station shall be responsible for the conduct of the election at that station and for the observance therein of the provisions of regulations and of instructions issued pursuant hereto.

He may expel from the station any person who disobeys any order or instructions made by him in conformity with this Proclamation. He may, when necessary, request the assistance of the police or guards assigned to the station; provided, however, that no member of the police or armed forces may enter a polling station during the balloting otherwise than for the purpose of voting or in response to a request for assistance made by the Presiding Official.

38. Inspection by Election Board:

(1) The Board shall, during the balloting, conduct such inspections of polling stations as it may deem appropriate to ensure compliance with the requirements of this Proclamation.

(2) It shall, in particular, inspect forthwith any polling station upon complaint of irregularities made by any observer mentioned in Article 11 of this Proclamation. Each such inspection shall be conducted by two (2) members of the Board and an observer selected by the Board.

39. Completion of Voting:

(1) Immediately upon completion of voting on the last day of the voting the two (2) officials shall sign a completion of voting form to be provided by the Board and shall together deposit the form in the ballot box in the polling station.

(2) The Presiding Official shall thereupon, in the presence of the other official, immediately seal each of the ballot boxes as provided in paragraph 10 of Article 35 hereof. The Presiding Official shall then prepare a statement indicating:

(a) the number of unused ballots remaining;

(b) the serial numbers of the ballots furnished and of the unused ballots remaining;

(c) the number of ballots used;

(d) the number of voters registered to vote at the station; and

(e) the number of voters noted in the voting register as having been issued ballots.

The statement shall be signed by him and by the other official.

(3) The Presiding Official, accompanied by appropriate guards, shall transport to the district office of the

Board all ballot boxes, unused ballots and the voting register, as well as the statement required by paragraph 2 of this Article. All of the aforementioned items shall be deposited with the Board which shall retain them as delivered in a locked and guarded room pending further action in accordance with this Proclamation.

CHAPTER XII — ELECTION RESULTS

40. Counting Procedure:

(1) All except tendered ballots shall be counted at each polling station. Tendered ballots shall be counted at electoral districts. All observers shall be entitled to be present while the ballots are being counted.

(2) Officials shall unlock each ballot without breaking the seal on the aperture. They shall compare the signatures on the seal with those appearing on the completion of voting form within the box and shall immediately report any irregularities to the Board for its action. They shall then immediately proceed to count the ballots in the box and shall continue until all the ballots therein have been counted. The ballots and the completion of voting form shall then be returned to the box and the number of valid ballots counted shall be clearly marked on the box. The box shall then again be locked, the seal on the aperture being retained thereon intact.

(3) A ballot shall be void and shall not be counted if it is not stamped with the official, dated seal of the appropriate polling station or if the number appearing on the ballot is not among the numbers on the ballots furnished by the Board to the polling station.

41. Determination and Declaration of the Referendum Results:

(1) If the difference between the number of voters counted for or against the proposition is less than three percent (3%) of the total number of ballots, then the ballots shall be recounted upon the request of an observer.

(2) A provisional result shall be announced as soon as the counting of the ballots is over. If no complaints concerning the referendum have been received within seventy-two (72) hours after the announcement of the provisional results, the provisional results shall become final.

42. Complaints:

(1) Any observer shall be entitled to submit to the Election Board, at any time up to and including the third (3rd) day after the posting of the provisional referendum results, any complaints which he may have concerning the conduct of the referendum. Each complaint shall be submitted in writing and shall include a clear statement of the grounds thereof.

(2) The Election Board shall consider each such complaint as submitted and shall within seventy-two (72) hours after the submission of the complaint forward it with its own comments to the Referendum Commissioner for his decision.

(3) The Referendum Commissioner shall within forty-eight (48) hours decide on the complaint and order appropriate action.

CHAPTER XIII — THE REFERENDUM COURT

43. Establishment, Composition and Powers:

(1) A Referendum Court is hereby established for the duration of the referendum process.

(2) The Court shall be composed of one presiding judge and two other judges to be appointed by the Referendum Commissioner with the prior approval of the Secretary General.

(3) The powers of the Court shall be limited to:

(a) the interpretation of the provisions of this Proclamation;

(b) hearing and deciding appeals from decisions made by the Referendum Commission;

(c) hearing and deciding cases related to the offences specified in Article 48 of this Proclamation.

(4) The Court shall adopt the Transitory Civil and Criminal Procedure codes of Eritrea. However, its decisions shall be final and may not be challenged by any other authority.

CHAPTER XIV — MISCELLANEOUS AND FINAL

44. Procedure:

(1) Unless otherwise stated in this Proclamation, the Referendum Commissioner makes all final decisions of the Referendum Commission, giving due respect to the advice and opinions of the other members of the Commission.

(2) The decisions of the various Boards of the Commission shall be by majority vote in the presence of a quorum. Three (3) members shall form a quorum. The chairman shall have a casting vote.

45. Material Resources:

The Referendum Commissioner shall solicit for all the material resources that the Commission needs in order to be able to perform its duties and to accomplish its mission.

46. Media:

(1) The Referendum Commissioner shall make sure that the referendum process is free, fair and impartial.

(2) (a) All Eritrean individuals and associations mentioned in Chapter X of this Proclamation shall have access to periods of air time on both radio and television.

(b) To this end, the Referendum Commissioner shall (i) establish a standing consultative committee composed of observers and the management of the mass media of the Government; (ii) ensure coverage of all important meetings, news conferences and media releases.

(3) The Referendum Commissioner shall make sure that programs related to the referendum will focus on familiarizing the electorate with all aspects of the referendum process.

(4) The Referendum Commissioner shall make sure that, as far as possible, daily radio and television broadcasts on the referendum are transmitted in all the main languages of Eritrea during the entire period of the referendum.

(5) The Referendum Commissioner shall make sure that all instructional and voter education films on the referendum process, as well as posters and leaflets on the referendum and voting process, are, as far as possible, prepared and disseminated in all the major languages of Eritrea.

(6) The Referendum Commissioner shall, as early as possible, employ all other available means to explain the referendum process and to ensure a big turnout during the referendum voting.

47. Proclamation of the Results of the Referendum:

(1) The result of the referendum shall be proclaimed as indicated in paragraph 2 of Article 41 of this Proclamation.

(2) The Referendum Commissioner shall notify the Secretary General as soon as the results of the referendum have been certified by him. The Government shall take the necessary action to give effect to the decision of the Eritrean people as expressed in the referendum.

48. Offences:

(1) Whosoever registers in more than one (1) place or in more than one (1) voter register or whosoever registers by more than one (1) name shall be sentenced to imprisonment not exceeding three (3) months or by a fine not exceeding Birr 3,000 or by both.

(2) Whosoever attempts to prevent, or disturbs, or obstructs, the registration or voting process of the referendum by force or the threat of force, intimidation, bribery or fraud shall be sentenced to imprisonment not exceeding six (6) months or by a fine not exceeding Birr 5,000 or by both.

49. Entry into Force:
This Proclamation shall enter into force on the date of its publication in the Gazette of Eritrean Laws.

Done at Asmara this 7th day of April 1992
The Provisional Government of Eritrea

Corrigendum No. 1/1992

Proclamation No. 22/1992 has been corrected as follows:
1. The second sentence of Art. 3 (3) is deleted and shall be replaced by the following sentence:

"The ballot shall be printed in different Eritrean languages."

2. The cross-reference in Art. 39 (2) shall be to paragraph 9 and not 10.

3. Art. 18 (5) (b) is deleted and shall be replaced by the following sentence:

"Prepare in different Eritrean languages copies of the proposition of the referendum as well as explanatory materials."

Asmara, 8 May 1992,
The Provisional Government of Eritrea

Document 18

Letter dated 9 April 1992 from Denmark, Finland, Iceland, Norway and Sweden to the Secretary-General of the United Nations concerning the dispatch of a technical survey mission to Eritrea and Ethiopia

Not issued as a United Nations document

In December last year, His Excellency, Meles Zenawi, president of the Transitional Government of Ethiopia, wrote to the Secretary-General of the United Nations requesting him to take steps in order to enable the United Nations to play an active role in verifying that the Eritrean referendum, planned to take place in 1993, would be free and fair.

In view of this request and of the fact that also the Provisional Government of Eritrea, on several occasions, has expressed a desire for a United Nations role in the referendum process, it is our hope that Your Excellency would send a technical survey mission of United Nations officials to Ethiopia and Eritrea to evaluate, with authorities concerned, how the United Nations could support the referendum process.

Please accept, Your Excellency, the assurances of our highest considerations.

Bent HAAKONSEN
Ambassador, Permanent Representative of Denmark
to the United Nations

Tauno KÄÄRIÄ
Ambassador, Permanent Representative of Finland
to the United Nations

Kornelius SIGMUNDSSON
Chargé d'affaires a.i. of the Permanent Mission
of Iceland to the United Nations

Martin HUSLID
Ambassador, Permanent Representative of Norway
to the United Nations

Lars-Göran ENGFELDT
Ambassador, Acting Permanent Representative
of Sweden to the United Nations

Document 19

Letter dated 19 May 1992 from the Commissioner of the Referendum Commission of Eritrea to the Secretary-General of the United Nations inviting the United Nations to observe and verify the referendum process

A/C.3/47/5, Annex III, 29 October 1992

In May 1991, the newly formed Provisional Government of Eritrea, meeting in London with delegations from Ethiopia under the auspices of the Government of the United States of America, reaffirmed its commitment to the holding of a referendum on the future of Eritrea within two years. The referendum is regarded as the culmination of all-Eritrean efforts to transform into reality the principles and purposes that had underlined the struggle of the Eritrean people.

The Conference on Peace and Democracy, organized by the Transitional Government of Ethiopia in July 1991 and attended by almost all the political parties, movements and social organizations of that country, welcomed the decision of the Provisional Government of Eritrea.

In the Transitional Charter of Ethiopia, which it adopted at the end of its session, it committed itself to respecting the results of an Eritrean referendum and further made it clear that the referendum shall entirely be an Eritrean affair.

On 7 April 1992, the Provisional Government of Eritrea issued a Referendum Proclamation, by which a commission to organize, conduct and supervise the said referendum was created.

The Referendum Commission is an independent organization which is committed to an internationally observed, free, fair and impartial referendum.

As Referendum Commissioner, and by the powers vested in me by article 6 of the Proclamation, I have the honour to invite Your Excellency to send a delegation of the United Nations Organization to observe, and to verify the freeness, fairness and impartiality of the entire referendum process from its beginning in July 1992 to its completion in April 1993.

(*Signed*) Amare TEKLE

Commissioner

Document 20

Letter dated 11 June 1992 from the Secretary-General of the United Nations to the President of the General Assembly concerning developments pertaining to the political status of Eritrea

A/C.3/47/5, Annex I, 29 October 1992

The General Assembly has had a historical involvement with issues pertaining to the political status of Eritrea. Recently, several Member States, including members of the European Community, the Nordic countries, the United States of America and Austria, have approached me to urge support for a United Nations role with regard to a referendum planned for 1993 in Eritrea. In view of the previous involvement of the Assembly and the renewed interest on the part of Member States, I consider it appropriate to apprise the Assembly of the following developments.

By a letter dated 13 December 1991 (annex II [reproduced here as Document 13]), Mr. Meles Zenawi, President of the Transitional Government of Ethiopia, provided information about the decisions of a Conference on Peace and Democracy in Ethiopia, held at Addis Ababa from 1 to 5 July 1991. That Conference had adopted a Charter affirming that freedom, equal rights and self-determination of all peoples are the cardinal principles governing state affairs in the new Ethiopia. In the light of this, the Conference formally recognized that the people of Eritrea have the right to determine their own future by themselves, and accepted that the future status of Eritrea should be decided by the Eritrean people in a referendum to be conducted in the presence of international observers.

Both the Transitional Government of Ethiopia and the Provisional Government of Eritrea had registered their commitment to respect the results of the referendum in Eritrea as the genuine choice of the people concerned, expressed in an exercise of self-determination. The Transitional Government of Ethiopia believed that the United Nations should play an active role in verifying that the referendum is, indeed, free and fair. The Transitional Government therefore requested that appropriate measures be initiated to enable the United Nations to play this role and make the necessary arrangements with the Provisional Government of Eritrea to facilitate the ways and means for United Nations supervision of the referendum.

Following receipt of the above-mentioned letter, contacts were undertaken with the Transitional Government of Ethiopia and the Provisional Government of Eritrea in order to clarify the nature of the United Nations involvement sought. Under-Secretary-General James O. C. Jonah met twice with the President of the Transitional Government of Ethiopia and has also been in touch with representatives of the Provisional Government of Eritrea. Pursuant to those contacts, further clarifications were obtained regarding the United Nations role envisaged.

By a letter dated 19 May 1992 (annex III [reproduced here as Document 19]), the Referendum Commissioner of Eritrea invited me "to send a delegation of the United Nations Organization to observe, and to verify the freeness, fairness and impartiality of the entire referendum process from its beginning in July 1992 to its completion in April 1993".

Taking into account the historical involvement of the General Assembly with the political evolution of Eritrea and the express invitation from both the Transitional Government of Ethiopia and the Referendum Commissioner of Eritrea, as well as the recent General Assembly resolution on the subject of electoral assistance to Member States at their request, the Assembly may wish, following informal consultations among the regional groups as may be required, to authorize involvement by the United Nations in the referendum in Eritrea. In the meantime, in view of the need for further information on which the General Assembly may base its decision and the limited time remaining before the referendum process starts in July 1992, I am dispatching a technical team to gather information for the preparation of a report to be submitted to the General Assembly on the details of potential involvement by the United Nations in the referendum in Eritrea.

(*Signed*) Boutros BOUTROS-GHALI

Document 21

Letter dated 18 June 1992 from the Secretary-General of the United Nations to the Secretary-General of the Provisional Government of Eritrea concerning United Nations involvement in the referendum process

Not issued as a United Nations document

Under-Secretary-General James O. C. Jonah has kept me informed of his many contacts with you, your representatives, and recently with the Commissioner of the Referendum Commission of Eritrea, regarding the referendum planned for 1993 in Eritrea. As Mr. Jonah has emphasized, there are certain basic procedural requirements that must be followed for the United Nations to be engaged in such a process. We have taken into account the historical involvement of the United Nations in the question of Eritrea, a factor which has now enabled us to find a formula which I believe can facilitate our task.

As you may know, I recently carried out a restructuring of the United Nations Secretariat. Among the changes that were announced was the appointment of Mr. Jonah as one of two Under-Secretaries-General for Political Affairs. Mr. Jonah has been assigned two geographic areas—Africa and the Middle East—and a functional task, co-ordination of United Nations electoral assistance. Consequently, he is responsible for political developments in Africa as well as the electoral process in your specific case. An Electoral Assistance Unit has been established in Mr. Jonah's department to assist him in carrying out his responsibilities relating to elections. Mr. Horacio Boneo has been designated head of the Unit.

We have made sufficient progress in our contacts with the various parties concerned to enable me to send on 11 June 1992 a letter to the President of the General Assembly, requesting him to initiate action in respect of the authorization of United Nations involvement in the referendum in Eritrea. In the letter, I also informed the President, and through him, the members of the General Assembly, that I had decided to dispatch a United Nations team to Eritrea to gather information for the preparation of a report to the Assembly on the details of potential involvement by the United Nations in the referendum. As you may know, Under-Secretary-General Jonah had already written to the Commissioner of the Referendum Commission of Eritrea regarding this matter.

I wish to take this opportunity to assure you that the United Nations stands ready to assist, and to be involved, in the referendum, as appropriate.

With my warmest regards.

Yours sincerely,

(*Signed*) Boutros BOUTROS-GHALI

Document 22

Letter dated 24 August 1992 from the Secretary-General of the United Nations to the President of the Transitional Government of Ethiopia concerning United Nations involvement in the referendum process in Eritrea

Not issued as a United Nations document

I have the honour to refer to your letter of 13 December 1991 in which you requested a United Nations role in the referendum to be held in Eritrea, as approved by the decision of the Conference on Peace and Democracy held in Addis Ababa on July 1991.

As Your excellency may be aware, following consultations on this matter, a technical team was sent to Eritrea from 30 July to 8 August 1992 to discuss the terms of reference of a United Nations observation mission that would verify the freeness, fairness and impartiality of the referendum, and to obtain the information necessary for a report to the General Assembly to enable it to approve a mandate for a verification mission.

A report on this question will be submitted to the Assembly for its consideration on a date to be determined. In the interim, I intend to assign two officers to Asmara to assist in the initial preparations and to provide such support to the Eritrean Referendum Commission as might be required. Once the Assembly takes a decision and the financial implications are approved, it is expected that full deployment of the mission would be completed during October 1992. At a later stage, I also intend to appoint a Special Representative.

Please accept, Mr. President, the assurances of my highest consideration.

(*Signed*) Boutros BOUTROS-GHALI

Document 23

Letter dated 24 August 1992 from the Secretary-General of the United Nations to the Secretary-General of the Provisional Government of Eritrea concerning United Nations involvement in the referendum process

Not issued as a United Nations document

I wish to refer to my letter to you of 18 June 1992 in which I informed you of the status of the United Nations involvement in the referendum to be held in Eritrea.

As you are aware, a technical team visited Eritrea from 30 July to 8 August 1992 to discuss the terms of reference of a United Nations observation mission that would verify the freeness, fairness and impartiality of the referendum, and to obtain the information necessary for a report to the General Assembly to enable it to approve a mandate for a verification mission. I understand that the team had the opportunity to meet with you and to exchange views on the matter.

A report on this question will be submitted to the Assembly for its consideration on a date to be determined.

In the interim, I intend to assign two officers to Asmara to assist in the initial preparations and to provide such support to the Eritrean Referendum Commission as might be required. Once the Assembly takes a decision and the financial implications are approved, it is expected that full deployment of the mission would be completed during October 1992. At a later stage, I also intend to appoint a Special Representative.

Your sincerely,

(*Signed*) Boutros BOUTROS-GHALI

Document 24

Report of the Secretary-General on the request to the United Nations to observe the referendum process

A/47/544, 19 October 1992

1. The present report is submitted further to my letter to the President of the General Assembly, of 11 June 1992, informing him of a number of developments with regard to the United Nations involvement in a referendum process in Eritrea. In the course of the 30-year war, the Eritreans had made repeated requests that an internationally observed referendum be held in Eritrea to determine the wishes of the Eritrean people regarding their political status. It will be recalled that the Referendum Commissioner of Eritrea had, on 12 May 1992, invited the Secretary-General to send a delegation of the United Nations to observe and to verify the freeness, fairness and impartiality of the entire referendum process, from its beginning in July 1992 to its completion in April 1993.

2. The Conference on Peace and Democracy, which assembled all the political parties and relevant social actors in Ethiopia, met at Addis Ababa from 1 to 5 July 1991 and formally recognized the right of the Eritrean people to determine its political future by the internationally supervised referendum. As indicated in my letter of 11 June 1992, I informed the President of the

General Assembly that, in view of the need for further information on which the General Assembly may base its decision and the limited time remaining before the referendum process starts in July 1992, I was dispatching a technical team to gather information for the preparation of a report to be submitted to the General Assembly on the details of a potential involvement by the United Nations in the Eritrean referendum.

3. In this connection a technical team headed by the Director of the Electoral Assistance Unit of the Department of Political Affairs and comprising a senior political officer from the Unit and an officer from the Field Operations Division visited Eritrea for the following purposes:

(a) To discuss with the Eritrean authorities the terms of reference of a possible observation mission to verify the freeness, fairness and impartiality of the entire referendum process, as requested by the Referendum Commissioner of Eritrea;

(b) To obtain information on the proposed organization of the referendum process and on geographical and communication aspects that would be necessary to prepare an operational plan for possible United Nations verification of the referendum process;

(c) To obtain information that would be necessary for the preparation of the cost estimates of the possible observation mission;

(d) On the basis of the previous items, to prepare a report to be submitted to the General Assembly.

4. The technical team, in accordance with its mandate, examined the situation in Eritrea through in-depth discussions with the Referendum Commission, members of the provisional Government of Eritrea and representatives of a wide spectrum of political, social and religious organizations. The team also visited the region of Seraye and the cities of Keren and Massawa, contacting there the local authorities.

5. The technical team was provided with a set of the legal instruments drawn up to regulate the conduct of the referendum and had ample occasion to discuss the matter with the Referendum Commission in long and productive working sessions. The members of the team, on the basis of their experience in other contexts, and of comments received from the Centre for Human Rights of the United Nations Secretariat, made a number of technical suggestions aiming at improving some operational aspects of the organization of the referendum or clarifying articles that might be susceptible of misinterpretation. The reaction of the Commission was positive in all cases. On the day of departure of the team, the Referendum Commission issued a press release, clarifying questions related to the participation of organizations and individuals in the campaign period that were raised by the mission.

6. During all their meetings with members of the provisional Government and with representatives of political, social and religious organizations, the mission detected a uniform and strong support for the presence of an observation mission and a desire to have a free and fair referendum process. The team provided the Referendum Commission with detailed information on the characteristics and procedures of a United Nations observation mission, including standard agreements related to the status of the mission as well as its terms of reference. As in the previous case, complete agreement was reached.

7. Given the fact that the referendum to be held in Eritrea and the notion of the international supervision thereof have been supported by the Addis Ababa agreements of July 1991, I conceive of it not only as an important step towards the establishment of democracy but also as an integral part of the consolidation of peace. I am furthermore firmly convinced that this step can contribute decisively to the stability of the region. It is for these reasons, and taking into consideration the historical involvement of the United Nations with Eritrea, that I have decided to recommend the establishment of a United Nations Observer Mission to Verify the Referendum in Eritrea (UNOVER). The terms of reference of such mission would, subject to the approval of the General Assembly, be as follows:

(a) To verify the impartiality of the referendum authorities and organs, including the Referendum Commission, in all aspects and stages of the referendum process;

(b) To verify that there exists complete freedom of organization, movement, assembly and expression without hindrance or intimidation;

(c) To verify that there is equal access to media facilities and that there is fairness in the allocation of both the timing and length of broadcasts;

(d) To verify that the referendum rolls are properly drawn up and that qualified voters are not denied identification and registration cards or the right to vote;

(e) To report to the referendum authorities on complaints, irregularities and interferences reported or observed and, if necessary, to request the referendum authorities to take action to resolve and rectify such complaints, irregularities or interference;

(f) To observe all activities related to the registration of voters, the organization of the poll, the referendum campaign, the poll itself and the counting, computation and announcement of the results.

8. In carrying out the above mandate, the Observer Mission will be expected to gather factual information

about the conduct of the referendum and, in particular, the decision of the electorate; to recognize that the ultimate judgement about the referendum process will be made by the electorate themselves and that its role will be to take note of the decision of the electorate as they determine their fate in a referendum; to recognize the independent character of the Referendum Commission and establish a relationship with it on that basis; and, in its capacity as observer, to make constructive contributions to ensure the success of the referendum at every stage of the process.

9. Subject to the approval of the General Assembly, the structure of UNOVER could be the following:

(a) Office of the Chief of the Mission (Asmara): a small unit could provide overall political direction to the verification mission. It could maintain contacts with the provisional Government and the Referendum Commission and could deal with political and electoral matters that might arise from the performance of the verification functions;

(b) Regional offices at Asmara, Keren and Mendefera: each regional office could be headed by a regional coordinator, who could be assisted by two electoral officers, and could be in charge of the verification activities in its jurisdiction;

(c) Mobile teams located at Asmara and Keren: there could be two teams of two persons each located in these cities to make periodic visits to areas that fall outside the jurisdiction of the regional offices, so as to cover the totality of the country.

10. Given the peaceful situation in Eritrea, the organization of the referendum effort already carried out by the Referendum Commission, and the lack of evidence of political tensions or conflictual positions in relation to the Referendum, it is considered that a total of 21 international staff, supported by local personnel, would be a sufficient number to fulfil adequately the verification functions.

11. If approved by the General Assembly, the UNOVER referendum observers, during all three phases, would monitor and evaluate the operations and impartiality of the referendum authorities at all levels. UNOVER would similarly evaluate the fairness of all significant decisions of the referendum authorities and would investigate disputed actions taken by them. The regional teams would have regular contact with community leaders and social organizations, and would visit municipalities and villages throughout the country; they would monitor registration by making random visits to registration centres; they would observe rallies and other referendum-related activities; and they would verify compliance by all parties with the referendum proclamation and with the code of conduct. The mechanisms through which broadcasting time would be allotted to those registered for its use and the content of information broadcasts would also be observed. A mechanism would be created to receive complaints by individuals or organizations participating in the referendum process, analyse their relevance and transmit them to the referendum authorities for appropriate action.

12. Three main phases of the referendum process are foreseen: the registration of voters (possibly starting during the second week of September); the referendum campaign and the poll itself, which is scheduled to take place in April 1993.

13. During the polling itself, 60 observation teams of two persons each, that is, a total of 120 persons, would be fielded. These teams would have full access to monitor all stages of the poll. The 120 personnel would consist of the approximately 21 staff mentioned in paragraph 10 above; about 50 additional observers to be selected from the United Nations Development Programme and other United Nations agency personnel at Asmara and in neighbouring countries, plus volunteers from the international personnel of selected non-governmental organizations operating in Eritrea; and 50 additional observers from abroad, contributed by the Secretariat and Member States.

14. Given the nature of the tasks for which UNOVER would be responsible, it would be essential to equip it with a small but reliable communication system to enhance its effectiveness and the security of its functions and personnel. Adequate transport resources would also be required to give it the mobility essential for its effective operation. The need to cover remote areas with the mobile teams makes it essential to include in the budget an amount for air operations. The provisional cost estimates are given in the annex to the present report. The total estimated cost of UNOVER for an eight-month period will be less than US$ 3 million.

15. In view of the imminent start of the registration process, should the General Assembly authorize the establishment of UNOVER, I intend to appoint a Special Representative to take charge of the exercise and to assign two officers to Asmara to undertake the initial stages of the process and provide such support to the Eritrean Referendum Commission as might be required. Once a decision is reached on the matter and the financial implications are approved, my objective is that the full deployment of the mission will be completed during October 1992.

16. In conclusion, I strongly recommend that the General Assembly give its approval for the establishment of UNOVER, on the basis of the considerations addressed above.

Annex
Provisional cost estimates of the United Nations Observer Mission to Verify the Referendum in Eritrea

A. Summary

(United States dollars)

Personnel costs	1 456 600
Vehicle operations	249 800
Air operations	48 100
Premises	76 100
Purchase of equipment	147 600
Miscellaneous supplies and services	72 100
Compensation	400 000
Freight and transportation	29 000
Communications	366 200
Subtotal	2 845 500
Contingency allowance of 5 per cent of subtotal cost estimate for unforeseen items and price increases (funds not to be expended without prior approval of the Director of the Field Operations Division)	(142 275)
Total	2 987 775
	(2 988 000 in round figures)

B. Details

1. *Personnel costs*

Staff members

1. The proposed staffing table for the mission allows for a total of 21 international staff members, as follows: one Special Representative of the Secretary-General (at Assistant Secretary-General level), from 1 September to 30 April; two at P-5 level (Chief Electoral Officer and Chief Administrative Officer), from 1 September to 31 May; one at P-4 level (Finance/Personnel/Procurement Officer); one at P-3/P-4 level (Political Affairs Officer); two Field Service Officers, one being a senior experienced member for the coordination of air movements, transport, accommodation, stores etc. and the other being a radio technician/assistant coordination officer, from 1 October to 31 May; three at P-4/P-5 as coordinators for each of the regional offices and 10 at P-2/P-4 level as observers, from 1 November to 30 April; and one at P-3 level (Assistant Political Affairs Officer), from 1 May to 30 April. Allowance is also made for 20 observers seconded from the Secretariat (10 from New York and 10 from Europe) for a period of 10 days only.

(a) *Salaries*. One Special Representative of the Secretary-General for eight months, two x P-5 for nine months, two x P-4 for eight months, two Field Service Officers for eight months, three x P-4/P-5 and 10 x P-2/P-4 for six months, and one x P-3 for two months: $610,000 (estimate);

(b) *Subsistence allowance*. 3,900 man-days for 19 staff, comprising 80 man-days for the Special Representative of the Secretary-General (eight visits each of 10 days) and 200 man-days for the 20 observers; the total number of man-days is 4,180, at $101 per person per day (current rate of mission subsistence allowance): $422,180;

(c) *Travel costs*. Estimates are based on return airfares from New York, with an allowance for each member to carry 10 kg excess air baggage and to send 100 kg of personal effects by air freight: $3,900 per member for airfares plus $500 per person for air freight; the 20 observers for 10 days are costed at $3,900 from New York and $1,900 from Europe: $150,400;

(d) *Official travel*. The estimate is based on the Special Representative of the Secretary-General visiting the mission once every month, from New York (one visit is already included in subparagraph (c) above); allowance is also made (airfares and subsistence allowance) for two visits (say four days in the country) by two officers from the Electoral Assistance Unit: 11 x $3,900 = $46,200.

Member State observers

2. Allowance is made for 30 observers from Member States, for whom costs are limited to travel to and from the mission and subsistence allowance for 10 days while in the area. The cost estimates are based on 20 observers coming from Europe and 10 from North America; for budget purposes, it is assumed that the United Nations is responsible for travel costs:

(a) *Travel costs*. (20 x $1,900) + (10 x $3,900) = $77,000;

(b) *Subsistence allowance*. For a total of 300 man-days at $101 per person per day: $30,300.

Other international observers

3. Allowance is made for 50 observers recruited from the international personnel of UNDP and selected non-governmental organizations located in Eritrea and neighbouring countries, and for 20 of these observers to travel from Addis Ababa; costs for subsistence allowance are estimated for five days only:

(a) *Travel from Ethiopia*. Twenty air tickets from Addis Ababa to Asmara and return: $24,000;

(b) *Subsistence allowance*. For a total of 250 man-days at $101 per person per day: $25,300.

Local employees

4. The proposed staffing table for the mission allows for a total of 123 local employees, comprising two secretaries/interpreters and two drivers from 1 September to 31 May (nine months); one secretary/interpreter and two drivers from 1 October to 31 May (eight months); five interpreters and five drivers from 1 November to 30 April (six months); and 53 interpreters and 53 drivers (these figures include an allowance for three reserve drivers and interpreters) for an estimated period of five days:

Salaries. Monthly salaries, in birr, are based on advice from the World Food Programme (WFP) representative in Asmara and are: secretary, 900; interpreter, 500; driver, 900, plus an extra 20 birr per day when away from Asmara. Total cost estimates, excluding estimates for time away from Asmara, are as follows:

Secretaries/interpreters: (2 x 9 x 900) + (1 x 8 x 900) = 23,400 birr

Interpreters: (5 x 6 x 500) + (53 x 500 x 5/30) = 19,500 birr

Drivers: (2 x 9 x 900) + (2 x 8 x 900) + (5 x 6 x 900) + (53 x 900 x 5/30) = 65,600 birr

The total cost is 108,500 birr. At the current official exchange rate (US$ 1 = approximately 2 birr), the total cost is $54,300, or $60,000 including allowance for time away from Asmara and hire of cleaners etc.

Consultancy service

5. Allowance is made for the services of a consultant, for about three weeks, to assist with the counting aspects of the referendum. The cost estimate is based on salary, travel and per diem: $11,121, approximately.

2. *Operating costs*
Vehicle operations

6. The proposed vehicle requirement is as follows: two four-wheel-drive vehicles from 1 September to 31 May; two from 1 October to 31 May; five from 1 November to 30 April; and 53 for a period of five days in April. The requirement for two vehicles in early September will probably be met by hiring vehicles in Asmara; in the early stages sedans will be adequate, possibly even taxis. However, a total of nine 4x4s need to be purchased by 1 November, five for the five observer teams and the other four to be used by the Headquarters support staff. The latter four vehicles will also provide a reserve holding for the observer teams, if required. The 53 4x4s required for the five-day period are to be hired locally, and the total also allows for a reserve of three vehicles. However, if this number is not available for hire, as is expected, the extra observers and interpreters for the actual referendum period can be transported as far as possible in hired mini-buses, and then ferried forward by the 4x4s available at the time; this is not considered to be a very satisfactory alternative.

(a) *Purchase of vehicles.* These vehicles will be available for reallocation to any future missions in this region; nine 4x4 vehicles at $19,000 each, plus $1,000 per vehicle for freight from Jeddah: $180,000;

(b) *Vehicle hire*

(i) Assuming the purchased vehicles can be delivered by 1 November, the cost estimate for hiring two sedans for the months of September and October is: (100 birr per day) x 60 days x 2 cars = 12,000 birr or $6,000;

(ii) Assuming 53 4x4s are available for hire at a rate of 150 birr per day, and over a three-day period each vehicle averages 400 kilometres at 1.50 birr per kilometre, the estimated cost is (53 x 150 x 3) + (53 x 400 x 1.50) = 55,650 birr or $27,900;

(c) *Petrol, oil and lubricants.* The estimated cost for about 78 vehicle months (purchased and hired vehicles) is: 78 x (eight refills per month) x (60 litres per refill) x 0.75 birr per litre = 28,080 birr or $14,000;

(d) *Vehicle repairs and maintenance.* Twenty-four maintenance staff are currently employed by WFP. These mechanics are servicing vehicles for other United Nations agencies in Asmara at a rate of $10 per hour or $15 per hour for overtime. The estimated cost for 3.5 hours of service per month, by WFP mechanics, for nine vehicles for eight months is $2,500;

(e) *Vehicle insurance.* Six vehicle years at $380 per vehicle is $2,300 (it is assumed that the hired vehicles have insurance cover included in the hire cost; consequently separate allowance is not made);

(f) *Spare parts.* As there are few spare parts available in the country, provision is made for fast-moving items (e.g., all types of filters, brake parts etc.) to be purchased and shipped at the same time as the nine 4x4s. The estimate is 10 per cent of the vehicle purchase price: 9 x 10 per cent x $19,000 = $17,100.

Air operations

7. Allowance is made for chartering a light fixed-wing aircraft, once a month, at a rate of $3,700 per month. The estimate is based on a recent charter by WFP for a flight from Asmara to Assab and Djibouti, and return. The aircraft was a Twin Otter from Eritrean Airways. Allowance is also made for chartering an aircraft on four separate occasions for medical evacuations. The total cost estimate is $3,700 x 13 = $48,100.

Premises

8. It is considered that there is adequate living accommodation (either hotels or private residences) for all personnel in receipt of mission subsistence allowance. No commitment was made by the provisional Government to provide accommodation free of charge to the mission. Therefore, allowance is made for renting office accommodation in Asmara (mission headquarters and Asmara regional centre) and for three teams in outlying regional centres, as a back-up. The estimated requirement in Asmara is 130 square metres (Special Representative of the Secretary-General, 20; two x P-5, 15 each; two x P-4, one Field Service Officer and three secretaries, 10 each; Asmara regional centre, two x P-3, 10 each). The estimated requirement in the outer areas is 20 m2 per region. The total requirement for office space is 190 m2. As there may be a requirement for a small stores building, allowance is made for the rental and minor repairs of an existing building within the WFP compound.

(a) *Rental.* The estimated cost is $6,000 per month for eight months for mission headquarters, $1,200 per month for seven months for the stores building and $1,200 per month for six months for the three regional centres: $63,600;

(b) *Maintenance.* Allowance is made for cleaning supplies and services as well as any necessary minor repairs (e.g., plumbing, electrical): $2,500 at five different locations, total $12,500.

Purchase of equipment

9. The equipment requirements are as follows:

(a) *Data-processing equipment.* Two desktop computers ($1,500 each), seven laptop computers ($3,100 each), six bubble-jet portable printers ($550 each), three desk jet printers ($500 each, one as a reserve) and various software and other accessories ($11,000); the five regional teams each require a laptop computer for report writing, leaving one laptop and two desktops for headquarters and one laptop as a reserve: total $40,500;

(b) *Office equipment.* Two electronic typewriters ($1,400); one medium-sized photocopier ($2,300); and one over-head projector ($400): total $4,100;

(c) *Generators.* As most provincial capitals have limited hours in which electricity is supplied (e.g., 1,800 hours to 2,400 hours) allowance is made for a total of five small, portable generators (e.g., Honda gasoline generators at $900 each), one for each of the three regional teams and two for headquarters. The two for headquarters will also provide the reserve for the field. Cost estimate for five generators, cables and spare parts: $6,500;

(d) *Office furniture.* Allowance is made for a small quantity of desks, chairs, filing cabinets etc. to be purchased locally if not provided by the local authorities: $13,000;

(e) *Miscellaneous equipment*

(i) Basic camping equipment for the five teams operating from 1 November to 30 April for areas in which accommodation may not be available (tents, stoves, camp cots, sheets/blankets, cooking utensils, jerry cans etc.): $11,500;

(ii) Allowance for camping equipment for 50 per cent of the teams during the referendum, who may be in areas where accommodation is not available: 25 x $2,200 = $55,000;

(iii) Miscellaneous other equipment, including small kerosene refrigerators: $17,000.

Miscellaneous supplies and services

10. Requirements for miscellaneous supplies and services are as follows:

(a) Stationery and office supplies: $7,000;

(b) Medical supplies and first-aid kits for vehicles: $1,800;

(c) Medical services: $7,000;

(d) Operational maps: $4,000 (it is understood that both Czechoslovakia and the Russian Federation were producing maps of Eritrea);

(e) Sanitation and cleaning supplies: $3,500;

(f) Purchase of water supplies: currently water is only available to each residence once a week. Allowance is made for water for toilets in rented office accommodation at the rate of 1,000 litres per day at a cost of one birr per 200 litres; the requirement for an eight-month period is 240,000 litres, $1,000, approximately;

(g) Minor water purification units: $25,000;

(h) Official hospitality: $2,500;

(i) General stores, including United Nations flags and decals, production of identification cards, vehicle number plates, fire extinguishers, compasses, loud hailers, batteries, flashlights and miscellaneous supplies: $17,000;

(j) Subscriptions to newspapers and periodicals: $1,300;

(k) Payment of electricity bills for rented premises; allowance is made for $100 per month for eight months for mission headquarters and $100 per month for three months for each of the three regional centres: $2,000, approximately.

Compensation claims

11. Contingency funds for the settlement of possible claims for death, injuries and disabilities in respect of personnel other than staff members: $400,000.

Freight and transportation

12. Allowance is made for the freight costs of supplies and equipment to be shipped to the mission, and any clearing charges to be paid, when the items are received in Eritrea. Estimated cost: $29,000.

Communications equipment and supplies

13. There is considered to be little requirement for reporting by radio throughout the duration of the mission. Moreover, the internal security situation throughout the country has been very calm for the past 12 months and it is not expected to change in the lead-up to the referendum. However, because isolated areas are to be visited, some form of radio communication is considered necessary for safety purposes only. Discussions with officials of the Telecommunications Authority of Eritrea indicated a requirement for high frequency (HF) radios. In the past month the telephone system, in some areas, has been resurrected and calls can now supposedly be made to all provincial capitals (Massawa direct, Keren through the operator) and overseas. However, there are few lines and consequently, many delays.

(a) *External communications.* Allowance is made for user charges for the WFP INMARSAT terminal. The estimate is based on a nine-month period, usage of one hour per day, at a cost of $10 per minute. The total estimate is 9 x 30 x 60 x 10 = $162,000;

(b) *Internal communications equipment to be purchased*

(i) Nine HF radios ($9,500 each), together with all the equipment needed to have them mounted in vehicles ($1,000 per vehicle): 9 x $10,500 = $94,500;

(ii) One HF base radio for use in a static role inside an office: $9,500

(HF radios may be available from existing missions in either Angola or Kuwait, or possibly from the United Nations Supply Depot at Pisa);

(c) *Communications supplies.* Spare parts, hardware, batteries, battery chargers, commercial repairs (if beyond the capabilities of the radio technician); the estimate is 7.5 per cent of the equipment cost: $78,000;

(d) *Miscellaneous items.* Allowance is made for contractual assistance for the installation and dismantling of the radio equipment (radio technicians will install an HF radio in one day for 200 birr); the estimate provides for nine radios and a base station: $3,000;

(e) *Commercial communications.* The estimates under this heading include:

(i) Telephone rental and call charges: $7,500;

(ii) Pouch services to and from New York: $7,200;

(iii) Commercial telex charges: $4,500.

Document 25

General Assembly resolution authorizing the Secretary-General to establish the United Nations Observer Mission to Verify the Referendum in Eritrea (UNOVER)

A/RES/47/114, 16 December 1992

The General Assembly,

Having considered the report of the Secretary-General concerning a request to the United Nations to observe the referendum process in Eritrea, 1/

Recalling that the authorities directly concerned have registered their commitment to respect the results of the referendum in Eritrea, 2/

Taking into account that the authorities directly concerned have requested the involvement of the United Nations to verify the referendum in Eritrea, 2/

1. *Takes note* of the report of the Secretary-General 1/ and of the recommendations contained therein for the establishment of a United Nations observer mission to verify the referendum scheduled to take place in Eritrea in April 1993;

2. *Decides* to authorize the Secretary-General to establish the United Nations Observer Mission to Verify the Referendum in Eritrea, which will have terms of reference as provided for in paragraph 7 of the report of the Secretary-General, and to appoint, as a matter of urgency, a Special Representative for the referendum, who will head the Observer Mission;

3. *Requests* the Secretary-General to arrange, as soon as possible, for the deployment of the Observer Mission so that it may commence its verification functions;

4. *Calls upon* the authorities directly concerned to extend their fullest cooperation to the Observer Mission

---
1/ A/47/544.
2/ See A/C.3/47/5.

in order to facilitate the accomplishment of its task, as requested by the United Nations;

5. *Requests* the Secretary-General to report to the General Assembly at its forty-eighth session on the implementation of the present resolution.

Document 26

United Nations 1993 Consolidated Inter-agency Appeal: Eritrea. Special Emergency Programme for the Horn of Africa (SEPHA) (excerpt)

January 1993

Executive summary

In 1992 Eritrea continued to enjoy a period of peace that contrasted starkly with the decades of warfare preceding it. That warfare damaged or destroyed much of the physical infrastructure in many parts of Eritrea, and, together with recurrent drought in recent years, produced major relief needs. In 1992, Eritrea also received the best rainfall in years. The November 1992 FAO/WFP Crop and Food Supply Assessment Mission estimated that the 1992 growing seasons will produce an excellent crop of some 260,000 mts of cereals and pulses.

Thus, overall Eritrea is continuing to move from a situation characterized primarily by massive emergency relief needs, to a more mixed situation. This new situation still includes significant emergency relief needs (e.g., even the improved 1992 crop will only meet half of the food needs of Eritrea in 1993) but also involves major post-disaster rehabilitation needs. Such rehabilitation efforts are especially needed in the health and health-related sectors, and in agricultural and pastoral production.

Within this context, the 1993 SEPHA (Special Emergency Programme for the Horn of Africa) appeal for Eritrea 1/ presents funding requests totalling US$ 80.5 million for relief and short term rehabilitation activities to be carried out by six UN agencies—FAO, UNICEF, UNV, WFP, WHO and DHA—during the 12 months of 1993. Of this total, the largest amount is sought for emergency food needs. This includes US$ 48 million for WFP's Emergency Food Aid project. WFP is also requesting US$ 3.3 million for logistics and rehabilitation projects related to the delivery of relief food.

UNICEF is seeking US$ 7.8 million for targeted efforts to reactivate part of the primary health care services and to establish adequate immunization programmes, for supplemental feeding, repair of the water system of Keren, reactivation of priority primary education services, and reunification of orphans and unaccompanied children. WHO requests US$ 10.4 million for the functional restoration of damaged health services, provision of essential drugs and support to the local drug production facilities, control of priority communicable diseases, installation of a health information system for reliable and efficient reporting and surveillance, the rehabilitation of war-disabled persons, and the integration of ex-combatants in the Primary Health Care structure through training programmes.

FAO will be working jointly with the Ministry of Agriculture in early 1993 to review, modify and finalize a project proposal which the Ministry has prepared concerning "Rehabilitation of the Eastern Lowlands of Eritrea". FAO is appealing to donors via this SEPHA appeal to earmark US$ 10 million for the first year of this two year project, including the immediate provision of funding needed for the project review and finalization mission and related activities.

The United Nations Volunteers Programme (UNV) is requesting US$ 620,000 to enable UNV to provide 20 UNV specialists to assist UN agencies in the implementation of relief and rehabilitation projects.

The Department of Humanitarian Affairs (DHA) is requesting US$ 225,000 for partial support of the operations of the SEPHA Unit in Geneva. This Unit coordinates the production of SEPHA appeals across the Horn of Africa, tracks donor inputs against these appeals, provides regular reporting on UN agency humanitarian assistance activities and on outstanding needs in the region, and provides support to those charged with UN inter-agency coordination in-country.

In 1992, Eritrea received US$ 135.8 million in SEPHA funding, constituting the highest per capita SEPHA funding of the six Horn of Africa countries. However, US$ 119.9 million of this total was provided

---

1/ For 1993, the decision has been made to split SEPHA appeals for the Horn of Africa countries into individual country appeals, rather than group them all together. This reflects primarily the wishes of the governments and UN agencies in the countries concerned, as well as the practical problem of needing to avoid holding up appeals for the rest of the Horn of Africa because of uncertainties about when, and through what process, an appeal for Somalia could be launched. The SEPHA Unit in DHA-Geneva will continue to monitor and report on UN humanitarian assistance efforts across all six countries of the Horn during 1993, as well as producing consolidated reporting on resource mobilization against the specific country appeals.

for emergency food aid efforts appealed for by WFP. Funding for the non-food aid sectors in 1992 was quite weak, as was funding for short term rehabilitation projects in general.

Overview and 1993 SEPHA strategies

SEPHA funds raised in 1992 and their use

Overall, funding for the activities included in the 1992 SEPHA appeals was reasonably good when compared to the traditional donor response to UN appeals of this type. Thus, as shown in Annex 1, overall pledges for SEPHA as of 31 December amounted to US$ 892.9 million, or 78% of the total funds requested for 1992. Of this total, US$ 135.8 million were provided for Eritrea. This represented the highest per capita figure of any of the Horn of Africa countries.

Of the six countries covered by the SEPHA mechanism, Eritrea received the highest percentage of contributions against the total funds requested for the first half of 1992. However, few additional funds were pledged for Eritrea during the second half of the year. Meanwhile, there was a marked increase in funding for the crises in Somalia, and for relief efforts in neighbouring countries, especially those that were related to the crisis in Somalia. Thus, by the end of December, the percentage of funds pledged against those requested for Eritrea, 71%, was actually lower than the average for the six countries of the Horn of Africa.

Funding for the emergency food aid needs of Eritrea was especially strong. Thus, of the US$ 135.8 million of SEPHA contributions for Eritrea in 1992, US$ 121.9 million (or 90%) were reported by WFP. Most of these contributions went for the provision of food aid. With these resources, over 300,000 mts of food were delivered to Eritrea as of end of December 1992, which represented over 100% of the amount WFP had requested for the year. In addition, US$ 1.3 million was spent on purchasing of equipment, such as tarps, pallets, forklifts, tyres and tubes, equipment for bagging machines and tractors, to upgrade facilities at the ports of Assab and Massawa.

However, funding for activities of UN agencies for areas outside of food aid was not strong. UNHCR received US$ 7.9 million in funding primarily in anticipation of the start of significant repatriation of refugees from the Sudan. However, this programme has not yet come into being, and these funds have not been used except for a portion for the establishment and operation of a UNHCR office in Asmara in anticipation of a repatriation programme.

In the health and health-related areas, UNICEF received US$ 1.48 million in funding. These funds were used to purchase vaccines against seven preventable diseases so as to launch a massive vaccination campaign in areas prone to epidemics and to cover some of the overall needs of the country for six months. Operational funds, vaccination supplies and vehicles have been released to contribute to a nation-wide campaign, and solar cold chain and other equipment have been ordered to equip vaccination sites in five regions. In the area of nutrition, 52 supplementary feeding centres have been set up throughout the country and serve about 54,500 children and women. The first phase of the rehabilitation of the Keren water supply system, which addresses the repair and upgrading of the existing system, is fully funded. Implementation started in December 1992 and will be completed by June 1993. A nation-wide water point survey is being conducted. UNICEF assistance to vulnerable groups included the provision of operational and logistical support to the Department of Social Affairs to conduct surveys on orphans and unaccompanied children and identify their priority needs.

WHO received US$ 1.38 million in 1992 SEPHA funds. These have been used for the provision of essential medical/surgical supplies and laboratory equipment delivered to the Eritrean Department of Health to ensure more effective functioning of health services. Selected essential drugs not available in the country have been purchased and delivered to cover urgent needs. The referral rehabilitation centre for care of people with physical disabilities has been supported through supplies in raw materials to the orthopaedic workshops and a grant for a three-year scholarship for a course in prosthetic/orthotic techniques. In order to plan and implement the malaria disease control programme, spraying equipment, insecticides, basic laboratory equipment and two vehicles have been supplied. Finally, funds have been used to cover the first six months of a health information system project for which a technical agreement has been signed with the Liverpool School of Tropical Medicine.

In the agricultural sector, FAO received US$ 3.09 million. The funds were used for the urgent supply of staple cereal seed (US$ 1.3 million) prior to the start of the rainy season in June 1992. The balance will be utilised for the provision of small-scale irrigation equipment, farm tools and implements.

Overview of relief and rehabilitation needs in 1993

Eritrea, which suffered from over 25 years of civil war, is now enjoying a period of overall political and security stability following the end of the war in May 1991. A further encouraging aspect is that the past rainy season was the best in years, as is the resulting harvest. Based on the results of the FAO/WFP Crop and Food Supply Assessment Mission, Eritrea's food assistance needs are projected as being approximately 147,000 mts, or less than half of those of 1992.

However, while overall emergency relief needs for 1993 will be less than in previous years, there will still be a need for significant emergency food-aid related activities in 1993. It will take at least several years for Eritrea to attain basic food self-sufficiency, assuming good rains (as opposed to the drought of the past several years), and that donors give the same high priority to promoting food self-sufficiency that the Provisional Government of Eritrea (PGE) does. Within this context, the humanitarian assistance priorities for Eritrea are shifting somewhat from the provision of emergency assistance to addressing the rehabilitation and recovery needs. The extent to which emergency food aid can be phased down or out is heavily related to the extent to which the necessary inputs are provided to agriculturalists and pastoralists. In terms of health and social services, the cumulative damage of over two decades of war has been tremendous. Priority needs to be given to putting back into place the basic functioning of key health, water and sanitation facilities and systems.

1993 SEPHA strategies

Activities to be carried out in Eritrea in 1993 via SEPHA funding are of two types: emergency relief and short-term rehabilitation.

Within this context, the largest amount of funding requested for SEPHA for Eritrea for 1993 is for emergency food aid and related activities. This includes direct emergency food distribution and supplemental feeding, as well as a markedly increased component of programme food aid, such as food-for-work and market projects. Funding is also sought for several projects needed to improve the provision of emergency food aid, such as warehouse facilities.

The second main component of the 1993 SEPHA portfolio is that of short-term rehabilitation projects. For Eritrea, the most important aspect of the SEPHA mandate is that it places a limit on rehabilitation activities, with the understanding that medium and longer term rehabilitation activities fall outside of this mandate. Meeting the full rehabilitation and recovery needs of Eritrea will take many years and tremendous amounts of funding. Such efforts will include entities such as the World Bank and related donors, providing approximately US$ 140 million for the support of the Recovery and Rehabilitation Programme of Eritrea (RRPE), including contributions from the International Development Association (US$ 20 million), EEC (US$ 26 million), Italy (US$ 21 million), Sweden (US$ 11 million), Netherlands (US$ 2.2 million), UNDP (US$ 2.2 million) and potential inputs from USA and Germany. For the UN system, UNDP will be expected to take the lead in assisting the Government in the development of overall rehabilitation planning, and in coordinating the involvement of the UN family in implementing medium and longer-term rehabilitation efforts.

However, pending the creation of a full national rehabilitation programme, the identification of the funding required for it, and the actual implementation of such large-scale efforts, there is an immediate and urgent need for the kind of quick impact, short-term rehabilitation projects that fall under the SEPHA mandate. Thus, from among the total rehabilitation activities which need to take place in Eritrea, the rehabilitation-oriented projects in the 1993 SEPHA portfolio involve ones that:

- address needs that are primarily due to the decades of war;
- can be implemented within 12 months;
- are focused on priority rehabilitation needs from among the total rehabilitation needs of the country;
- address needs that are not being covered by other aid mechanisms; and
- produce results that in the main are sustainable even if subsequent rehabilitation funding is not forthcoming.

Unlike in 1992, the 1993 SEPHA appeal contains no request for funds for refugee or returnee programmes, as the agreements required to begin the formal repatriation of Eritrean refugees from Sudan have not yet been reached. Discussions between UNHCR and the Commission for Eritrean Refugee Affairs (CERA) are continuing on the modalities of such an undertaking.

The programme currently proposed by CERA entails a budget of US$ 209 million, and would involve substantial rehabilitation efforts of the areas that the refugees would return to. As most of these rehabilitation efforts would fall outside of the mandate of UNHCR, it is envisioned that a range of UN and other agencies would be heavily involved in such a programme. Such an undertaking will require a special appeal of its own, in addition to the current SEPHA appeal. However, some of the activities proposed in the 1993 SEPHA appeal will be implemented in areas where sizable numbers of refugees are expected to return, and would thus help lay the groundwork for the repatriation programme.

The activities for which funding is being sought via this SEPHA appeal by no means represent the total relief and short term rehabilitation needs of Eritrea. Rather, they represent that portion that the UN agencies feel that they have the capacity to address in 1993 via SEPHA. A major part of the strategy of SEPHA is to ensure that SEPHA requests fit into the larger context of humanitarian assistance efforts, without duplicating the activities of entities. Within Eritrea, this larger context includes the activities of the Provisional Government of Eritrea, of bilateral donor inputs via channels other than the UN, of non-governmental organizations, and of the World Bank, among others.

The projects proposed in this SEPHA appeal have been developed in close collaboration with the relevant line ministries and coordinating authorities of the Provisional Government of Eritrea, and are presented with their approval.

Total funding requests for 1993

This appeal presents a total of US$ 80.5 million in funding requests by six UN agencies—FAO, UNICEF, UNV, WFP, WHO and DHA—for relief and short-term rehabilitation activities to be carried out in 1993. This includes US$ 10 million for FAO, US$ 51.4 million for WFP, US$ 10.4 million for WHO, US$ 7.8 million for UNICEF, US$ 620,000 for UNV and US$ 225,000 for DHA. An overview of the priority activities to be undertaken with these funds is provided in the subsequent section. The specific projects are then presented in the Project Summaries section that forms the remainder of this appeal document.

1993 SEPHA
UN Agency Budget Requirements for Eritrea

FAO	10,000,000
UNICEF	7,828,255
UNV	620,000
WFP	51,422,100
WHO	10,416,500
DHA	225,000
TOTAL	80,511,855

Eritrea 1993
Summary of Project Activities

Code	Activity	Agency	Requirements
1	Emergency rehabilitation of the eastern lowlands of Eritrea	FAO	10,000,000
2	Re-activation of primary health care services/immunization (EPI)	UNICEF	2,896,400
3	Emergency supplementary feeding programme	UNICEF	1,656,355
4	Rehabilitation of Keren's water supply system	UNICEF	860,500
5	Rehabilitation and reactivation of basic primary education	UNICEF	1,000,000
6	Reunification of orphans and unaccompanied children	UNICEF	1,415,000
7	UNV support to relief and rehab. programmes of UN agencies and NGOs	UNV	620,000
8	Emergency food aid	WFP	48,098,700
9	Rural warehouse construction	WFP	1,994,250
10	Strengthening of ERRA's food aid monitoring unit	WFP	179,150
11	Equipment for Port Rehabilitation	WFP	1,150,000
12	Recovery and reactivation of emergency health services	WHO	5,300,000
13	Control of priority communicable diseases	WHO	2,139,200
14	Provision of essential drugs and support to local drug production facilities	WHO	1,350,000
15	Rehabilitation of war-disabled persons	WHO	1,225,000
16	Crisis management, institution building, health information/coordination	WHO	150,000
17	Integration of ex-combatants in the primary health care structures	WHO	252,300
18	Support of SEPHA unit	DHA	225,000

Priority activities

Food aid and logistics

The report of the FAO/WFP Crop and Food Supply Assessment Mission to Eritrea in November 1992 forecast that the cereal and pulses harvest for 1992 would be "excellent", amounting to 260,000 mts. Taking into account a stock drawdown of 50,000 tons for commercial use, approximately 190,000 mts of food will still need to be imported in 1993. Given an estimated 50,000 mts of commercial food imports, the food aid requirement for 1993 is estimated at 147,000 mts, or less than half of the 1992 requirement. WFP is therefore requesting US$ 48.09 million in donations and procurement of food, and related transport costs to provide 146,900 mts of food aid, comprising 60,900 mts for relief distribution, 42,000 mts for food-for-work programmes, and 44,000 tons for market sales. It is proposed that counterpart funds generated from the sale of 44,000 tons of cereals can be used to support the proposed food-for-work programme, given the Government's lack of revenue and inadequate budget.

US$ 2 million in funds are being requested by WFP to help alleviate the problem of damage and loss of food aid due to lack of adequate warehouse capacity in the rural areas. In addition, WFP requests US$ 1,150,000 for an emergency contingency fund for essential equipment and the purchase of four bagging machines.

Health and nutrition

In spite of the emergency supplementary feeding programme established by UNICEF in 52 feeding centres throughout the country, serving 32,500 children and 10,000 women, the nutritional status of vulnerable groups is still very precarious. While still awaiting economic recovery, and with the threat of prolonged spells of drought still not fully removed, a continuation of such supplementary feeding programme for the coming year will be necessary. Health services are still under extreme pressure and are unable to cope with new demands. Most health facilities have been damaged, especially in the five lowland provinces, and their basic rehabilitation is beyond the resources now available to the Government. Four hospitals have been completely destroyed. Functioning health facilities are overcrowded and lack essential drugs as well as basic medical equipment. Those injured during the war still do not receive adequate health care.

WHO is seeking US$ 5.3 million for the physical rehabilitation of damaged hospitals and health centres that have been identified as priority targets in the provinces of Gash and Setit and Barka. The same facilities will also be provided with essential medical and surgical supplies, equipment, training, and supervisory and logistical support. US$ 2.1 million will be required to strengthen the capacity of the Department of Health to control priority communicable diseases, in particular malaria, tuberculosis, AIDS and meningococcal meningitis. A project for the provision of essential drugs and support to the development of local drug production facilities will need funding of US$ 1.35 million. The WHO health information system project, which was initiated in 1992 to support to the Department of Health in crisis management, institution building and health emergency coordination, needs US$ 150,000 to implement the second phase in 1993.

Efforts for the rehabilitation of war-disabled persons are badly needed. The requested amount of US$ 1.2 million will cover essential inputs to referral rehabilitation facilities, supplies to orthopaedic workshops, and rehabilitation aids. Assistance will focus on a community-based rehabilitation (CBR) approach and will include the training of specialized personnel.

The integration of EPLF ex-combatants in the Primary Health Care structure through training courses to become public health nurses, health assistants and senior laboratory technicians will be an important contribution to improving health service delivery, including in remote provinces which suffered from the war. WHO is seeking US$ 252,300 for the implementation of this project.

Health sector activities foreseen by UNICEF will complement those planned by WHO. UNICEF will need US$ 2.9 million to rehabilitate key provincial hospitals, health centres and stations in seven provinces not covered by WHO, and to ensure that expanded immunization coverage is being provided as part of essential Primary Health Care for around 750,000 children and women of childbearing age. The continuation of the supplementary feeding programme will be necessary for the benefit of 45,000 children and 15,000 pregnant and lactating mothers. The operation of 60 feeding centres and related support will require financial input of US$ 1.7 million. A nation-wide nutrition survey will be implemented as part of this project.

Water and sanitation

Less than 12% of the rural population of Eritrea have access to clean water. Thus, there is a continual major risk from water-borne and water related diseases. Less than 3% of the rural areas have access to latrines and only 2% are served by adequate waste disposal systems. In large urban centres such as Massawa and Keren, water supply systems are either completely destroyed or suffer from high leakage rates (30-50%). Less than 30% of the urban population have access to clean water and to basic sanitation facilities.

Full implementation of the project for the rehabilitation of Keren's water supply system continues to be a top priority. Keren, the capital of Senhit province, is the largest city in Eritrea. Its population of 50,000 is expected to grow in the near future with the resettlement of returnees from the Sudan. After completion of the project, the water supply system will have the capacity to provide safe drinking water for 70,000 people. The first phase of the project received funding under the 1992 SEPHA appeal and will be completed by June 1993. The second phase entails the rehabilitation of the existing water distribution system, the expansion of water distribution lines to unserved areas of the town (about 60%), and increased water pumping and storage capacity, as well as the construction of new water distribution points. Funding for this phase is sought within this appeal, totalling US$ 860,500. The project will eventually benefit 80,000-90,000 people, including the returnees from the Sudan who are expected to resettle in Keren.

Special assistance to children

While children will be the priority target group of some of the projects mentioned above, UNICEF is presenting two additional projects which address certain specific needs of children. Regarding the educational sector, 80% of schools have been seriously damaged or have steadily deteriorated as a result of the complex emergency. Access to education is therefore extremely restricted, with a primary school enrolment rate not exceeding 30%. UNICEF is requesting US$ 1 million to be able to relaunch and support pre-primary and primary education for 85,000 children by rehabilitating facilities, providing educational materials, organizing teacher-training and supporting curriculum development. A pilot adult literacy initiative will complement the assistance to children.

The reunification of orphans and unaccompanied or displaced children—currently estimated at 90,000—with their relatives or foster families and their integration into society continues to be a priority concern. US$ 1.4 million will be required to conduct family tracing activities, reunify an initial 5,000 orphans and unaccompanied children with their relatives, and provide some basic counselling and material support.

Agriculture

FAO will be working jointly with the Ministry of Agriculture in early 1993 to review, modify and finalize a project proposal which the Ministry has prepared concerning "Rehabilitation of Eastern Lowlands of Eritrea". The proposed project areas are ones that have been particularly hard hit by the combination of war and drought. The proposed project would have five main components:

- re-afforestation
- soil conservation
- construction activities
- livestock development
- agricultural inputs

FAO is appealing to donors via this SEPHA appeal to earmark US$ 10 million for the first year of this two year project (which has a preliminary two year budget of US$ 21.3 million). This includes the immediate provision of the funding needed to field an interdisciplinary formulation mission which would—in consultation with the PGE—finalize the project plan and the specific requirements for the first year of project implementation.

Use of UN volunteers

Use will be made of UN specialists by UN agencies in the implementation of a number of relief and rehabilitation activities in Eritrea. Many of these could be qualified expatriate specialists of Eritrean origin prepared to return from the Eritrean Diaspora and serve as UNVs. By using experienced specialists on volunteer terms to fill expertise requirements, UN Agencies, and the international donor community, will keep international personnel costs at cost-effective affordable levels. UNVs will continue to play important roles as outreach support to beneficiaries, and as trainers to develop local capacities, especially at the level of local communities and institutions. They will also support technical and programme monitoring functions.

Drawing on UNV's special roster of experienced relief and rehabilitation specialists, which was set up in 1992 in response to GA resolution 46/182, UNVs will be fielded in support of WHO projects in the health sector. Scope also exists for utilizing UNVs in some other projects, especially related to training of social workers, teachers, and technical specialists, as well as other areas, and the UN Agencies concerned will in due course specify the needs.

...

Appealing Agency:	FAO
Activity:	Rehabilitation of the Eastern Lowlands of Eritrea
Code:	ERI-93-1/N01
Target Population:	16,000 war- and drought-affected farm families
Implementing Agency:	FAO and the Ministry of Agriculture
Time-frame:	January - December 1993
Objective:	Rehabilitation of sectors of the eastern lowlands of Eritrea through urgent interventions aimed at soil conservation/afforestation programmes, construction activities to control flood waters and increase irrigated areas, and provision of livestock and agricultural inputs.
Funds Requested:	US$ 10,000,000

Summary:

The people in the Eastern lowlands, who are agro-pastoralists, have suffered much due to war and recurrent droughts. They have lost much of their cattle, their agricultural inputs and other belongings. The average rainfall of the area is around 200 mm per annum which is insufficient to support the growth of agricultural crops. Soil erosion due to flood waters from the highlands during summer rains is quite heavy. There are more than 20 streams and small rivers that flow from the highlands to the alluvial plains of the project area. So far, no control measures have been implemented to use the flood waters for irrigation purposes.

The Ministry of Agriculture has now developed a proposed two year project to address the main agriculture and livestock rehabilitation needs of those areas. The urgent introduction of soil conservation and afforestation activities, construction of diversion structures, the provision of agricultural and foundation stock for dairy cows, milk goats, chicken and other related activities is expected to positively change the life of the 16,000 farmers in the project area.

In order to assess and formulate the emergency component of this rehabilitation project, FAO requires funding for a multi-disciplinary mission, including experts in the fields of plant production and protection, animal husbandry, agricultural mechanisation, forestry and soil management. The mission's objective will be to define immediate interventions which can be carried out successfully within a time-frame of twelve months. An initial planning figure for immediate requirements is of US$ 10 million (inclusive of missions costs). FAO thus appeals to the international donor community to earmark US$ 10 million to implement activities within this period of time. The PGE has estimated overall requirements for external assistance at US$ 21.3 million, covering also a successive one-year development phase of this project.

Financial summary

Budget Item	Amount (US$)
Project formulation mission 2/	120,000
Estimated requirements, subject to assessment	9,880,000
Total	10,000,000

2/ FAO requests urgent provision of this priority funding.

Appealing Agency:	UNICEF
Activity:	Re-Activation of Primary Health Care Services and Expanded Programme of Immunization (EPI)
Code:	ERI-93-1/N02
Target Population:	Children under 1 year 74,250 Children 1 to 5 years 296,850 Women 15 to 45 years <u>371,200</u> Total beneficiaries in 7 provinces of Eritrea: 742,300
Implementing Agency:	Department of Health
Time-frame:	January - December 1993
Objectives:	To reduce morbidity and mortality of children, infants and women of childbearing age by: a) immunizing all Eritrean children under one year of age against prevalent communicable diseases; and b) providing all Eritrean under-five children and all women of childbearing age with a broad spectrum of quality and cost-effective preventive and curative health services.
Funds Requested:	US$ 2,896,400

Summary:

Following the liberation of Eritrea in May 1991, EPLF health services staff immediately took over from the former administration at both national and regional levels. To serve the Eritrean population, the EPLF started to implement a Primary Health Care System. The Department of Health is currently in the process of applying this model to the entire country.

It is estimated that 60% of health facilities have been either entirely destroyed or seriously damaged during the war. Malaria, malnutrition, diarrhoeal diseases, respiratory infections and vaccine-preventable diseases contribute to a very high level of infant mortality and morbidity. Neo-natal tetanus is responsible for up to 30% of neo-natal deaths in Eritrea and might amount to 20% of all infant deaths.

The central point of this project is that for child and maternal survival, EPI has to be firmly fitted into the already existing health network. This implies that the Primary Health Care System must be rehabilitated and upgraded to enable the Department of Health to reach every child and every mother.

Experience has shown that rapid gains in infant and child mortality can be obtained through EPI as well as proper case management of acute respiratory infections and malaria, and prevention and correct treatment of dehydration caused by diarrhoeal disease. To reach its objectives, this project will be composed of three major components.

The first component will address the rehabilitation of 15 health centres and 48 health stations, as well as providing the basic equipment still needed for 7 provincial hospitals, 24 health centres and 87 health stations in seven provinces of Eritrea.

EPI will constitute the second component of the project. This will involve both immunization campaigns and regular vaccinations at fixed sites against diphtheria, polio, pertussis, tuberculosis and neo-natal tetanus. The purpose of the mass vaccination campaign will be to catch up on the backlog of 724,500 non-immunised children under five and women of child-bearing age. The establishment of fixed vaccination sites in 7 regional hospitals, 24 health centres and 82 health stations aims at sustaining immunization coverage over the long term.

The integration of EPI with other PHC services within a rehabilitated and upgraded PHC structure will constitute the third part of this project. The restoration of PHC services will be achieved through provision of essential drugs, training, social mobilization and supervision as well as close monitoring and evaluation.

Financial budget

Budget Item	Amount (US$)
Rehabilitation of 15 health centres and 48 health stations	780,000
Equipment for 7 provincial hospitals, 24 health centres and 82 health stations	548,800
Establishment of fixed vaccination sites in provincial hospitals, 24 health centres and 82 health stations	417,600
Immunization campaigns	96,200
Supply of vaccines and immunization materials	399,400
Supply of essential drugs	122,500
Supply of transportation equipment	164,000
Training costs	66,900
Social mobilization	50,000
Monitoring, reporting and evaluation	65,000
Programme support	186,000
Total	2,896,400

Appealing Agency:	UNICEF	
Activity:	Emergency Supplementary Feeding Programme	
Code:	ERI-93-1/N03	
Target Population:	Children	45,000
	Pregnant/Lactating Women	15,000
	Total	60,000
Implementing Agencies:	Department of Health and UNICEF	
Time-frame:	January - December 1993	
Objectives:	To stop, and hopefully reverse, the deterioration of the nutritional status of especially vulnerable groups	
Funds Requested:	US$ 1,656,355	

Summary:

The effects of conflict and drought in Eritrea have pushed the margins of affected groups beyond the bounds of mere vulnerability to a state of critical impoverishment. Famine, massive population displacement, disruption of the already inadequate social services and, in some cases, loss of traditional coping mechanisms have created unprecedented levels of hardship and household stress in the country. It is estimated that about 80% of the Eritrean population depended on food aid in 1992. Under such circumstances, the nutritional status of children, women, returnees and other vulnerable groups has become extremely precarious. In 1992, the Department of Health implemented two emergency supplementary feeding programmes supported by UNICEF. These programmes have cumulatively served about 54,500 children and pregnant/lactating women. While there is an improved harvest for 1992, at least half of Eritrea's food needs will have to be met in 1993 via food aid. In addition, the damaged state of the economy and the possibility of drought in 1993 provide further reasons for special efforts to address the food needs of identified vulnerable groups.

The proposed project would: (a) provide wet and dry ration feeding in seven provinces in Eritrea to a total of 45,000 children under five years of age and 15,000 pregnant and lactating women; (b) strengthen 60 emergency supplementary feeding centres by providing locally produced supplementary food and cash support for operational costs; (c) conduct nutrition screening and maintain nutrition status records; (d) provide regular medical check-up to children attending the feeding centres; (e) provide primary health care services and use the emergency supplementary feeding centres as entry points for promoting integrated health and nutrition activities; and (f) conduct a nationwide nutrition survey and thereby formulate a National Food and Nutrition Strategy (NFNS).

These activities will be targeted on the following seven provinces: Asmara, Hamassien, Seraye, Senhit, Akele Guzai, Sahel and Semhar.

Financial summary

Budget Item	mts	Amount (US$)
Procurement of 1320 mts DMK 3/ at US$ 868/mts	1,320	1,145,760
Salary and per diem of 7 provincial supervisory teams		7,980
Salary of 60 feeding centre supervisors, measurers, store-keepers and guards		317,460
Cost of transport (rental truck)		40,400
Fuel		14,545
Nutritional survey		97,080
Programme support		33,130
Total	1,320	1,656,355

3/ A locally produced food supplement for children composed of wheat, chickpeas, full creamed milk, sugar, vitamin A, vitamin C, and iron.

Appealing Agency:	UNICEF
Activity:	Rehabilitation of Keren's Water Supply System (Phase Two)
Code:	ERI-93-1/N04
Target Population:	Local Population 50,000 Returnees 20,000 Total 70,000
Implementing Agencies:	Water Resources Department
Time-frame:	June - December 1993
Objectives:	To substantially reduce mortality and morbidity rates due to water-borne and water-related diseases, especially among children, women and other vulnerable groups, by providing safe drinking water to the entire population of Keren
Funds Requested:	US$ 860,500

Summary:

Keren, the capital of Senhit Province, is located 91 km north of Asmara. The rehabilitation and expansion of its water supply system is regarded as a top priority as it is the second largest city in Eritrea, whose population of 50,000 is expected to grow in the near future with the resettlement of returnees from the Sudan. In the absence of an organized repatriation programme, several thousand spontaneous returnees have already resettled in Keren. During the 1992 dry season, the water supply situation in town has been extremely critical. Only one-third of the population has access to minimum water supply. The entire distribution system suffers from a high leakage rate (30 to 50%). Most pumps and generators fitted on the various wells and boreholes of the system are not functioning properly due to past neglect and lack of spare parts. The present water storage capacity is not sufficient to address the needs of the population. And finally, two-thirds of the city are not connected to the existing water distribution lines. Health statistics collected during the last quarter of 1992 show a significant increase (50%) in the number of patients treated for diarrhoeal diseases. All this demonstrates that it is urgent to rehabilitate and expand the water supply system of Keren prior to the return of refugees, so that an adequate quantity of water can be supplied to each family, and that mortality and morbidity due to water-borne diseases will remain under control.

The project is designed to be implemented in three phases over an eighteen-month period. The first phase (15 December 1992 - 15 June 1993) addresses the rehabilitation of the existing water supply system (piping network, water tanks, pumps, generators) and is already funded. The second phase (15 June 1993 to December 1993) deals with the expansion of the water supply system (extension of distribution lines to unserved areas, increased water pumping and storage capacity, construction of new water distribution points) and is the one for which funding is sought.

The second phase of the project will include the following activities:
a) 25 drilling tests will be undertaken in Keren and surrounding areas;
b) 2 new wells will be dug close to the Anseba river;
c) A new pipeline (8 km) with pumping equipment will be installed to link the new wells to the main water reservoir;
d) A total of 16.1 km of pipes and 40 new water distribution points will be installed in the unserved areas of the town; and
e) Tools, equipment and spare parts for two years will be provided to the Provincial Water Resources Department—a Government institution which will no longer be subsidized by the Central Water Resources Department upon completion of this project. Its capacity therefore needs to be strengthened to enable it to raise income from water supply and eventually become self-sufficient.

The third phase (sanitation, health education, institutional capacity building and establishment of a cost-recover system) will be implemented at a later stage (15 December 1993 - 15 June 1994) and is not part of the present appeal.

Financial summary

Budget Item	US$
Pipes, fittings and related spare parts	570,750
Water equipment, pumps, generators and related spare parts	69,000
Manpower (local)	37,500
Transportation of equipment and construction materials	10,000
Expatriate staff (water engineer, consultants)	70,000
Freight/Contingency	91,250
Programme Support	12,000
Total	860,500

Appealing Agency:	UNICEF
Activity:	Rehabilitation and Reactivation of Basic Primary Education
Code:	ERI-93-1/N05
Target Population:	Pre-primary students: 6,000 Primary school students: 78,830 Adult learners: 30,000 Total 114,830
Implementing Agencies:	Department of Education and UNICEF
Time-frame:	January - December 1993
Objectives:	To provide basic education to children of pre-school and primary school age and adults in Eritrea by restoring the primary education system
Funds Requested:	US$ 1,000,000

Summary:

Eritrea inherited an educational system which was highly inappropriate and grossly detached from reality and the needs of the country. The educational system in Eritrea is still characterized by poor and inadequate school facilities, inappropriate curriculum, lack of teaching and learning resources and low numbers and quality of staff.

As a result of the 30-year-old conflict and the neglect of the past regime, 80% of schools have been seriously damaged or have steadily deteriorated. Most of them lack qualified professional staff, education equipment and supplies. As a consequence, thousands of Eritrean school-age children have been denied access to basic education. The Provisional Government of Eritrea has, in an environment of scarce resources, made a firm commitment to meeting the basic learning needs of all Eritreans. This is reflected in the education policy of the Government where free and compulsory primary education is prescribed. With about 151,000 children currently enrolled in the primary education system, the current primary school enrolment rate does not exceed 30%.

The following activities are foreseen under this project:

a) rehabilitate, furnish and equip 5 damaged primary schools in Gash/Setit, Barka, Semhar, Sahel and Senhit provinces;
b) provide basic educational supplies (e.g. exercise books, pencils, pens, teaching aids) to 192 functioning elementary schools in seven priority provinces;
c) train 1,160 pre-primary and primary school teachers, 69 schools supervisors, 92 school directors;
d) support curriculum development for pre-primary, elementary and adult education (consultants, printing of text-books, technical support);
e) carry out an adult literacy and kindergarten pilot projects in 35 villages; and
f) improve the institutional capacity of the Department of Education.

Financial summary

Budget Item	Amount (US$)
Rehabilitation, furnishing and equipment of 5 elementary schools	335,000
Educational supplies for 192 elementary schools	125,000
Training costs	220,000
Curriculum development	150,000
Adult literacy pilot project	35,000
Kindergarten pilot project	35,000
Programme support	100,000
Total	1,000,000

Appealing Agency:	UNICEF
Activity:	Reunification of Orphans and Unaccompanied Children
Code:	ERI-93-1/N06
Target Population:	5,000 orphans and unaccompanied children
Implementing Agency:	Department of Social Affairs
Time-frame:	January - December 1993
Objectives:	To reintegrate orphaned and unaccompanied children into the society, and provide opportunities that enable them to become productive and self-reliant members of their community
Funds Requested:	US$ 1,415,000

Summary:

The 30-year-old Ethio-Eritrean conflict has caused extensive human and material devastations demanding enormous resources for rehabilitation and reconstruction. Children and youth represent a socially and numerically significant portion of the deaths, injuries, tortures and social problems associated with the conflict. Eritrean children were subjected to constant threats of aerial bombardment, parental separation or loss and repeated internal and external displacement. As a result of this protracted war, there are currently over 90,000 orphans and unaccompanied or displaced children in Eritrea.

This project plans to implement the following activities:

a) conduct family tracing activities and thereby locate blood relatives of the children to be reunified;
b) reunify an initial 5,000 orphans and unaccompanied children with their relatives;
c) train 250 social workers who will be assigned in the various branches of the Department of Social Affairs to implement and monitor the child reunification programme;
d) provide basic school supplies and household effects, clothing materials and a one-year food supply. A reunification kit composed of 20 exercise books, 12 ball-point pens, 2 geometry sets, 2 erasers, 2 pencil sharpeners, 1 schoolbag, 1 blanket, 1 jerrycan, 1 cooking set, 25 soaps, 1 trouser, 1 coat, 1 shirt and 300 gms supplementary food/day will be offered to each family adopting/receiving a child; and
e) provide logistic support (transportation for the project).

Financial summary

Budget item	Amount (US$)
School supplies	55,000
Household effects	235,000
Clothing materials	335,000
Food supplies to support children	475,000
Training 180 social workers for 3 months	55,000
Tracing of families and relatives	50,000
Logistics/transport support (one vehicle)	25,000
Transport cost	70,000
Medical treatment	25,000
Monitoring and evaluation of project	25,000
Programme support	65,000
Total	1,415,000

(At US$ 283 per child per year)

Appealing Agency:	**UN Volunteers Programme (UNV)**
Activity:	UNV support to strengthening the relief and rehabilitation programmes implemented by UN Agencies and NGOs
Code:	ERI-93-1/N07
Target Population:	War- and drought-affected persons
Implementing Agencies:	UN agencies and NGOs
Time-frame:	January - December 1993
Objectives:	To provide technical expertise to strengthen the implementation capacity of operational agencies in relief and rehabilitation focused on following sectors: agriculture, water and health
Funds Requested:	US$ 620,000

Summary:

The devastating impact of the prolonged drought has affected Eritrea's agriculture. The decades of warfare damaged or destroyed much of the physical infrastructure in many parts of Eritrea. Special efforts will be required in Eritrea to strengthen its capacity in the following sectors: livestock, agriculture, water and sanitation, and health.

UNV specialists will assist in agricultural recovery and rehabilitation programmes, emergency programmes combining nutrition and health care services, epidemiological survey programmes, rehabilitation of water supply, and operational support service to strengthen implementation capacity of UN Agencies.

Technical support will equally be provided in order to strengthen the capacity of indigenous NGOs involved in the relief and rehabilitation operations.

Financial summary

Budget Item	*Amount (US$)*
20 UNV Specialists	600,000
Contingencies	20,000
Total	620,000

Appealing Agency:	WFP
Activity:	Emergency Food Aid
Code:	ERI-93-1/N08
Target Population:	1,560,000 war and drought victims, returnees and displaced persons
Implementing Agencies:	WFP, NGOs and Eritrean Relief and Rehabilitation Agency (ERRA)
Time-frame:	January - December 1993
Objectives:	To deliver required food supplies for general and supplementary rations to war- and drought-affected, displaced persons and refugees returning from Sudan
Funds Requested:	US$ 48,098,700

Summary:

After years of war, an extended drought and the collapse of much of the agricultural sector, Eritrea will need significant food aid in 1993.

In 1991, the harvest was 70,000 mts. In 1992, the harvest was estimated at 260,000 mts. After 3 years of extreme drought, the rainfall was much improved with amounts 150% higher than in 1991 in most areas and reasonably well distributed during the main growing seasons. Due to the good harvest and an estimated 110,000 mts of opening stocks, and taking into account an estimated 50,000 mts of commercial food imports, the food aid requirements in cereals will amount to 140,000 mts. Supplementary, blended food aid needs are estimated at 6,900 mts. In addition, UNICEF will require 1,320 mts of supplementary, blended food for their own MCH activities which is appealed for separately by UNICEF under project ERI-93-1/N03 .

Food aid for the general distribution and supplementary feeding is provided through Eritrean Relief and Rehabilitation Agency (ERRA) which is designated by the Provisional Government of Eritrea to receive and coordinate all relief food coming to Eritrea. WFP, other UN agencies and the NGOs have delivered and distributed through ERRA over 300,000 mts of food aid in 1992.

Logistically, it is possible to manage these amounts of food aid in Eritrea both in terms of port handling and internal transport.

Financial summary

Budget Item	mts	Amount (US$)
CIF delivery including ocean freight		
– 140,000 mts cereals	140,000	28,000,000
– 6,900 of supplementary foods (oil, pulses, blended food)	6,900	4,968,000
ITSH for 146,900 mts (US$ 103/mt)		15,130,700
Total	146,900	48,098,700

Appealing Agency:	WFP
Activity:	Rural Warehouse Construction
Code:	ERI-93-1/N09
Target Population:	1.5 million war and drought victims, returnees and displaced persons
Implementing Agency:	ERRA (Eritrean Relief and Rehabilitation Agency)
Time-frame:	January - December 1993
Objectives:	To reduce the loss of food aid provided by donors, and delays in the delivery of such food, by building 39 semi-permanent warehouses in rural Eritrea with total storage capacity of 63,000 mts
Funds Requested:	US$ 1,994,250

Summary:

Warehouse capacities are severely lacking in Eritrea. It is estimated that only 17,200 mts of warehouse space is available in rural Eritrea. Most food distribution sites lack warehousing facilities, leaving large amounts of commodities in the open. In 1992, ERRA estimated that 90% of food aid was stored in the open which caused significant commodity losses, and delays of distribution to beneficiaries. Thus, the provision of adequate storage facilities remains a top priority. Such warehouses could be used not only for storing food aid, but also agricultural inputs such as seeds, fertilizer and tools.

It is proposed that 39 rural warehouse structures, with a total capacity of 63,000 mts be constructed throughout Eritrea, of which 30 would be in the districts and 9 in the provinces. Each district store would have a 300 mts capacity, while each provincial store would have a 6,000 mts capacity. The warehouse sites in rural Eritrea would be selected in conjunction with the Department of Agriculture and the Department of Construction. Warehouses would be semi-permanent structures made from corrugated metal bolted to a concrete basement frame.

Financial budget

Budget Item	Amount (US$)
9 Provincial stores x US$ 110,000	990,000
30 District stores x US$ 16,000	480,000
Supplies including cement (39 stores x US$ 2,000)	78,000
Travel and transport costs (39 stores x US$ 2,000)	78,000
Assembly, equipment and tools	343,250
Other costs	25,000
Total	1,994,250

Appealing Agency:	WFP
Activity:	Strengthening of ERRA's Food Aid Monitoring Unit
Code:	ERI-93-1/N10
Target Population:	1.5 million war and drought victims, returnees and displaced persons
Implementing Agency:	ERRA (Eritrean Relief and Rehabilitation Agency)
Time-frame:	January - December 1993
Objectives:	To establish a Food Aid Monitoring Unit with the capacity to: a) produce regular arrival, shipment and distribution reports for donors; b) establish a monitoring system for all food aid in Eritrea; c) develop a complete food aid database tracking unit for ERRA; and d) train ERRA staff in food aid management.
Funds Requested:	US$ 179,150

Summary:

ERRA has received an estimated 752,561 mts of food aid in the past three years, including 300,000 mts in 1992 alone. However, there is no central mechanism in place to track and monitor this substantial amount of emergency food aid.

It is therefore proposed to develop a Food Aid Monitoring Unit within ERRA, which is the agency designated by the Provisional Government of Eritrea to receive and coordinate all emergency food aid. The unit would collect reports from the 108 ERRA distribution sites and compile that data into one reporting system. Special attention would be paid to the ERRA/Massawa office as most food aid passes through Massawa. With accurate data collected from these sources, and systems for data processing and analysis developed at a relatively low cost, ERRA could better ensure that food stocks would be adequate in all provinces, proper reports would be prepared for the donors, and food could be better programmed into food shortage regions.

A consultant familiar with ERRA operations and food aid management would set up software and hardware for ERRA. The project would include training, software development, and the obtaining of printers and other computer-related equipment, as well as three vehicles for the unit. Project implementation would involve extensive field site visits to distribution sites, warehouses and Massawa to collect and compile data on a timely basis. The start-up costs for this project are being requested via this SEPHA project, while the subsequent operational costs will be covered by ERRA.

Financial budget

Budget Item	Amount (US$)
3 Landcruisers and stock of basic spare parts x 30,000	90,000
Office equipment and supplies	55,950
1 Consultant x 31,200	31,200
Field trips	2,000
Total	179,150

Appealing Agency:	WFP
Activity:	Equipment for Port Rehabilitation
Code:	ERI-93-1/N11
Implementing Agency:	WFP and NGOs
Time-frame:	January - December 1993
Objectives:	To maintain the relief cargo handling capacity of Massawa and Assab ports
Funds Requested:	US$ 1,150,000

Summary:

In 1992, over US$ 1.3 million was spent on port equipment, such as tarps, pallets, tyres and tubes, tractors, and bagging machine equipment for Assab.

In 1993, the need to maintain the efficiency of port operations at Massawa and Assab for the timely delivery of shipments to Eritrea and Ethiopia will continue. WFP proposes a contingency fund of US$ 500,000 for essential equipment, such as bags, twine, spare parts and other materials to ensure smooth operations in the ports.

In addition, 4 new bagging machines for the port of Assab are required to replace old and depreciated machines which constantly break down and affect offtake capacity.

Financial summary

Budget Item	Amount (US$)
Port Contingency Fund for Massawa and Assab	500,000
4 bagging machines for Assab	650,000
Total	1,150,000

Appealing Agency:	WHO
Activity:	Recovery and Reactivation of Emergency Health Services
Code:	ERI-93-1/N12
Target Population:	1,200,000 in the most war-affected areas in the country
Implementing Agencies:	WHO and the Department of Health
Time-frame:	January - December 1993
Objectives:	a) To provide urgent functional restoration of damaged health services on the basis of a detailed assessment; b) To provide essential medical and surgical supplies and equipment to ensure effective function of the health facilities; and c) To strengthen health services, including manpower training, supervision and logistics.
Funds Requested:	US$ 5,300,000

Summary:

Most of the Health Service Infrastructure in Eritrea that existed in the 1950s has been either completely or partially destroyed as a result of the long conflict and a lack of maintenance for 30 years. For example, in Gash and Senhit province, for a population of 253,500 there is one temporary hospital in Tesseney, one support hospital in Barentu recently upgraded from a health centre and three other health posts. These health services are isolated from each other as vehicles, telephone or radio communication facilities are not available to them, which makes the concept of a referral system a theoretical one. The condition of the health services in Barka, Senhit, Sahel and Semhar provinces are similar, and additionally strained from inadequate medical supplies and an increasing patient load. The hospital in Tesseney town is completely destroyed and the "temporary hospital" is accommodated in privately owned residential buildings. A total of four hospitals have been completely destroyed, whereas most of the remaining health facilities have been seriously damaged.

The hospital facilities, already overstretched to accommodate local patients, are further strained by the influx of populations spontaneously arriving from outside Eritrea. It is reported that the population of Tesseney town has increased from 2,000 to 10,000 within a year, following the end of the war. Similar population increases are reported in most major towns. The project targets a portion of those hospitals and health centres to rehabilitate them immediately and to bring them back to their basic level of functioning. US$ 4,000,000 are required for the physical rehabilitation of health services to meet the basic requirements for the first year, though the overall requirements for rehabilitating damaged facilities is estimated to be at least twice as much.

Funds so far have been used for the delivery of medical and surgical supplies and equipment benefitting some 300,000 people in affected areas. But this is still largely insufficient to meet the basic needs of the population served by the currently functioning health services, let alone the future needs with a possible influx of returnees.

In order to alleviate the tremendous effects of war in the short term and bridge the gap until medium and long-term rehabilitation projects will bring about extensive and fundamental improvements, the project's main focus will be:
- a) the physical rehabilitation of structures based on a detailed assessment of most urgent priority needs; construction work is to start within the second quarter of 1993, aiming to complete major rehabilitations by the end of the year; and
- b) the provision of supplies and equipment to reactivate the basic working level of the same structures that will be rehabilitated. At present, no major interventions on the international side have been initiated to tackle this situation.

WHO also intends to provide scholarships in health planning/management for the strengthening of health services capacities at the central level

Financial summary

Budget Item	Amount (US$)
Recovery of war-damaged hospitals in the 5 northern districts	4,000,000
Medical and surgical hospital supplies, equipment, logistics and professional expertise	1,300,000
Total	5,300,000

Appealing Agency:	WHO
Activity:	Control of Priority Communicable Diseases
Code:	ERI-93-1/N13
Target Population:	1,200,000 in the most war-affected area in the country
Implementing Agencies:	WHO, in collaboration with the Department of Health, UNICEF and local organizations working in the health sector
Time-frame:	January - December 1993
Objectives:	a) To strengthen the DOH's capacity to investigate and to control disease outbreaks; b) To plan and implement a communicable disease control (malaria/leishmaniasis, tuberculosis, aids, meningitis, etc.); and c) To strengthen local capacity for emergency preparedness and response through the Health Information System.
Funds Requested:	US$ 2,139,200

Summary:

After 30 years of protracted war, most of the health infrastructure in Eritrea is either partly or totally demolished and due to insecurity the health manpower has left the country. Having restructured the overall health services in the country, the Department of Health has proclaimed a nationwide Primary Health Care (PHC) policy. Communicable Disease Control (CDC) is an essential component of the Department's PHC policy, with priority given to major diseases such as malaria, tuberculosis, AIDS, leishmaniasis and meningococcal meningitis.

Malaria is endemic in Eritrea affecting two-thirds of the total population with high incidence of epidemics. It is also of serious concern that 92% of the total malarial infections in Eritrea are due to plasmodium falciparum, the most fatal form of malaria.

Although tuberculosis is one of the most common causes of out-patient attendance, with an annual infection rate estimated to be 2.5% per year, no infrastructure for the control of this disease is currently in place.

In 1988, there were 8 recorded cases of AIDS in Eritrea, while in 1992, there were 180 recorded cases. Schistosomiasis mansoni, leishmania and meningitis remain major causes of morbidity.

In view of the possible imminent arrival of 500,000 Eritrean returnees presently in the Sudan, and projected to be resettled heavily in the lowland malarious provinces, WHO has made a Plan of Action for malaria control. Equipment and supplies for the Malaria Control Programme (MCP) have already been provided by WHO. However, needs are still substantial. The plan of action for malaria is based on (a) Vector control activities and (b) case management. Vector control will be carried out at 6 centres in 5 northern provinces. Prompt diagnosis and facilities for microscopical examination, and availability and accessibility of antimalarial drugs at all levels, will be pursued.

An infrastructure for a tuberculosis control programme will be established at district/sub-district level, following an assessment by an external advisor.

The CDC unit of the Department of Health who conducted a health education programme on AIDS in all provinces of Eritrea needs further strengthening as does the health services generally in this capacity.

In-service training is planned for capacity building in epidemiological surveillance and diagnosis of leishmania and meningocele meningitis.

Financial summary

Budget Item	Amount (US$)
Malaria: spraying and laboratory equipment, insecticide, drugs, vehicles, maintenance, petrol, expertise; training workshops and educational material	673,200
	70,000
Plan of action for returnees: spraying equipment, bednets drugs, tools, computers, tents, operational costs and manpower	480,000
Tuberculosis: training and materials, laboratory equipment, drugs, vehicles, expertise	60,000
	149,000
AIDS: training, visual aids, test kits, vehicle, expertise	487,000
Leishmaniasis, schistosomiasis, meningitis: training, equipment, drugs, vaccine, operational costs	220,000
Total	2,139,200

Appealing Agency:	WHO
Activity:	Provision of Essential Drugs and Support to Local Drug Production Facilities
Code:	ERI-93-1/N14
Target Population:	1,200,000 in the most war-affected area in the country
Implementing Agencies:	WHO and Department of Health
Time-frame:	January - December 1993
Objectives:	(a) To provide basic inputs of essential drugs not available in the country until national facilities are ready for their own production; (b) To support local drug production; and (c) To ensure adequate distribution and rational use of the drugs and supplies.
Funds Requested:	US$ 1,350,000

Summary:

As a result of the war, an acute shortage of drugs, vaccines and medical supplies is prevailing throughout the country. The local production of drugs covers only 23% of the total needs, and a significant increase in the incidence of diarrhoeal diseases, malnutrition, malaria, tuberculosis and leishmaniasis has led to increased shortages of essential drugs in the stores.

In 1992, with funding provided by the Netherlands, WHO purchased selected essential drugs not available in the country and delivered them to cover the most urgent needs. However, most of the requirements remain unmet, and there will still be a great demand to import essential drugs throughout 1993.

Under this project WHO plans to purchase standard WHO emergency kits and other essential drugs not available in the country for distribution to selected health facilities in order to help bridge the gap until the country has finalized the construction of a new local production facility. It is expected that this facility will be operational by the end of 1993 and will considerably reduce the need for future import of drugs. WHO also hopes to reactivate and increase local drug production by providing the required raw materials to facilities which are already in existence as well as technical assistance to the Department of Health.

To promote adequate distribution and use of drugs and supplies, a WHO consultancy is foreseen to provide technical support to the Department of Health's initiatives to strengthen drug legislation and to ensure drug registration, inspectorate and quality control. Computer-based management of the drug regulation authority is also envisaged, with particular attention to monitoring drug import and consumption. Training will be provided in this context and to strengthen quality control of imported drugs, and of those produced in the country.

Financial summary

Budget Item	Amount (US$)
Essential drug kits and selected drugs	550,000
Raw materials	600,000
Monitoring system, training and expertise	200,000
Total	1,350,000

Appealing Agency:	WHO
Activity:	Rehabilitation of War-Disabled persons
Code:	ERI-93-1/N15
Target Population:	60,000 disabled people within the country
Implementing Agency:	WHO in collaboration with the Department of Social Affairs and local organizations working with the war-disabled
Time-frame:	January - December 1993
Objective:	a) To support the referral rehabilitation centre for the care of people with physical and sensory disabilities and to equip the orthopaedic workshops; b) To support training courses for social workers in order to introduce a community-based rehabilitation programme in the country; and c) To facilitate the coordination of UN Agencies who intervene in favour of these populations in aspects related to health and social welfare.
Funds Requested:	US$ 1,225,000

Summary:

The Department of Social Affairs conducted a survey in 1992 that reported approximately 60,000 disabled people within the country, comprising civil population, ex-combatants, and approximately 40,000 orphans. Types of war disabilities include multiple trauma, brain trauma, spinal cord injuries, blindness, hemi- and paraplegia and a large number of amputees. An estimated 3,000-4,000 amputees are on the waiting list for receiving prothesis, pending receipt of funds to buy supplies in raw materials to the orthopaedic workshops. The number of disabled is expected to rise in the coming years due to inevitable accidents that will occur from remaining unexploded bullets, mines and shells. The large gap between the services needed and those provided presents a very serious dilemma.

It is generally recognized that an institution-based approach does not present a solution to the problem of rehabilitation. Successful rehabilitation has to be community-based. Only if communities are involved will they recognize and accept people with disabilities. 70% of disabled persons' needs could be dealt with in the community through a community-based rehabilitation programme (CBR) as opposed to the 2-3% that are presently being met in many developing countries. In countries where CBR has been implemented, a positive impact on the lives of disabled could be recorded, although economic constraints have hindered the expansion of CBR during the past 10 years.

This project under the SEPHA appeal advocates a community-based approach, and it is hoped that its funding will give war-disabled persons in Eritrea the possibility of returning to their homes and receiving support at the same time. Thus, the introduction of new institutions would be avoided.

Funding received under the 1992 SEPHA appeal from the Italian Government has been utilized for the provision of equipment and supplies to a referral rehabilitation centre and to orthopaedic workshops, as well as for the provision of a three-year scholarship for a prothesis/orthosis technician.

The referral rehabilitation centre for the care of people with physical and sensory disabilities and the orthopaedic workshops will need further support with equipment and supplies throughout 1993. With regard to needs of orthopaedic workshops in terms of trained manpower, a new curriculum for a one-year diploma course for prothesis technicians has been designed at the TATCOT International Training Centre - Moshi. This would meet the needs in the short term provided that funds can be made available to grant scholarships to students from Eritrea.

In tandem with the above measures, this project plans to introduce a WHO-CBR programme in Eritrea, if funding is received to assist the Department of Social Affairs in developing a master plan for CBR, as a strategy for the integration of rehabilitation into Primary Health Care. Within the CBR programme, community resources will be used for the rehabilitation of people with disabilities, including the disabled themselves, their families, community members and organizations, local schools, workplaces and recreational centres in a large-scale transfer of knowledge and skills to rehabilitate the war-disabled. Village or social workers will be trained in a three-month course, supported by a short-term consultant as Community Rehabilitation Workers (CRW), with the required skills to identify people with disabilities and to provide basic information about self-care, mobility and communication. At least one mid-level rehabilitation worker (MLRW) needs to be trained for each province. The MLRW will serve as a link between the CRW and the various referral rehabilitation services needed supporting the CRW to guide the community on steps to be taken to help disabled children to attend school, and disabled adults to obtain work and to participate in community activities, thus promoting social integration.

Financial summary

Budget Item	Amount (US$)
Support of referral rehabilitation facilities	500,000
Essential rehabilitation equipment (hearing aids, sight aids, wheelchairs, medical supplies)	400,000
Supplies for orthopaedic workshops	165,000
CBR programme and expertise	120,000
Scholarships (4 students)	40,000
Total	1,225,000

Appealing Agency:	WHO
Activity:	Crisis Management, Institution Building, Health Information System and Health Emergency Coordination
Code:	ERI-93-1/N16
Target Population:	1,200,000 in the most war-affected areas in the country
Implementing Agencies:	WHO, Department of Health and Social Affairs, UN Agencies, NGOs
Time-frame:	January - December 1993
Objectives:	a) To build institutional capacity of the planning and evaluation divisions of the Department of Health to enable them to take appropriate emergency preparedness and response action;
	b) To create efficient and reliable systems for routine reporting and surveillance and to facilitate coordination with NGOs and UN Agencies in information collection to guide health emergency response; and
	c) To equip the staff working in the health sector with skills required to assess needs, and to monitor and report according to established procedures.
Funds Requested:	US$ 150,000

Summary:

The health information system in Eritrea has been completely disrupted following 30 years of war. Effective implementation of disease control programmes and national strategies depends on the availability of a functioning health system. It must be emphasized that common health problems will continue to become emergencies until the health system serving the community has the basic capacity to provide preventive and curative care.

There is an urgent need to develop the institutional capacity of the newly established Department of Health with priority attention to the capacity to plan and implement emergency preparedness and response programmes. In this context, the strengthening of managerial capability and the establishment of adequate reporting and surveillance systems at central, provincial and district levels are required as a matter of urgency.

A consultant from Liverpool School of Tropical Medicine (LSTM) completed a mission to Eritrea, resulting in a detailed project proposal for a health information system project. In 1992, with funding received under the SEPHA appeal, an initial phase of the project was implemented by WHO, the Department of Health and LSTM. The health information office within the DOH has been equipped with 5 computers, and a set of reporting forms have been designed. A project coordinator, as well as a research officer, have been appointed. The latter will attend a three-month course in epidemiology at LSTM starting in January 1993.

The funding sought under this SEPHA appeal is for the second phase of this project, with the following activities to be implemented in 1993:

a) The designed reporting forms will be distributed to all provinces. A Health Information Officer and fifteen health information assistants are to be appointed;

b) The forms will be evaluated and a computer software developed for efficient data processing and analysis in the information and documentation centre of the Department of Health;

c) Four pilot provinces have been selected (Gash and Setit, Semhar, Seraye and Hamassien) for evaluation of the system. The provincial health authorities will be equipped with radio and computer equipment to increase speed of reporting and response;

d) There will be a training course in epidemiology for senior level staff to be followed by a baseline health and nutrition survey.

Financial summary

Budget Item	Amount (US$)
Health information system and expertise, development of computer software	25,000
Training course in epidemiology	20,000
National and provincial surveys	50,000
Radio and computer equipment	55,000
Total	150,000

Appealing Agency:	WHO
Activity:	Integration of Ex-Combatants in the Primary Health Care Structures
Code:	ERI-93-1/N17
Target Population:	1,200,000 in the most war-affected areas in the country
Implementing Agencies:	WHO, UNICEF in collaboration with the Department of Health
Time-frame:	January - December 1993
Objectives:	a) To improve health service delivery through an upgrading training programme for EPLF ex-combatants who will be integrated into the Primary Health Care system; b) To cope with the increased need of the rural population for health services in those provinces mostly effected by war, drought and the imminent arrival of returnees from Sudan; and c) To strengthen the training capacity of central institutions by supporting the development of curricula and providing supplies and equipment.

Funds Requested: US$ 252,300

Summary:

During the 30 years of war, government health services were accessible to the military and their families, at the expense of the Eritrean population. With the end of the war, health priorities have shifted towards the development of a National Plan for Primary Health Care throughout the whole territory. It aims to make health services available to all people in Eritrea, especially to those population groups living in remote areas accounting for about 84% of the total population.

An assessment of current health training needs in Eritrea accomplished by WHO in collaboration with the Department of Health identified the urgent need for a programme to retrain and rehabilitate EPLF ex-combatants and to integrate them into the basic PHC services at district and sub-district levels. With their newly acquired skills, they are expected to upgrade and strengthen the health care delivery system. Their impact will be important in particular for vulnerable communities that have been affected by war and drought, and in those remote areas where resources are inadequate to meet the needs of returnees, as well as those of the local residents (i.e. the Provinces of Gash and Setit, Barka, Sahel, Semhar and part of Senhit). The transition from emergency relief towards a long-term development would thus be facilitated.

WHO and the Department of Health initiated the revision of the nursing curriculum and the development of teaching, assessment and evaluation methods to be applied in the one-year course which would specifically prepare students for their future responsibilities as public health nurses. A one-year health assistant course will also be set up in collaboration with UNICEF following a revision of the job description for this function, the design of an appropriate curriculum and introduction of new teaching methodology. The course for Junior Laboratory Technicians will be upgraded to train Senior Laboratory Technicians. During 1993, with SEPHA funding, it is planned to implement the initial phase of this essential training programme that is urgently required to lead the way into longer-term recovery. 150 public health nurses, 100 health assistants and 25 senior laboratory technicians should be trained during this phase. The entire programme for the upgrading of a total number of 1,500 EPLF health personnel (750 nurses, 400 health assistants and 350 specialized personnel) is planned over a period of five years. It is hoped that the resources needed for the period 1994 to 1997 will become available through longer-term rehabilitation programmes.

Financial summary

Budget Item	Amount (US$)
Food and lodging for 150 nurses x 12 month course:	
150 x 300 Birr x 12 months	110,000
Supplies, equipment, models, for Nursing School	30,000
Sub Total	140,000
Food and lodging for 100 health assistants x 12 months:	
100 x 300 Birr x 12 months	73,000
Supplies and equipment for Health Assistant School	15,000
Sub Total	88,000
Food and lodging for 25 lab. technicians x 12 months:	
25 x 300 Birr x 12 months	18,000
Supplies and laboratory equipment (5 microscopes)	6,300
Sub Total	24,300
Total training cost of 275 students for 1993	252,300

Appealing Agency:	DHA
Activity:	Support to SEPHA Unit
Code:	ERI-93-1/N18
Target Population:	Persons in need of humanitarian assistance in the Horn of Africa
Implementing Agency:	DHA (SEPHA Unit)
Time-frame:	January - December 1993
Objectives:	To facilitate UN Inter-Agency coordination of humanitarian assistance
Funds Requested:	US$ 225,000

Summary:

Within the Department of Humanitarian Affairs office in Geneva, the Special Emergency Unit for the Horn of Africa (SEPHA) covers the six countries of the Horn: Sudan, Ethiopia, Eritrea, Djibouti, Somalia and Kenya. The original SEPHA Unit was set up in September 1991, but was dismantled in January 1992, prior to the creation of DHA. The present SEPHA Unit began its work in October 1992, but has been greatly constrained by lack of adequate donor funding. The funds requested for 1993 are for a SEPHA Unit approximately half the size of the 1991 version. The total funding needs for the SEPHA Unit are divided between the various 1993 individual country appeals for the Horn of Africa countries.

The main task of SEPHA is to support the coordination of UN relief and short-term rehabilitation efforts in the Horn of Africa. This includes, *inter alia*:

- the creation of UN inter-agency consolidated appeals;

- tracking and reporting on donor inputs;

- the production of quarterly monitoring reports regarding ongoing and proposed humanitarian aid efforts, and identification of outstanding needs;

- support for relevant meetings, conferences, etc. in the Horn of Africa (e.g., the 1992 and planned 1993 conferences in Addis Ababa regarding Somalia); and

- support and backstopping of the in-country operational coordination efforts of the offices of the various UN Resident Coordinators and Special Coordinators in the region.

Financial summary

Budget Item	Amount (US$)
Staff and Consultants 4/	1,180,000
Travel	222,000
Communications and Publications	48,000
Office expenses and equipment	50,000
Total	1,500,000
Total DHA Requirements: Eritrea Component (15%)	225,000

4/ Includes 50% of staff costs of the financial tracking section, which tracks donations against both the SEPHA appeals as well as the appeals for the Drought Emergency in Southern Africa (DESA).

Annex I: SEPHA 1992
Total Contributions/Income
1 January – 31 December 1992

Compiled by DHA Geneva on the basis of information provided by the respective appealing agencies.

	SEPHA Regional Projects	Djibouti	Eritrea	Ethiopia	Kenya	Somalia	Sudan	Unearmarked for SEPHA Region	TOTAL (US$)
FAO	—	—	3,093,564	7,636,939	—	1,850,000	1,300,904	—	13,881,407
UNDP	—	—	—	50,420	—	—	1,400,000	—	1,450,420
UNHCR	—	2,009,600	7,911,714	39,284,875	58,505,613	8,863,107	10,138,197	—	126,713,106
UNICEF	2,440,336	188,780	1,479,446	7,609,744	14,642,242	30,099,656	13,278,657	—	69,738,861
UNV	—	—	—	—	—	1,060,000	—	310,476	1,370,476
WFP	60,000	896,000	121,966,670	210,334,940	83,446,810	74,051,160	177,423,464	—	668,179,044
WHO	—	75,668	1,380,056	4,541,003	—	3,575,081	558,048	—	10,129,856
DHA	—	—	—	—	—	1,430,000	—	—	1,430,000
TOTAL INCOME*	2,500,336	3,170,048	135,831,450	269,457,921	156,594,665	120,929,004	204,099,270	310,476	892,893,170
1992 SEPHA Requirements**	16,980,000	4,960,200	190,746,300	338,766,300	159,726,306	153,087,830	281,498,150	—	1,145,765,086
SHORTFALL	14,479,664	1,790,152	54,914,850	69,308,379	3,131,641	32,158,826	77,398,880	(310,476)	252,871,916

* An additional quantity of food was contributed to WFP Somalia with an estimated dollar value of $37,245,176 and to Kenya US$ 13,088,088. However, this is not reflected in the shortfall as a food surplus cannot fund non-food activities.

** These requirements include the revised budgets and additional projects introduced by the 100-Day Programme of Action for Somalia of 15 October 1992. As of 1 February 1993, UNDP has not updated inputs since November 30th.

Annex II: 1993 SEPHA Appeals
Eritrea, Ethiopia, Kenya, Sudan

Compiled by DHA Geneva on the basis of information provided by the respective appealing agencies.

	Eritrea	Ethiopia	Kenya	Sudan	TOTAL (US$)
FAO	10,000,000	40,611,000	8,933,000	8,093,000	67,637,000
UNDP	——	1,708,666	185,000	6,253,800	8,147,466
UNHCR	——	43,835,100	78,569,800	8,532,500	130,937,400
UNICEF	7,828,255	17,612,157	32,301,300	40,773,000	98,514,712
UNV	620,000	620,000	520,000	720,000	2,480,000
WFP	51,422,100	185,032,656	67,923,370	116,184,460	420,562,586
WHO	10,416,500	10,152,169	3,000,000	8,933,000	32,501,669
WMO	——	——	460,000	——	460,000
DHA	225,000	300,000	300,000	300,000	1,125,000
TOTAL:	80,511,855	299,871,748	192,192,470	189,789,760	762,365,833

Document 27

Statement of 26 April 1993 by the Organization of African Unity Observer Mission to the Eritrean Referendum

Not issued as a United Nations document

OAU observer team declares polling in Eritrea free and fair

The eighteen-man strong Organization of African Unity Observer Mission to the Eritrean Referendum has declared that the manner in which polling was conducted in Eritrea was generally free, fair and devoid of significant irregularities.

This decision was announced today, Monday 26 April 1993 by the leader of OAU observer team, H.E. Papa Louis Fall, the Ambassador of Senegal to East Africa and the OAU, after holding a two-hour appraisal meeting with members of his Observer Mission who had covered 13 different locations within the nine provinces of Eritrea.

Ambassador Fall also stated that the Referendum marked a happy occasion for all the people of Eritrea in particular and for Africa in general considering how the Eritrean people had exercised their freedom of choice through the ballot box in a peaceful manner without any fear of intimidation and harassment.

He noted that the OAU observer team was particularly impressed with the high degree of enthusiasm, discipline and maturity exhibited by the Eritrean electorate and people in view of the warm reception they extended to the OAU team in spite of previous misperceptions and misunderstanding.

The Secretary-General of the Provisional Government of Eritrea, Mr. Issaias Afwerki, had earlier stated that Eritrea would join the Organization of African Unity and other international Organizations if the results of the Referendum were positive. Mr. Afwerki made these remarks when the OAU team paid him a visit on Friday 23 April 1993, to express its sympathy over the hurricane that struck part of Semhar Province and destroyed 60-70% of the polling stations along with a number of houses and property.

It should be recalled that following the Dakar Summit in 1992, the Council of Ministers at its last session held in February, this year, approved full participation of the OAU in the Eritrean Referendum, so that the Organization would contribute towards the establishment of peace and stability in the region.

Document 28

Announcement of 27 April 1993 by the Special Representative of the Secretary-General on the referendum

Not issued as a United Nations document

The United Nations Observer Mission to Verify the Referendum in Eritrea (UNOVER) was established pursuant to General Assembly resolution 47/114 of 16 December 1992.

The mandate of UNOVER was to verify the impartiality of the referendum authorities and organs, including the Referendum Commission, in all aspects and stages of the referendum process; to verify that there existed complete freedom of organization, movement, assembly and expression without hindrance or intimidation; to verify that there was equal access to media facilities and that there was fairness in the allocation of both the timing and length of broadcasts; to verify that the referendum rolls were properly drawn up and that qualified voters were not denied identification and registration cards or the right to vote; to report to the referendum authorities on complaints, irregularities and interferences reported or observed and, if necessary, to request the referendum authorities to take action to resolve and rectify such complaints, irregularities and interference; and to observe all activities related to the registration of voters, the organization of the poll, the referendum campaign, the poll itself and the counting, computation and announcement of the results.

UNOVER deployed observers in all districts of Eritrea, and covered, from 23 to 25 April, most if not all, of the 1,014 polling stations. The core observer team, composed of 21 members from 21 countries, arrived in early February. They were joined the week before the vote by 100 UN observers. A total of 38 countries were represented.

In addition, more than 40 observers were deployed in Ethiopia and in the Sudan to verify the vote of the Eritreans in those countries. United Nations designated representatives also observed the referendum in several other countries including Canada, Italy, Saudi Arabia, the Scandinavian countries and the United States.

On the basis of the evaluation performed by UNOVER, I have the honour, in my capacity as Special Representative of the Secretary-General, to certify that on the whole, the referendum process in Eritrea can be considered to have been free and fair at every stage, and that it has been conducted to my satisfaction.

I would like to take this opportunity to thank all Eritreans who helped UNOVER perform its mission. This of course includes members of the Referendum Commission and the Eritrean authorities as well as all Eritreans.

Document 29

Statement of 27 April 1993 by the Secretary-General of the Provisional Government of Eritrea on the referendum

Not issued as a United Nations document

The Eritrean people were compelled to suffer an imposed and destructive war deprived as they were of their right to self-determination and statehood. But, after a bitter struggle and precious sacrifices, they have managed to express their democratic choice through a referendum conducted in the full presence of the international community. It is thus with boundless pleasure that I express on this momentous juncture and on behalf of the Provisional Government of Eritrea, my congratulations to the Eritrean people for their historic achievement.

The express choice of the Eritrean people for full independence was never in doubt, and had indeed been long demonstrated without equivocation, through the peaceful and armed struggle that they waged for almost half a century. But although they were able to achieve their liberation two years ago in May 1991 by confronting the spiral of aggressive designs meted out on them to suppress their rights and crush their resistance, the victorious EPLF nonetheless refrained from declaring outright independence and opted to form a provisional government. This decision was taken because the EPLF was keenly aware that the issues of sovereignty and membership in the international community were predicated on a democratic and legal conclusion to the conflict. In this spirit, the EPLF decided that the free and fair choice of the Eritrean people would be determined through a referendum and formed an Independent Commission to carry out the task.

Laws and regulations that govern the process were subsequently ratified and the necessary preparations undertaken. Efforts were made to ensure the fairness and freeness of the referendum process by soliciting the presence of observers as well as the active participation of the United Nations. And in spite of the hostile attempts carried out to deny the Eritrean people this historic opportunity and to impede the participation of observers—and especially to prevent the participation of the United Nations, the OAU and other regional organizations—the referendum process elicited in due time the international response that it merited. Moreover, thanks to the full cooperation of the Eritrean people, the preparations and organization of the referendum were accomplished peacefully and with least expenditure; by all standards.

As earlier announced by the Referendum Commissioner, Dr. Amare Tekle, the preliminary result of the referendum carried out in the past three rainy days with gratifying enthusiasm and propriety is 99.8% in favor of independence. The freeness and fairness of the process has been certified by the observers and notably by Mr. Samir Sanbar, the Head of the United Nations Observer Mission to Verify the Referendum in Eritrea. This outcome is not surprising or unexpected. Indeed, the issue at stake was not some political contest but the very survival, the question of to be or not to be, of a people. As such, the result was obvious and a foregone conclusion from the outset. In the event, it constitutes a delightful and sacrosanct historical conclusion to the choice of the Eritrean people. And although it has been decided that formal independence will be declared on 24 May 1993, Eritrea is a sovereign country as of today, April 27, 1993.

Finally, congratulating the Eritrean people who have persevered with heroism, patience and civilized norms to shoulder their national responsibility and pay the heavy price of the lives of their best sons and daughters to make this democratic process a reality, I express my deepest thanks to the representatives of Governments, international organizations and individuals who have participated in the observation process. I also wish that the new phase and future ushered in by this democratic choice will herald a period of enduring peace and prosperity.

Glory to Eritrean Martyrs

Victory to the Masses

Document 30

Statement of 4 May 1993 by the Ministry of Foreign Affairs of the Transitional Government of Ethiopia on the recognition by Ethiopia of the sovereignty and independence of Eritrea

Not issued as a United Nations document

The Ministry of Foreign Affairs of the Transitional Government of Ethiopia wishes to make it known to the international community that the Transitional Government of Ethiopia welcomes and accepts the near unanimous choice of independence by the Eritrean people confirmed in the UN-OAU–supervised referendum held from 23 to 25 April, 1993.

It is to be recalled that the Conference on Peace and Democracy of July 1991 had resolved that Ethiopia would accept the decision of the Eritrean people regarding their political future as expressed in an internationally supervised referendum, regardless of what the outcome of such a referendum may be.

The referendum held in Eritrea from 23 to 25 April 1993 has been pronounced to have been free and fair by observers from the UN, the OAU as well as by all those from various sectors of the international community who have participated in the referendum as observers. The report of the high-level Ethiopian delegation which was sent to observe the same fully confirms this unanimous verdict of the international observers.

It was in light of the foregoing that the Council of Representatives at its 68th session held on 29 April 1993 resolved to accept and respect the choice of the Eritrean people for an independent and free Eritrea.

Accordingly, the Transitional Government of Ethiopia wishes to make it known to the international community that Ethiopia accepts and recognizes Eritrea as a sovereign state.

It is the conviction of the Transitional Government of Ethiopia that the independence of Eritrea represents a new landmark in relations between two peoples, ushering in a period of far more enhanced cooperation and the further strengthening of the bonds of brotherhood between them. The new phase in relations between Eritrea and Ethiopia takes off from the closed chapter of war which had caused so much destruction of life and property and contributed to the undermining of the so many bonds between the two peoples.

The past two years of peace and co-operation between the Transitional Government of Ethiopia and the Provisional Government of Eritrea have made it abundantly clear that the opportunities for expanding the areas of co-operation between Ethiopia and Eritrea in all fields are limitless and that the prospects for further enhancing harmonious relationship between the two are bright.

Both the peoples of Ethiopia and Eritrea have demonstrated their maturity by the way they have met the challenges of the past two years and the Transitional Government of Ethiopia is convinced that this same demonstrated quality will serve the two peoples forge exemplary ties based on equality and the pursuit of mutual benefits. This constitutes one of the top priorities of the Transitional Government of Ethiopia.

Document 31

Letter dated 12 May 1993 from the Secretary-General of the Provisional Government of Eritrea to the Secretary-General of the United Nations submitting Eritrea's application for membership in the United Nations

A/47/948-S/25793, 18 May 1993

In accordance with rule 135 of the rules of procedure of the General Assembly and rule 59 of the provisional rules of procedure of the Security Council, the Secretary-General has the honour to circulate herewith the application of Eritrea for admission to membership in the United Nations, contained in a letter from the Secretary-General of the Provisional Government of Eritrea received by the Secretary-General on 12 May 1993.

Annex
Letter from the Secretary-General of the Provisional Government of Eritrea received by the Secretary-General of the United Nations on 12 May 1993

As you are aware, the Eritrean referendum on independence held from 23 to 25 April 1993 resulted in a resounding "yes" to independence by 99.8 per cent of the voters in a turnout of 98.5 per cent. You also know that this referendum was observed by the United Nations, the Organization of African Unity, the League of Arab States, the Movement of Non-Aligned Countries and a host of other international as well as national bodies, all of which have witnessed to its freeness and fairness. On the basis of this outcome in favour of independence, announced by the head of the independent Referendum Commission on 27 April 1993, the Provisional Government of Eritrea declared Eritrea to be an independent and sovereign State on the same day. Several countries have already recognized the independent Eritrean State.

We believe that the peaceful and democratic resolution of the Eritrean case through the referendum will not only consolidate peace and stability, but also greatly contribute to cooperation and progress in our subregion and thus our continent. In the two years of its free existence, Eritrea has indeed demonstrated its commitment to peace, stability and cooperation by engaging actively in contributing to the peaceful resolution of conflicts in the Horn of Africa.

Eritrea accepts the obligations under the Charter of the United Nations and is prepared to carry out these obligations, and, on the basis of the articles of the Charter of the United Nations concerning admission, which I believe Eritrea fulfils, I should like, on behalf of the State of Eritrea, to apply for the country's full and immediate membership to the United Nations, the World community of States.

(*Signed*) Issaias AFWERKI
Secretary-General
Provisional Government of Eritrea

Document 32

Message of 24 May 1993 by the Secretary-General of the United Nations on the occasion of the independence celebrations in Eritrea

Not issued as a United Nations document

It gives me great pleasure to send my warmest congratulations to the People of Eritrea on this joyous and historic occasion.

Today marks the turning point in the history of Eritrea and indeed the Horn of Africa region as a whole. The spirit of independence was kept alive by Eritreans for nearly two decades, often under very difficult circumstances. Eritreans have made great sacrifices in order to determine the future of their country as free people. That objective has now been achieved.

The near unanimous participation of registered Eritreans in the recent referendum, and the equally resounding endorsement they gave to Eritrean independence were truly epic events which will be so recorded in the history of the country. The referendum not only affirmed the aspirations of the Eritrean people for independence but its outcome also provided an auspicious beginning for a new era, one in which the benefits of independence and peace, of hard work and resolve, should enhance the search for a better way of life, for sustained development and the enjoyment of fundamental rights and freedoms.

The United Nations is proud to have been involved in the referendum process in Eritrea and to have provided technical assistance to the Eritrean Referendum Commission which had overall responsibility for organizing and conducting the referendum. In the course of observing the referendum process, the United Nations Observer Mission in Eritrea was greatly impressed by the seriousness and maturity of the Eritrean people and their leadership and by their commitment to the democratic process and to the historic task at hand.

As the experience of other countries has amply shown, independence will confront Eritreans and their leaders with daunting challenges as well as great opportunities. The onerous responsibilities of nation-building, of consolidating the political victory, of revitalizing the Eritrean economy, among others, are important and challenging tasks that await Eritreans. Eritreans should not be asked to face these challenges alone. I intend to ask the international community to provide generous and timely assistance in support of Eritrea's reconstruction and development priorities.

It is a widely held view that Eritrea's independence will contribute appreciably to the stability and peace of the Horn of Africa region. There are already very encouraging signs of enhanced and broad-based cooperation between Eritrea and its immediate neighbours. These possibilities and efforts need to be further developed and built upon in order to lay a firm foundation and framework for enduring peace and cooperation in the region.

The people of the region stand today on the threshold of a new and promising era. A period of sustained peace, enhanced cooperation and meaningful development lies within their grasp. This is a challenge that the people and leadership of the region must rise to meet.

I wish to assure the people of Eritrea that, for my part, I will do whatever is possible to ensure that the United Nations system will provide coordinated assistance to Eritrea to facilitate its development efforts and to help it achieve its rightful place in the community of nations.

Once more, I extend my heartfelt congratulations to the people of Eritrea and to their leaders on this momentous day.

(*Signed*) Boutros BOUTROS-GHALI

Document 33

Security Council resolution recommending to the General Assembly that Eritrea be admitted to membership in the United Nations

S/RES/828 (1993), 26 May 1993

The Security Council,

Having examined the application of Eritrea for admission to the United Nations, 1/

Recommends to the General Assembly that Eritrea be admitted to membership in the United Nations.

1/ *Official Records of the Security Council, Forty-eighth Year, Supplement for April, May and June 1993,* document S/25793.

Document 34

Statement by the President of the Security Council concerning the Council's recommendation to the General Assembly that Eritrea be admitted to membership in the United Nations

S/25847, 26 May 1993

At the same meeting, following the adoption of resolution 828 (1993), the President made the following statement on behalf of the members: 1/

"The Security Council has decided to recommend to the General Assembly that Eritrea be admitted as a Member of the United Nations. On behalf of the members of the Security Council, I wish to extend my congratulations to Eritrea on this historic occasion.

"The Council notes with great satisfaction Eritrea's solemn commitment to uphold the purposes and principles of the Charter of the United Nations and to fulfil all the obligations contained therein. We look forward to the day in the near future when Eritrea will join us as a Member of the United Nations and to working closely with its representatives."

1/ S/25847.

Document 35

General Assembly resolution admitting Eritrea to membership in the United Nations

A/RES/47/230, 28 May 1993

The General Assembly,

Having received the recommendation of the Security Council of 26 May 1993 that Eritrea should be admitted to membership in the United Nations, 1/

Having considered the application for membership of Eritrea, 2/

Decides to admit Eritrea to membership in the United Nations.

1/ *Official Records of the General Assembly, Forty-seventh Session, Annexes,* agenda item 19, document A/47/953.
2/ Ibid., document A/47/948-S/25793, annex.

Document 36

Provisional verbatim record of the 104th meeting of the 47th session of the General Assembly, at which Eritrea was admitted to membership in the United Nations

A/47/PV.104, 28 May 1993

Held at Headquarters, New York, on Friday, 28 May 1993, at 10 a.m.

President: Mr. GANEV (Bulgaria)
- Admission of new members to the United Nations [19] (*continued*)
- (a) Applications for admission
- (b) Letters from the President of the Security Council
- (c) Draft resolutions
    Address by Mr. Haji Ali, Chairman of the Delegation of Eritrea
    Address by Mr. Jacques Dupont, Minister of State of the Principality of Monaco
- Adoption of the agenda and organization of work: request for the inclusion of additional items submitted by the Secretary-General [8] (*continued*)

The meeting was called to order at 10.35 a.m.

AGENDA ITEM 19 (*continued*)

ADMISSION OF NEW MEMBERS TO THE UNITED NATIONS

(a) APPLICATIONS FOR ADMISSION (A/47/948 and A/47/950)

(b) LETTERS FROM THE PRESIDENT OF THE SECURITY COUNCIL (A/47/953 and A/47/954)

(c) DRAFT RESOLUTIONS (A/47/L.61 and A/47/L.62)

THE PRESIDENT: This morning I should like to invite the General Assembly to consider, under agenda item 19, "Admission of new Members to the United Nations", the positive recommendations by the Security Council on the applications for admission to membership in the United Nations of Eritrea and the Principality of Monaco.

The Security Council has recommended the admission of Eritrea in document A/47/953 and the Principality of Monaco in document A/47/954. The draft resolutions concerning the admission of these new members are contained in documents A/47/L.61 and A/47/L.62.

In connection with draft resolution A/47/L.61 on the admission to membership in the United Nations of Eritrea, in addition to the countries listed in that document, the following countries have become sponsors: Algeria, Australia, the Bahamas, Bahrain, Bhutan, Canada, Chile, China, Colombia, Costa Rica, Cyprus, the Czech Republic, the Democratic People's Republic of Korea, Denmark, Egypt, El Salvador, Estonia, Finland, France, Gabon, Germany, Greece, Guatemala, Guinea, India, Indonesia, the Islamic Republic of Iran, Ireland, Israel, Italy, Japan, Jordan, Kenya, Kuwait, Latvia, Lebanon, Lesotho, the Libyan Arab Jamahiriya, Liechtenstein, Luxembourg, Madagascar, Malawi, Malaysia, Maldives, Mali, Malta, Myanmar, Namibia, the Netherlands, New Zealand, Nicaragua, Nigeria, Norway, Oman, Panama, the Philippines, Poland, Portugal, Qatar, the Republic of Korea, Romania, the Russian Federation, Saudi Arabia, Senegal, Singapore, Slovenia, Sudan, Suriname, Sweden, the Syrian Arab Republic, Thailand, Turkey, Uganda, the United Arab Emirates, the United Republic of Tanzania, the United States of America, Uruguay, Venezuela and Yemen.

In connection with draft resolution A/47/L.62 on the admission to membership in the United Nations of the Principality of Monaco, in addition to the countries listed in that document the following countries have become sponsors: Australia, the Bahamas, Bahrain, Bhutan, Bulgaria, Canada, China, Colombia, Costa Rica, Cyprus, the Czech Republic, Denmark, El Salvador, Estonia, Finland, Gabon, Germany, Greece, Guatemala, India, Indonesia, Ireland, Israel, Jordan, Kuwait, Latvia, Lebanon, Liechtenstein, Luxembourg, Madagascar, Maldives, Mali, Malta, Myanmar, Namibia, the Netherlands, New Zealand, Nicaragua, Norway, Oman, Panama, the Philippines, Poland, Portugal, Qatar, Romania, the Russian Federation, Senegal, Singapore, Slovenia, Suriname, Sweden, Thailand, Turkey, the United Arab Emirates, the United Republic of Tanzania, the United States of America, Uruguay, Venezuela and Yemen.

We shall consider first draft resolution A/47/L.61 on the admission of Eritrea to membership in the United Nations.

May I take it that the General Assembly accepts the recommendation of the Security Council and adopts draft resolution A/47/L.61 by acclamation?

Draft resolution A/47/L.61 was adopted (resolution 47/230).

The PRESIDENT: I therefore declare Eritrea admitted to membership in the United Nations.

I request Protocol to escort the delegation of Eritrea to its place.

The delegation of Eritrea was escorted to its place.

The PRESIDENT: We shall now consider draft resolution A/47/L.62 on the admission of the Principality of Monaco to membership in the United Nations.

May I take it that the General Assembly accepts the recommendation of the Security Council and adopts draft resolution A/47/L.62 by acclamation?

I request Protocol to escort the delegation to its place.

The PRESIDENT: I therefore declare the Principality of Monaco admitted to membership in the United Nations.

Draft resolution A/47/L.62 was adopted (resolution 47/231).

I request Protocol to escort the delegation of the Principality of Monaco to its place.

The delegation of the Principality of Monaco was escorted to its place.

The PRESIDENT: It is my pleasure on this historic occasion to welcome, on behalf of the General Assembly, Eritrea and the Principality of Monaco as full Members of the United Nations.

I congratulate Eritrea and the Principality of Monaco, as well as the United Nations, on the admission of its 182nd and 183rd Member States. I am confident that these newly admitted Member States will contribute to the General Assembly and to the United Nations efforts in addressing the issues in international relations that lie ahead.

I wish the Governments and the peoples of Eritrea and the Principality of Monaco peace, prosperity and success in the future. On behalf of the United Nations and the General Assembly, I wish to assure you of our full support as you take your rightful places in the international community as free, independent, sovereign and peace-loving States.

I now call on the representative of Senegal, who will speak on behalf of the Group of African States.

Mr. CISSÉ (Senegal) (interpretation from French): On behalf of the Group of African States, over which I have the honour to preside in the month of May, it is a personal pleasure for me to convey our warm congratulations to the peoples and the Governments of Eritrea and the Principality of Monaco on their admission as the 182nd and 183rd members of the United Nations.

The admission of Eritrea, which has come about precisely one month after the proclamation of the independence of that country, is the international community's formal recognition of the Eritrean people's freely expressed will at the referendum of 23-25 April 1993, by an overwhelming majority, to take its place in the concert of nations as an independent and sovereign country.

After several years of fratricidal war, a peaceful and democratic settlement prevailed. Thus, the way has opened up to the consolidation of peace, stability and cooperation in the subregion of the Horn of Africa and throughout the whole continent.

The Group of African States bids welcome to the newly independent and sovereign State of Eritrea to the United Nations and assures it of its wholehearted solidarity. We are convinced that the international community will extend all necessary assistance to the Eritrean people for the consolidation of its independence and the achievement of its objectives of economic and social development.

We have no doubt that as a Member of the United Nations Eritrea will make a valuable contribution to the achievement of the noble ideals of the Charter.

Allow me to convey to President Issaias Afwerki, and to the Government and the people of Eritrea, our congratulations and wishes for success in the Assembly.

As I extend once again, on behalf of the President of the Republic of Senegal, current Chairman of the Organization of African Unity (OAU), the congratulations of the Senegalese nation and its Government, I should like to add my own personal sentiments.

It is a great honour for Senegal to have sponsored the admission of Eritrea to the United Nations.

The admission of the Principality of Monaco today as the 183rd Member of the United Nations undoubtedly paves the way towards the achievement of the principle of universality for our Organization.

It also reflects the international community's recognition of and respect for the independence and sovereignty of the Principality of Monaco and the already remarkable role it has been playing for so long in the world arena. Its admission to the United Nations will enhance the promotion of the noble ideals and objectives of our Charter.

The States members of the African Group are convinced that this new Member State, which today is taking its rightful place in the Assembly, will make an exemplary contribution to the strengthening of international peace and cooperation.

Senegal, which since its independence has maintained excellent relations with the Principality, is happy to see it admitted to the United Nations. President Abdou Diouf has asked me to convey to the delegation of Monaco his feelings of friendship and good wishes.

To Eritrea and the Principality of Monaco, whose presence we hail in the Assembly, Africa says: welcome.

The PRESIDENT: I call on the representative of China, who will speak on behalf of the Group of Asian States.

Mr. CHEN Jian (China) (interpretation from Chinese): On behalf of the Asian Group, I wish to express our warm congratulations to the Government and the peoples of Eritrea and the Principality of Monaco on their admission to membership of our Organization. This marks a significant event in the political life of both countries.

What is worth mentioning in particular is the fact that with United Nations assistance Eritrea attained its independence through a plebiscite not long ago and today has become a State Member of this august world Organization. This is indeed a double happiness.

In the present international situation both the status and the role of the United Nations are becoming increasingly important. The admission of Eritrea and Monaco at this time has further strengthened the world Organization and enhanced its universal representation.

I sincerely hope and believe that Eritrea and Monaco, having become Members of the United Nations, will be guided by the purposes and principles of the United Nations Charter in making their own contributions to the noble objectives of the United Nations and to the promotion of world peace and development.

The Asian countries are looking forward to a fruitful cooperation with Eritrea and Monaco.

The PRESIDENT: I call on the representative of Latvia, who will speak on behalf of the Group of Eastern European States.

Mr. BAUMANIS (Latvia): As the current Chairman of the Group of Eastern European States, I have the honour, on behalf of the members of the Group, to address our best wishes to the Government and the people of Eritrea and to the Government and the people of the Principality of Monaco on the occasion of the admission of Eritrea and the Principality of Monaco to membership of the United Nations. The admittance of a new State is always an extraordinary occasion because it marks another step forward in the process of completing the universality of the United Nations.

The Group of Eastern European States looks forward to working together with Eritrea and the Principality of Monaco in the United Nations. The admission of these new Members will bring new perspectives and ideas which will ameliorate future discussions and contribute to the fulfilment of our common objectives as set forth in the Charter of the United Nations.

The PRESIDENT: I call on the representative of Bolivia, who will speak on behalf of the Latin American and Caribbean Group.

Mr. SERRATE CUELLAR (Bolivia) (interpretation from Spanish): It is most gratifying for me to participate in this meeting of the General Assembly on behalf of the Latin American and Caribbean Group to express our satisfaction at the admission to the United Nations of both Eritrea and the Principality of Monaco.

The inclusion of these two countries once again reflects the universality of our Organization. The coincidence of their simultaneous admission bears witness to the democratic identity that today characterizes the international community.

On the one hand, Eritrea, an emerging country, for its independence has had to pay the price of all heroic actions: blood, sweat and tears. From the dawn of its history, it lived through a situation of dependency, alternating between empire and colony, until the civil war, which it endured for 15 years to consolidate its existence as a sovereign State.

On the other hand, Monaco, so closely linked since the twelfth century to the process of the formulation of the so-called Old World, today is coming to us bringing, like letters of introduction, the modernity of its institutions, the soundness of its economy and its commitment to the principles that guide our Organization.

The peoples of Latin America and the Caribbean have always seen the peoples of these two countries as brotherly, although from conceptually different standpoints. As for Eritrea, the land of courageous people, we associated them in our minds with the nightmare of war, and we shared their social and human tragedy. As to Monaco, we identified them as an extraordinary crossroads of Latin cultures and traditions that made us dream of marvelous visions of castles and fairy tales.

Nevertheless, two countries that are so distant yet so similar, so different and yet now united under the umbrella of this institution, two countries, each with its own specific features and its own problems, were seeking their space in the world and their legitimate place in the sun.

The symbol of their admission to this universal forum, coincidentally on the same date, also reflects the outlook of the community of nations at this moment. Today we all know that peace is development, development is justice, justice is equity; and in the vast ocean of differences, in the final analysis, all of us are in the same boat—a participatory boat.

In accepting them into our midst, we are also committing ourselves to work together under the sign of solidarity. For Eritrea, hope; for Monaco, the standing of its presence here; for both, the path to integration; and for all of us, the challenge of unity. We know that our new colleagues will become part of the climate of cooperation enshrined in the Charter. We know that they will join in the common effort to achieve the goals that form the philosophy guiding us all, seeking an equality that goes beyond formal positions to become an endeavour designed to eradicate poverty, which is today the principal discriminatory barrier still affecting all of humankind—those who endure it and those who tolerate it.

Both States, Eritrea and Monaco, contemporaries in their timeless maturity and now in their adherence to the Charter, represent, in a sense, the two poles under which the problems of the world are being debated today, a world deeply committed to finding global solutions. The future is theirs.

We are certain that both will play an active part in the process of peace and of human and sustainable development, as is increasingly characteristic of the United Nations, and that they will bring to this task not just their historic experience but a true determination to serve the ideals that the United Nations represents. We welcome them.

The PRESIDENT: I now call on the representative of Italy, who will speak on behalf of the Group of Western European and Other States.

Mr. FULCI (Italy): On behalf of the Group of Western European and Other States, I have the honour and the privilege to welcome the two new Members to the United Nations family.

Their admission constitutes a further step by our Organization on the path towards universality. It bears testimony to the strength and vitality of the values and ideas embodied in the Charter. It demonstrates a readiness on the part of the new Members to work together with all other nations of the world for the enhancement of international political, economic and social cooperation.

We are especially pleased that Eritrea, after 30 years of hostilities and war, is taking its place in the international community. Its admission marks the end of a long and painful struggle in the Horn of Africa, culminating in the incontrovertible outcome of a referendum which was carried out democratically and monitored by the United Nations and other international bodies.

The political maturity demonstrated by the people of Eritrea, as well as their commitment to peace, stability, democracy and cooperation, augurs well for the destiny of the new State.

The other new Member is the Principality of Monaco. It is one of the smallest States of Europe, yet also one of the most ancient and beautiful ones. Its founding dates back to the thirteenth century. Since then, it has been able to preserve or, following times of adversity, to regain its cherished independence. Among its many contributions to the international community, its distinguished tradition in the field of oceanography is appreciated by scientists the world over.

We are certain that both new Members, each in its own way, will participate actively and positively in the work of our Organization.

In this time of rapid change, all Member States—be they large or small, ancient or new—bear a responsibility to strengthen the role of the United Nations as the only universal instrument for fostering political, economic and social development, for ensuring the respect of human rights and for preserving international peace and security. It is in this spirit and with these feelings that we warmly welcome Eritrea and the Principality of Monaco as new Members of the United Nations. We wish them well.

The PRESIDENT: I call now on the representative of the United States of America, the host country.

Mrs. ALBRIGHT: (United States of America): As the host country of the United Nations, the United States, with great satisfaction, joins the other members of the General Assembly in welcoming Eritrea and the Principality of Monaco to membership in the United Nations.

The free and fair United Nations–monitored independence referendum held in Eritrea was a fitting conclusion to the peaceful negotiated settlement of its long-standing dispute with Ethiopia. Our fervent wish is that parties involved in conflict in other areas of the globe will learn from the example set recently by Eritrea and Ethiopia and will seek peaceful solutions to their differences, solutions that will enable their citizens to resume normal, productive lives.

We wish Eritrea the greatest success in its endeavours to establish a democratic form of government and a free market economy.

The Principality of Monaco and the United States have historically enjoyed excellent relations. Our friendship is grounded upon a shared commitment to advancing the cause of peace and prosperity for all the world's people.

Although new to this Organization, the Principality of Monaco is not new to international affairs. Over the years it has participated with a great sense of responsibility in a number of international bodies, including the International Atomic Energy Agency, the United Nations Educational, Scientific and Cultural Organization and the World Health Organization. We therefore welcome the Principality of Monaco to membership in the United Nations today.

We believe that the world community will benefit from the contributions of these two new Members.

ADDRESS BY MR. HAJI ALI, CHAIRMAN OF THE DELEGATION OF ERITREA

Mr. Haji Ali, Chairman of the delegation of Eritrea, was escorted to the rostrum.

The PRESIDENT: I now have the pleasure of inviting the Chairman of the delegation of Eritrea, Mr. Ahmed Haji Ali, to address the General Assembly.

Mr. HAJI ALI (Eritrea): On this historic day for Eritrea, permit me on behalf of the people and the State of Eritrea to express appreciation for the action taken by the General Assembly and for the kind words representatives have spoken about my country.

The people and the Government of the State of Eritrea are pleased to accept membership in the United Nations—the world community of States.

In a referendum held from 23 to 25 April—which was determined to have been free and fair by a variety of observers, notably the United Nations—99.8 per cent of the voters in a turnout of 98.5 per cent of the Eritrean people voted for independence. The peaceful and democratic resolution of the Eritrean case through the referendum has consolidated peace and stability in the region and will contribute to future cooperation and progress in the region and in the continent of Africa.

Membership in the United Nations is of special significance for Eritrea, because of the United Nations role in deciding Eritrea's future in the 1950s, and because of the Organization's special responsibility.

We thank Secretary-General Boutros Boutros-Ghali and the Member States for their role in supporting the referendum and our membership in the United Nations. We hope the United Nations and its Member States will also play an active role in supporting reconstruction in our country, which has been devastated by 30 years of war.

Once again, we are pleased to accept membership in the United Nations, and we wish to express our commitment to fulfilling our obligations as a State member of the world community.

...

The PRESIDENT: I should like to announce that the flags of Eritrea and Monaco will be raised at a ceremony which will take place in front of the delegates' entrance immediately after the adjournment of this plenary meeting.

Document 37

Joint Government of Eritrea and United Nations Appeal for Eritrea: Programme for Refugee Reintegration and Rehabilitation of Resettlement Areas in Eritrea (PROFERI)

June 1993 (Volume I: Main Appeal Document)

Executive summary

During the 30 years of war, much of the population of Eritrea was forced to flee to neighbouring Sudan. The majority of these refugees fled from the western provinces, where the effects of the war were particularly severe and prolonged. Some remained in refugee settlements, while others found places in the cities, towns and villages of Sudan. Many have grown old in exile, while others have been born in a foreign country and have never seen their homeland.

Since the end of the war in May 1991, around 70,000 people have returned spontaneously to Eritrea. Many more are now poised for return. Given the necessary help, they can succeed not only in starting their new lives, but also in being a powerful force for helping to re-build a country devastated by the effects of war and repeated droughts.

Through this appeal, the Government of Eritrea and the United Nations are seeking the resources required to implement the Programme for Refugee Reintegration and Rehabilitation of Resettlements Areas in Eritrea (PROFERI). This Programme aims to repatriate the projected 430,000 refugees still in the Sudan who wish to return to Eritrea. It further involves carrying out short and medium term rehabilitation efforts in the areas where most of the resettlement will take place, so that both the returnees and the existing population can sustain themselves once PROFERI ends.

The Programme will last for three years and seven months. This period will be divided into three phases:

Phase One: 1 July 1993 – 31 January 1995 (19 months)

Phase Two: 1 Feb 1995 – 31 January 1996 (12 months)

Phase Three: 1 Feb 1996 – 31 January 1997
(12 months)

During Phase One, up to 150,000 refugees will be repatriated from Sudan, and will receive assistance together with the 70,000 who have already spontaneously repatriated. It is projected that up to 150,000 refugees will be repatriated in Phase Two and 130,000 in Phase Three. Thus, up to 500,000 returnees will be assisted via PROFERI, of whom an estimated 430,000 will be repatriated during the course of the programme.

A pledging conference for PROFERI will take place in Geneva on 6 July 1993. At that time, funds will be sought for Phase One of PROFERI, which has a budget of US$ 110,927,900. A major review of the progress of PROFERI will be undertaken in mid-1994, which will lead to a revised request for Phase Two. The present budget for Phase Two is US$ 79,867,958, and that of Phase Three is US$ 71,406,331. This brings the total projected cost of PROFERI to US$ 262,202,279.

A central principle of PROFERI is that of national execution. This means that most of the programme activities will be implemented by the various parts of the Government of Eritrea, including the relevant sectoral departments and provincial and local government entities. PROFERI will be coordinated by the Government's Commission for Eritrean Refugee Affairs (CERA). Within this overall framework, UNHCR, WFP and UNV will approach donors directly for certain portions of the programme. It is also understood that certain donors may wish to channel some of their funds via other United Nations agencies or through nongovernmental organizations, based on the standard policies and procedures of these donors. Such donations are certainly welcomed, as long as they are consistent with the goal of building up national capacities, and not substituting for them.

It is projected that five western lowland provinces of Eritrea—Gash Setit, Sahel, Barka, Senhit and Semhar—will receive 88% of the returnees. Perhaps 10% will go to the capital city of Asmara, with a few percent also resettling in the highland areas. The relevant infrastructure of these five lowland provinces is less developed than that of the highland regions, and will be greatly overstretched by the number of returnees unless significant additional inputs are provided. Thus, PROFERI will target these five provinces in particular, with less assistance being provided to the other resettlement areas. For many sectors, such as health and water, the Government itself will seek to provide the additional resources needed to absorb the returnees to Asmara and the highlands.

Beneficiaries of PROFERI include local residents in the resettlement areas as well as the returnees themselves. These local residents will benefit in a number of different ways. One is through being the direct recipient of programme inputs, e.g., the needy local families who will receive a portion of the relief aid packages. Another, is through sharing the use of the new infrastructure, such as the health facilities and schools to be created, equipped and staffed. The implementation of PROFERI will also provide considerable opportunities for wage and food-for-work labour for local residents. In some components, it is assumed that the returnees and local residents themselves will share benefits through their own social systems. One example is the provision of livestock in the Agriculture component, which presumes that traditional mechanisms will ensure that substantial numbers of these livestock, in particular plough animals, will be shared among the larger community in the resettlement sites. Lastly, many of the PROFERI inputs, such as the repair and maintenance of secondary roads and the range of productive activities associated with the programme, will markedly increase the economy of the five main target provinces, with benefits accruing to all citizens, returnees and local residents alike.

Within PROFERI there are eleven main components. These are briefly summarized in the main appeal document, Volume I. More details are provided in the Component Descriptions that constitute Volume II [not reproduced here]. These eleven components include:

- Repatriation and Initial Relief
- Food Aid
- Water
- Health
- Education
- Agriculture
- Environment
- Marine Resources/Fisheries
- Shelter
- Roads
- Institutional Support/Capacity-Building

A summary of the financial requirements for each of these components, divided into each of the three phases, is included as an annex at the back of the present Volume.

I. Main objectives of PROFERI: reintegration and rehabilitation

On 27 April 1993, following a national referendum (which included Eritreans still abroad), Eritrea was officially declared a sovereign country. After thirty years of war, the new nation faces the tremendous challenge of re-building itself, and of reintegrating the hundreds of thousands of Eritreans who can now finally return to their homeland.

Much of the country has been impoverished, especially most of the areas formerly inhabited by the refugees who are currently in Sudan. As a result of the war and their forced departure, little remains of many of their former villages. In many of these areas, the severe droughts of recent years, including the famed drought in the mid-1980's, have devastated animal holdings and agricultural production.

The first objective of the proposed Programme for Refugee Reintegration and Rehabilitation of Resettlement Areas in Eritrea (PROFERI) is the repatriation and reintegration of the estimated 430,000 refugees who are expected to return from Sudan, and the reintegration of the estimated 70,000 who have already returned. This programme will require the provision of transportation and initial relief packages for those returning from Sudan, as well as programme activities in the areas of food aid, shelter, agriculture, environment, fisheries, education, health, water, and rehabilitation of certain secondary roads.

By the improvement of infrastructure and the injection of new resources, the programme will also provide both direct and indirect benefits to many of the local population in the areas to which the refugees will return. For example, rehabilitation or construction of health facilities and schools, and the creation of new wells and water systems will increase the level of such services available to local populations. Thus, PROFERI will provide an essential first step in the longer-term process of economic and social development in areas where the returnees will settle.

While some returnees are expected to settle in the highland areas and in the capital of Asmara, the plan is for the western lowlands to absorb the majority of the returning refugees from Sudan. The province of Gash Setit, for example, is expected to more than double in population once the returnees have arrived. However, it is precisely these areas where the war was most prolonged and its effects especially severe. Thus, while adequate arable land and water is available, most of the basic infrastructure, from houses to agricultural assets and health and education services, will have to be reconstructed from a very limited base.

The challenge, therefore, is not just to repatriate and reintegrate the refugees from Sudan. It is also to rehabilitate and rebuild the areas to which they will return, and to do so in a way that does not create a privileged class of returnees amidst a deprived local population, but rather helps to improve the lives and supporting infrastructure for these persons as well.

Thus, the Government of Eritrea (GOE) includes PROFERI as an important component of its overall recovery and rehabilitation programme. PROFERI is also complementary to the US$ 155 million "Recovery and Rehabilitation Programme for Eritrea" (RRPE) recently approved by a consortium of donors led by the World Bank (with UNDP, EEC, Italy, Sweden, Germany, the Netherlands), and in particular to its US$ 7 million Community Rehabilitation Fund. However, it should be noted that the PROFERI programme addresses rehabilitation needs of these areas only up to January 1997, and not the full, longer-term needs.

Ironically, the same war that has so devastated Eritrea has also helped to forge some of its most important assets. These include a strong sense of national unity and tolerance, a tradition of self-sufficiency and of popular participation, and a reputation for efficiency and honesty. These qualities offer a strong basis on which reintegration and rehabilitation efforts can be undertaken, and provide assurance that international assistance can be effectively utilized.

II. Overview of the programme

Through this appeal document, the Government of Eritrea (GOE) and the United Nations are seeking funding for PROFERI—a three year and seven month programme that seeks to repatriate and reintegrate up to 500,000 Eritrean refugees from the Sudan and help rehabilitate the main areas to which they will return.

The programme is multi-sectoral, including the initial transport and related logistics of the physical return of the refugees (e.g., creation of reception and transit centres), an initial relief package to the returnees, and rehabilitation of the necessary secondary roads. Further activities include food aid, shelter, water, health, education, agriculture and environment, fisheries, and institutional support/capacity building. PROFERI focuses on the five provinces in which it is anticipated that the great majority of returnees will resettle. These include (in order of projected numbers of returnees) Gash Setit, Sahel, Barka, Senhit and Semhar. Significant numbers are also foreseen as resettling in the capital of Asmara, which is expected to be able to absorb such persons with much less additional assistance than that required in the lowlands areas.

The programme is scheduled to begin on 1 July 1993 and finish on 31 January 1997. Phase One begins with a Preparatory Period of seven months. During this time the more detailed Operations Plan will be completed, registration of refugees in Sudan will occur, and the necessary additional preparatory actions will be undertaken, in particular at the intended resettlement sites. The Repatriation Period of Phase One will then begin on 1 February 1994 and will last 12 months. This will involve the movement of approximately 150,000 returnees from Sudan, as well as initial assistance to the estimated 70,000 persons who have already spontaneously returned from Sudan.

As shown in Table 1, the funds requested for Phase One total US$ 110,927,990. Phases Two and Three will each last 12 months, and are projected to involve the return of up to 150,000 and 130,000 persons respectively. US$ 79,867,958 is requested for Phase Two and US$ 71,406,331 for Phase Three, bringing the total cost of the programme to US$ 262,202,279 .

This appeal information is divided into two documents. The present document—Volume I—is the main appeal document. The following sections of Volume I review aspects of the appeal process and a number of important planning issues, discuss several important principles which underlie the entire programme, and describe the coordination and implementation principles and modalities. This is followed by brief summaries of each of the main components of PROFERI. The annexes of this main appeal document provides financial summary tables which break out the funding requested by component and phase. The longer companion appeal document—Volume II [not reproduced here]—contains Component Descriptions. These provide more information about each of the main components that make up the PROFERI programme.

Table 1
Summary of Funding Requirements for PROFERI

Component	Phase I	Phase II	Phase III	Total (US$)
1. Repatriation	18,822,600	6,250,100	6,515,100	31,587,800
2. Food Aid	14,575,364	12,581,114	11,125,376	38,281,854
3. Water	5,758,453	4,458,645	3,793,835	14,010,933
4. Health	4,497,000	4,447,000	1,936,000	10,880,000
5. Education	7,945,000	9,403,000	12,602,000	29,950,000
6. Agriculture	18,462,972	11,121,727	9,662,821	39,247,520
7. Environment	3,704,828	2,458,519	1,701,717	7,865,064
8. Marine Resources Fisheries	607,643	653,412	61,518	1,322,573
9. Shelter	19,545,662	20,570,279	20,559,79	60,675,720
10. Roads	9,606,750	1,961,350	1,921,350	13,489,450
11. Institutional Support/ Capacity Building	7,401,718	5,962,812	1,526,835	14,891,365
TOTAL (US$)	110,927,990	79,867,958	71,406,331	$262,202,279

III. The appeal process

In January 1993 the Commission for Eritrean Refugee Affairs (CERA), the section of the Government of Eritrea responsible for refugee matters, produced a programme for "Repatriation and Reintegration of 500,000 Eritrean Refugees in the Sudan." This document revised and updated earlier formulations by CERA, and was based on the planning information available to CERA and on input from the relevant sectoral departments of the GOE. In May 1993, a three week joint mission, composed of members of the GOE, UN agencies, donor governments, NGOs, and other interested parties reviewed the earlier programme proposal and revised it into its present form and content.

On 6 July 1993 a pledging conference for this programme will be convened in Geneva, chaired by the United Nations Under-Secretary-General for Humanitarian Affairs, Mr. Jan Eliasson. While the conference will consider the entire PROFERI programme, the focus will be on pledges for Phase One. The pledging conference immediately follows the opening of the 1993 UN Economic and Social Council (ECOSOC), which will include consideration on 1-2 July of the subject of "Coordination of Humanitarian Assistance: Emergency Assistance and the Continuum to Rehabilitation and Development".

The PROFERI programme and process provides an excellent example of how programming that bridges this continuum can actually be conceived and carried out, through a joint effort of the GOE, donor governments, the UN, NGOs, the local communities, and other interested parties. The pledging conference should also provide a unique opportunity for Eritrea to make a first, and high profile, presentation to the international community soon after the country's independence.

A full review of the PROFERI programme will be undertaken during mid-1994. This will include the review of the rate of return of refugees to date, the updated projections regarding the numbers still likely to come, and the progress of the implementation of all progamme activities. Based on this review, a revised appeal for Phase Two of the programme is planned for late 1994.

This appeal is presented jointly by the Government of Eritrea (through CERA) and the United Nations (through the Department of Humanitarian Affairs). As described further in Section V of this paper ("Coordination and Implementation Mechanisms") a central principle of this programme is national execution. Thus, it is anticipated that most funding will be bilateral donations channelled to the GOE via CERA.

Within the total budget requested via this appeal, UNHCR will seek funds from donors for the activities to be carried out in the repatriation and initial relief component, as well as for a number of Quick Impact Projects that it will develop jointly with CERA that fall within a number of the other component areas. It should be noted that this PROFERI appeal does not include requests for those activities based in Sudan that will be undertaken as part of the repatriation of Eritreans. UNHCR will appeal for these additional funds once the necessary tripartite agreements among the Sudanese Government, the Eritrean Government, and UNHCR are established and the relevant budgets finalized.

Within the overall PROFERI framework, WFP will seek funds from donors for the food aid portion of this appeal. It is also understood that certain donors will wish to channel some of their funds via other United Nations agencies or through non-governmental organizations, due to existing standard policies and procedures of these donors. Such donations are certainly welcomed, as long as these are consistent with the GOE policies discussed in Section V. In this context, the establishment of a UNDP support project for capacity-building to the PROFERI operation through which bilateral funds could be channelled via cost-sharing mechanisms, is under consideration by the Government.

IV. Important planning issues

A. Projecting Returnee Numbers and Resettlement Patterns

In order to make reasonable plans at this point for assistance to the returnees, it is important to consider three planning parameters in particular:
- The total number of returnees who may return from Sudan (plus those who already have since the end of the war);
- The most likely geographic distribution of the these returnees once they have resettled into Eritrea; and
- The likely rate of return of these persons over the course of the programme.

CERA estimates that 430,000 Eritrean refugees will return via this formal repatriation programme, based on the best information available to it. This information includes registration data from the recent referendum on nationhood and independence (in which Eritreans in Sudan also participated) and active dialogue with refugee leaders in Sudan. 165,000 Eritreans in Sudan registered to vote in the referendum. The experience in Asmara showed that registered voters constituted about 40% of the total population (i.e., of all ages). If this percentage is applied to the population in Sudan, and account is taken of the numbers who may not have registered, this supports the CERA overall estimation.

In addition to those refugees still in Sudan, CERA estimates that approximately 70,000 refugees have already returned spontaneously from Sudan, the majority of whom have registered with CERA. CERA, in collaboration with several non-governmental organizations, has taken the responsibility to establish transit and reception centres for many of these persons. After registering the returnees, it provides them with the basic essential needs (including food aid provided via the national programme coordinated by ERRA—the Eritrean Relief and Rehabilitation Agency) and accommodates many of them in various refugee centres.

Following the 6 July 1993 pledging conference, UNHCR, in coordination with the Sudanese Commissioner for Refugees and CERA, will undertake a formal registration for repatriation among Eritrean refugees in Sudan (assuming that sufficient indications of funding are received to allow preparations for the PROFERI programme to commence). It will also undertake related surveys to obtain other information needed for planning purposes (e.g., the specific locations to which people wish to return, their economic preferences and skills, etc.). Pending receipt of the registration data, the most useful projections that can be made at present are based on the distribution pattern of those refugees from Sudan who have already spontaneously returned to Eritrea. Projecting these patterns across the 500,000 who may potentially return to Eritrea gives the following distribution:

Table 2
Projected Returnees by Province

Province	Percentage of Total Spontaneous Returnees/Province	Projected Total Number Returnees
Barka	9.4	47,000
Gash Setit	43.5	217,500
Sahel	23.9	119,500
Semhar	3.3	16,500
Senhit	8.2	41,000
Highlands	1.6	8,000
Asmara	10.1	50,500
Total	100.0	500,000

It is obvious that the actual pattern of return by province will vary from the above projections. However, CERA's analysis of the pattern of location of Eritreans in

Sudan who registered for the April referendum, together with information about their ethnic background and areas of origin, support the general pattern of projections given above, as does information about returnee preferences obtained by Eritrean officials through dialogue with refugee leaders in the Sudan. Such changes as do take place in the actual pattern of return are not likely to greatly affect the total resource levels required for the programme, but will require adaptations and flexibility within programme implementation.

The above projections indicate that the great majority of the returnees will resettle into five provinces—Gash Setit, Sahel, Barka, Senhit and Semhar. Gash Setit and Sahel together are projected to receive two thirds of the total returnees. While these areas are fortunate in having generally adequate amounts of arable land for the returnees to use for agricultural purposes, they are also areas that have been particularly devastated by war and drought. Thus, they will be the primary areas of geographic focus of PROFERI. In the interests of keeping the overall costs of PROFERI lower, and based on the relatively higher level of infrastructure already existing in Asmara, less international assistance is sought for returnees to the capital itself.

Planning for Phases Two and Three, including refinement of the projections for the total number of returnees, will be much easier by the time of the planned mid-1994 review of PROFERI. Not only will more information be available about the intentions of those still in Sudan, but there will also be concrete repatriation experience to draw on. However, it should be noted that while there are some differences of opinion concerning the total number of persons who may return to Eritrea, there are virtually no observers who expect this total to be less than the 220,000 who will be assisted in Phase One (150,000 to be repatriated plus the 70,000 who have already returned), which is the main focus of the current appeal.

In terms of rate of repatriation of the up to 430,000 refugees still to come from Sudan, the programme plans are as follows:

- Phase One: 150,000
- Phase Two: 150,000
- Phase Three: 130,000

UNHCR, the Government of Sudan, and the Government of Eritrea will work with refugee leaders to enlist their aid in persuading returning refugees to repatriate in a planned and staged fashion. It is hoped that the combination of linking the provision of transportation to participation in the official repatriation programme, and education about the need to ensure that adequate preparations are made prior to the arrival of the returnees (e.g., the provision of wells for drinking water) will further encourage acceptance of a more orderly pattern of return.

The exact timing of the return movements to specific locations in Eritrea will be determined to a large extent by the rainy season. These rains make most of the roads in the major resettlement sites impassable for much of the rainy season. Thus, the western lowlands, with a rainy season from June to September, will receive returnees mostly during the period between October and May. To maximise the use of the truck fleet during the remaining months of June to September, the repatriation operation will concentrate during those months on the coastal areas, where the rainy season begins in October. Many of these persons will arrive by ship in Massawa from Port Sudan and will need onward transportation.

Efforts will be made to return as many refugees as possible well ahead of the beginning of the rainy season, so that they will be able to participate fully in the coming agricultural cycle. The provision of agricultural packages such as seeds and tools to the returnees will be coordinated accordingly.

B. Phasing and Prioritization of the Programme Activities

PROFERI will be divided into three phases:

- Phase One: 1 July 1993 – 31 January 1995 (19 months)
- Phase Two: 1 February 1995 – 31 January 1996 (12 months)
- Phase Three: 1 February 1996 – 31 January 1997 (12 months)

Phase One will be further sub-divided into two periods. The first, the Preparatory Period, will last for seven months, from 1 July 1993 to 31 January 1994. This period will be used to carry out those actions that must be taken before starting to actually repatriate returnees. Examples include the registration of returnees in Sudan, the creation of a more detailed Operations Plan (as described in the following section) including the formulation of individual project proposals, further mobilization of adequate funding, and the initiation of work on essential infrastructure (e.g., roads, medical facilities, schools, and shelter) at the specific resettlement sites to be used in Phase One.

The second part of Phase One, the Repatriation Period, will last from 1 February 1994 to 31 January 1995. During these 12 months, up to 150,000 refugees from Sudan will be transported back to their eventual settlement sites in Eritrea, in addition to the estimated 70,000 who have already spontaneously returned. These persons will receive their relief packages (including such items as cooking utensils) and necessary food aid, and further work will be undertaken in the various component areas.

It should be noted that in implementing Phase One, the number of returnees who spontaneously return between 1 July 1993 and the beginning of the Repatriation Period on 1 February 1994 will be deducted from the total to be moved from Sudan in Phase One. Thus, the total population to be assisted in Phase One will remain constant at approximately 220,000 persons.

C. Development of the Operations Plan

The planning information contained in the present appeal document will be further refined by the development of a more detailed Operations Plan. The development of this plan will begin in July 1993, and is expected to be completed during September. This work will be a joint endeavour of the Eritrean and Sudanese Governments and the United Nations. In Eritrea, it will include the participation of relevant sectoral departments and provincial and local government officials, as well as UNHCR (focusing especially on the initial repatriation and relief aspects) and UNDP on behalf of DHA (focusing for the UN on the more rehabilitation oriented aspects).

The Operations Plan will concentrate in particular on Phase One, although further refinement of the plan for Phases Two and Three will also be undertaken. The preparation of the Plan will include, among other actions:

- The identification of the specific sites where most of those returning in Phase One will go.
- Further clarification of the priority actions to be undertaken during the Preparatory Period and Repatriation Period of Phase One, as well as those actions related to the Phase One returnees that will be carried over into subsequent phases.
- The elaboration of the information contained in this appeal document concerning activities to take place within each province into geographic area based plans.
- Review of the implementation mechanisms for the full range of activities, with the joint identification of any specific areas (geographic and institutional) where additional capacity-building support may be needed.
- Revision of any particular budget requests as appropriate, based on the above information.

An update on the status of the development of the Operations Plan will be provided at the 6 July 1993 pledging conference.

D. Local Residents as Programme Beneficiaries

Beneficiaries of PROFERI in the resettlement areas will include local residents as well as the returnees themselves. Local residents will benefit in a number of different ways.

One way is through being the direct recipient of programme inputs, e.g., the needy local families who will receive a portion of the relief aid packages. Another is through sharing the use of the new infrastructure to be created. For example, the hospitals, health posts and new school facilities to be created, equipped and staffed, will be shared between the returnees and the local population.

The implementation of PROFERI will also provide considerable opportunities for wage and food-for-work labour for local residents, e.g., in the soil conservation activities in the Environment component and as skilled labour for housing and other construction efforts. In some cases, it is assumed that the returnees and local residents themselves will share PROFERI benefits through using their own social systems. One example is the provision of livestock in the Agriculture component, which presumes that traditional mechanisms will ensure that substantial numbers of these livestock, in particular plough animals, will be shared among the larger community in the resettlement sites. Lastly, many of the PROFERI inputs such as repair and maintenance of secondary roads and the range of productive activities associated with the programme will markedly increase the economy of the five main target provinces, with benefits accruing to all citizens, returnees and local residents alike.

V. Key principles of PROFERI

A. Gender Concerns

The Government of Eritrea has an official commitment to equality of women and men, and has shown this in concrete ways during the liberation struggle, including the involvement of women in combat and in officer rank positions. In planning for PROFERI, explicit consideration has been given to how the various proposed activities will impact on women, and can best address their needs. This is especially important given the high number of women-headed households among the returnees. Such households constitute 35.7 % of those returnees to date who have registered with CERA.

A fuller discussion of how issues of special importance to women will be addressed in this programme is contained within the relevant Component Descriptions in Volume II. However, some concrete examples may be usefully noted here. Within the agriculture component, lowland women-headed households will be given priority access to tractors while highland women-headed households will be provided with money during their first year of return in order to hire needed labour until they can fund this cost from receipt of their first harvest. Within the shelter component, women-headed households will have priority to receipt of shelter materials. By increasing the number of primary education facilities in settlement sites, the programme seeks to increase the proportion of children attending such schools from the current national average of one third (and often much lower in the lowlands) to two thirds in the settlement areas. This would markedly increase access by girls, who often find their brothers given preference by their parents when school spaces are limited.

B. *The Relief to Development Continuum*

Practical experience has shown that humanitarian and development assistance should not be viewed or implemented as if they were separate operations. Rather, relief, rehabilitation, and development should be recognized as being parts of a continuum. Unfortunately, relief work still continues to be dealt with in most instances in isolation from rehabilitation, involving separate programmes implemented by agencies with very different implementation modalities and using different technologies.

The problem of having internal administrative divisions between those responsible for relief and those handling rehabilitation and development also exists in most governments. It is especially problematic within many donor governments, where it can lead to a number of problems. Sections of the same donor government can have very different ideas not only about the best approaches and technologies to be used, but also about what is required for programme approval and for reporting requirements. Furthermore, these differences can lead to significant lapses in the provision of funding, as the situation moves from a relief focus to a more rehabilitation-oriented one.

In this context, the PROFERI effort offers an opportunity to overcome such problems of compartmentalization and to implement the concept of the relief to development continuum in a practical and effective manner. From the onset of the planning of this programme, those concerned have endeavoured to take the longer view. Such planning has focused on issues such as the sustainability of inputs and the maximizing of community participation. It has also concentrated on ensuring that the approaches and technologies used in the initial return and reintegration of the refugees are consistent with those planned for longer-term efforts, and are built into the planning for those efforts.

Within the Government of Eritrea, coordination throughout this continuum will be maximized by having one entity—CERA—take responsibility for overall coordination throughout the programme, and by involving the same sectoral departments and local government entities from the beginning to the end of the programme. Within the UN system, both UNHCR (focusing on the initial return of the refugees and on Quick Impact Projects) and UNDP on behalf of DHA (focusing on the rehabilitation aspects) will assist the government in the creation of a single Plan of Operations that will integrate both relief and rehabilitation aspects from the very beginning of the programme.

C. *Sustainability of Inputs*

In planning and implementing this programme, conscious efforts are being made to ensure the sustainability of the inputs made, and of the existing economic and environmental context. For example, the technologies proposed for shelter construction seek to minimize the impact on the already fragile environment by using stabilized earth blocks for the walls and fibre reinforced tiles for the roof, rather than extensive use of thatch and wood. The drawing of water from wells and boreholes will use hand pumps where the population and recharge of water is small, and solar powered pumps (which have minimal maintenance) where the concentration of people and the recharge is high. The returnees' preference for resettlement in the lowlands, where, unlike the highlands, ample arable land is available, will reduce the problem of depletion of the soils through over-use.

For social services such as health and education, the GOE has committed itself to covering the recurrent and operating costs of the additional activities required for the returnees, and has built this into its regular operations plans and budgets. The implementation of PROFERI activities have been designed to maximize community participation in the actual work involved, and incorporate community participation in ongoing decision-making (which will be especially important in prioritizing programme activities, given the inevitable shortages and delays in funding). This should increase the extent to which the returnees and local population feel ownership and responsibility for these activities and inputs. Lastly, the programme will seek to develop the use of credit mechanisms within this programme. However, this will be subject to the limitations of the relative unfamiliarity of many Eritreans with such approaches and the need to avoid over-burdening those who are only now starting to rebuild their communities and their economic base.

VI. **Programme coordination and implementation**

More detailed information concerning the coordination and implementation modalities for each main component are noted in the Component Summaries in Section VIII of this document and in Volume II [not reproduced here]. Overall, there are four important principles which underlie the coordination and implementation of this programme:

A. *National Execution*

Overall coordination responsibility for this programme will lie with CERA, while the actual implementation of most programme activities (beyond those undertaken by the returnees and the local communities themselves) will be undertaken by the Government. Such implementation will be done either through the relevant sectoral departments or through the local government entities, with assistance, as appropriate, from multilateral, bilateral, and non-governmental donors.

Within this context, the Government recognizes the effective role which non-governmental organizations (NGOs) have played in relief operations, including during the liberation struggle, and encourages the contribution of NGOs in this kind of reintegration and rehabilitation work. It intends to enhance the effective role of NGOs in the formulation and implementation of projects in accordance with guidelines and modalities set by the Government and its institutions. However, NGO activities must not be a substitute for existing national human resources, and should aid in strengthening national institutional capacity and execution.

B. *Decentralization*

De-centralization is a relatively new Government policy, as the need for a military chain of command, together with limited resources, necessitated a more centralized approach during much of the liberation struggle. In practice, de-centralization regarding political representation and local decision-making is already relatively far advanced, with most of the decision-making mechanisms already in place (e.g., provincial assemblies). A major constraint on implementing this policy has been the lack of sufficient resources to allow for significant distribution of such resources to the local areas. Thus, the implementation opportunities and resources that will be provided via PROFERI will offer an opportunity to put this policy into fuller practice.

C. *Community Participation*

Eritreans have strong experience in community participation, both in mobilizing the population behind needed activities and in local level decision-making. The GOE is strongly committed to continuing such approaches in this programme as well. Most programme activities have been planned to include substantial inputs from the returnees and local communities in provision of labour, and anticipate extensive sharing of the resources provided to the returnees among the local population as well.

D. *Capacity-building*

Clearly the scale and complexity of the activities foreseen in this programme will strain the implementation and management capacity of the relevant institutions, especially at the field level. The Government is very concerned to see that this programme helps to build up these capacities. The GOE will take a number of steps to strengthen CERA and the sectoral departments, as well as provincial administrations. This will include increasing the number of teachers via crash-training programmes and increasing the number of qualified health personnel via training programmes for former combatants with practical health care experience. The identification of further capacity-building steps will be part of the Preparatory Period of Phase One, especially within the development of the Operations Plan.

VII. Resource mobilisation

In order for the PROFERI programme to be implemented, substantial resources will be required, for which the financial and technical support of the international donor community is solicited. These resources should be used essentially to strengthen national capacity to implement the programme.

Support generated for various components should be provided in forms which are mutually agreeable to the government and donors alike, whereby the comparative advantages of each can be fully used and built upon in the context of a joint collaborative partnership.

In addition, external agencies, particularly NGOs and those which provide technical support, are encouraged to mobilize funds from all appropriate sources, including governments, foundations, etc. UNHCR, WFP and UNV will also organise their own appeals, lobbying their regular donors.

VIII. Summaries of main components

The following sections provide summaries of the eleven main components of the PROFERI programme. Fuller information on each component is contained in the "Component Descriptions" that constitute Volume II.

1. *Repatriation and Initial Relief*

Main activities:

Six transit centres and seven reception centres will to be constructed to facilitate the transfer and management of up to 150,000 returnees per 12 month period from the Sudan to their final destinations in Eritrea.

Transportation, in the form of 50 trucks and trailers, two buses, two water-tankers and two mobile workshops will be provided by the UNHCR and turned over to CERA who will be responsible for the running and the maintenance of the fleet.

Relief items (e.g. kitchen utensils) will be provided to needy returnees as well as to other needy members of the community, mainly through NGOs. It is expected that up to 40,000 families will receive relief and household items during Phase One and a similar proportion during the next two phases. Female-headed households will also have access to grinding mills which will lessen the burden of their tasks significantly.

Implementation arrangements:

CERA is the coordinating agency for the Repatriation and Initial Relief component, and will be responsible for overall management of the transit and reception centres, including related logistics concerns and registration of the returnees. It is anticipated that NGOs will assist in the actual running of these centres, and will provide some of the required inputs as well.

Funding requested (US$):

Phase One:	18,822,600
Phase Two:	6,250,100
Phase Three:	6,515,100
Total:	$ 31,587,800

2. Food Aid

Main activities:

Food rations will be provided to returnees for a period of twelve months, until the first harvest, or until the returnee enters gainful employment (whichever comes first). Approximately 25% of returnees are expected to fall into the category of vulnerable groups and to require supplementary feeding. Important concerns for this component are monitoring the proper storage of food and facilitating its distribution.

Implementation arrangements:

Much of the food will be obtained via WFP and provided to ERRA and CERA which will both distribute the food and monitor its distribution. CERA will coordinate the programme while ERRA is responsible for regularly screening returnees to ensure that those who no longer fit the criteria for food distribution are removed from the registers. Under the aegis of CERA, NGOs may be invited to assist in the handling of food distribution and warehousing. Supplementary feeding in many locations will be carried out through UNICEF and NGO feeding centres which are already in place in the areas of resettlement.

Funding requested (US$):

Phase One:	14,575,364
Phase Two:	12,581,114
Phase Three:	11,125,376
Total:	$ 38,281,854

3. Water

The recurrent drought in Eritrea has had a significant impact on the availability of water throughout the country. With the large numbers of former refugees who have begun returning to the country, the provision of potable water is an even greater priority. Water supply systems in much of Eritrea are in poor condition and require extensive rehabilitation. To enable the resettlement of the returnees there is an urgent need to ensure the availability of water before the process of repatriation is underway. The PROFERI programme aims to supply sufficient water for the needs of 300,000 returnees (60% of the estimated returnee population) in areas with inadequate or non-existent water systems in five target provinces. These new water points will be shared with the local residents.

It should be noted that in the planning for PROFERI, considerable attention was given to the related question of sanitation. While sanitation facilities will be constructed as part of all new schools and health facilities, the Government concluded that the current rate of provision of latrine facilities for homes in the non-urban areas (estimated at about 3 %) would make the inclusion of a latrine sub-component in the Shelter component inappropriate and too expensive.

Main activities:

A projected 185 boreholes and 53 hand-dug wells will be constructed in the selected sites, according to local conditions. Boreholes will be drilled by Water Resources Department teams, primarily using a drilling rig to be procured via PROFERI and assigned to this programme. Boreholes and wells will be equipped with either motorized pumps powered by solar energy or hand-pumps, depending on the relative concentration of people to be served and the level of recharge for the borehole or well. Caretakers for the wells and pump attendants, preferably women, will be trained and provided with basic maintenance kits (in the case of the hand-pumps).

Implementation arrangements:

The Water Resources Department is the main implementing body of this programme. Because the task of providing water for the large numbers of returnees is such an extensive and urgent one, the Water Resources Department with the support of the Eritrea Inter Agency Consortium (EIAC) and UNICEF is currently creating regional offices in all the provinces of Eritrea.

Funding requested (US$):

Phase One:	5,758,453
Phase Two:	4,458,645
Phase Three:	3,793,835
Total:	$ 14,010,933

4. Health

The planned resettlement of most of the Eritrean returnees to the under-developed lowland regions highlights the urgency for adequate health care provision. The existing community health services in the planned resettlement areas are clearly inadequate to deal with such large influxes of people. During the three year period over which the returnees will be repatriated and rehabilitated, more extensive infrastructure and facilities will need to be developed.

Main activities:

Additional health facilities will be constructed in the five main target provinces, including two hospitals, seven health centres, and fifteen health stations. The supply of essential drugs and medical supplies for these new facilities will be provided. Control of communicable diseases, which are especially dangerous during periods of large-scale population movements, will include implementing the Expanded Programme of Immunization for the returnee population, and taking actions to control the crucial diseases of malaria, meningitis, and cholera.

Implementation arrangements:

The Department of Health of the Government of Eritrea will implement the projects linked to this development, train and assign personnel to staff facilities, and monitor, evaluate, and report on the funds expended. The Department of Health will meet all running costs and operational expenses generated by this proposal from its own budget.

Funding requested (US$):

Phase One:	4,497,000
Phase Two:	4,447,000
Phase Three:	1,936,000
Total:	$ 10,880,000

5. Education

The planned repatriation over three years of 500,000 Eritreans from Sudan, the majority of whom are expected to settle in the lowlands, will clearly place a strain on the government's limited resources and on the infrastructures which are in the process of being established after the years of war. It is estimated that approximately 30% of the returnees, or 91,000 persons, will be between 6 and 15 years of age, and will thus be of special concern to those responsible for the Education component.

Main activities:

The primary objective of the Education component of the PROFERI programme is to provide educational opportunities for the 91,000 students among the returnees, continuing education to early school-leavers, literacy skills to women, and skills related to income-generating activities for young people and adults.

The main activities of the PROFERI programme will be to:

(a) Support the formal school system with trained teachers, basic school supplies, textbooks and adequate physical facilities.

(b) Improve the quality of training programmes for literacy and continuing education activities and expand the coverage of these programmes. A skills-development component for income-generating activities has been included.

(c) Provide resources and technical assistance at the provincial level for a school construction and rehabilitation programme in the targeted provinces.

(d) Support institutional capacity-building through teacher-training activities and the training of educational planners, managers and administrators, as well as through developing the capacity of textbook production.

During the three-year period over which the programme will be implemented, 265 schools will be built in the targeted provinces, 2171 teachers will be trained, and the capacity of textbook production in the country enhanced, thus significantly increasing the human and institutional capacity of the educational sector.

Implementation arrangements:

CERA, in cooperation with the Department of Education, is responsible for programme implementation. The existing structure for provincial management of the education system will be used for operations in the various settlement areas, and detailed plans for decentralized implementation will be finalized during the Preparatory Period of Phase I. Eritreans abroad who will return via a programme to be implemented by the United Nations Volunteers, will be deployed as site supervisors for the school construction programme in six provinces.

Funding requested (US$):

Phase One:	7,945,000
Phase Two:	9,403,000
Phase Three:	12,602,000
Total:	$ 29,950,000

6. Agriculture

Main activities:

The PROFERI programme aims to enable 72,819 returnee agricultural and pastoral households to meet their food needs through their agricultural and pastoral pursuits. Agriculturalists will be provided with land (an average of two hectares per family in the lowlands and one hectare per family in the highlands), and farming inputs such as seed, livestock, fertilizer and tools which will enable them to begin farming.

Pastoralists will receive a package of one camel, two cows, and five sheep or goats on which to begin building up a sufficient herd to reach economic self-sufficiency. Tractor services for ploughing will be made available to women-headed households and other vulnerable groups in the lowlands for their first year, and funds will be made available to such persons in the highlands for their first year in order to cover the labour costs of ploughing.

The following table summarizes the inputs to be provided:

Item	Highland	Lowland	Pastoralist	Total
Seed (MT)	89	2,134	-	2,223
Fertilizer (MT)	195	8,003	-	8,198
Tools (pce.)	16,848	674,966	-	691,814
Livestock (no.)	6,480	248,110	145,328	399,918
Tractors (no.)	-	80	-	80

Implementation arrangements:

The Department of Agriculture is the implementing body which will be responsible for providing agricultural inputs and transportation services as well as for the storage of inputs. The Department of Agriculture will also be responsible for tractor service and maintenance through their existing regional service and maintenance facilities.

Funding requested (US$):

Phase One:	18,462,972
Phase Two:	11,121,727
Phase Three:	9,662,821
Total:	$ 39,247,520

7. Environment

Environmental degradation is especially pronounced in parts of Eritrea, especially in the highland areas. However, even in the lowland areas, care needs to be taken to avoid further damage to the environment. This is especially a concern given the movement of large numbers of people and livestock into these areas via PROFERI.

Main activities:

This component will focus on activities related to the estimated 55,000 returnee households whose main economic base will be agriculture, most of whom will resettle in the five target lowland provinces. The design of these activities is based on ongoing programmes of the same type already being carried out by the Department of Agriculture. Large numbers of returnees, as well as smaller numbers of local residents, will participate in soil conservation activities (including farmland and hillside terracing, construction of check dams, and afforestation) as well as in the production and planting of fuelwood seedlings. 32 large ponds will also be excavated by machines in order to provide water for up to 200,000 head of livestock in areas where there will be large numbers of additional livestock belonging to the returnees, but where local water resources inadequate.

The following table summarizes the planned outputs of this component:

Activity	Highland	Lowland	Total
Farmland terracing (km)	720	22,800	23,520
Hillside terracing (km)	936	2,880	3,816
Check dams (km)	17	120	137
Afforestation (ha)	234	960	1,194
Seedling production	129,600	40,018,500	40,148,100
Fuelwood sites	648	26,679	27,327
Ponds for livestock	0	32	32

Implementation Arrangements:

The soil conservation and fuelwood activities will be coordinated by the Department of Agriculture and implemented through local institutions such as the Village Councils, as is already the practice in Eritrea. Construction of the livestock ponds will be contracted via the Department of Agriculture, while access and priority to ponds will be administered by the Village Councils with the help of DOA extension agents.

8. *Fisheries*

Although fishing has traditionally occurred along the Red Sea coast, the combination of drought and war has had a devastating effect on the Eritrean coastal communities. Farming and marine activities ceased when people were forced to flee. Nevertheless, the large marine resources present on the Red Sea coast offer excellent opportunities for returnees to earn a livelihood and to become self-sustaining within a relatively short period.

This component will establish coastal fishing villages which will accommodate returnees from the Sudan. The re-introduction of fishing as a mode of production will not only help to alleviate the food shortage by providing the returnees with readily available sources of protein, but will also enhance the long-term economic development of coastal communities.

Main activities:

Two villages will be established along the Sahel coast, each capable of sustaining approximately 200 families, or about 700-800 people. It is expected that other persons will follow once basic facilities have been established. A total of 50 of the returnees will be trained in the special areas of mechanical trades, commerce and management. A fisheries infrastructure will be created through the provision of boats, fishing gear, drying facilities, transportation and cold storage. 40 women will be trained in net-making and repair, thus integrating them into the paid economic sector. Community infrastructure in the form of housing, a school and health clinic will also be established for the returnees during Phase One. The construction of these infrastructures will be undertaken by unskilled labourers. The Government has indicated that it will repair existing roads and construct others to allow access to the villages.

Implementation arrangements:

The Department of Marine Resources and Inland Fisheries (DMRIF) will be the principal government body responsible for the project in cooperation with CERA.

Funding requested (US$):

Phase One:	607,643
Phase Two:	653,412
Phase Three:	61,518
Total:	$ 1,322,573

9. *Shelter*

This component will be implemented in the five target provinces of Gash Setit, Sahel, Barka, Senhit and Semhar. The main beneficiaries of houses to be provided through this component will be needy returnee households, totalling over half of the returnee population in these five provinces. This will include virtually all of the women-headed households and those headed by elderly persons. The remaining houses, up to the target figure of 75,700 homes, will be provided to the other most needy returnees and local residents, as determined by CERA, local officials, and returnees and local leaders. During 1993, further study will be undertaken of possible mechanisms to provide some amount of housing materials to the other returnees on a generous cost-recovery basis, including those resettling in Asmara and in the highland province.

Main activities:

Building materials production units will be established at the village level for the construction of stabilised earth blocks and for making fibre-reinforced cement tiles for roofing. At the district level, these units will utilize power-driven equipment. Given the environmental concerns, wood for the housing construction will be imported. The projected target is the construction of 75,700 homes. Many of the returnees will initially be accommodated in tents of the type manufactured in Pakistan, pending completion of their homes. The returnees themselves will carry out most of the unskilled labour, while skilled labour will be funded by PROFERI. Persons carrying out their National Service are also expected to assist in this component.

Implementation arrangements:

CERA will be the main implementing agency for this component. CERA will work with the coordinating committees at the provincial level, the local Government structures, and those of the refugees themselves in actual implementation. CERA will establish project management units at the central, regional and site levels, and will be assisted by the Department of Construction regarding any additional technical assistance required. NGOs are encouraged to assist with this component, and several have expressed an interest in doing so.

Funding requested (US$):

Phase One:	19,545,662
Phase Two:	20,570,279
Phase Three:	20,559,779
Total:	$ 60,675,720

10. Roads

Much of the road network in the main resettlement areas is in urgent need of rehabilitation and reconstruction. This work is needed in order to enable the return of refugees and the regrowth of the economy to sustain the population as a whole in these areas. This component of PROFERI is mainly directed towards the relevant portions of the secondary road system, as main roads are the focus of the Relief and Rehabilitation Programme for Eritrea being funded via the World Bank.

Main activities:

Approximately 2600 kms of secondary roads will be repaired and maintained in the five provinces which will receive the great majority of returnees (Gash Setit, Barka, Sahel, Senhit, and Semhar). This work will include reconstruction of earthworks, repair and reconstruction of drainage systems and river crossings, resurfacing and realignment if necessary. In addition, some new feeder roads will be constructed to settlement sites.

Implementation arrangements:

The Road Works Branch (RWB) of the Department of Roads will be responsible for the programme of construction which will be carried out by both labour intensive and equipment based means. Six teams will be established for this purpose which will be supported by existing regional offices. Technical design and supervision of labour will be provided by the Government, and communities will be mobilised to provide their own labour in support of the programme.

The bulk of the costs of this component will be incurred in Phase One, as the heavy equipment needed throughout the programme will be bought during the first year. The equipment to be purchased includes bulldozers, graders, compactors and trucks as well as tools. Operational costs, which include fuel, lubricants and spare parts are included in the budget together with some cement for use in the repair or rehabilitation of structures.

Funding requested (US$):

Phase One:	9,606,750
Phase Two:	1,961,350
Phase Three:	1,921,350
Total:	$ 13,489,450

11. Institutional Support/Capacity Building

The size and complexity of PROFERI will clearly strain key portions of the Government infrastucture. Part of the development of the Plan of Operations will entail identification of those portions which will be most in need of capacity-building efforts to help them carry out their work, and recommending actions for addressing these needs. It is anticipated that UNDP in particular will be of special help to the Government in coordinating such capacity-building assistance.

Within the present PROFERI plan, there are two sub-components related to institutional support and capacity-building for which funds are sought. The first is support for the operations of CERA headquarters. The other is the provision of professional expertise via the return of qualified expatriate Eritreans, to be carried out through a special programme of the United Nations Volunteers.

a. Support for CERA Headquarters Operations

As the agency with responsibility for overall coordination of PROFERI, CERA will require a considerable field presence. These costs are covered within the budgets of the respective components. However, funding is needed for the necessary CERA headquarters operations to supervise and support CERA staff in the field and to carry out its overall coordination functions. In addition, over two thirds the total US$ 5.87 million requested for this sub-component is to cover the costs of CERA providing the transportation needed for the Shelter sub-component.

Funding requested (US$):

Phase One:	2,332,318
Phase Two:	2,011,662
Phase Three:	1,526,835
Total:	$ 5,870,815

b. Specialist Eritrean Returnee Volunteers

This programme, to be carried out by UNV in collaboration with CERA and the relevant government departments, will mobilize 300 qualified and experienced Eritrean specialists from abroad on volunteer terms. These persons will be placed for a two year period within the various departments involved with PROFERI, after which time the Government will assume the costs for integrating them within the Government structure.

Funding requested (US$):

Phase One:	5,069,400
Phase Two:	3,951,150
Phase Three:	0
Total:	$9,020,550

IX. Concluding Remarks

After 30 years of war, Eritrea is now beginning the long, hard process of rebuilding itself. The energy and enthusiasm of the returnees can be a powerful force not only for starting new lives in their homeland, but also for helping rebuild their country. However, if the framework and resources required to reintegrate these returnees, and to rehabilitate the areas to which they will return, are not provided, this opportunity will be lost. This in turn could make the returnees a burden instead of an asset, with the added danger that they could even become a divisive factor for the new nation at a time when national unity and healing are essential.

These reintegration and rehabilitation processes will take time. The programme described in this appeal document will need to be modified as the needs and wishes of the returnees become clearer, especially through their own decisions and actions. However, while acknowledging the need for such flexibility, the Government of Eritrea and the United Nations are confident that the activities described this appeal document offer a sound basis for initiating PROFERI, and for the commitment of donor funds.

It is therefore hoped that at the 6 July 1993 pledging, conference in Geneva, and in the months immediately following it, the donors will provide the support needed for Phase One of PROFERI. It is further hoped that these donors will also become active participants themselves in the process of making PROFERI the strong, flexible programme that is needed to successfully meet the reintegration and rehabilitation challenge facing the new nation of Eritrea.

Annex I
PROFERI Budget by Sub-Component and Phase

Component	Phase I	Phase II	Phase III	Total (US$)
1. Repatriation	18,822,600	6,250,100	6,515,100	31,587,800
a. Transit and Reception Centres	5,886,000	994,500	1,259,500	8,140,000
b. Transportation and other Logistical Issues	10,911,000	3,230,000	3,230,000	17,371,000
c. Emergency Relief Needs and Installation of Grinding Mills	2,025,600	2,025,600	2,025,600	6,076,800
2. Food Aid	14,575,364	12,581,114	11,125,376	38,281,854
a. Standard Rations	6,537,520	6,537,520	5,790,410	18,865,450
b. Supplementary Food	588,650	588,650	509,900	1,687,200
c. Dried Skim Milk	77,900	77,900	68,400	224,200
d. Ocean Freight	1,979,280	1,979,280	1,750,920	5,709,480
e. ITSH	3,397,764	3,397,764	3,005,746	9,801,274
f. Warehouse/Store Costs	1,994,250	0	0	1,994,250
3. Water	5,758,453	4,458,645	3,793,835	14,010,933
a. Machinery & Vehicles	1,168,844	0	0	1,168,844
b. Boreholes	586,344	586,344	470,852	1,643,540
c. Wells & Well Rehabilitation	125,094	166,229	146,792	438,115
d. Pumps and Micro Distribution System	3,312,366	3,182,668	2,721,668	9,216,722
e. Maintenance & Programme Support	565,805	523,404	454,503	1,543,712
Component	Phase I	Phase II	Phase III	Total (US$)
4. Health	4,497,000	4,447,000	1,936,000	10,880,000
a. Provincial Hospitals	0	3,000,000	0	3,000,000
b. Supporting Hospitals	0	0	500,000	500,000
c. Health Centres and Stations	3,050,000	0	0	3,050,000
d. Communicable Disease Control	600,000	600,000	590,000	1,790,000
e. Expanded Programme of Immunization	347,000	347,000	346,000	1,040,000
f. Essential Drugs and Supplies	500,000	500,000	500,000	1,500,000
5. Education	7,945,000	9,403,000	12,602,000	29,950,000
a. Staff Development	393,000	170,000	230,000	793,000

b. Textbook Production/Learning Materials	1,715,000	720,000	939,000	3,374,000
c. Physical Facilities	3,929,000	6,679,000	9,035,000	19,643,000
d. Adult Education	872,000	1,140,000	1,538,000	3,550,000
e. Early Childhood Development	64,000	58,000	78,000	200,000
f. Programme Support	752,000	416,000	557,000	1,725,000
g. Contingencies	220,000	220,000	225,000	665,000
6. Agriculture	18,462,972	11,121,727	9,662,821	39,247,520
a. Seeds	639,250	435,852	377,738	1,452,840
b. Tools	1,196,329	815,679	706,922	2,718,930
c. Fertilizer	961,893	655,836	568,391	2,186,120
d. Livestock	12,462,340	8,497,050	7,364,110	28,323,500
e. Tractors	2,300,000	171,360	171,360	2,642,720
f. Labour Hire	23,971	16,344	14,165	54,480
g. Operational Costs (5%)	879,189	529,606	460,135	1,868,930
7. Environment	3,704,828	2,458,519	1,701,717	7,865,064
a. Soil Conservation	1,958,387	1,335,264	1,157,229	4,450,880
b. Fuelwood Production	756,649	515,897	447,111	1,719,657
c. Pond Construction	825,000	495,000	0	1,320,000
d. Operational Cost	164,792	112,358	97,377	374,527
8. Marine Resources/Fisheries	607,643	653,412	61,518	1,322,573
a. Project Personnel and Stipends	45,613	32,360	33,177	111,150
b. Operating Costs	39,520	48,752	16,617	104,889
c. Equipment	456,520	502,172	6,050	946,742
d. Marketing	7,500	8,250	0	15,750
e. Indirect Costs & Contingency	58,490	61,878	5,674	126,042
9. Shelter	19,545,662	20,570,279	20,559,779	60,675,720
a. Building Materials	8,089,083	10,716,558	10,716,559	29,522,200
b. Equipment	550,400	0	0	550,400
c. Transport	3,525,996	4,671,302	4,671,302	12,868,600
d. Skilled Labour	2,986,737	3,956,882	3,956,881	10,900,500
e. Temporary Shelter	3,096,700	0	0	3,096,700
f. Technical Assistance	150,000	30,000	20,000	200,000
g. Programme Support	216,000	216,000	216,000	648,000
h. Contingencies	930,746	979,537	979,037	2,889,320

Component	Phase I	Phase II	Phase III	Total (US$)
10. Roads	9,606,750	1,961,350	1,921,350	13,489,450
a. Equipment	7,525,400	0	0	7,525,400
b. Hand Tools	120,000	0	0	120,000
c. Materials, Cement	80,000	80,000	40,000	200,000
d. Fuel, Lubricants, Parts Based On Equipment Cost	1,881,350	1,881,350	1,881,350	5,644,050
11. Institutional Support/ Capacity Building	7,401,718	5,962,812	1,526,835	14,891,365
a. CERA	2,332,318	2,011,662	1,526,835	5,870,815
b. UNV	5,069,400	3,951,150	0	9,020,550
TOTAL (US$)	$110,927,990	$79,867,958	$71,406,331	$262,202,279

Annex II
List of Acronyms

CERA	Commission for Eritrean Refugee Affairs	PHC	Primary Health Care
DHA	Department of Humanitarian Affairs	RRP	Recovery and Rehabilitation Programme
DMRIF	Department of Marine Resources and Inland Fisheries	RWB	Road Works Branch
		TBA	Traditional Birth Attendant
DOE	Department of Education	UNDP	United Nations Development Programme
DOA	Department of Agriculture	UNESCO	United Nations Educational, Scientific and Cultural Organisation
DOC	Department of Construction		
DOH	Department of Health	UNHCR	United Nations High Comissioner for Refugees
ECS	Eritrean Catholic Secretariat		
EC	European Community	UNICEF	United Nations Children's Fund
EIAC	Eritrea Inter-Agency Consortium	UNV	United Nations Volunteers
ERRA	Eritrean Relief and Rehabilitation Agency	UNV-SERVs	United Nations Volunteers/Specialist Eritrean Returnee Volunteers Organisation
EPI	Expanded Programme of Immunisation		
EPLF	Eritrean People's Liberation Front		
GOE	Government of Eritrea	VHW	Village Health Worker
GTZ	Gesellschaft fur technisch zusammenarbeite	WFP	World Food Programme
LWF	Lutheran World Federation	WRD	Water Resources Department
MCH	Maternal and Child Health	WB/IDA	World Bank/International Development Organisation
NGO	Non-Governmental Organisation		
NUEW	National Union of Eritrean Women		

Document 38

Statements made by the President of Eritrea and by the United Nations Under-Secretary-General for Humanitarian Affairs at the Pledging Conference for the Programme for Refugee Reintegration and Rehabilitation of Resettlement Areas in Eritrea (PROFERI), held in Geneva on 6 July 1993

10 August 1993

Annex I
Speech of H.E. Mr. Issaias Afwerki, President of the State of Eritrea, at the Eritrea Pledging Conference, Geneva, 6 July 1993

Mr. Chairman, Excellencies, Ladies and Gentlemen,

I wish to express first deep gratitude to all those who have worked hard to prepare the PROFERI programme and make this meeting a reality. We are also grateful for the representatives of the donor and international community who have come to attend this conference.

The PROFERI programme has been submitted to you with sufficient detail. Accordingly, I have no intention to waste your time by dwelling on it again here. But allow me to emphasize some of its salient aspects and underlying considerations.

The reality in Eritrea—which has just emerged after three decades of a costly and devastating war—is appalling by all standards. These grim statistics offer a glimpse of the gravity of the situation.

Out of a population of 3 million:

- 500,000 or about one sixth are refugees (there are over 750,000 refugees scattered all over the world) in the Sudan;

- Among the population residing inside the country, 70% or 1.5 million are destitute and dependent on relief handouts for their daily survival;

- A programme to demobilize a substantial number of the 90,000 former combatants who continue to serve the country without monthly pay is also on the offing. The main problem with this category of the needy is not the difficulties they have to endure at the individual level, but the emotional pressures they face from their incapacity to help their families and dependents under distress.

All these problems are compounded several fold because there is no real economy one can speak of in Eritrea today. As a result, the fruits of rehabilitation, reconstruction and development programmes already underway or those that the Government hopes to launch in the period ahead will not be felt for some years to come.

The situation is desperate to the extent that even the most urgent economic rehabilitation and reconstruction programmes that cannot be postponed any longer cannot be initiated without substantial resources.

Under these bleak realities where virtually the entire society is in a very precarious and vulnerable situation, the repatriation process cannot be contemplated as a separate undertaking which can be pursued in its own right in the usual, conventional sense.

Indeed, to embark on repatriation, desirable and urgent as this is, without creating the conducive environment would be tantamount to damping the returnees into a much more worse predicament. Such an exercise will immensely aggravate the overall situation of the recipient communities and exacerbate the precarious reality perhaps to a degree beyond any remedy.

These consideration dictate that the repatriation of refugees be firmly rooted on, and be linked with, programmes of rehabilitation and recovery of the society as a whole. The exercise must also be framed within the long-term development strategies and plans of the country. This is why the Government has earnestly sought to develop, with its international partners, a comprehensive and integrated programme of repatriation, rehabilitation and re-integration. These are, I believe, the basic tenets that underline the spirit of the PROFERI programme.

My Government harbours a great hope and expectation that the international community will accept the validity of these cogent considerations. We harbour, likewise, a great faith and trust in its political will to shoulder the obligations and mobilize the necessary funds for its implementation. Such action will not only help the Eritrean people stand on their own two feet, but extricate the international community from the vicious circle of emergency assistance. I might as well add that a measure of this type will constitute an appropriate gesture of reparation for damages incurred in the past.

Your Excellencies,

Happily, the Cold War has come to an end. The enormous expenditure on armaments made exigent yesterday by the threat of global war can be funneled today to constructive purposes and worthy aims. The peace dividend can be employed to advance noble purposes; to save the disadvantaged sections of humanity from the scourges that afflict them.

This is, of course, neither to underrate the prevailing economic recession nor to put under the rug the multiple, costly, conflicts that are raging today in various parts of the globe. But surely, these problems and setbacks are not overwhelming to the extent that they can deter or paralyze the international community from acting to resolve the disasters in question.

The programmes of rehabilitation and peace-building might also appear inordinately expensive since they have a higher initial price tag. But, as Your Excellencies will agree with me, this is more than offset by the long-term dividends that they will help engender. These programmes will, indeed, lay the basis for the viability and stability of generations to come.

The aggregate funds being requested both for the overall rehabilitation, reconstruction and development programmes in Eritrea, and for PROFERI in particular, are modest in comparison to programmes underway elsewhere.

Although this may sound rather immodest or self-serving, it must also be stated that Eritrea has a good track record of effective use of funds. The smooth and efficient conduct of the referendum within an incomparably small amount of money is a recent evidence of this record. The factor of selfless commitment, obviously engendered by a keen awareness of the mess the country finds itself in, that prevails over a wide section of the population must also be taken into account or recognized for its beneficial impact.

The last remark I wish to make is in regard to modalities of implementation.

The Government believes that the programme must be participatory in spirit and orientation. The population at large, and especially the returnees who are the direct beneficiaries, must participate in the whole undertaking in a manner that will relieve them from being permanently dependent on aid and enable them, gradually, to manage and control their own affairs.

Moreover, the implementation modalities devised must not be at loggerheads but be compatible with and complement the existing and effective working patterns of the Government. In this connection, we note that decentralisation is a cornerstone of Government policy. This is hinged on two basic pillars and approaches: regional and sectoral. And as Your Excellencies will agree with me, it would be unwise and harmful to superimpose alternative or parallel structures and resources to these structures and institutions.

The Government nonetheless faces shortages and constraints in terms of expertise and professionals in various areas. Recourse to international consultants and experts in the fields and sectors where there is no local expertise, and, assistance in institution and capacity building will therefore be crucial.

The implementation modality must further be designed in a way that ensures and enhances transparency, accountability and efficiency in financial matters and the use and allocation of resources. To this end, there must be clear mechanisms that allow UN agencies and individual donors (Governments as well as NGOs) to monitor and supervise the implementation and progress of projects as well as the overall programmes.

The understanding already reached to open a UN integrated office in Eritrea will no doubt contribute to reinforce these mechanisms and interactive environment.

Within the framework of these three component parts, we think that CERA would be the Government Agency entrusted with the overall task of programme execution. But as the programme will be realized only through the donation of funds by the international community, I appeal to all donors to contribute generously so as to ensure the success of this humanitarian undertaking.

Thank you.

Annex II
Opening Statement of Mr. Jan Eliasson, Under-Secretary-General for Humanitarian Affairs at the Eritrea Pledging Conference, Geneva, 6 July 1993

Mr. President, Ladies and Gentlemen,

May I first of all take this opportunity to congratulate you, Mr. President, on the results of the recent referendum in Eritrea and on the achievement of your country's independence on 24 May, after thirty long years of struggle. May I also, on behalf of the United Nations Secretary-General, welcome your country's accession as the 182nd member state of the United Nations.

I would also like to welcome you, Mr. President, to Geneva, and to say how honoured we are that you have been able to come here to lead your country's delegation to the first United Nations meeting for the new and independent Eritrea. We were particularly pleased that you were able to address the ECOSOC meeting last Friday. You spoke, in a very impressive and dignified way, about your country's situations, and future direction. You also dealt with the important subject of the relief to development continuum, a subject that has obvious relevance to your country and to our conference today.

Mr. President, Ladies and Gentlemen,

With the ending of the Cold War, the whole world hoped that the time had come for a new era in which many of the tensions and conflicts of the previous decades would lessen, and that we would finally deal seriously with the global survival issues. There was hope that a new era of peace, development and a life in dignity for all would come into being.

Sadly, this has not been the case. Instead, many long-simmering disputes have broken into open conflict, making development efforts extremely difficult and adding even more to the burden on those who attempt to provide assistance and those who provide the resources for such efforts.

While the headlines are dominated by the growing list of conflicts, there are some bright spots on the international scene, too often obscured by the conflict situations. These are places where conflicts, after many years of suffering, have finally ended. In such countries, humanitarian efforts can shift from reducing the magnitude of death and destruction, to helping people to rebuild new lives out of the wreckage of the war. In places like El Salvador, Mozambique, and Cambodia, the focus is now on re-building, and on returning and re-integrating those uprooted by the conflict.

The focus of our meeting today is another place, the new nation of Eritrea, where peace has finally been achieved. After decades of war, the building of a nation can begin. In Sudan, hundreds of thousands of Eritrean refugees now stand ready to come home. But to what?

The lowland areas of Eritrea where the refugees are to resettle were the scene for many years of some of the most intense fighting of the war. Towns and villages were destroyed, crops and animal herds were decimated, and much of the population was forced to flee. Even with the best efforts of the new Government to maximize the use of limited financial resources available, basic infrastructure such as schools, health facilities and water wells are gravely inadequate for the local population, and much more so for the returning refugees. Major deliveries of seeds, tools and livestock, must be provided if farming and herding the productive activities that underlie self-sufficiency of most of the population are to become economically viable for returnees and local residents.

This is the background for the Programme for Refugee Reintegration and Rehabilitation of Resettlement Areas in Eritrea (PROFERI). Over the three years and seven months of this programme, it is envisaged that up to 500,000 returning refugees will be reintegrated into their homeland. Furthermore, it is foreseen that the main resettlement areas will benefit from a solid foundation of basic services. Finally, it is envisaged that the economies of these areas will have been given a basis for sustainable self-sufficiency.

Mr. President, Ladies and Gentlemen,

You have, I hope, been able to appraise the appeal document for PROFERI, which my Representative in

Eritrea, Mr. Michael Askwith, will present in a few moments. I shall not attempt to delve into the details of the programme at this time. Let me only make a few general comments.

We all know that the challenge of implementing this reintegration and rehabilitation programme is a formidable one. But there are good reasons for believing that the resources being sought from the donor community can be well and efficiently used. These reasons have to do both with the soundness of the programme itself, and with the qualities that have been universally observed in Eritrea—qualities like a strong sense of national unity, a tradition of self-reliance, efficiency, honesty and tolerance.

At a time when donors are particularly concerned about getting the maximum value out of their contributions, these are indeed important assets and qualities. As for funding for reintegration/rehabilitation, it must be recognized that such programmes require considerable resources. We know this from experiences in Cambodia and Mozambique.

Today, we are discussing a request for US$ 111 million for the first 19 months of PROFERI. In May of this year, the joint Government-UN agency-donor-NGO mission reduced the earlier budget for the total programme by approximately US$ 80 million. In addition, the launching of the PROFERI operation in Eritrea will make possible a progressive reduction in the cost to the international community in maintaining camps for Eritrean refugees in the Sudan. However, the total budget request is still a substantial US$ 262 million over a three and a half year period.

Here it is important to recognize the efforts that have been made to keep the level of inputs to be provided to a reasonable level. For example, the education package would allow 60% of the returnee children to attend primary school. Farming and pastoralist families would receive a kind of "starter kit" of animals that would represent less than half the amount needed for sustained economic viability. Half of the returnees would receive permanent shelter while the others would have to make their own arrangements, perhaps through receiving building materials on a payback basis.

We know that at a time when many donor countries have economic difficulties and their aid budgets are under heavy pressure, their ability is much strained to meet the substantial present needs as well as those generated by the growing list of new and dramatic emergencies. Nevertheless, by building on the good-will that Eritrea enjoys in the international community, a good start can now be made to generate the core of assistance which will enable repatriation, reintegration, and rehabilitation activities to begin as soon as possible. In addition to any pledges or commitments that may be possible today, we would be especially interested to hear from donors as to what further steps regarding programme and project formulation you consider useful and which might in turn allow you to make further commitments later.

All of those concerned with the development of this programme recognize that this programme will require flexibility through an ongoing process of review, if it is to be effective. We hope that the donors will be full partners in this process as well. I would therefore ask you, if possible, to make your position known today as to the role your government or organization intends to play in the context of the PROFERI operation.

Mr. President, Ladies and Gentlemen,

Lastly, I would like to review certain aspects regarding the role of the various institutions involved with PROFERI, as well as the programme's relationship to other aid efforts in Eritrea.

Unlike the other appeals which the Department of Humanitarian Affairs has facilitated in 1993 under the rubric of SEPHA—the Special Emergency Programme for the Horn of Africa—the present appeal is not a strict UN inter-agency appeal. Rather, it is a joint Government of Eritrea–United Nations Appeal for a programme with national execution as a central tenet. This means that it is the various sectoral departments of the Government, under the overall coordination of the Commission for Eritrean Refugee Affairs, that will carry out most of the programme implementation of PROFERI.

Within the overall framework of PROFERI, several UN agencies, i.e., UNHCR, WFP and the United Nations Volunteer program, will appeal directly to donors for components of the programme. Their role in programme implementation will be familiar to donors. I expect that a number of donors are likely to wish to channel some of their funds through these and other UN agencies. I understand that most of the UN agencies stand ready to play such a role, consistent of course with their own policies and procedures, and if requested to do so by the Government of Eritrea and the donors.

The Department of Humanitarian Affairs was asked by the Eritrean Government to help get this programme under way through the mobilization of international support, and to ensure that the transition from relief to rehabilitation would be firmly established. This role is consistent with our view that humanitarian assistance involves the range from early warning, preventive actions and relief to short-term rehabilitation, when humanitarian aid agencies hand the baton over to the development organizations. In the case of Eritrea, it is advantageous that my Representative in Asmara is also the head of UNDP. I look to UNDP to take over the UN inter-agency coordination aspects of this programme once it is under way in 1994.

I am gratified that the Government encourages the participation of non-governmental organizations in this programme, particularly as regards strengthening national capacity. This attitude of the Government is built on recognition of the effective role which many NGOs have already played both during the liberation struggle and in its aftermath, facing the period of nation-building in solidarity with the people of Eritrea.

In designing this programme, attention has been given to ensuring that existing or planned programmes in Eritrea, complement the PROFERI operation. This has included ensuring that there is no duplication of funding sought via the SEPHA appeal for Eritrea, or with the World Bank and bilateral aid programmes.

In conclusion, I would like to thank you all for actively participating in this meeting. It is an expression of the interest in co-operating with the Government of Eritrea in what must be considered as a shared collective venture to address the most critical and urgent problems faced by the world's newest independent state.

We know the problem. We also know what needs to be done. But we do not yet know, in a comprehensive way, how the international community can help. I hope that this meeting will play a useful role in clarifying this matter, and in broadening and deepening the discussion about the crucial transition from relief to development.

At the same time we can make important contributions to the solution of problems which are severely straining the capacity, but not the will, of the new Eritrea.

Document 39

Report of the Secretary-General on UNOVER

A/48/283, 11 August 1993

I. Introduction

1. By its resolution 47/114 of 16 December 1992, the General Assembly authorized, by consensus, the establishment of the United Nations Observer Mission to Verify the Referendum in Eritrea (UNOVER). In its resolution 47/114, the Assembly took into account that the authorities directly concerned had requested the involvement of the United Nations in verifying the referendum and registered their commitment to respect its results. The present report is submitted in pursuance of paragraph 5 of General Assembly resolution 47/114. It presents the findings of the Secretary-General on the referendum and the activities of UNOVER from its establishment in January 1993 until its conclusion in April 1993.

A. *Background*

2. With a geographical area of nearly 125,000 square kilometres, Eritrea has a population estimated between 3 million and 3.5 million. Close to 85 per cent of the population lives in rural areas, of which 25 to 30 per cent is nomadic or semi-nomadic. The population consists of nine groupings: Afar, Bilen, Hadareb, Kunama, Nara, Rashaida, Saho, Tigre and Tigrinya. Nine languages are spoken.

3. Located on the Red Sea Coast just above the Horn of Africa, Eritrea was an Italian colony from 1890 to 1911, when it became a British Protectorate. Its federation with Ethiopia took place in 1952. That arrangement ended in 1962 when Eritrea's federal status was abrogated and the territory was incorporated into Ethiopia as a province. For three decades thereafter, Eritreans struggled for self-determination, first within a federation and then in full independence.

4. In May 1991, the Eritrean People's Liberation Front (EPLF) took control of the Eritrean capital of Asmara and established itself as the Provisional Government of Eritrea. The Provisional Government of Eritrea consisted of legislative, executive and judicial bodies. The executive was responsible, among other things, for issuing and implementing proclamations.

B. *Eritrean request and United Nations response*

5. In May 1991, the newly formed Provisional Government of Eritrea met with delegations from Ethiopia and made a commitment to hold a referendum on the future of Eritrea within two years. The meeting took place in London under the auspices of the United States of America.

6. In July 1991, a Conference on Peace and Democracy held at Addis Ababa brought together all the Ethiopian political parties and other social groups. It formally recognized the right of the Eritrean people to determine their political future by an internationally supervised referendum.

7. In a letter dated 13 December 1991, Mr. Meles Zenawi, the President of the Transitional Government of

Ethiopia, informed the Secretary-General about the decisions of the Conference on Peace and Democracy. President Zenawi noted that both the Transitional Government of Ethiopia and the Provisional Government of Eritrea had registered their commitment to respect the results of the referendum in Eritrea. He asked that the United Nations play an active role in verifying a free and fair referendum. In May 1992, the Referendum Commissioner of Eritrea invited the Secretary-General to send a United Nations delegation to observe and to verify the freedom, fairness and impartiality of the entire referendum process which was to begin in July 1992 and end in April 1993.

8. The Secretary-General brought the matter to the attention of the President of the General Assembly and asked for informal consultations among the regional groups to ascertain their views on this invitation. Subsequently, a technical team visited Eritrea between 30 July and 8 August 1992 to gather information about a possible United Nations role in the referendum and thereafter submitted a report to the Secretary-General. The findings of the team were contained in the Secretary-General's report to the General Assembly of 19 October 1992 (A/47/544).

9. The Secretary-General's report to the General Assembly took note that international supervision of the referendum in Eritrea had been supported by the Addis Ababa Agreements of 1991. Since the Secretary-General considered the referendum process an important step towards the establishment of democracy, and for the promotion of regional stability, he recommended the establishment of a United Nations Observer Mission to Verify the Referendum in Eritrea.

C. *Establishment of the United Nations Observer Mission to Verify the Referendum in Eritrea*

10. Based upon these recommendations of the Secretary-General, the General Assembly, in its resolution 47/114, declared its decision to establish UNOVER with the following mandate:

"(a) To verify the impartiality of the referendum authorities and organs, including the Referendum Commission, in all aspects and stages of the referendum process;

"(b) To verify that there exists complete freedom of organization, movement, assembly and expression without hindrance or intimidation;

"(c) To verify that there is equal access to media facilities and that there is fairness in the allocation of both the timing and length of broadcasts;

"(d) To verify that the referendum rolls are properly drawn up and that qualified voters are not denied identification and registration cards or the right to vote;

"(e) To report to the referendum authorities on complaints, irregularities and interferences reported or observed and, if necessary, to request the referendum authorities to take action to resolve and rectify such complaints, irregularities or interference;

"(f) To observe all activities related to the registration of voters, the organization of the poll, the referendum campaign, the poll itself and the counting, computation and announcement of the results." (A/47/544, para. 7)

1. *Structure and composition of the United Nations Observer Mission to Verify the Referendum in Eritrea*

11. On 6 January 1993, the Secretary-General, accompanied by Under-Secretary-General James O. C. Jonah, visited Eritrea for a first-hand appraisal of the referendum process. Upon his return, he appointed Mr. Samir Sanbar as his Special Representative and Chief of the UNOVER with its headquarters at Asmara. UNOVER also set up its headquarters and a regional office at Asmara, and other regional offices at Keren and Mendefera.

12. In the composition of UNOVER, several considerations were borne in mind. There was peace in Eritrea. The decision to hold a referendum had been taken by the concerned Eritrean authorities. The organization of the referendum effort by the Eritrean Referendum Commission was already under way. There was little evidence of political tensions or conflicting positions over the referendum. In fact, civic peace and security in Eritrea were remarkable for a society emerging from a prolonged conflict. Asmara, with a population of 400,000, for example, had only 123 policemen. Accordingly, the Secretary-General decided that a relatively small international staff of civilians, supported by local personnel, would be sufficient to fulfil the mandate of UNOVER.

13. The UNOVER core team consisted of 21 international staff, headed by the Special Representative of the Secretary-General. Sixteen different nationalities were represented. As Chief of the Mission, the Special Representative was to provide overall political direction to the observation and verification mission. The Asmara headquarters was made up of a small team, including the Chief Electoral Observer, the Special Assistant of the Special Representative, a Political Affairs Officer, and an Administration Unit comprising four officers. Each of the

UNOVER regional offices at Asmara, Keren and Mendefera, was headed by a regional coordinator and assisted by three to four electoral officers organized in two mobile teams of two persons each.

14. During 12 and 18 April 1993, 86 observers joined the 21 members of the UNOVER core team for the last phase of the referendum process. Of the additional 86 observers, 57 were seconded by Member States, 8 from United Nations specialized agencies and project personnel, 3 from the United Nations Secretariat, 5 from the Economic Commission for Africa, 3 from international non-governmental organizations, and 10 qualified local international staff. At its maximum strength, UNOVER had observers from the following 35 countries: Afghanistan, Argentina, Austria, Canada, Côte d'Ivoire, Finland, France, Germany, Iceland, Ireland, Italy, Japan, Jordan, Lebanon, Madagascar, Mexico, Netherlands, New Zealand, Norway, Peru, Portugal, Russia, Somalia, Sri Lanka, Sweden, Switzerland, Togo, Turkey, Uganda, United Kingdom of Great Britain and Northern Ireland, United States of America, Venezuela, Viet Nam, Zaire and Zambia. These were deployed in 16 teams in the Asmara region, 15 teams in the Keren region, and 14 teams in the Mendefera region. Each team included two observers, one driver and one interpreter.

15. UNOVER held training seminars in order to brief the observers on the code of conduct, on the UNOVER *modus operandi*, and to provide them with specific instructions for the observation of the voting and the counting of the ballots. The core team of 21 UNOVER observers received intensive in-depth training at the beginning of the mission before being deployed to their respective regions.

2. *Guidelines for the United Nations Observer Mission to Verify the Referendum in Eritrea*

16. UNOVER was given clear guidelines for carrying out its mandate. As provided in the Secretary-General's report of 19 October 1992 (A/47/544), UNOVER was expected "to gather factual information about the conduct of the referendum and, in particular, the decision of the electorate; to recognize that the ultimate judgement about the referendum process will be made by the electorate themselves and that its role will be to take note of the decision of the electorate, as they determine their fate in a referendum; to recognize the independent character of the Referendum Commission and establish a relationship with it on that basis; and, in its capacity as observer, to make constructive contributions to ensure the success of the referendum at every stage of the process" (para. 8).

17. Three main phases of the referendum process were foreseen: the registration of voters; the referendum campaign; and the poll itself. The first priority for all activities undertaken by UNOVER was to support, monitor and evaluate the impartiality of the referendum in all its phases.

II. Referendum process in Eritrea

18. The referendum process in Eritrea had started much earlier than the establishment of UNOVER in December 1992. Thus, on 7 April 1992, the Provisional Government of Eritrea issued a Referendum Proclamation which laid down the rules and regulations to govern the referendum process. The Proclamation also established a Referendum Commission and a Referendum Court, in addition to setting out the referendum's terms of reference.

A. *Referendum Commission*

19. The Referendum Commission consisted of a Referendum Commissioner and four Deputy Commissioners designated by the Secretary-General of the Provisional Government of Eritrea. The work of the Commission was carried out by: a secretariat; an Identification and Registration Board; a Publicity and Information Board; and an Election Board. Each was headed by a Deputy Commissioner. At the regional level, the Commission's activities were organized into 10 provincial and 140 district offices.

20. The main functions of the Referendum Commission, according to the Referendum Proclamation, were to:

(a) Guarantee a referendum that was free and fair;

(b) Identify and register eligible voters;

(c) Create the procedures for the referendum itself;

(d) Publicize the referendum and inform the voters.

21. To create the proper environment for preparing and carrying out the election, the Referendum Commission was entrusted with making arrangements to:

(a) Guarantee freedom of speech, assembly, movement and press for the purposes of the referendum;

(b) Ensure the security of voters;

(c) Publicize the referendum and encourage the free exchange of views;

(d) Facilitate the return and vote of all eligible voters;

(e) Address promptly, adequately and fairly all complaints regarding rules and instructions about the referendum and its conduct;

(f) Ensure law and order during the referendum campaign and voting.

B. Referendum Court

22. The Referendum Proclamation established a Referendum Court consisting of a Presiding Judge and two others. The appeal procedure for a person denied participation in the referendum allowed him or her to petition the Election Board until four weeks before the first polling day. If rejected by the Board, the appellant could appeal to the Referendum Court until two weeks before the first day of voting. The Proclamation stated that decisions handed down by the Court "... shall be final and may not be challenged by any other authority". International verification of this procedure for appeal was an important element in the responsibilities of UNOVER.

C. Terms of reference

23. Under article 3 of the Eritrean Referendum Proclamation, the referendum put a single question to the electorate: "Do you approve that Eritrea should become an independent sovereign State?" Voters were to respond either in the affirmative or the negative.

D. Phases of referendum

24. The actual conduct of the referendum was divided into three phases. The first phase corresponded to the registration of voters which started in mid-October 1992 and was completed on 1 March 1993. The referendum campaign constituting the second phase began on 17 February 1993 and ended two days before the first day of voting. The final and third phase was the voting itself which lasted for three days, starting on 23 April and ending on 25 April 1993. The official results were announced on 28 April 1993.

25. Throughout all three phases, the Referendum Commission faced two major tasks: to make each and every citizen an informed and consciously responsible voter; and to make certain each voter mastered the voting techniques so as to ensure a truly free choice and to thwart fraud.

26. The first task was indeed not easy. The low levels of literacy in a multilingual population produced considerable difficulties of communication and administration. For instance, the Referendum Commission found very few literate Afar speakers to be its officials.

27. Furthermore, for a long time Eritreans had been excluded from decision-making on central issues and deprived of direct participation as "conscious voters" in elections. This absence of electoral practice presented an additional challenge to creating informed and knowledgeable voters.

28. Organizationally, the consequences of three decades of conflict further complicated the work of creating institutions to carry out the elections and inform voters on voting procedures. The lack of a reliable census, the absence of a civil register and, hence, of an electoral register, and the scarcity of persons qualified in conducting elections were among the obstacles to fulfilling this task.

1. Registration

29. The Eritrean Referendum Proclamation made the Referendum Commission responsible for "verifying the identity and eligibility of the people of Eritrea, residing in Eritrea or abroad, who may wish to participate in the referendum". According to the Proclamation, any person having Eritrean citizenship and who was of the age of 18 years or older or attained that age at any time during the registration period, was qualified to be a voter. The general conditions for qualifying as an Eritrean citizen were defined in the Nationality Proclamation issued by the Provisional Government of Eritrea on 6 April 1992. For verifying the identity or eligibility of citizens, the Referendum Commission relied on the investigations and decisions of the Department of Internal Affairs. The Commission therefore registered as a voter any person eligible under the Referendum Proclamation who possessed a citizen's identity card issued by the Department.

30. Registration was extended from 22 February to 1 March 1993 in order to process a backlog of 2,000 Eritrean nationals wishing to register. Overall, a total of 1.1 million Eritreans registered to vote: 861,074 persons in Eritrea, 154,136 persons in the Sudan, 66,022 in Ethiopia, 43,765 in Saudi Arabia and 76,000 in all other countries combined. These countries included Djibouti, Germany, India, Kuwait, Qatar, the United Arab Emirates and the United States of America.

31. Of Eritrea's estimated population of 3 million to 3.5 million, 50 per cent are under the minimum voting age of 18 years. Accordingly, there were only 1.5 million to 1.75 million eligible Eritreans from which the eventual electorate of 1.1 million voters were registered. In addition, the relative remoteness of some regions, and traditional restrictions against public activities for women in some places, may also have reduced the number of people taking part in the referendum.

32. The presence of UNOVER and other international observers helped to deal with some problems of cultural practices. For example, upon receiving reports that some women in the Gash and Setit province had been forbidden to register by their male relatives, a UNOVER team raised the issue in a visit to the area. Eventually, the UNOVER team was informed that women there would be allowed to register from then on.

33. As part of the verification of the registration campaign, UNOVER asked the Referendum Commission about the status of participants in the Referendum of certain prisoners awaiting trial for collaboration with the Ethiopian authorities during the war. The Referendum Commission immediately took up the matter with the Department of Internal Affairs. It was subsequently understood that all such prisoners who had not been tried and convicted would be provided with registration cards and be allowed to exercise their right to vote in the Referendum. Shortly thereafter, UNOVER Regional Coordinators were invited to visit the prisons, in order to interview prisoners in this category awaiting trial and to ensure that they had been registered to vote. A number of these visits by the three Regional Offices confirmed that this class of prisoners had indeed registered, and would be able to vote in prison. The UNOVER observers were informed that 462 prisoners in Senbel and Hazhaz prisons at Asmara City were registered. This constituted an important and successful assertion by UNOVER of a fundamental electoral principle.

34. The members of the Eritrean Popular Liberation Army (EPLA) registered directly in barracks, whether in the main provinces such as Asmara, Mendefera, Barentu and Afabet, or in numerous small villages close to the frontiers, like Sirdaka, Forto, Tessenei and Ghirmaika. In agreement with UNOVER, the Referendum Commission decided to authorize EPLA members to cast their vote one week prior to the official Referendum days, since most of them had to be deployed for duty during those days. It was also agreed that observers would be present during this exceptional voting and that ballot boxes would be kept sealed until 7 p.m. of 25 April 1993, the last regular day of the referendum. UNOVER observers were present at the voting in the barracks at Asmara, Mendefera and Keren.

35. The Referendum Commission also made special arrangements to register those freedom fighters, not belonging to EPLA, who were at their duty stations. They numbered 79,295 of the 861,074 registered voters in Eritrea.

36. On the basis of UNOVER observation, the registration campaign was conducted smoothly, notwithstanding that nationality identification was simultaneous with the registration of eligible voters. In conducting the registration, those Commission representatives encountered by UNOVER observers acted with due impartiality.

2. *Referendum campaign*

37. The referendum campaign officially began on 17 February 1993, and ended on 21 April, two days before the first polling day. All interested parties were urged to freely organize, form movements, and assemble and express their views for or against the independence of Eritrea without hindrance or intimidation. To that end, three groups registered with the Referendum Commission to campaign in favour of independence: the National Union of Eritrean Women, the National Union of Eritrean Youth, and the National Union of Eritrean Workers. No organization registered to campaign for a "no" vote.

38. During the last several weeks preceding the polling days, political rallies were observed in the form of gatherings, festivities, concerts and dances. It was reported and observed that members of EPLF had been campaigning throughout Eritrea, often travelling in small groups around the countryside.

39. For its part, the Referendum Commission's efforts at this time were devoted to a civic education campaign. Thus, the primary purpose of the Publicity and Information Board of the Referendum Commission during this period was to explain voting procedures and techniques to as many of the electorate as possible. A significant effort was devoted to producing public education materials: 800,000 posters in four main languages; voter manuals of which 10,000 were printed in Arabic and Tigrigna; and videos for television in nine languages. The media, schools, youth and women's associations, and a touring theatre group also disseminated information. Ten mobile teams of two to three persons travelled to remote areas of the country where there was no access to the media.

40. Although the media consisted of one newspaper, published twice weekly, one television station and one radio, coverage of the referendum process was thorough. The wider outreach of the national radio station, broadcasting in Arabic and Tigrigna, made it the most effective medium. The referendum comprehensive education programme, including a question-and-answer portion, was aired every day in Arabic and Tigrigna for 10 minutes in each language. There was a transmission three days a week at Kunama and Tigre, also for 10 minutes each. Television in Eritrea has three weekly broadcasts of three hours each. The Referendum Commission was allotted 10 minutes in each broadcast.

41. With respect to free access to the media and equal allocation of resources among the campaigning parties, UNOVER received no reports of complaints, nor did it observe any flagrant violations. In the absence of opposing parties, the relevance of equal allocation of time to the impartiality of the process was rather limited.

42. Voting simulations were undertaken throughout Eritrea. Their degree of sophistication varied according to the people's level of understanding. In remote, rural areas, the programme was usually limited to the basic

essential information, such as the meaning of the "red" and the "blue" ballots, and practice voting. At the same time, in other areas, voters were taught about such issues as absentee ballots and tender ballots. Community leaders, village elders, youth volunteers and other civilian groups were visibly involved in civic education campaigns.

3. Voting procedure

43. A total of 1,560,000 ballot papers were printed, numbered, perforated and bound for official use. UNOVER observers made frequent visits to the printing press to verify that the preparation of ballots was lawful and procedurally correct.

44. The ballot paper was printed on opaque brown paper to enhance the privacy of the vote. It had three detachable segments. The first two parts were red and the last blue. The first portion was numbered and retained by the second officer as a control measure to guard against repeat voting. The second red portion was a negative vote and the third blue portion was for an affirmative vote. Inside the private booth, voters made their choice and detached one portion from the other. The portion of the ballot paper corresponding to the choice made by the voter was deposited in the ballot box. The remaining portion was deposited inside the booth in a cardboard "trash" box. The contents of this box were emptied out at the end of each of three polling days and burned along with the voter registration cards.

45. Forty-five persons received instruction as polling officer trainers at Asmara. Using the multiplier training methodology they, in turn, trained 6,000 polling station officials for the provinces.

46. Two polling officials were in charge of each electoral table. The first officer verified that the potential voter possessed an orange voter-registration card and was on the electoral roll. Both officers carried out cross-check and double vote control procedures. Finally, the second officer received the voter-registration card and supplied the voter with a ballot paper.

47. The building of polling stations—mat huts called "agnets" constructed from local materials—had been completed in most provinces by the beginning of April. In the cities, the polling station sites were identified in administrative offices, schools and other appropriate buildings, and structural changes necessary for the polling stations were made. In the provinces of Barka, Gash and Setit and Sahel, there was some delay in building the polling stations. In the coastal areas of Semhar province, a hurricane in mid-April completely destroyed 60 per cent to 70 per cent of the polling stations. However, new "agnets" were built or other alternative arrangements were made before polling began.

III. Referendum

48. All necessary electoral materials left Asmara in early April for the respective destinations in Eritrea and abroad. Inadequate transportation and communications had to be overcome in achieving their delivery on time.

49. For the actual voting, a total of 1,012 polling stations were set up by province:

Achele Guzai	157
Asmara	146
Barca	87
Dankalia	47
Gash and Setit	91
Hamasien	104
Sahel	59
Semhar	44
Senhit	120
Serae	157

50. On 22 April 1993, the Secretary-General's Special Representative and the Referendum Commissioner officially announced the beginning of the referendum. The referendum took place on 23, 24 and 25 April 1993. The polling stations stayed opened from 7 a.m. to 7 p.m.

51. During the three days of the referendum, UNOVER teams covered almost all of the 1,012 polling stations. The number of polling stations visited in the Asmara region was 351 (96 per cent coverage); in the Keren region, 278 (88 per cent coverage); and in the Mendefera region, 257 (84 per cent coverage). Some of the polling stations were visited more than once, especially in the urban areas.

52. On 27 April, the Referendum Commission announced the official provisional results of the referendum. Total number of registered voters was 1,174,654. Of these, 1,154,001 participated in the referendum voting, constituting voter turnout of 98.24 per cent.

53. Of those who cast their votes, 1,098,015 voted "yes", 1,825 voted "no", 323 votes were invalid and 53,838 were cast by tendered ballots. This revealed that 99.805 per cent of those who participated in the vote had voted for independence and only 0.17 per cent voted against independence.

54. Reports of UNOVER observers indicated that, in general, the referendum was well organized and conducted in an orderly and smooth manner. The officials of the Referendum Commission were present, without exception, and there were no essential electoral materials missing in the polling stations. No cases of intimidation were reported or observed. The secrecy of the vote was generally respected although the lack of electoral practice created some minor procedural difficulties.

55. Also, it was reported that in certain polling stations the ballots were counted on the evening of 24 April, before the end of the referendum. Appropriate corrective measures were suggested by UNOVER and taken by the Referendum Commission. These incidents did not, however, affect the outcome of the vote.

56. On the basis of the information and observations of UNOVER, on 27 April 1993, the Secretary-General's Special Representative officially announced that "On the whole, the referendum process in Eritrea can be considered to have been free and fair at every stage, and that it has been conducted to my satisfaction".

IV. Activities of the United Nations Observer Mission to verify the referendum in Eritrea

A. Regional activities

57. The electoral teams from the three regional offices of UNOVER, based at Asmara, Keren and Mendefera, made visits to polling station sites in their respective regions of responsibility. The purpose of these visits was:

(a) To develop and maintain an effective working relationship with the local authorities and the local population;

(b) To observe and verify the final stage of the registration campaign, and the distribution of citizen identification cards and voter registration cards;

(c) To verify the information provided by the Referendum Commission on the names and locations of the polling stations, and on the number of registered voters;

(d) To observe and verify voter education and the political campaigns;

(e) To assess road conditions and logistical needs for UNOVER observers during the last phase of the referendum;

(f) To prepare plans, road maps and itineraries for the deployment of UNOVER observers during the polling days.

58. The provinces of Asmara, Dankalia, Hamasien and Semhar constituted the region of responsibility under the Asmara Regional Office. The office was consistently staffed with four officers, including one Regional Coordinator. Of the total of 365 polling stations located in the region, 335 were visited by UNOVER electoral teams, constituting a coverage of 92 per cent.

59. The Keren Regional Office had under its responsibility the western provinces of Barka, Gash and Setit, and Senhit, as well as the province of Sahel. The office was also staffed with four officers, including the Regional Coordinator. Each team member was assigned a province of responsibility, whereby he/she was expected to draw up the deployment plan for the observers during the referendum days. Of the total 339 polling stations located in the region, 216 were visited by Keren teams, constituting a coverage of 64 per cent.

60. The Mendefera Regional Office was responsible for the provinces of Achele Guzai and Serae. The office was initially staffed with three electoral officers. At the end of March, an additional member joined the team. Of the total 210 polling station sites in the region, 113 were visited by UNOVER electoral teams, constituting a coverage of 54 per cent, or 80 per cent of the accessible polling stations.

61. The UNOVER observers combed through the provinces, visited polling station sites, assessed road conditions, prepared detailed directions and planned travel itineraries for the observers of the final phase. Particularly hazardous areas, owing to poor surface conditions or land mines, were identified and duly reported. In many parts of Eritrea, road conditions are poor even for the use of four-wheel-drive vehicles. In the absence of up-to-date maps, observers relied heavily on local assistance and self-drawn maps.

62. The UNOVER observers maintained constant dialogue with members of the local authorities, including the Governors of all 10 provinces, sub-province administrators, administrators and village administrators. Observers met regularly with the local representatives of the Referendum Commission to discuss the various aspects of the referendum preparations. These meetings were held in an informal and cooperative atmosphere, which allowed the parties to discuss freely issues of significance to the referendum and to UNOVER. These local contacts were effective in conveying the purpose of the UNOVER mission, as well as in learning about the developments in the field with respect to the preparation for the referendum.

63. The UNOVER observers also made extensive contacts with the local population, which enhanced the latter's understanding of the referendum and the UNOVER mission. The most common encounters were with elders who usually came forward as the village representatives to speak with the observers. Many were aware that the United Nations had been invited to verify the referendum, and expressed their sincere welcome of UNOVER in that role.

64. The Secretary-General's Special Representative travelled to all UNOVER regional office sites, as well as to the towns of Agordat, Massawa and Assab. He was welcomed with great enthusiasm everywhere, particularly at Keren, where he was received by over 100,000 people from the town and the surrounding villages. In these areas, his visit symbolized the return of the United Nations to the region in a renewed and helpful role. This was especially important for winning over those with

another impression of the United Nations from the 1950s and 1960s when Eritrea became first a part of the Ethiopian Federation, and then its province. Indeed, throughout Eritrea, UNOVER observers were extended an overwhelming popular welcome, and noted a positive reversal in the public perception of the United Nations.

65. UNOVER actively participated in sharpening the sense of free and fair choice among potential voters. This was emphasized during all public visits of the UNOVER Chief and other officers. A prevailing feature of UNOVER involvement in the education campaign was the teaching of the concept of every citizen's right to vote and of one vote per citizen. It also highlighted the secrecy of the vote as a basic principle of a democratic system. Certain groups of voters wondered about the need for the secrecy of the vote, and whenever possible and appropriate, UNOVER teams explained its significance and necessity.

B. Overseas activities

66. In an official communication to UNOVER, the Referendum Commission reaffirmed its commitment to facilitate and guarantee the return home of all eligible voters. Nevertheless, many voters remained abroad and the UNOVER mandate also included observation of the voting process for them. Accordingly, UNOVER conducted two large-scale operations in Ethiopia and the Sudan. Other overseas polling sites, for example, in Egypt, Iraq, Kuwait and Saudi Arabia, were monitored by observers from United Nations agencies, United Nations Information Centres, the diplomatic community and non-governmental organizations. In Saudi Arabia and the other countries, arrangements to conduct polls were made in consultations between the government and local United Nations representatives.

67. The registration of voters had progressed smoothly at Addis Ababa, and was completed by early April. Identification and registration cards were distributed after experiencing some delays, but without any reports of complaints or known cases of fraud. Of 63,803 voters registered to vote in Ethiopia, 40,278 registered at Addis Ababa. The procedure for tendered ballots applied to overseas polling stations as well as within Eritrea, thus allowing voters registered in Ethiopia to vote at a polling station in Eritrea.

68. The referendum campaign was also carried out in Ethiopia, although in a relatively low-profile manner. At Addis Ababa, radio programmes broadcast voting procedures and other pertinent information. Posters explaining the referendum were observed in certain areas of Addis Ababa. No organizations publicly conducted political rallies either in favour of or against Eritrean independence.

69. For the voting in Ethiopia, UNOVER organized 10 teams to observe 202 polling stations. With the willing cooperation of all parties involved, 20 observers coordinated by the Economic Commission for Africa (ECA) were deployed from ECA, the United Nations Development Programme (UNDP), the United Nations Children's Fund (UNICEF) and the World Food Programme (WFP). The operation was coordinated by the Chief of the Administration Division of ECA. During the first week of April, a training seminar was organized and given at Addis Ababa by UNOVER core staff based at Asmara.

70. In the Sudan, 12 teams were planned to observe 335 polling stations located in five separate areas of the Sudan. Twenty-four observers were fielded in these teams with the cooperation and logistical support of United Nations agencies, in particular considerable assistance from the Office of the United Nations High Commissioner for Refugees (UNHCR) and UNDP, and from diplomatic missions at Khartoum. The Director of the United Nations Information Centre at Khartoum coordinated the preparatory aspects of the operation, and a UNOVER core staff member was appointed to oversee the observer operation during the polling days. In both Ethiopia and the Sudan, these activities coordinated by UNOVER helped to create a peaceful environment for the safe and smooth conduct of the voting.

71. In other countries where the referendum was to take place, the polling days were scheduled on different dates, as indicated by the following examples:

Australia	24-25 April 1993
Djibouti	17 April 1993
Germany	24 April 1993
India	18 April 1993
Kuwait	23 April 1993
New Zealand	24-25 April 1993
Nordic countries	17-18 April 1993
Qatar	23 April 1993
Saudi Arabia	24-25 April 1993
United Arab Emirates	16 April 1993
United States of America	24 April 1993
Yemen:	
Sanaa and El Kouka	16-18 April 1993
Taiz	16 April 1993
Houdaida	17-18 April 1993

C. Coordination with independent observers

72. At the invitation of the Referendum Commission, international observers from around the world arrived in Eritrea a few days before the referendum. These observers were to operate independently of UNOVER, and represented Governments, regional organizations,

non-governmental organizations and other organizations. They included delegations from the Organization of African Unity (OAU), the non-aligned countries, the European Community (EC) and the League of Arab States. With the UNOVER observers, the total number of international observers in Eritrea exceeded 300.

73. UNOVER cooperated closely with the independent observers, and in particular with OAU, which had sent a preparatory mission to Asmara in early April in order to coordinate activities with UNOVER. The Secretary-General authorized United Nations support for 15 OAU observers of the Eritrean referendum, although they were to remain entirely independent from UNOVER operationally.

74. Cooperation with the independent observers included coordination of deployment plans and exchanges of information. There was also discussion of evaluation standards for the referendum so as to avoid inconsistent criteria that might impair the credibility of international observation. It was agreed that one of the common objectives of international observers should be to give Eritreans confidence in a free, fair and impartial referendum.

D. *Coordination with national observers*

75. National observers were elected or appointed by community residents to watch over the impartiality of the voting process during the polling days. They were placed inside and outside the polling stations. Village elders and other community leaders were common among those selected. They were trained by the Referendum Commission and were supported by the "Citizens Referendum Monitoring Group". This was a national non-governmental organization committed to ensuring a free, fair and impartial referendum through a network of national observers. UNOVER was invited to attend the training seminars for national observers.

76. The main objective of the national observers was to monitor the voting process, and to point out any irregularities or anomalies that might arise from voters' unfamiliarity with the referendum. The national observers, as individuals of acknowledged standing in their respective villages, also verified the legitimacy of individual voters when questioned, and acted as impartial advisers. In addition, before the referendum, they were among the most important civic educators on the voting process. It is estimated that more than 2,000 national observers attended the referendum during the polling days. UNOVER observers exchanged information with the national observers during the referendum days, and cooperated with them to ensure smooth conduct of the polling.

E. *Coordination within the United Nations system*

77. Considerable importance was given to the early establishment of a unified United Nations presence in Eritrea through close contact among the various United Nations agencies based at Asmara. The Secretary-General's Special Representative reported that the local authorities welcomed this coordination. They hoped especially that this would lead to an active United Nations role in post-conflict peace-building in Eritrea as well as elsewhere in the region.

V. Financial arrangements

78. The Eritrean contribution to the Referendum Commission's budget amounted to US$ 480,000, accrued through a combination of funds made available by the Provisional Government, fund-raising events, and public donations.

79. Multilateral funds were channelled through the UNDP/indicative planning figure cost-sharing project, "Support for the Eritrea Referendum". Total contributions both in cash and in kind amounted to about US$ 4.3 million. In addition, US$ 171,698 was made available through a fund established by non-governmental organizations from Ireland, the Netherlands and the United Kingdom.

80. Australia, Belgium, Canada, Denmark, France, Germany, Ireland, Italy, Netherlands, Norway, South Korea, Spain, Sweden, Switzerland, the United Kingdom, the European Community and UNDP, provided equipment, training and technical assistance. In particular, Norway generously contributed three of the four satellite terminals which constituted UNOVER's major communication equipment.

81. UNOVER itself was estimated to cost a total of US$ 3 million. Thanks in part to those contributions, the actual cost was less than US$ 2 million.

VI. Concluding observations

82. UNOVER was given a clearly defined mandate which remained essentially unchanged. This mandate was carried out on time and well within the estimated budget. Neither the difficulties of establishing and explaining voting techniques, nor logistical problems, became insurmountable obstacles. The success of UNOVER came from: a coordinated United Nations presence, reliance upon local resources, the Eritreans' commitment to support the referendum process, the cooperation of Eritrea's neighbouring countries, and the support and contributions of Member States and international and non-governmental organizations. I wish to pay warm tribute to all concerned in the preparation and execution of the very successful mission of UNOVER.

Particular appreciation is due to my Special Representative, Mr. Samir Sanbar, for his skilful leadership of UNOVER. Above all, however, the Observer Mission's accomplishment was made possible by the Eritrean people's own voluntary decision to make popular participation a foundation of their political system. The United Nations stands proud to have helped them in carrying out this decision so effectively and in peace.

83. Eritrea has much still to do in building on this achievement. Three quarters of Eritrea's population today is partly dependent on food aid. Over 500,000 refugees returning to Eritrea from the neighbouring countries must be rehabilitated. After being damaged by three decades of protracted conflict, Eritrea's infrastructure needs to be rebuilt. In facing these multiple challenges, Eritrea will require the active cooperation and assistance of the United Nations and an uninterrupted period of peace and harmony in the surrounding region.

84. It is, therefore, particularly gratifying that Ethiopia was one of the very first countries to recognize Eritrea's independence, opening the way to its membership in the international community. On 28 May 1993, the Eritrean flag was raised for the first time at the United Nations, and Eritrea was welcomed as the 182nd State Member of the United Nations. The determination of Ethiopia and Eritrea to work together in meeting the challenges of the future is a source of great encouragement and a bright omen for the region.

Document 40

Statement dated 30 September 1993 by the President of Eritrea at the 48th session of the United Nations General Assembly

Not issued as a United Nations document

Mr. President,

Let me begin by congratulating you upon your election to the presidency of the 48th session of the General Assembly.

Mr. President,
Distinguished Delegates,

I feel special privilege and honor to address the General Assembly of the United Nations on behalf of a people who struggled for half a century to regain their fundamental human and national rights and who, despite the outright military victory that they won, took the unprecedented step of organizing a free and fair referendum, so as to join the community of independent states on the basis of their freely expressed wish and on solid legal grounds.

As I speak here today, I cannot help but remember the appeals that we sent year in and out to this Assembly and the member countries of the United Nations, describing the plight of our people and asking for legitimate sympathy, support and recognition. We appealed to the United Nations not only in its capacity as a representative of the international community, but also because of its special responsibility to Eritrea. For it was the United Nations that decided in 1950, at the beginning of the Cold War, to deny the colonized people of Eritrea their right to self-determination, thereby sacrificing their national and human rights on the altar of the strategic interests of the superpowers.

In passing that resolution, the UN affirmed that it "remained an international instrument" which the General Assembly "could be seized of" at anytime. But for the next 41 years, as a brutal war of aggression was conducted against the Eritrean people, initially with the active support of the United States and later with a much worse and massive involvement of the Soviet Union, and despite the repeated appeals of the Eritrean people, the United Nations refused to raise its voice in the defense of a people whose future it had unjustly decided and whom it pledged to protect. Not once in 41 years did Eritrea, scene of the longest war in Africa, and victim of some of the grossest violations of human rights, figure in the agenda of the United Nations.

This deafening silence pained our people. It also gave a free hand to the aggressors, thereby prolonging our suffering and increasing the sacrifices we had to pay. But it neither shook our resolve nor undermined our belief in the justness of our cause and the inevitability of our victory. As an Eritrean proverb says, "The rod of truth may become thinner but it cannot be broken." Indeed, justice has finally prevailed. This is a source of hope and happiness not only for the Eritrean people, but for all those who cherish justice and peace.

Mr. President,

While we rejoice at the peace and freedom that has been attained and the promising prospects that lie ahead, we are confronted with the reality of a devastated country and population. The extent of physical and economic destruction visited on our country (in terms of infrastructure, industry, agriculture, education, health services) as well as the more harmful human losses (death of over 150,000 people, exile of a quarter of the population, massive displacement, over 100,000 disabled and orphaned) are appalling by any standard, especially when measured against the meagre resources and small size of our population.

Formidable as our problems are, we are confident that we can and will rebuild our devastated country and provide for a decent life for ourselves. It is our firm conviction that outside assistance, no matter how generous, cannot of itself, solve our problems. Ultimately, deliverance will depend on our own efforts, on the mobilization and efficient utilization of our resources. But as we start to clear the rubble and pick the pieces after three decades of war and destruction, we find that our resources are too limited for the awesome task of rehabilitation and jump-starting our economy. We cannot help but ask: Will the United Nations and the international community come to our assistance this time or will our pleas once again go unheeded?

At this critical juncture of our history, Eritrea needs and deserves international support and assistance, not only because the United Nations and the international community bear special responsibility for Eritrea, but also because it is a test case for the United Nations' Agenda for Peace and the whole concept of peacebuilding. Eritrea has not only secured peace and stability, it has made the rare achievement of establishing warm relations of cooperation with its former enemy, Ethiopia. And it is tackling the task of reconstruction with popular support and participation, with commitment and determination, with sound and flexible policies, with prudent and efficient utilization of limited resources, with a demonstrated readiness to promote regional understanding and cooperation.

Unfortunately, the response of the United Nations and the international community so far has not been encouraging. UN contributions to the Eritrean referendum—one of the most successful electoral processes that the UN has been involved in—was less than 2 million dollars, a meager sum compared to the tens of millions of dollars devoted to similar exercises, many of which were dismal failures. Similarly, the response of the international community to the program for the repatriation of half a million Eritrea refugees from the Sudan fell far short of reasonable expectation and the Government has found no alternative but to start the program regardless of funds and expected problems. Eritrea has also embarked on a crucial demobilization program—it has demobilized close to one third of its 90,000 army in the first phase—without UN or other contribution. It had to cut back some of its rehabilitation and development projects and borrow money to finance this first phase.

In our efforts at mobilizing international resources, we have repeatedly come up with explanations of "lack of funds", "competing demands","more pressing priorities" and "donor fatigue". There well may be some truth in all of this. And we are appreciative of the constraints and commendable efforts of some donors. But, I believe, we cannot and should not hesitate from acknowledging that, by and large, the international aid programme is deeply flawed, unfair and unjust, ill-structured to respond to the vital needs of recipient communities. Assistance and amounts of assistance appear to be decided not on the basis of needs or capacity to use the assistance to good use, but—even after the proclamation of the end of the cold war—on the basis of the interests and agendas of donors. Moreover, the international community tends to be more responsive to putting out fires than preventing them, and once fires are put out it often turns its back on the smouldering combustible remains.

Mr. President,
Honorable Delegates,

One of the most disquieting features of the present international situation is the marginalization of the entire continent of Africa. Every indicator shows that Africa is sliding back and being left behind, resulting in intolerable poverty, suffering and desperation for millions of its people. There is no denying that the onus of the responsibility for these problems falls first and foremost on us Africans. But, I believe, the international community must squarely face the fact that it also bears responsibility for Africa's plight. Many of the dictators who have sown so much havoc and suffering were in fact brought to power and sustained during the years of the cold war by sections of the international community. Perhaps more significant, the now discredited economic policies and the failed projects were generally designed, and approved of, by international donors and implemented under the direction an army of foreign experts and advisors.

In our present highly interlinked world, Africa's marginalization, the poverty and desperation of its people, of its youth, cannot be walled within the continent's boundaries. It is bound to threaten global prosperity and stability. The frustration and resentment that continues to swell and may well explode must be defused in time. Once again, it is Africa that must seize its own destiny. Its people and leaders must tap deep into their human and material resources and come up with the wisdom, strategy and commitment to lift up Africa from the mire. But as they embark on this difficult road, the international community needs to come to their assistance, not with hand outs that only increase dependency, not with the familiar packages and projects that have gone down the drain, not with pre-conceived formulas and attitudes of "We know what is best", but in a spirit of partnership dedicated to helping Africa to stand on its own feet and contribute to the enrichment of human life and protection of the environment.

Of course, not everything in Africa has been bleak. Just as gross human failure is not limited to Africa—witness events in Bosnia-Hercogovina, the former Soviet Union and elsewhere—Africa has its share of positive and uplifting developments and successes. We are following with much interest the determined and promising efforts of several African countries, both on an individual country level and within a regional context. Despite the neglect and inequities of the international community, many African peoples are making a determined assault on poverty and social injustice. In our part of the continent, Eritrea and Ethiopia have already started mutually beneficial economic cooperation and together with the other countries of the Horn, are working to set up a regional mechanism to foster peace and cooperation. We strongly believe all of the many positive developments in Africa should be duly recognized.

Mr. President,
Honorable Delegates,

In view of the positive developments in the Horn Africa, the tragedy that has gripped Somalia has been profoundly disturbing. As the bloodletting among our Somali brothers assumed harrowing proportions, and at a time when many were hesitating, we strongly advocated the constructive intervention of the international community, under the umbrella of the United Nations, to save lives and help extricate Somalia from the destruction it was heading for. Despite our opposition, in principle, to external military intervention, we realized early on that the extraordinary situation in Somalia demanded extraordinary measures.

It was, therefore, with great relief that we welcomed the decision of the United States Administration to intervene in Somalia. Encouraged, we sought—individually and in conjunction with our regional partners—to ensure that the intervention be guided by clear and comprehensive security, humanitarian and political objectives. And we did not hesitate to share our views on the size, type and stay of the intervention force needed for the success of the mission. But unfortunately, our views were not heeded, although we were, and still are, better placed to understand and work in the realities of neighbouring Somalia.

Be that as it may, we do recognize and appreciate the achievements of the international intervention in Somalia. The improvement of the humanitarian situation and the March 1993 Addis Ababa Accords on national reconciliation are major steps forward. At the same time, the worsening security situation in Mogadishu and the increasing toll in civilian lives, including women and children, have cast a long shadow on the Somali intervention. Repeated mistakes in handling the situation have led some people to openly call for an immediate end to the intervention.

It is our conviction that a precipitate withdrawal of the United States troops—which we strongly warned against from the beginning—will not only signal a lack of US commitment to the intervention, but it will eventually make the position of UNOSOM untenable. This will plunge Somalia into a catastrophe much worse than the anarchy that prompted the intervention in the first place. We, therefore, urge the United States and the international community at large to stay the course in Somalia and to shoulder their responsibility to the Somali people at the hour of their greatest need. We also urge them to review, frankly and dispassionately, the intervention to date, build up on successes and achievements, and more importantly admit and correct mistakes.

We sincerely believe that the countries of the region, whose role has so far been deliberately or otherwise neglected, can make a constructive contribution to the international effort. Consulting them informally, every once in a while, as has been the case in the past is clearly not enough. They need to become part of the process in a more meaningful and formalized way, as it concerns and affects them directly and more than anyone outside the Region.

Mr. President,
Honorable Delegates,

The advent of the new State of Eritrea happily coincided with the end of the cold war, the era of superpower rivalry that caused so much human misery and led to the virtual paralysis of the United Nations. Like the rest of humanity, we place much hope on the new era, on the prospects of an enhanced role for the United Nations, a role that would make it truly representative of "We, the peoples of the world". And yet, we have no illusions that a new, just and equitable world order has dawned on us. We see too many old habits and practices to entertain any illusions—inside the United Nations and outside it. In as much as we hope for successes, we see that the failures of the UN initiatives far outnumber any of its successes. Injustice endures within nations and between nations.

We are awed by the challenges that continue to face humanity and are deeply aware of our minuscule capabilities. Still, Eritrea is determined to make its own small contribution to the betterment of human life, in its own corner of the world.

Thank you.

Document 41

Formulating the master plan for rehabilitation, reconstruction and development of Eritrea: A report by the United Nations Economic Commission for Africa, the United Nations Development Programme and the Department of Humanitarian Affairs (excerpt)

October 1993

Executive summary

Following the discussions in Geneva (at the Joint Government of Eritrea and United Nations Appeal for Eritrea, Pledging Conference, 6 July 1993) between H.E. Issaias Afwerki, President of the State of Eritrea, and the UNECA Executive Secretary, and further to their discussions during the Summit of Head of States and Governments of the member countries of IGADD in Addis Ababa (6 and 7 September 1993), the President of the State of Eritrea requested UNECA to send a Mission to Eritrea to help prepare a Master Plan for the Rehabilitation, Reconstruction and Development of Eritrea. The UNECA Executive Secretary decided to send a Reconnaissance mission to Asmara from the 14 to 21 September 1993.

The objectives of the mission were based on: the necessity of maintaining a continuum between Rehabilitation, Reconstruction and Development in order to ensure the appropriate link between the short, medium and long term in the development process of the country; the necessity to maintain a continuum from national to sub-regional and regional in the development process of Eritrea which future is closely linked to the Horn of Africa as the window to the Middle East and to the African continent as a whole, in fact, it is necessary for Eritrea to search for economic cooperation and integration within the spirit of the Abuja Treaty establishing the Pan-African Economic Community; the necessity of achieving a decentralization of the economic development process from national level to regional or provincial, with the aim of involving the whole population especially at the grass-roots level; UNECA was also of the view that, in order for the donor community to see the interface which exists between the different blocks constituting the national economic and social development programme of Eritrea, there must be a Master Plan which can also serve as a coordinating instrument for the implementation of such national programme. The other equally important objective is to develop an institutional capacity able to translate medium and long term visions into immediate actions; to support the on-going relief efforts; to coordinate short-term relief, and rehabilitation, reconstruction and development efforts so as to ensure consistency with long term goals and objectives; and to provide a local permanent technical expertise for follow-up and coordination. Over the last year or more a number of efforts have been made by different bilateral and multilateral donors, UN Agencies and other international organizations to identify the areas of need in different sectors of the economy. At present, as indicated by the UNDP, there are plans for a number of technical missions to be fielded. These missions will look into the areas of needs assessment for the rehabilitation, reconstruction and development of Eritrea. A coordinated effort for rehabilitation, reconstruction and development requires an umbrella that should take the individual efforts and integrate them in a meaningful manner, to bring these efforts together in a manner so as to avoid duplication, unnecessary overlapping of suggestions, recommendations and operations, and contradictory course of actions which some of the future operations may entail. The objective of the UNECA/UNDP/DHA mission to Eritrea was to prepare the groundwork and draw up a framework for long-term reconstruction and rehabilitation, planning in an independent Eritrea. The purpose of the mission, therefore, was to: (a) Establish the scope of work that would be required for long-term rehabilitation, reconstruction and development planning process in the country; (b) Establish the modalities and time frame for implementing, directing, monitoring, and coordinating the exercise by the Eritrean authorities in collaboration with UNECA/UNDP/DHA; (c) Establish the modalities for a Eritrean-lead and UNECA/UNDP/DHA supported continuous consultative process which will involve all parties interested in providing assistance to the country for reconstruction and rehabilitation.

The final goal of UNECA mission was, therefore, to help the Eritrean authorities formulate such a Master Plan as UNECA was convinced that the Master Plan must be *owned* by Eritreans themselves.

The present report is the result of the work undertaken by the mission. It provides a layout and the plan of operation for the formulation of the Master Plan. It also presents a consultative process to facilitate coordination between the international organization, bilateral donors, the international NGOs and the Eritreans for the preparation of the Master Plan. The report also proposes a methodology and format as well as a timetable for the preparation of the Master Plan.

The report proposes that the planning exercise be pursued under the auspices and overall guidance of the (projected) Planning Unit at the President's Office which will act as an umbrella and coordinating organization for all the national programmes being assisted by the UN system and international (bilateral and NGOs) community in Eritrea.

The Planning Unit in the Office of the President should assume principal responsibility for the preparation of the Master Plan based on its own analysis and technical input provided by international organizations and donors (bilateral and NGOs). The Planning Unit by its position should ensure active political participation of the Provinces and since the credibility of the Master Plan will also depend on its acceptance by Eritreans, it should try to receive the broadest possible technical support of Eritreans. The Planning Unit should also assume the overall responsibility for the coordination between donors, international organizations, NGOs and facilitate the interaction between Eritreans and the international community so that Eritreans have voice and receive advice. There is a need for continuous coordination, including assistance in coordinating among NGOs operating in different regions of Eritrea, particularly in the health and education sector; coordination leading to a consistent set of sector and development priorities; coordination in preparing a budgetary framework and resource constraints for missions different sectors.

It is clear that the rehabilitation, reconstruction and development of Eritrea is not waiting for the conclusion of the present planning process before starting. Decisions are being made daily regarding revenue generation and taxation, institutional development, operation and administration of facilities, and the rebuilding of government. Because of its position, the Planning Unit is to assist in making these decisions through position and issue papers that have an immediate impact and lead to immediate actions, while keeping into account the plan priorities. The Planning Unit must also remain abreast of new developments, translate plans into immediate course of actions and project proposals as opportunities arise.

The preparation of the Master Plan is to be directed by a "Steering Committee" made up of representatives of the Ministry of Finance and Development (MFD) and relevant Government Departments, the World Bank, UNDP, UNECA, DHA, the Planning Unit and possible others. The Planning Unit would be the Project office with inputs from and active participation of the members of the "Steering Committee". The central objective of the planning component of the EFMP would be to assist the "Steering Committee" and Planning Unit in making an optimum use of technical assistance provided by the donors including the World Bank, UNDP, UNECA, Italy, and other UN and bilateral donors.

One of the principal features of the proposed planning process will be the effective participation of Eritreans. Any planning must take place with the active participation of those who later will implement the Master Plan and bear its consequences on their lives. The participation of the Eritreans in deciding their future economic development process is indeed essential and a prerequisite to the *Eritrea Ownership of the Master Plan*.

The planning principles should be the general guidelines affecting all aspects of the development of the Master Plan and must be considered as: identifying national programmes to address specific problems as the main framework for coordinating national and international resources, thus putting into practice the principle of the "Programme Approach"; supporting the emergency activities, the decentralization and good governance process; and the efficient public sector management; encouraging the establishment of efficient markets rather than re-establish the command economy of the pre–civil war; promoting the role of private sector and of regional and rural communities' self reliance through an institutional and regulatory framework that supports private initiative and re-enforces the process of privatization already underway; seeking economic and financial sustainability as an important element in defining viable economic development activities by not committing Eritrea to development projects beyond its institutional, technical and financial capacity; encouraging efforts at domestic resource mobilization and ensuring efficient utilization; ensuring that sectoral components are internally consistent; addressing the historic apparent regional imbalances between regions and provinces in their entire natural strengths and their potential in the allocation of resources, reach all regions and involve all segments of society including women (while it is not always efficient to distribute investments equally among regions, a distribution without taking into account certain balance has led to instability and greater loss than would have otherwise been the case); encouraging environmentally sound policies and practices throughout the economy to ensure a balanced and sustainable development; giving preference to projects for which Eritreans are willing to invest and commit their own development and operating funds, so as to reinforce and sustain a sense of Eritrean ownership and to provide a credible indicator of Eritrean priorities; and encouraging the sub-regional and regional cooperation and integration as an element of paramount importance in the development process of Eritrea.

The above principles highlight the common themes that should be pursued in the design of the different segments or building blocks of the Master Plan for Eritrea.

The Master Plan, it is proposed, will comprise eight building blocks or segments. Each segment would tackle the specific issues pertinent to its own tasks. Issues which are not covered by the segment but are considered essential to the planning efforts will be covered by individual experts or by the project coordinator, who will put together the Master Plan's building blocks.

The proposed segments are:
1. Immediate regeneration of the economy;
2. Macroeconomic framework;
3. Decentralization, good governance and institutional development including data base requirements;
4. Agriculture, livestock, fisheries, and environment and soil conversation;
5. Human development, capacity building including gender issues and social services (health, education, etc.);
6. Industry, mining, tourism and commerce;
7. Infrastructure; and
8. Regional cooperation and integration.

This format should be adjusted so as to ensure that the Plan also reflects the essential components and orientations of the CEM and PFP. For each segment, the report provides an overview of the present condition, discussion on the planning objectives, and terms of reference for all the required experts for each sector.

It is, therefore, correct to say that the envisaged Master Plan should provide the coordination mechanism that Eritrea needs for planning its immediate and future rehabilitation, reconstruction and development. This will enable the entire process and available resources for Eritrea to be oriented (utilized) in an efficient way.

The proposed time frame is in part determined by discussions with UNDP and the Government whereby the Master Plan would constitute the basic document for the proposed Donors' Conference on Eritrea in June 1994 which was called for by President Issaias Afwerki in his speech to ECOSOC in July 1993 in Geneva. This could call for completion of the Master Plan by late April 1994. There is no doubt that the proposed time schedule is extremely tight. Nonetheless, it is feasible if one considers that the Plan should reflect information already generated by prior missions and studies and present it in an action oriented way. The Plan should also be conceived as one of the series of rolling plans, each building on the next, with additional information added to annual revisions as they are prepared.

It is clear that the tight schedule is not without risks. In the absence of a constitution, progress in the development of regional or provincial administrative structures may be slow. Therefore, the capacity and interest of the provinces or regions in participating in the planning process may be uncertain. There is also the possibility of delays because of the need to coordinate between some donors and international organizations called upon to provide technical assistance inputs in the preparation of the Master Plan.

While these risks are recognized, they could be considered manageable, if it is agreed and accepted that the Master Plan represents a working document that will be updated and/or adjusted as time goes on, especially since peace and stability prevail in Eritrea, which is an extremely important asset. The alternative of extending the preparation process also carries risks, indicating that short term decisions without consistent macro-framework could forestall options for the future as stressed by the President of the State of Eritrea during the Eritrean Pledging Conference last July in Geneva. We know that development with structural transformation and stabilization programmes are not sustainable without peace, and durable peace is not possible without development with structural transformation and stabilization.

...

Document 42

Letter from Chargé d'affaires a.i. of the Permanent Mission of Eritrea to the United Nations addressed to the Secretary-General of the United Nations concerning UNOVER

A/48/643, 24 November 1993

The Permanent Mission of Eritrea has the honour to draw the attention of the Secretary-General to the report of the Secretary-General on the United Nations Observer Mission to Verify the Referendum in Eritrea (A/48/283), dated 11 August 1993, and the report of the Secretary-General on the work of the Organization (A/48/1), dated 10 September 1993, for certain inaccuracies of fact and observation.

I wish to assure you that the Permanent Mission of Eritrea to the United Nations makes the following observations in good faith and to protect the general credibility of the reports.

The following observations are made regarding A/48/283:

1. Eritreans struggled for their right to self-determination. There was never a time during the struggle in which they declared that they were fighting for a federation, as suggested in the last sentence of paragraph 3. Any such reference is incorrect.

2. Paragraph 5 implies that the newly formed Provisional Government of Eritrea made a commitment to holding a referendum on the future of Eritrea, for the first time, as a result of the London Conference. We wish to point out that the Eritrean People's Liberation Front (EPLF), which formed the Provisional Government, had proposed a referendum in 1980.

3. In paragraph 30, the statement "... 2,000 Eritrean nationals wishing to register" is incorrect. The 2,000 persons are non-Eritrean residents who had duly registered for naturalization with the objective of making them eligible voters in the referendum.

4. The third sentence of paragraph 30 should also include the following countries: Australia, Belgium, Canada, Côte d'Ivoire, Denmark, Egypt, Finland, France, Greece, Iceland, Iraq, Italy, Kenya, Netherlands, Nigeria, Norway, Russian Federation, Sweden, Switzerland, Syrian Arab Republic, Uganda, United Kingdom of Great Britain and Northern Ireland, United Republic of Tanzania, Yemen, Zambia and Zimbabwe. They were omitted from the report.

5. In the first and second sentences of paragraph 31, the realistic figures are 60-65 per cent, not 50 per cent, and 1.1 to 1.3 million, not 1.5 to 1.75. These figures are borne out by accurate statistical evidence collected by the Referendum Commission of Eritrea.

6. In connection with the first sentence of paragraph 33, we wish to elaborate that the Referendum Commission informed UNOVER that the Government was already committed to allowing all political and non-political prisoners who had not yet been convicted by a lawfully recognized court of law to vote. This in effect makes the third sentence unnecessary.

7. In paragraph 35, the figure cited represents the actual combatants and not the freedom fighters serving in a civilian capacity.

8. In paragraph 38, we feel that it is worth qualifying the second sentence by stating that members of EPLF had been campaigning as ordinary citizens, in an individual capacity, not representing EPLF and bearing no arms, often travelling in small groups around the countryside.

9. In paragraph 40, the second sentence should include Afar, Kunama and Tigre, because the radio broadcast in those languages also.

10. In the fourth sentence of paragraph 64, the words "when Eritrea became first a part of the Ethiopian Federation" might lead to the understanding that Ethiopia had been a federal State. We believe that "when Eritrea was first federated with Ethiopia" would better explain the point made in that regard.

The following observations are made regarding A/48/1:

1. There are two factual errors in the first sentence of paragraph 466. The "25 years of civil war" should actually read "30 years of war".

2. It is to be recalled that the substance of the second sentence of that paragraph was the cause of a protracted diplomatic intercourse between the United Nations and the then Provisional Government of Eritrea. Considering the letters exchanged between the competent authorities of the United Nations and the Provisional Government, we are convinced that paragraph 7 of document A/48/283, quoted here, better explains the point made in the second sentence:

> "In a letter dated 13 December 1991, Mr. Meles Zenawi, President of the Transitional Government of Ethiopia, informed the Secretary-General about the decisions of the Conference on Peace and Democracy. President Zenawi noted that both the Transitional Government of Ethiopia and the Provisional Government of Eritrea had registered their commitment to respect the results of the referendum in Eritrea. He asked that the United Nations play an active role in verifying a free and fair referendum. In May 1992, the Referendum Commissioner of Eritrea invited the Secretary-General to send a United Nations delegation to observe and to verify the freedom, fairness and impartiality of the entire referendum process which was to begin in July 1992 and end in April 1993".

I should be grateful if you would have the present letter circulated as a document of the General Assembly, under agenda items 10 and 114.

(*Signed*) Ghirmai GHEBREMARIAM
Chargé d'affaires a.i.

Document 43

Activities of the United Nations High Commissioner for Refugees financed by voluntary funds: Report on Eritrea for 1993-1994 and proposed programmes and budget for 1995

A/AC.96/825/Part I/8, 23 August 1994

I.8 Eritrea

Country Overview

Characteristics of the refugee population

1. At 31 July 1994, Eritrea hosted 1,240 refugees, of whom some 500 were from Djibouti, 450 from Yemen, 282 from Somalia and eight from various other countries. The refugees from Somalia and other countries are assisted by UNHCR in Asmara and Assab, and the Djiboutians are assisted by the Government. No assistance has as yet been provided to the Yemenis. None of the refugees are economically self-reliant.

2. An estimated 100,000 Eritrean refugees from the Sudan have repatriated spontaneously to mainly rural areas of Eritrea since its independence in 1991. A further 430,000 are poised to return.

Major developments (1993 and first quarter 1994)

3. After 30 years of war, a massive majority voted in favour of independence, bringing the State of Eritrea into being on 24 May 1994. Eritrea being a new country, the Government has not yet ratified the 1951 Convention relating to the Status of Refugees or the 1969 Organization of African Unity Convention Governing the Specific Aspects of Refugee Problems in Africa.

4. Following an inter-agency mission to Eritrea, composed of United Nations agencies (including UNHCR), non-governmental organization (NGOs) and bilateral donor representatives under the auspices of the Department of Humanitarian Affairs (DHA), the Government of Eritrea agreed, in May 1993, to a repatriation/reintegration/rehabilitation project known as PROFERI (Programme for Refugee Reintegration and Rehabilitation of Resettlement Areas in Eritrea) covering all of the estimated 500,000 Eritrean returnees from the Sudan. The total PROFERI budget is estimated at some $262 million, with UNHCR's part budgeted at some $32 million covering, *inter alia*, transport, reception and initial integration. The more developmental activities in the fields of health, education, agriculture, shelter, water and roads are left to the other participants in the programme.

5. The initial response by the donor community to this programme (some $32 million) was considered by the Eritrean Government as insufficient to embark on a large-scale repatriation. Instead, it was agreed by the Government and DHA to start with a pilot project for the return and integration of some 4,500 families (15,000 to 20,000 persons) in nine reception areas in Eritrea. Preparations to receive this group were started by the Eritrean authorities in early 1994, including the construction of reception facilities. In addition, an agreement was signed, in April 1994, between the Government of Eritrea and UNHCR establishing a legal framework for the return in safety and dignity of the refugees. Discussions between UNHCR and the Government of the Sudan are taking place to establish modalities of registration of repatriants, assuring the voluntary nature of the repatriation and guaranteeing the right of each refugee to return to his country of origin. It is hoped that the first organized movement of returnees can take place after the rainy season in September 1994, and that the entire group of 4,500 families will have arrived in Eritrea before the end of 1994.

6. The Governments of Yemen and Eritrea agreed, in early 1994, to stop the flow of Somali refugees/job-seekers passing through Assab on their way to Yemen, which had resulted in their permanent stay in Assab. UNHCR agreed to provide assistance to genuine refugees only, and not to persons in transit. However, before an assistance programme could be established, Assab experienced a reverse movement of Somalis fleeing Yemen, together with the arrival of Yemenis. UNHCR is therefore modifying its assistance programme in Assab accordingly, including through the construction of a reception centre.

Programme objectives and priorities

7. Care and maintenance assistance will continue to be provided to the refugee caseload during 1995, including improved provision of services such as shelter, health care, potable water supply and sanitation facilities, as well as basic education opportunities. At the same time, possibilities for voluntary repatriation and increasing self-reliance will be explored.

8. During the latter half of 1994, UNHCR is taking necessary measures to prepare basic infrastructure and services to receive the returnees from the Sudan within the context of PROFERI. A limited number of organized movements will be executed during 1994.

9. UNHCR will place emphasis on enabling the returnees to become self-reliant/sufficient in the shortest feasible time. Quick impact projects (QIPs) will focus on major areas of return by providing assistance which will benefit the local population in those areas, as well as in increasing the capacity for the reintegration of returnees.

Arrangements for implementation/related inputs

10. The implementing agency for the programme for refugees in Eritrea is the Ministry of Interior.

11. The Government of Eritrea has opted for a policy of national execution which calls for foreign-supported programmes to be implemented directly by governmental agencies. For PROFERI and for the coordination of the implementation of the returnee programme, the Commissioner of Eritrean Refugees Affairs (CERA) is UNHCR's counterpart, with appropriate ministries acting as executing agencies. Thus, the reception centres and the resettlement sites will be established and operated directly by CERA.

12. Within PROFERI, several United Nations agencies have made provisions for the following related inputs:

UNDP: overall coordination and support to institutions and operations
WHO: health related support
WFP: food assistance
FAO: agriculture, livestock, afforestation
UNICEF: water supply

13. Bilateral donors and NGOs will participate in some activities directly with line ministries, and coordinated by CERA.

General Programmes

Care and maintenance

(a) *1994 planned implementation*

14. Up to the end of May 1994, the Ministry of Interior implemented all assistance activities for asylum-seekers. In the second half of 1994, UNHCR will start funding a project for emergency assistance to refugees in Eritrea.

(b) *1995 programme proposals*

15. UNHCR, in cooperation with the Ministry of Interior, will establish a programme for the delivery of relief goods and services. The provision of social and community services as well as basic education facilities is also planned. The levels of assistance in 1995 and 1996 are not yet determined but will be based on an expected return to political stability and a normal security situation in Somalia and other neighbouring countries, which in turn will facilitate implementation of a voluntary repatriation programme.

Special Programmes

Eritrean Repatriation Programme

(a) *1994 planned implementation*

16. Subject to an agreement between the Government of Sudan and UNHCR, the PROFERI pilot project will be implemented as of September 1994. This would allow for UNHCR and CERA to receive and reintegrate 4,500 returnee families at nine selected sites in four different provinces.

17. UNHCR is also assessing the possibility of starting QIPs in the areas of return before the end of 1994.

(b) *1995 programme proposals*

18. According to the original plan for the repatriation of Eritrean refugees from the Sudan, presented in July 1993, the first phase of PROFERI would have allowed for the voluntary repatriation of 150,000 refugees. Since the programme has been delayed, the current plan is that between 120,000 and 150,000 persons will return before the end of 1995. UNHCR will support the returnees, through CERA, with basic food commodities, in-country transport, and the establishment of resettlement sites, transport and distribution of non-food items, construction of temporary shelters and continued institutional support to CERA and implementing line ministries. Depending upon progress in the implementation of QIPs in 1994, the project will be expanded to cover larger areas during 1995.

19. During 1996, UNHCR will continue to support voluntary repatriation of Eritrean refugees from the Sudan. It is anticipated that, by the end of 1996, all the refugees living in camps/settlements and urban areas in the Sudan will have repatriated to Eritrea.

Programme Delivery and Administrative Support Costs

(a) *Variations in planned activities in 1993*

20. During 1993, UNHCR maintained a minimal presence in Asmara pending the commencement of the organized repatriation operation. The main expenditures incurred were for salaries of staff, travel costs, rental of premises, communications and other general operating expenses.

(b) *1994 planned implementation*

21. At the beginning of the year, the Office continued to maintain a minimal staff presence as the country agreement had not yet been entered into. Hence, only minimal activities were undertaken, although contingency plans were made for the provision of care and maintenance assistance to approximately 600 Somali

refugees, as well as for the repatriation of some 430,000 Eritrean returnees from the Sudan, to be implemented once an agreement is finalized. The Office was operating during this period under the care of the Administration Officer. Subsequent to discussions with the Government of Eritrea, a Chargé de Mission was assigned to Asmara in March. The signature of the agreement with the Government in mid-April 1994 enabled UNHCR to finalize the budgetary requirements for the assistance projects and to commence the construction of a camp in the Assab area. Subsequently, a Senior Programme Officer and a Protection Officer were also appointed. The posts of two guards were discontinued effective 1 January 1994. Higher travel costs are foreseen in the revised 1994 budget to ensure appropriate monitoring of the returnee operation from the Sudan. The anticipated move of the UNHCR Office to United Nations common premises is expected to be delayed as the necessary works have not yet commenced. Meanwhile, in April 1994, the Office of the Chargé de Mission moved to temporary premises which required minor alterations and repairs. The revised 1994 estimate includes these costs, as well as UNHCR's contribution to the common premises.

(c) *1995 programme proposals*

22. At this juncture, the initial 1995 estimates are similar to the revised 1994 estimates.

23. New Field Offices will be established at the reception centres in Tessenei, Ghirmaika and Mahmimet. These will be staffed by the Programme Monitoring Assistants, who should travel by motorcycle to eliminate the necessity of stationing vehicles in these sites and employing additional drivers. The Programme Assistant for Tessenei will also cover the Office of Ghirmaika.

24. The care and maintenance programme for refugees will continue as the situation requires. The monitoring of this programme will most probably be undertaken by the Protection Officer and Assistant.

UNHCR Expenditure in Eritrea
(in thousands of United States dollars)

1993	1994		1995	
Amount obligated	Allocation approved by 1993 EXCOM	Proposed revised allocation	Source of funds and type of assistance	Proposed allocation/ projection
			SPECIAL PROGRAMMES	
–	25,000.0	–	Horn of Africa	–
–	–	519.0	Programme delivery See Annexes I a and II a*	520.3
–	–	137.9	Administrative support See Annexes I b and II b*	181.1
0.0	25,000.0	656.9	Grand Total	701.4

*Editor's Note: The Annexes to this Report have not been reproduced.

Document 44

Activities of the United Nations High Commissioner for Refugees financed by voluntary funds: Report on Eritrea for 1994-1995 and proposed programmes and budget for 1996

A/AC.96/846/Part I/7, 24 July 1995

Eritrea

1. *Beneficiary population*

1. At 31 December 1994, Eritrea hosted 706 refugees consisting of 704 Somalis and 2 Sudanese. By 1 April 1995, this number had increased to 867 mainly due to a further influx from Somalia. These refugees are sheltered in a temporary camp in Assab and are fully dependent on UNHCR assistance for all their material needs. The majority of them are below the age of 18.

2. Since November 1994, some 24,200 Eritrean refugees from the Sudan have been assisted to repatriate under a project designed for the repatriation of 25,000 persons. It is estimated that since 1991 over 100,000 refugees have spontaneously repatriated, mainly to rural areas in Eritrea.

2. *Developments in 1994 and 1995*

3. Since early 1995, the influx of Somali refugees has continued to increase. The refugee population fluctuated on account of illegal migration of Somalis to Yemen via Assab. Although the Eritrean authorities no longer allow the Somalis to embark on vessels destined for Yemen within the port of Assab, it appears difficult to bring the illegal migration to a halt. Assuming stability in North-West Somalia, it is envisaged that the refugee population in Assab will stabilize at around 1,000. Following the increase in the refugee population, the shelter situation in the transit camp in Assab, where the refugees are temporarily accommodated, has become untenable. Therefore, construction of new facilities is under way in the Harsile camp in Assab. The construction itself was delayed due to significant design and implementation problems.

4. During the course of 1994 two separate Memoranda of Understanding were signed by UNHCR with the Governments of Eritrea and the Sudan which provide the framework for voluntary repatriation of Eritrean refugees. The pilot phase planned for the repatriation of 25,000 Eritreans from the Sudan within the Programme for Refugee Reintegration and Rehabilitation of Resettlement Areas in Eritrea (PROFERI) began in November 1994. Some 24,200 Eritreans were assisted to return at the end of the pilot project.

5. The start of the pilot phase was delayed due to late finalization of the Memoranda of Understanding as well as some logistical problems. Furthermore, as registration for repatriation proceeded, it became evident that the majority of the returnees were requesting to return to only one of the four provinces foreseen in the plan of operation. Moreover, a substantial number of returnees requested inland transportation to 73 different sites, against the originally planned 9 sites. This resulted in a significant modification in overall planning and preparation by the Commission for Eritrean Refugee Affairs (CERA) and UNHCR, and consequently only 8,706 returnees could be received and resettled between mid-November 1994 and December 1994. Thus the pilot operation planned for the repatriation of 25,000 refugees by December 1994 was extended to May 1995. Meanwhile preparation for Phase I of the operation to repatriate some 100,000 returnees is under way following a successful conclusion of the pilot phase.

6. An appeal for funds was launched by UNHCR in March 1995 for its part in the Phase I of PROFERI.

3. *1996 country programmes*

(a) *Objectives*

7. The construction of the Harsile camp in Assab to accommodate the refugee population will be finalized during the course of 1995. During 1996, care and maintenance assistance will continue to be provided to an estimated 1,000 Somali refugees in Assab. Meanwhile possibilities for durable solutions for this caseload will be pursued.

8. Phase II of the operation under PROFERI, which foresees repatriation and reintegration of up to 150,000 Eritreans, will begin in 1996. UNHCR will assist the returnees, through CERA, with basic food commodities (supplied by WFP), in-country transport, the establishment of resettlement sites, provision of temporary shelter, transport and distribution of non-food items, as well as institutional support to CERA. Provision is also made for continuation of quick impact projects (QIPs) in 1996. However, progress in repatriation will very much depend upon the donor support that the Eritrean Government will receive in rehabilitating the war-damaged country in order to build up the absorption capacity for the returnees. Therefore, planning assumptions may require adjusting through periodic reviews.

(b) *Proposed budgets for 1996*

(i) *General Programmes*

9. *Care and maintenance*: The refugee assistance programme in 1996 will include improved provision of services such as shelter, food, health care, potable water supply and sanitation, basic education, and other community services for an estimated 1,000 Somali refugees.

(ii) *Special Programmes*

10. *Horn of Africa*: The sectoral breakdown of the revised 1995 and initial 1996 allocation for the reintegration programme in Eritrea is as follows (in US dollars):

Sector	Revised 1995	Initial 1996
Food	585,370	659,950
Transport/logistics	4,130,945	1,291,885
Domestic needs	1,067,500	1,067,500
Water	172,700	111,000
Sanitation	245,000	200,000
Health	243,976	225,157
Construction/shelter	3,837,063	4,251,440
Community services	119,200	117,500
Education	119,200	117,500
Crop production	180,000	65,600
Livestock	253,870	212,425
Agency op. support	462,576	348,543
Total	11,417,400*	8,668,500

* Including $ 3,000,000 allocated from the General Allocation for Voluntary Repatriation.

(c) *Implementing partners*

11. In the case of PROFERI, the responsible government body and UNHCR's implementing partner is CERA. This Commission is mandated by the Government of Eritrea to coordinate the returnee programme, working closely with the line ministries in the implementation of a wide range of sectoral activities. Bilateral funding towards PROFERI is channelled through CERA and allocated to the line ministries. Similarly, the Ministry of Internal Affairs is mandated by the Government of Eritrea as a body responsible for refugee issues and is UNHCR's implementing partner for the ongoing refugee assistance programme.

(d) *Programme delivery and administrative support costs*

(i) *1994 expenditure (all sources of funds)*

12. The 1994 expenditure was lower than revised estimates due to savings made following the prolonged vacancies in two professional posts at the Office of the Chargé de Mission in Asmara.

(ii) *Revised 1995 requirements (all sources of funds)*

13. To ensure appropriate monitoring of the returnee operation from the Sudan, a Field Office was opened in Tesseni in early 1995. This Field Office is manned by a Head of Sub-Office, a National Field Officer and eleven General Service staff. The revised 1995 requirements therefore include provisions for the cost of these posts as well as for the purchase of vehicles and basic office furniture and equipment which was not foreseen in the initial 1995 estimates. Replacement costs for two vehicles in the Office of the Chargé de Mission in Asmara are also included in the revised 1995 requirements. Furthermore, the UNHCR presence in Asmara has been strengthened to support the repatriation through the creation of one National Officer and eight General Service posts.

(iii) *Initial 1996 estimates (all sources of funds)*

14. In the proposed 1996 requirements, reduced provisions for non-expendable property have been made on the assumption that most of the required purchases will take place during 1995 as planned. However, a modest provision is proposed for the replacement in 1996 of old office equipment.

UNHCR Expenditure in Eritrea
(in thousands of United States dollars)

1994	1995		1996	
Amount obligated	Allocation approved by 1994 EXCOM	Proposed revised allocation	Source of funds and type of assistance	Proposed allocation/ projection
GENERAL PROGRAMMES (1)				
446.8	–	–	Emergency fund	–
3.0 a/	–	599.4	Care and maintenance	539.2
2.3 a/	–	3,000.0 b/	Voluntary repatriation	–
1.9 a/	–	–	Resettlement	
454.0		3,599.4	Sub-total operations	539.2
454.0		3,599.4	Total (1)	539.2
SPECIAL PROGRAMMES				
2,820.2	–	8,417.4	Horn of Africa	8,668.5
361.5	–	799.9	Programme delivery See Overview Tables (Part II)*	746.5
137.5	–	159.0	Administrative support See Overview Tables (Part II)*	146.3
3,319.2		9,376.3	Total (2)	9,561.3
3,773.2		12,975.7	Grand Total (1+2)	10,100.5

a/ Obligation incurred against Other Programmes

b/ Allocated from the General Allocation for Voluntary Repatriation

*Editor's Note: The Overview Tables to this Report have not been reproduced.

V Subject index to documents

[This subject index to the documents reproduced in this book should be used in conjunction with the index on pages 271-275. A complete listing of the documents indexed below appears on pages 45-48.]

A

Agricultural technology.
– Document 37

Agriculture
– Documents 4, 26, 37

Aid coordination.
See: Coordination within UN system. Development assistance.

Aid programmes.
See: Development assistance. Economic assistance. Emergency relief. Food aid. Humanitarian assistance. Refugees.

Amnesty.
– Document 7

Appointment of officials.
– Documents 4, 6-7, 9-10, 21, 25

Autonomy.
See: Self-government.

B

Boundaries.
– Document 4

Boutros-Ghali, Boutros.
– Documents 14-15, 20-24, 32, 39, 42

British administration in Eritrea.
– Documents 4, 6-10

Burma.
– Documents 3- 4, 7

C

Chief Administrator of Eritrea.
– Documents 4, 7, 9-10

Citizenship.
See: Nationality.

Civil and political rights.
– Documents 6-7, 9

Colonialism.
See: Italian Colonization of Eritrea. Self-determination of peoples.

Commissions of inquiry.
See: Special missions. UN Commission for Eritrea.

Conference on Peace and Democracy in Ethiopia (1991 : Addis Ababa).
– Documents 13, 19-20, 22, 24, 30

Constitutions.
– Documents 6-7, 9-10

Consultations.
– Documents 4, 6
See also: Dispute settlement. Negotiation.

Coordination within UN system.
– Documents 26, 38

Customs administration.
– Documents 4, 6-7

D

Decolonization.
See: Independence. Political status. Self-determination of peoples. Self-government.

Democratic and Independent Front.
– Documents 7, 9

Democracy.
See: Self-government.

Denmark.
– Document 18

Deportation.
– Document 6
See also: Nationality.

Detention.
– Document 6

Development assistance.
– Documents 26, 32, 37, 40
See also: Economic assistance.

Development planning.
– Document 41

Diplomacy.
See: Consultations. Dispute settlement. Negotiation.

Displaced persons.
See: Humanitarian assistance.

Dispute settlement.
– Document 8
See also: Consultations. Negotiation. Special missions.

E

Economic assistance.
– Documents 4, 7-8, 37
See also: Development assistance. Humanitarian assistance. Reconstruction.

Economic conditions.
– Document 4

Economic, social and cultural rights.
– Documents 6, 8-9

Educational assistance.
– Documents 4, 26, 37

Egypt.
– Documents 4, 7

Elections.
– Documents 7, 9
See also: Referendum. Voting. Political representation.

Electoral assistance.
– Documents 13, 15, 19-25, 27-28, 32, 39, 42
See also: Referendum. Voter registration.

Emergency relief.
– Documents 26, 37
See also: Humanitarian assistance.

Environmental protection.
– Document 37

Eritrean People's Liberation Front (EPLF).
– Documents 13, 29, 42

Eritrea. Assembly.
– Documents 6-7, 9

Eritrea. President.
– Documents 38, 40

Ethiopia.
– Documents 4, 6-15, 18, 20, 24-25, 30, 39

European Community (EC).
– Documents 37, 39

Exiles.
See: Deportation.

Expulsion.
See: Deportation.

F

Fact-finding missions.
See: Dispute settlement. Special missions. Visiting missions.

Federal Act.
– Documents 6—11

Federal Government (1952-1962).
– Documents 6-7, 9-10

Financing.
– Documents 15, 22, 24, 26, 37, 39, 43

Finland.
– Document 18

Food aid.
– Documents 26, 37

Food and Agriculture Organization (FAO).
– Documents 26, 43

France.
– Documents 1, 4, 7

Franchise.
See: Political representation

G

Government.
See: Federal Government (1952-1962). Provisional government. Self-government. Transitional government.

Guatemala.
– Documents 3-4, 7

H

Health services.
– Documents 26, 37

Hearings.
See: Consultations.

Human rights.
– Documents 6, 9, 12
See also: Civil and political rights. Economic, social and cultural rights.

Humanitarian assistance.
– Document 26
See also: Economic assistance. Emergency relief. Refugees. Special missions.

I

Iceland.
– Document 18

Imprisonment.
See: Detention.

Independence.
– Documents 3, 7, 30, 32
See also: Political conditions. Political status. Self-determination of peoples. Self-government. Sovereignty.

Independent Muslim League.
– Documents 4, 7, 9

Interim governments.
See: Provisional government. Transitional government.

Internal security.
– Documents 7, 9

International courts.
– Document 8
See also: Dispute settlement.

Italian colonization of Eritrea.
– Documents 1-4, 7-8

Italy.
– Documents 4, 7-8, 26

L

Laws and regulations.
– Documents 4, 8-10, 16-17

Living conditions.
See: Economic conditions.

League of Arab States.
– Document 39

M

Maps.
– Document 37

Marine resources.
– Document 37

Mediation.
See: Consultations. Dispute settlement. Negotiation.

Military pensions.
– Document 8

Movement of the Non-Aligned Countries.
– Document 39

Muslim League of the Western Province.
– Documents 4, 7, 9

Myanmar.
See: Burma

N

National Party.
– Documents 4, 7, 9

National security.
See: Internal security. Regional security.

National territory.
See: Boundaries.

Nationality.
– Documents 6-7, 9, 16

Natural resources.
See: Marine resources.

Naturalization.
– Document 16
See also: Nationality.

Negotiation.
– Document 6
See also: Consultations. Dispute settlement.

Non-citizens.
See: Deportation. Nationality.

Non-self-governing territories.
– Documents 1-5, 7, 9

Norway.
– Documents 4, 7, 18

O

Organization of African Unity (OAU).
– Documents 27, 39

P

Pakistan.
– Documents 3-4, 7

Pardon.
See: Amnesty.

Peaceful settlement of disputes.
See: Dispute settlement.

Plebiscites.
See: Referendum.

Political conditions.
– Documents 4, 7, 9-13
See also: Independence. Self-determination of peoples. Self-government.

Political prisoners.
See: Amnesty.

Political representation.
– Documents 6, 9
See also: Federal Government (1952-1962).

Political rights.
See: Civil and political rights.

Political status.
– Documents 5, 7, 9, 13, 20
See also: Independence. Self-determination of peoples. Self-government.

Preventive diplomacy.
See: Dispute settlement. Negotiation.

Programme for Refugee Reintegration and Rehabilitation of Resettlement Areas in Eritrea (PROFERI).
– Documents 37-38, 43-44

Property rights.
– Document 8

Proportional representation.
See: Political representation

Provisional government.
– Documents 13-15, 20, 26-27, 31-32

Provisional Government. Secretary-General.
– Documents 23, 27, 29, 31

Public administration.
See: Customs administration. Tax administration.

Punishment.
– Documents 6-7
See also: Amnesty.

R

Reconstruction.
– Documents 26, 37, 40-41
See also: Economic assistance.

Referendum.
– Documents 13-15, 17-25, 27-30, 32, 39-40, 42

Referendum Commission of Eritrea.
– Documents 17, 19, 21-23, 42

Referendum Commission of Eritrea. Commissioner.
– Documents 19, 21, 24, 29

Refugees.
– Documents 26, 37-38, 40, 43-44
See also: Humanitarian assistance. Repatriation.

Regional security.
– Document 4

Regulations.
See: Laws and regulations.

Rehabilitation projects.
See: Economic assistance. Reconstruction.

Relief transport.
See: Emergency relief. Food aid. Humanitarian assistance. Refugees.

Repatriation.
– Documents 26, 37-38, 40, 43-44

Representative government.
See: Constitutions. Federal Government (1952-1962). Political representation. Self-government.

Resettlement.
– Documents 37-38, 43
See also: Repatriation.

Road construction.
– Document 37

Rules and regulations.
See: Laws and regulations.

S

Salaries and allowances.
– Document 6

Secession.
See: Independence. Political conditions.

Self-determination of peoples.
– Document 13
See also: Civil and political rights. Independence. Political conditions. Political status. Self-government.

Self-government.
– Documents 4, 6-7, 9-10
See also: Independence. Political conditions. Political status. Self-determination of peoples. Sovereignty.

Ships.
– Document 8

Social welfare.
– Document 8

Sovereignty.
– Documents 7, 30
See also: Independence. Self-government.

Special Emergency Programme for the Horn of Africa (SEPHA).
– Documents 26, 38

Special missions.
– Documents 18-23
See also: Dispute settlement. Humanitarian assistance. UN Commission for Eritrea. Visiting missions.

State government.
See: Political representation. Self-government.

State property.
– Document 8

Statelessness.
See: Nationality.

Statutes.
See: Laws and regulations.

Sudan.
– Documents 37-39, 43-44

Sweden.
– Documents 18, 26

T

Tax administration.
– Documents 4, 6

Technical cooperation.
See: Development assistance. Economic assistance. Electoral assistance.

Territorial asylum.
See: Deportation.

Territorial claims.
See: Political status.

Transitional government.
– Documents 13-15, 20, 30, 42

Transitional Government. President.
– Documents 13-15, 20, 22

Travel reimbursement.
– Document 3

Treaty of Peace with Italy (1947).
– Documents 1, 3-6, 8

Trusteeship agreements.
– Documents 3-4

U

UN—Membership.
– Documents 31, 33-36

UN. Committee to Nominate a Candidate for the Office of United Nations Commissioner in Eritrea.
– Document 6

UN. Department of Humanitarian Affairs (DHA).
– Documents 26, 37-38, 41, 43

UN. Economic Commission for Africa (ECA).
– Documents 39, 41

UN. General Assembly.
– Documents 1-11, 20, 24-25, 31, 33-36, 39-40

UN. General Assembly. Interim Committee on the Report of the United Nations Commission for Eritrea.
– Documents 4-7

UN. Secretary-General.
– Documents 14-15, 20-25, 32, 39, 42

UN. Security Council.
– Documents 33-34

UN. Security Council. President.
– Document 34

UN. Special Representative for the Referendum in Eritrea.
– Documents 25, 28, 39

UN. Trusteeship Council.
– Documents 3-4

UN. Under-Secretary-General for Humanitarian Affairs.
– Documents 37-38

UN. Under-Secretary-General for Political Affairs.
– Documents 15, 21, 24

UN Commission for Eritrea.
– Documents 3-7, 9-10

UN Commissioner in Eritrea.
– Documents 6-7, 9-11, 42

UN Observer Mission to Verify the Referendum in Eritrea (UNOVER).
– Documents 23-25, 28, 39, 42

UN Observer Mission to Verify the Referendum in Eritrea (UNOVER)—Financing.
– Document 24

UN Tribunal in Eritrea.
– Document 8

Union of South Africa.
– Documents 3-4, 7

Union of Soviet Socialist Republics (USSR).
– Documents 1, 4, 7

Unionist Party.
– Documents 4, 7, 9

United Kingdom.
– Documents 1, 4, 7, 9-10
See also: British administration in Eritrea.

United Nations Children's Fund (UNICEF).
– Documents 26, 37, 39, 43

United Nations Development Programme (UNDP).
– Documents 26, 37-39, 41, 43

United Nations High Commissioner for Refugees (UNHCR).
– Documents 37-39, 43-44

United Nations Volunteers (UNV).
– Documents 26, 37-38

United States.
– Documents 1, 4, 7

Visiting missions.
– Documents 3-4
See also: UN Commission for Eritrea. Non-self-governing territories. Special missions.

Voter registration.
– Document 17
See also: Electoral assistance.

Voting.
– Documents 9, 20
See also: Elections. Electoral assistance. Referendum.

Water supply.
– Documents 4, 26, 37

World Bank.
– Documents 26, 38, 41

World Food Programme (WFP).
– Documents 26, 37-39, 43-44

World Health Organization (WHO).
– Documents 26, 43

VI Index

[*The numbers following the entries refer to paragraph numbers in the Introduction.*]

A

Access to the sea, 15, 24, 50
Addis Ababa, 28, 33, 45-46, 49
Adi Qaih, 66
Administration of territory, 4, 9-10, 13-19, 21, 23, 28, 30, 33-35, 43-44.
    See also British administration of Eritrea; Federation; International Trusteeship System; Trusteeship agreements
African-American Institute, 81
Afwerki, Issaias, 6, 46, 52, 54-55, 89-90
Agnets, 79
Agriculture, 11, 102, 104
Amharic language, 35
Annexation of territory, 4, 15, 26
Arabic language, 32, 35
Asmara, 28, 37, 44, 46, 56, 62, 64, 66, 77, 89, 101, 112
Assab, 15, 44, 50, 56
Axumite kingdom, 10

B

Boundaries, 2, 110
Bretton Woods institutions, 7, 104, 112
British administration of Eritrea, 13, 34
Burma, 19, 21-22

C

Cairo, 54
Canadian NGO Observation Delegation, 81
Carter Center (Atlanta, Georgia), 44
Carter, Jimmy, 44
Catholic Fund for Overseas Development, 81
Charter of the Organization of African Unity (1963), 2
Charter of the United Nations (1945), 14, 94

Child immunization, 56
Christian population, 11, 31
Cold war, 61
Conference on Peace and Democracy in Ethiopia (1991 : Addis Ababa), 48-50, 52
Charter, 49
Constitution, 23, 27, 29, 32-35, 92
    adoption, 32
    Art. 1, 32
    draft, 32
Consultations, 13, 20, 28-30, 54, 58, 72, 78
Culture, 4, 29

D

Decolonization, 61, 112
Democracy, 1-2, 6, 37, 61, 66, 74, 110
    Democratic and Independent Front, 31
Denmark, 22, 73, 81
Diplomatic recognition of Eritrea, 92
Displaced persons, 42, 100.
    See also Refugees
Djibouti, 73, 79, 92, 112

E

Early-warning system, 106
East Africa, 20.
    See also Horn of Africa
Eastern Eritrea, 15
ECA.
    See UN. Economic Commission for Africa (ECA)
Economic recovery, 7, 90, 96, 102-104
Egypt, 10, 20, 73, 81, 92
Elections for Eritrean Representative Assembly (1952), 30-31.
    See also Political representation; Referendum; Right to vote

ELF.
    See Eritrean Liberation Front (ELF)
Emergency relief.
    See Humanitarian assistance
English language, 32
EPDM.
    See Ethiopian People's Democratic Movement (EPDM)
EPLA.
    See Eritrean People's Liberation Army (EPLA)
EPLF.
    See Eritrean People's Liberation Front (EPLF)
EPRDF.
    See Ethiopian People's Revolutionary Democratic Front (EPRDF)
Eritrea
    Department of Internal Affairs, 72
    Government, 33, 35, 98, 100-101
    Chief Executive, 33
    membership
        in OAU, 92, 112
        in UN, 7, 51, 92, 94-95, 112
    President, 99
    Provisional Government, 5-6, 46, 50, 52-54, 58-59, 62, 85, 92
        Secretary-General, 6, 46, 52, 54-55, 89-90
    Referendum Commission, 59, 62-64, 67-69, 72, 74, 80-81, 84-87
    Representative Assembly (1952-1962), 23, 30, 32, 34-35
        President, 33
    transition period, 23, 92
Eritrean Citizens' Referendum Monitoring Group, 81
Eritrean Liberation Front (ELF), 38
Eritrean People's Liberation Army (EPLA), 84, 86

271

Eritrean People's Liberation Front (EPLF), 38, 40-41, 43-48, 50, 84, 89, 92, 102.
  See also People's Front for Democracy and Justice
  leaders, 46-48
Ethiopia, 2-5, 7, 12, 15-16, 18-21, 23, 29, 35, 51-53, 56, 73, 81, 109, 112
  access to the sea, 15, 24, 50
  army, 43-46
  coalition of non-Eritrean groups, 37, 43
  Council of Representatives, 91
  coup d'état, 39, 43
  Dergue, 39
  drought, 42
  Emperor, 10, 29, 33, 35, 39
  famine, 39, 42
  flag, 29, 35, 95
  Government, 3, 15, 23-24, 40-41, 43-46, 58, 77, 109
  independence, 10, 13
  interim Government, 46-47
  land reform, 39
  military leaders, 39
  Ministry of Foreign Affairs, 91
  monarchy, 39
  Provisional Military Administrative Council (PMAC), 39
  President, 39
  socialist State, 39
  Transitional Government, 48, 50, 54, 58, 60
  President, 49, 53
  Transitional Parliament, 49
    Council of Representatives, 49
  transition period, 49
  voting in referendum, 77, 79, 86
  war with Eritrea, 1, 3, 7, 9, 37-40, 55, 70, 72, 76, 90, 97, 107, 113
  war with Italy, 10
Ethiopian Crown, 4, 9, 21-23
Ethiopian People's Democratic Movement (EPDM), 41, 43
Ethiopian People's Revolutionary Democratic Front (EPRDF), 43-46, 49
  leader, 49

Ethnic groups, 11, 41.
  See also Racial groups
European Community, 81, 104
Expatriates, 3, 69, 113

F

Famine, 39, 42, 102
Federal Government, 33
Federation of Eritrea with Ethiopia, 4, 7, 9, 15-16, 18, 21-24, 26-28, 32-36.
  See also Administration of territory; International Trusteeship System; Trusteeship agreements
  Act (1952), 32-33
    abrogation, 35-36
  agreement, 4, 9, 35
  local autonomy, 23, 28, 34
Financial assistance, 99-100, 103-104.
  See also Humanitarian assistance
Food aid, 44, 55-56, 98, 103, 106.
  See also Humanitarian assistance; World Food Programme (WFP)
Food and Agriculture Organization of the United Nations (FAO), 103, 105-106
Food production, 103, 106
Food-for-work programmes, 102
France, 13, 20, 73

G

Germany, 73, 79, 104
Guatemala, 19, 21, 25

H

Haile Selassie I, Emperor of Ethiopia, 35
Horn of Africa, 1, 42, 54, 56, 93, 99, 103, 106, 109
Humanitarian assistance, 7, 42, 56, 99, 106, 109.
  See also Financial assistance; Food aid
  financing, 56

I

IGAD.
  See Intergovernmental Authority for Development (IGAD)
IGADD.
  See Intergovernmental Authority for Drought and Development (IGADD)
Illiteracy, 3, 69
ILO.
  See International Labour Organization (ILO)
Immigration, 50
Independence, 1-4, 7-9, 14-16, 18, 21, 24-26, 37, 47-48, 59, 77, 89-93, 109, 112
  ceremonies, 92
  war, 1, 9, 37-38
Independent Muslim League of Eritrea, 26, 31
Inter-agency cooperation, 42, 64, 80, 106
Intergovernmental Authority for Development (IGAD), 112
Intergovernmental Authority for Drought and Development (IGADD), 112
International community, 48, 55, 90, 96, 98-99, 103, 112-113
International Labour Organization (ILO), 112
International security, 2, 20
International Trusteeship System, 14-15, 21.
  See also Administration of territory; Federation; Trusteeship agreements
Investment code, 104
Islam, 11.
  See also Muslim population
Italian colonies, 4, 9-10, 12, 17, 19.
  See also Italian Somaliland; Libya
Italian East Africa, 12
Italian Somaliland, 4, 12-13, 15, 17, 19, 25.
  See also Italian colonies
Italo-Eritrean Association, 16

Italy, 4, 9-13, 15, 19-20, 25, 92, 104
  settlers, 11
  Treaty of Peace
    (Paris : 10 February 1947), 13
  war with Ethiopia, 10

K

Kenya, 73, 112
Keren, 44, 66, 76
Kuwait, 73, 79

L

Land-mines, 79
Languages, 11, 74
  Amharic, 35
  Arabic, 32, 35
  English, 32
  official, 29, 32, 35
  Tigrinya, 32, 35
Latin American countries, 15
League of Arab States, 81
League of Nations, 12
  sanctions, 12
Libya, 4, 13, 15, 17, 19, 25.
  See also Italian colonies
Lie, Trygve, 14
Literacy, 3, 69, 105
Livestock, 98, 106
London negotiations, 45
London peace talks, 47-48

M

Mass media, 42, 74-76, 85, 92
Massawa, 10, 44, 50, 56
Mendefera, 66
Mengistu Haile Mariam, 39, 46
  regime, 39-40
Military assistance, 41
Movement of Non-Aligned
  Countries, 81
Muslim League of Eritrea, 16, 26, 31
Muslim League of the Western
  Province, 31
Muslim population, 31, 38, 41.
  See also Islam

N

Nairobi negotiations, 44

National liberation movements.
  See also Political parties
  Eritrean Liberation Front (ELF), 38
  Eritrean People's Liberation
    Front (EPLF), 38, 40-41,
    43-48, 50, 84, 89, 92, 102
  Omoro Liberation Front, 41
  Tigre People's Liberation Front
    (TPLF), 41, 43, 47
Nationalism, 11
Nationality, 59
  Proclamation, 59
Negotiation, 43-45, 47.
  See also Consultations;
    Peace talks
Netherlands, 73, 104
New Eritrea Pro-Italia Party, 16
Non-governmental organizations,
  64, 80-81, 112
Norway, 19, 21, 73

O

OAU.
  See Organization of African
    Unity (OAU)
Office of the United Nations High
  Commissioner for Refugees
  (UNHCR), 100
Official languages, 29, 32, 35
Omoro Liberation Front, 41
Organization of African Unity
  (OAU), 2, 58, 81, 88, 109, 112
Ottoman Empire, 10

P

Pakistan, 19, 21, 25
Partition of territory, 15, 26
Peace, 7, 20
  Conference (1991 : Addis
    Ababa), 48-50, 52
  Charter, 49
Peace-building, 2, 61, 110
Peace talks, 45, 47-48.
  See also Negotiation
People's Front for Democracy and
  Justice, 92.
  See also Eritrean People's
    Liberation Front (EPLF)
Pérez de Cuéllar, Javier, 52

PMAC.
  See Ethiopia Provisional
    Military Administrative
    Council (PMAC)
Political parties, 16, 18, 20, 28-29,
  31, 49, 62, 92.
  See also National liberation
    movements
  Democratic and Independent
    Front, 31
  Ethiopian People's Democratic
    Movement (EPDM), 41, 43
  Ethiopian People's
    Revolutionary Democratic
    Front (EPRDF), 43-46, 49
    leader, 49
  Independent Muslim League of
    Eritrea, 26, 31
  Italo-Eritrean Association, 16
  Muslim League of Eritrea, 16,
    26, 31
  Muslim League of the Western
    Province, 31
  New Eritrea Pro-Italia Party, 16
  People's Front for Democracy
    and Justice, 92
  Union and Liberal Unionist
    Parties, 31
  Unionist Party, 16, 26
Political representation, 30-31
Popular participation, 2
Population of Eritrea, 3, 24, 28, 96
Ports, 10, 15, 44, 50, 56
Poverty, 21
Press, 92
Prisoners, 72
Programme for Refugee Reintegration
  and Rehabilitation of
  Resettlement Areas in Eritrea
  (PROFERI), 98-100, 103
Provisional Government of Eritrea,
  5-6, 46, 50, 52-54, 58-59, 62,
  85, 92
  Secretary-General, 6, 46, 52,
    54-55, 89-90

R

Racial groups, 20.
  See also Ethnic groups
Radio broadcasting, 74-76

Rallies, 75
Reconstruction, 7, 55, 90, 96, 98.
    See also Rehabilitation
Recovery, 7, 90, 96, 102-104
Recovery and Rehabilitation Programme for Eritrea, 104
Red Sea, 15
Referendum, 1-3, 5, 7, 37, 47-48, 50-53, 57-59, 62, 67, 69, 87-88, 108, 110.
    See also Elections; Right to vote
    campaign, 6, 51, 63, 74, 77
    Commission, 59, 62-64, 67-69, 72, 74, 80-81, 84-87
    Commissioner, 59-60, 82
    electoral campaign, 6, 51, 63, 74, 77
    civic education programme, 6, 74-75, 77
    media coverage, 63, 85
    observation by UN, 57, 60
    observers, 2, 51, 64, 66-67, 75, 80-83, 85, 87
    poll, 51, 63, 83-84
    polling stations, 74, 79, 82-83, 85, 87
    registration cards, 72
    results, 3, 63, 85-86
    technical assistance, 2, 37, 57, 61, 110
    verification by UN, 51-53, 57-58, 60, 63
    voter identification, 59, 63, 70
    voter participation, 83
    voter registration, 51, 63, 70-74
        prisoners, 72
        soldiers, 84
        women, 71
    voting
        expatriates, 3, 69
        Ethiopia, 77, 79, 86
        Kuwait, 73, 79
        refugees, 3, 77
        Saudi Arabia, 78-79
        Sudan, 77, 79, 83, 86
        Yemen, 84
    voting supplies, 82
    voting techniques, 3, 6-7, 68-69, 74, 76

Refugees, 3, 69.
    See also Displaced persons
    repatriation, 96, 99-100
    resettlement, 97, 100, 111
    return, 97
    statistics, 3, 55, 97, 100
    voting, 3, 77
Rehabilitation, 97-99, 103-104.
    See also Reconstruction
Religious freedom, 29
Religious groups, 11, 20, 31, 62
Religious leaders, 6, 29, 75
Representative Assembly of Eritrea (1952-1962), 23, 30, 32, 34-35
Resistance movements, 4, 6, 9, 36, 38
Right to vote, 30
RRP.
    See Recovery and Rehabilitation Programme for Eritrea

S

Sanbar, Samir, 6, 64, 66, 76, 78, 82, 87
Saudi Arabia, 3, 69, 73, 78-79, 92
Secession, 2, 36, 41, 58, 109
Second World War (1939-1945).
    See World War (1939-1945)
Self-determination of peoples, 1, 4-5, 25, 36-37, 47, 49, 58, 61, 76
Self-government, 20-21
Self-sufficiency, 21, 102-103
SEPHA.
    See Special Emergency Programme for the Horn of Africa (SEPHA)
Social organizations, 11, 29, 49, 62
Soldiers, 84
    demobilization, 96
    reintegration, 55
South Africa.
    See Union of South Africa
Soviet Union.
    See Union of Soviet Socialist Republics (USSR)
Special Emergency Programme for the Horn of Africa (SEPHA), 56, 103

Special Representative.
    See UN. Special Representative for the Referendum in Eritrea
Statistics
    displaced persons, 42
    famine victims, 42
    food aid, 55
    observers, 80
    population, 3
    refugees, 3, 55, 97, 100
    soldier reintegration, 55
    voting registration, 73
Sudan, 3, 44, 51, 55, 69, 73, 77, 79, 83, 86, 92, 97, 100, 109, 112
Sweden, 73, 104

T

Teachers, 6, 74
Television, 74, 76
Theatre groups, 74
Tigre People's Liberation Front (TPLF), 41, 43, 47
Tigre Region, 41
Tigrinya language, 32, 35
TPLF.
    See Tigre People's Liberation Front (TPLF)
Trade unions, 11
Treaty of Peace with Italy (Paris : 10 February 1947), 13
Treaty of Wich'alē (Uccialli), 4, 9-10
Trust Territories, 14
Trusteeship agreements, 4, 14-16, 19.
    See also Administration of territory; Federation; International Trusteeship System

U

Uganda, 73, 107
UN
    Integrated office, 101
    membership, 7, 51, 92, 94-96, 112
UN agencies.
    See Inter-agency cooperation

UN Commission for Eritrea, 18-22
UN Observer Mission to Verify the Referendum in Eritrea (UNOVER), 2-3, 5, 7, 51, 63-67, 71-72, 74, 76-77, 107-108, 109, 113
 Chief, 66
 civilian component, 64
 cost, 64
 deployment, 3, 51
 establishment, 51, 63, 65
 headquarters, 66
 information campaign, 75
 mandate, 6, 52, 63, 69
 observers, 5, 51, 64, 67, 71, 75, 79-80, 82-83, 85, 87
 regional offices, 66, 76
 training, 66, 80
UN Pledging Conference for the Programme for Refugee Reintegration and Rehabilitation of Resettlement Areas in Eritrea (PROFERI) (1993 : Geneva), 99-100
UN Volunteers, 103
UN. Centre for Human Rights, 62
UN. Commissioner in Eritrea, 23, 27-30, 32-34
UN. Department of Humanitarian Affairs (DHA), 98, 100, 103
UN. Economic and Social Council (ECOSOC), 17
UN. Economic Commission for Africa (ECA), 80
UN. Four-Power Commission of Investigation, 13
UN. General Assembly, 17, 19-20, 34, 51, 58, 60-63, 65, 67, 87, 94
 (4th sess. : 1949), 17-18
 (5th sess. : 1950-1951), 22
 (47th sess. : 1992-1993), 95
 Ad Hoc Political Committee, 22, 26-27
 decision (1950), 4
 First Committee, 14, 16, 18
 res. 266 (III), 17
 res. 287 (III), 17
 res. 289 (IV), 19
 res. 390 (V), 27-28, 30, 32, 34
 res. 46/137, 61

res. 47/114, 61
res. 47/230, 94
UN. Group of African States, 58
UN. Resident Coordinator, 101
UN. Secretary-General, 14, 20, 52, 54, 57, 66
UN. Secretary-General, political representatives, 58
UN. Security Council, 95
 President, 94
 res. 828 (1993), 94
UN. Special Representative for the Referendum in Eritrea, 6, 64, 66, 76, 78, 82, 87
UN. Technical team to Eritrea, 62
UN. Under-Secretary-General for Humanitarian Affairs, 99
UNDP.
 See United Nations Development Programme (UNDP)
UNESCO.
 See United Nations Educational, Scientific and Cultural Organization (UNESCO)
UNHCR.
 See Office of the United Nations High Commissioner for Refugees (UNHCR)
UNICEF.
 See United Nations Children's Fund (UNICEF)
Union of South Africa, 19, 21-22
Union of Soviet Socialist Republics (USSR), 13, 15, 25, 39-40
Union with Ethiopia.
 See Federation
Unionist Party, 16, 26
United Kingdom. 13, 15, 20, 28-30, 33, 81, 92.
 See also British administration of Eritrea.
United Nations Children's Fund (UNICEF), 56, 103, 105
United Nations Development Programme (UNDP), 64, 104
United Nations Educational, Scientific and Cultural Organization (UNESCO), 105, 107
United States, 13, 15, 39, 45, 47, 81, 92

President (1977-1981), 44
UNOVER.
 See UN Observer Mission to Verify the Referendum in Eritrea (UNOVER)
UNV.
 See UN Volunteers

V

Village elders, 6, 71, 75, 85
Voting.
 See Elections; Referendum; Right to vote

W

War, 9-10, 37-38
 cold war, 61
 Ethiopia-Eritrea, 1, 3, 7, 9, 37-40, 55, 70, 72, 76, 90, 97, 108, 113
 Ethiopia-Italy, 10
 Second World War (1939-1945), 4, 7, 9, 13, 42
Water supply, 105
Western Eritrea, 15
WFP.
 See World Food Programme (WFP)
WHO.
 See World Health Organization (WHO)
Women, 71
Women's groups, 6
World Bank, 104, 112
World Bank Consultative Group on Eritrea (1994), 104
World Food Programme (WFP), 44, 56, 103, 106
World Health Organization (WHO), 103, 105, 112
World War (1939-1945), 4, 7, 9, 13, 42

Y

Yemen, 73, 79, 81, 84, 92

Z

Zenawi, Meles, 49

The United Nations Blue Books Series

The following titles have also been published in the Blue Books series and can be obtained from the addresses provided below or at your local distributor:

The United Nations and Apartheid, 1948-1994
E.95.I.7   92-1-100546-9   565 pp. $29.95

The United Nations and Cambodia, 1991-1995
E.95.I.9   92-1-100548-5   352 pp. $29.95

The United Nations and Nuclear Non-Proliferation
E.95.I.17   92-1-100557-4   199 pp. $29.95

The United Nations and El Salvador, 1990-1995
E.95.I.12   92-1-100552-3   611 pp. $29.95

The United Nations and Mozambique, 1992-1995
E.95.I.20   92-1-100559-0   321 pp. $29.95

The United Nations and the Advancement of Women, 1945-1996
E.96.I.9   92-1-100603-1   846 pp. $49.95

The United Nations and Human Rights, 1945-1995
E.95.I.21   92-1-100560-4   536 pp. $29.95

The United Nations and Somalia, 1992-1996
E.96.I.8   92-1-100566-3   516 pp. $29.95

The United Nations and the Iraq-Kuwait Conflict, 1990-1996
E.96.I.3   92-1-100596-5   864 pp. $49.95

The United Nations and Rwanda, 1993-1996
E.96.I.20   92-1-100561-2   739 pp. $29.95

Les Nations Unies et Haïti, 1990-1996
F.96.I.11   92-1-200196-3   648 pp. $29.95

Other United Nations publications of related interest

An Agenda for Peace
Second edition, 1995
By Boutros Boutros-Ghali,
Secretary-General of the United Nations
E.95.I.15   92-1-100555-8   155 pp. $7.50

An Agenda for Development
By Boutros Boutros-Ghali,
Secretary-General of the United Nations
E.95.I.16   92-1-100556-6   132 pp. $7.50

The 50th Anniversary Annual Report on the Work of the Organization, 1996
By Boutros Boutros-Ghali,
Secretary-General of the United Nations
E.96.I.19   92-1-100615-5 $7.50

New Dimensions of Arms Regulation and Disarmament in the Post–Cold War Era
By Boutros Boutros-Ghali,
Secretary-General of the United Nations
E.95.IX.8   92-1-142192-6   53 pp. $9.95

United Nations Publications
2 United Nations Plaza, Room DC2-853
New York, NY 10017
United States of America
Tel.: (212) 963-8302; 1 (800) 253-9646
Fax: (212) 963-3489

Women: Challenges to the Year 2000
E.91.I.21   92-1-100458-6 $12.95

Basic Facts About the United Nations
E.95.I.31   92-1-100570-1   341 pp. $7.50

World Economic and Social Survey 1996
E.96.II.C.1   92-1-109131-4   354 pp. $55.00

Yearbook of the United Nations, Vol. 48
E.95.I.1   90-411-0172-1   1994   1,564 pp. $150.00

Yearbook of the United Nations, Special Edition, UN Fiftieth Anniversary, 1945-1995
E.95.I.50   0-7923-3112-5   1995   443 pp. $95.00

Collection of International Instruments and Other Legal Texts Concerning Refugees and Displaced Persons, Volume I, *Universal Instruments* and Volume II, *Regional Instruments*
E.GV.96.0.2   92-1-100713-5   1,176 pp. $125.00

United Nations Publications
Sales Office and Bookshop
CH-1211 Geneva 10
Switzerland
Tel.: 41 (22) 917-26-13;
       41 (22) 917-26-14
Fax: 41 (22) 917-00-27

Printed on recycled paper